Street by Street

BRADFORD
HALIFAX

BINGLEY, BRIGHOUSE, KEIGHLEY, SHIPLEY

Baildon, Calverley, Cleckheaton, Cullingworth, Elland, Guiseley, Haworth, Hipperholme, Queensbury, Saltaire, Sowerby Bridge, Wyke, Yeadon

2nd edition February 2003
© Automobile Association Developments Limited 2003

Ordnance Survey® This product includes map data licensed from Ordnance Survey® with the permission of the Controller of Her Majesty's Stationery Office. © Crown copyright 2003. All rights reserved. Licence No: 399221.

Published by AA Publishing (a trading name of Automobile Association Developments Limited, whose registered office is Millstream, Maidenhead Road, Windsor, Berkshire SL4 5GD. Registered number 1878835).

The Post Office is a registered trademark of Post Office Ltd. in the UK and other countries.

Schools address data provided by Education Direct.

One-way street data provided by:

Tele Atlas   © Tele Atlas N.V.

Mapping produced by the Cartographic Department of The Automobile Association. A01539

A CIP Catalogue record for this book is available from the British Library.

Printed by GRAFIASA S.A., Porto, Portugal

Ref: ML013z

Key to map pages ii-iii

Key to map symbols iv-1

Enlarged scale pages 2-5

Street by Street 6-79

Index – towns & villages 80

Index – streets 81-110

Index – featured places 110-113

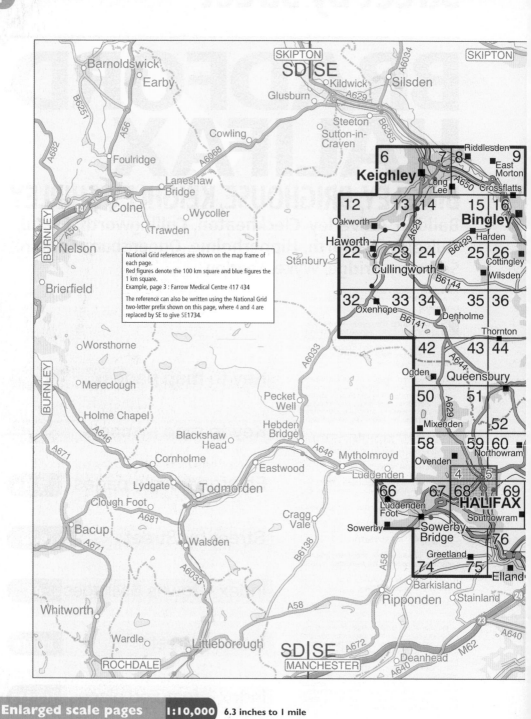

Barnoldswick
Earby
Glusburn
SKIPTON
SD | SE
Kildwick
Silsden
SKIPTON
Steeton
Sutton-in-Craven
Cowling
Riddlesden
Foulridge
6 **7** **8** **9** East Morton
Keighley
Long Lee
Crossflatts
Laneshaw Bridge
Colne
Wycoller
12 **13** **14** **15** **16**
Trawden
Oakworth
Bingley
Harden
Nelson
Haworth
22 **23** **24** **25** **26** Cottingley
Stanbury
Cullingworth
Wilsden
Brierfield

National Grid references are shown on the map frame of each page.
Red figures denote the 100 km square and blue figures the 1 km square.
Example, page 3 : Farrow Medical Centre 417 434

The reference can also be written using the National Grid two-letter prefix shown on this page, where 4 and 4 are replaced by SE to give SE1734.

32 Oxenhope **33** **34** **35** **36**
Denholme
Worsthorne
Thornton
42 **43** **44**
Ogden
Queensbury
Mereclough
50 **51**
Holme Chapel
Mixenden
52
Pecket Well
Blackshaw Head
Hebden Bridge
58 **59** **60** Northowram
Cornholme
Mytholmroyd
Ovenden
Eastwood
4 **5**
Luddenden
Lydgate
Todmorden
66 **67** **68** **69**
Clough Foot
Luddenden Foot
HALIFAX
Southowram
Cragg Vale
Sowerby
Bacup
Sowerby Bridge
76
Walsden
Greetland
74 **75**
Elland
Whitworth
Barkisland
Ripponden
Stainland
Wardle
A58
SD | SE
Littleborough
MANCHESTER
ROCHDALE
Deanhead
M62

Enlarged scale pages **1:10,000** 6.3 inches to 1 mile

0 1/4 miles 1/2
0 1/4 1/2 kilometres 3/4 1

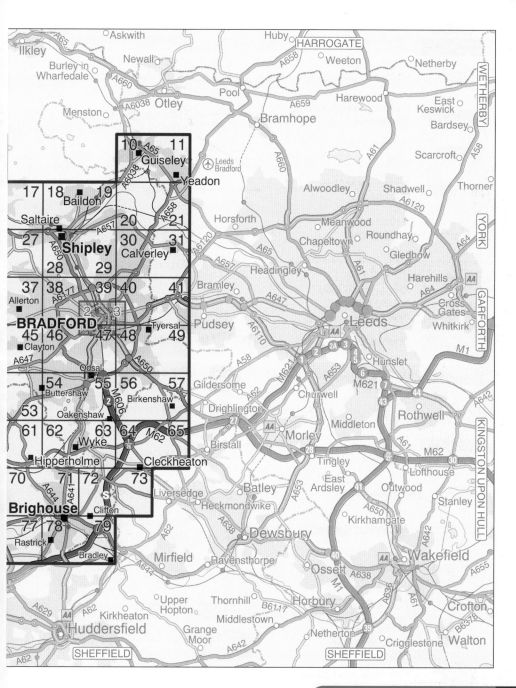

Junction 9	Motorway & junction	⊖	Underground station
Services	Motorway service area	⊖	Light railway & station
	Primary road single/dual carriageway	+++++++++	Preserved private railway
Services	Primary road service area	_LC_	Level crossing
	A road single/dual carriageway	•—•—•—•	Tramway
	B road single/dual carriageway	- - - - - - -	Ferry route
	Other road single/dual carriageway	....	Airport runway
	Minor/private road, access may be restricted	— · — · — · —	County, administrative boundary
← ←	One-way street	ᐯᐯᐯᐯᐯ	Mounds
	Pedestrian area	**17**	Page continuation 1:15,000
============	Track or footpath	**3**	Page continuation to enlarged scale 1:10,000
	Road under construction		River/canal, lake, pier
⌐ - - = = ⌐	Road tunnel		Aqueduct, lock, weir
AA	AA Service Centre	465 ▲ Winter Hill	Peak (with height in metres)
P	Parking		Beach
P+	Park & Ride		Woodland
	Bus/coach station		Park
	Railway & main railway station		Cemetery
	Railway & minor railway station		Built-up area

Featured building	Abbey, cathedral or priory
City wall	Castle
Hospital with 24-hour A&E department	Historic house or building
Post Office	Wakehurst Place NT — National Trust property
Public library	Museum or art gallery
Tourist Information Centre	Roman antiquity
Petrol station Major suppliers only	Ancient site, battlefield or monument
Church/chapel	Industrial interest
Public toilets	Garden
Toilet with disabled facilities	Arboretum
Public house AA recommended	Farm or animal centre
Restaurant AA inspected	Zoological or wildlife collection
Theatre or performing arts centre	Bird collection
Cinema	Nature reserve
Golf course	Visitor or heritage centre
Camping AA inspected	Country park
Caravan Site AA inspected	Cave
Camping & caravan site AA inspected	Windmill
Theme park	Distillery, brewery or vineyard

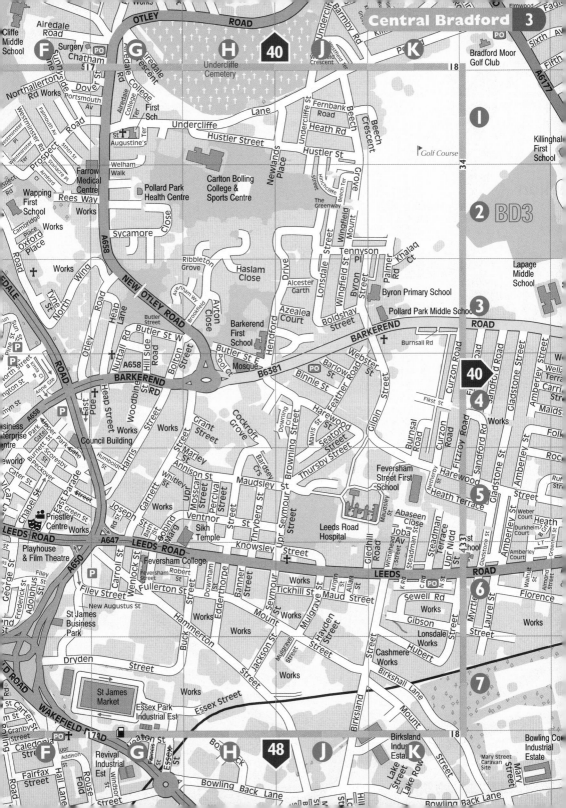

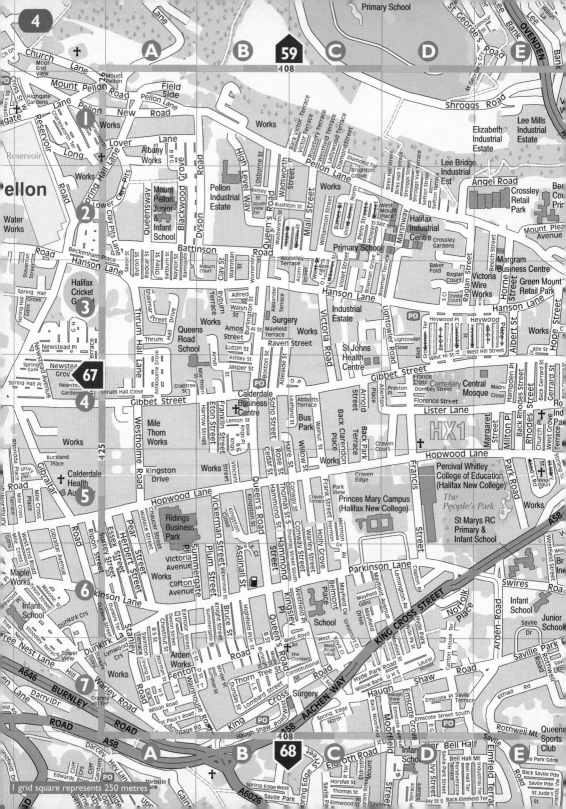

HX3

F **G** **H** 59 **J** **K**

1

Woodside Place
Bath Place
Woodside View
Woodside Crescent
Woodside
Victoria Old Lane
Lake View
Richmond Works
Range Court Ter
Eldon
Akroyd Court
Haley Court
Range Street
R St
Poplar
Lytton Street
All Souls Street
Ada St
Laura St
Side Hill
Church Side
School

Claremount

Prospect Street
Colwyn Place
Paragon Street
Turne
Brerwood Hill Close
Belgrave Mount
Belgrave Gardens
Belcross Street
Belgrave Grove
Belgrave Dr
Belgrave Cr5

Lee
ROAD
Bridge
HALEY HILL
Dean Clough Office Park
Stoney Batter
Crib Lane
Akroyd Place
Portland Road
Claremount Road
Lucy Street
Webb's Terrace
New Bank
The Incline
Belgrave Avenue
A58
Belmont St
Works

1

Dean
Clough
Corporation Street
A629
A58-BURDOCK WAY
North Bridge
Bowling Dyke
N Pollard
Garden Street
Gledcliffe
Spring Ter
NEW BANK A58
GODLEY ROAD
Beacon Hill Road
Lister's Road
A58

2

Richmond Rd
Condina Works
Cobden Court
Richmond Cl
Lewis
Police Stn
Laura Mitchell Health Centre
St James Court
Great Albion Street
Town Hall
St James Road
Albion Street
North Bridge Street
Foundry Street
Cross Street
North Bridge Leisure Centre
Charlestown
Caledonia Works
Old Bank
Godley Branch Road

2

Thompson Street
West Brook Court
Dene Court
Stannary Place
Richmond Way
Northgate
North Parade
Culver Street
Winding Rd
Lister Street
Lower Cross Street
Wade Street
Superstore
Works
Hall Road
Mulcure

3

West Grove
Bedford St North
Pellon Lane
Chapeltown Road
Pecketwell College
Lister Court
Crown St
Top Rank Theatre
BVS
Victoria St
Broad Street
Wade St
Crossley St
Old Market
Cncl Bldgs
Gaol Ln
King Street
PO Sorting Office
Well Lane
Smithy St
Superstore
Causeway
Works
Bank Bottom
Cripplegate
Southowram

69

3

Clarence St
Works
Mount St
Lister Lane
BURDOCK WAY
Boyne
Brunswick Gardens
Lord St
Surgery
George St
Silver St
Princess St
Corn Market
Crown St
Woolshops Square
Borough Market
Woolshops Shopping Centre
Calderdale Industrial Museum
Charles Square
Church Street
Berwick St
Berry Lane
War Memorial
Kirkgate
Lower
Baldwin Terrace

4

New Bond St
Culver Works
Playhouse Theatre
Council Building
Clinic
Cadney
COMMERCIAL ST
FOUNTAIN ST
Rawson St
The Victoria Theatre
Alexandra Place
Piece Hall Art Gallery
Albion
Westgate
Blackledge
Spire
Discovery Road
Bailey Hall
Bailey Hall Road
Southowram Bank

4

King Cross Street
Paradise St
Henry St
Kent St
Mag Court
Bull Close Lane
Ward's
Harrison Road
Ferguson Street
Carlton Street
St John's Lane
Trinity Road
ABC
Leisure Cen
Horton Street
Deal Street
Church Street
School Road
Wellington Street S
Hotel
Navigation
Halifax Station
Eureka the Museum for Children
Bank

5

Blackwall
Carlton Works
Balmoral Place
Halifax Bldg Soc
St John's Lane
Coleridge St
Prescott Street
County Court
Clare
New Road
Union Street
Discovery Road
Works
Lister Lane
High Grove
Blathroyd Lane
The Beaconsfield Centre

5

Saville Park Road
Savile Crescent
Hill St
Halifax High School
Pine
Hill Lane
Halifax Swimming Pool
Prescott Street
Surgery
Hope Hall La
South Parade
Waterside
Canal St
Trinity View
Trooper La
Cronfield
Albany Terrace
Trooper Terr

6

Central
Wellgarth
Heath Lea
Well Head
Old Well Head
Oxford Rd
Clare Road Flats
Heath View St
Sun Fold
Water Lane
Swan
Bank Lane
Albion Street
High Grove
Trooper Lane

6

Love Lane
Central
Wellgarth
Cavgill Terrace
Stoney Royd
Hunger Hill
Halifax Town FC Blue Sox RLFC (The Shay) Stadium
Shay Syke
Sedburgh Road
Calderdale
Hebble Works
The Beaconsfield Centre

7

Daisy Bank
Glen View
Clover Hill View
Glen Terrace
The Gardens
Clover Hill
Heath Park Avenue
SKIRCOAT ROAD
A629
Shaw Hill
Huddersf
Baldswort
Boys Lane
Siddal New Road
Siddal Lane
Cemetery

F **G** **H** 69 **J** **K**

A&E
Royal Halifax Infirmary

HALIFAX

09

10

A   B   C   D

404

| 05 B6265

SKIPTON
ROAD
LC

Keighley
RUFC

The
Hollins

Bar

Hollins

House

Hollins Cl

Hollins
Lane

Parker's

Brooklyn Street

Ferncliffe Drive

Hotel

Rowan St

PO

Fern Ct

Gn Head Dr

Green Head Lane

Elder St

Manor Rd

Grammar
Scho

1

Redcar

Tarn House

Whinburn
Residential
School

Four
Oaks
Lodge

Gleniyon
Av

Glenlyon
Drive

Cairn
Close

Airvw

Spring Gardens

Maple
Grove

Lime
Cl

Greenthw
Close

Westview
Grove

Holy
Fam
Sch

2

Redcar
Tarn

Black Hill Lane

Hawkstone
Drive

Uplands

Greenathorn
Garth

Pine Crt

Westway

The Chase

Shann

Broadlands

Sandy

Springfield Road

High Spring Gardens

View Rd

Tarn Lane

Braithwaite

Black
Hill

Braithwaite

Raymram Crs

Wimborne Dr

Kenva
Mount

Shann Av

Whin Knoll Avenue

Shann Crs

Edge

The Hallows

Clayton
Rl

Margaret La

Highfield

3

Far Laithe
Farm

Edge   Road

Ryan Gv

Sunnymount

Exley
Head
View

Braithwaite
Special
School

Bankfield
Street

Whinfield Dr

Coronation

Whinfield Av

Whinfield Cl

W Bank Cl

W Bank
Bn

Way

West
Bank

Wardle

Calver Av

Highfield Road

Smith St

Midd
Scho

4

Braithwaite

ll Clough

North Dean Av

Braithwaite

Avenue

Bankfield
Drive

Braithwaite
Gv

Braithwaite
Wk

Brigg
Gardens

Broster

School Walk

Infant
School

Braithwaite
Avenue

PO

Whin St

Guard
House
Drive

Guard House
Av

Redcliffe   Street

Guard House
Works

Airey St

Redcliffe Rd

Waterhouse

West

The
Gables

Devon

Guard
House

Guard
House

aycock
irst School

Calversyke
Middle Sch

Foster
Gardens

North   Dean   Road

School

5

North Becks

Fell
Lane

Works

Thorncliffe Rd

Holme
La

Durrance
St

Raglan
Av

Raglan
St

Rishworth

Becks

Branshaw
Sch

shapla Cl

Carlby

Litton Rd

Clifton St

Nashville
Terrace

Ryal

13

Meadow
Croft

Fell Lane

Rose Mdw

Fell Crs

Nile
Crs

Westfell

Westfell Rd

St Johns St

Feyrigg Av

Mannville Gv

Mannville

Industrial St

Greenfield
Close

OAKWORTH

Mannville Rd

Lund
Park

A   B   C   D

404   405

House   Lane   Stell Hill

Prospect Mount

Highfell Rise

Browfield
Vw

Wheathead Crs

Bunker's Hill
Lane

Wheathead
Lane

Westburn

Westbu
Lane

Newsfield
First School

Westbu
Mt

Nessfield Rd

Nessfield
Dr

Exley Mt

Sunny Hl

Sunny Hl GV

Whitley
Rd

Grafton
Rd

Oswood Rd

Selbo

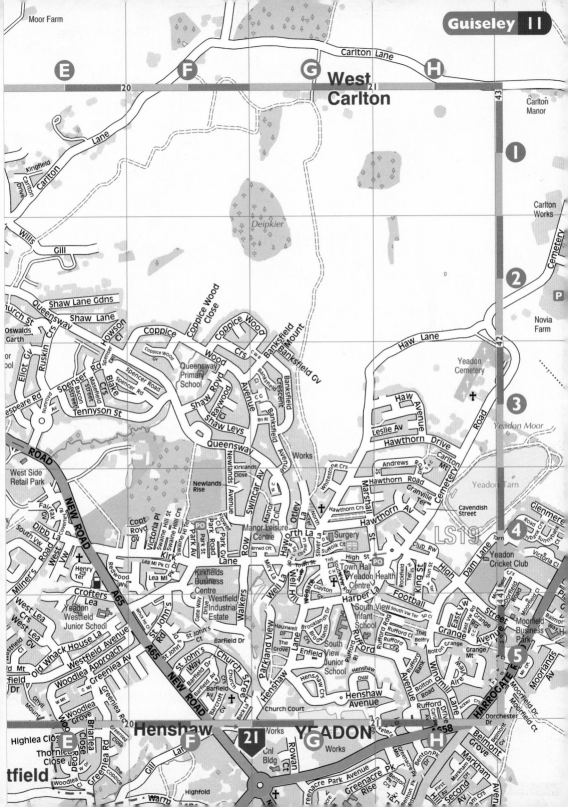

Moor Farm

Carlton Lane

E F G **West Carlton** H

20 21 43

Carlton Manor

Carlton Lane

I

Carlton Works

Kingfield

Carlton Drive

Carlton Lane

Wills

Gill

Deipkier

Cemetery

2

P

Novia Farm

Church St

Queensway

Shaw Lane Gdns

Shaw Lane

Howson Ct

Coppice

Coppice Wood Close

Coppice Wood Crs

Banksfield Mount

Haw Lane

Yeadon Cemetery

Oswalds Garth

Eliot Gv

Ruskin Crs

Spenser Rd

Coppice Wood Gv

Wood Crs

Queensway Primary School

Banksfield Gv

Banksfield Crescent

Banksfield Avenue

3

Yeadon Moor

Spesheare Rd

Spenser Crs

Masefield Street

Bacon Street

Blake Av

Spencer Road

Shaw Royd

Wood Avenue

Haw Avenue

Nunroyd Av

Tennyson St

Shaw Leys

Bn Rd

Haw

Leslie Av

Works

Hawthorn Drive

Cemetery Road

Queensway

Newlands Close

Whitestone Crs

Hawthorn Road

Andrews Rd

Granville Ter

Carlton Mt

Yeadon Tarn

West Side Retail Park

Newlands Rise

Newlands Avenue

Swincar Av

Hawthorn Crs

Hawthorn Av

Cavendish Street

LS19

Glenmere

4

Falcrax

Dibb La

Copt Royd Gv

Victoria Pl

Swaine Hill St

Swaine Hill Crs

Otley

Manor

Fflower

Park Avenue

Marshall St

Club RW

Tarn

Victoria Gv

south Vw

West Vw

Coventry Rd

Kirk

Park St

PO

Manor Leisure Centre

North La

Silver La

Surgery

Suffolk Ct

High St

Yeadon Cricket Club

Dam Lane

ROAD

NEW ROAD

A65

Henry Ter

Redwood

Lea MI Pk Cl

Lea MI

Kirkfields Business Centre

Gate Way

Westfield Industrial Estate

Mill Ya

Well La

Well Hill

Brrwd Crt

Town St

Clayton

High St

THS

Town Hall

Yeadon Health Centre

PO

Rockfield

King St

Football

High St

Moorfield

Yeadon Cricket Club

Crofters Lea

Yeadon Westfield Junior School

Old Whack House La

Westfield Approach

Woodlea Avenue

Greenlea Av

St John's Rd

St John's Ct

St John's Way

Barfield Dr

Church Street

Barfield Dr

Barfield Av

Hauxwell Dr

The Grove

Parkland View

Brooklands Dr

Enfield

South View Infant School

Harper La

South Vw Ter

SP Cl

Rufford Rd

Rufford

The Belfry

Grange

East Vw

Grange Mt

Grange

Bolton Grange

Moorfield Business Park

5

Milners

West Lea Crs

West Lea Gv

Old Whack House La

Greenlea Grove

Woodlea Grove

Briarlea

Greenlea Rd

St John's Way

Barfield Dr

Barcroft

Back La

South View Junior School

Henshaw Oval

Hens Haw Crs

Henshaw Avenue

Rufford Av

Rufford Bank

Windmill Lane

Bolton Road

Rufford Drive

Maltre

HARROGATE RD

Moorfield Dr

Moorfield Ct

Dorchester Dr

A658

Highlea Close

Thornlea Close

tfield

Highlea Close

E

Gill Lar

The Coppice

Woodlea Cl

Henshaw

F

21

Cnl Bldg

Rowan

Highfold

Church Court

Works

YEADON

G

Works

Peters

H

Greenacre Park Avenue

Greenacre Rise

Benton Pk

Belmont Grove

Markham Avenue

First Av

Second Av

Belmont

Warm

reenacre Park Avenue

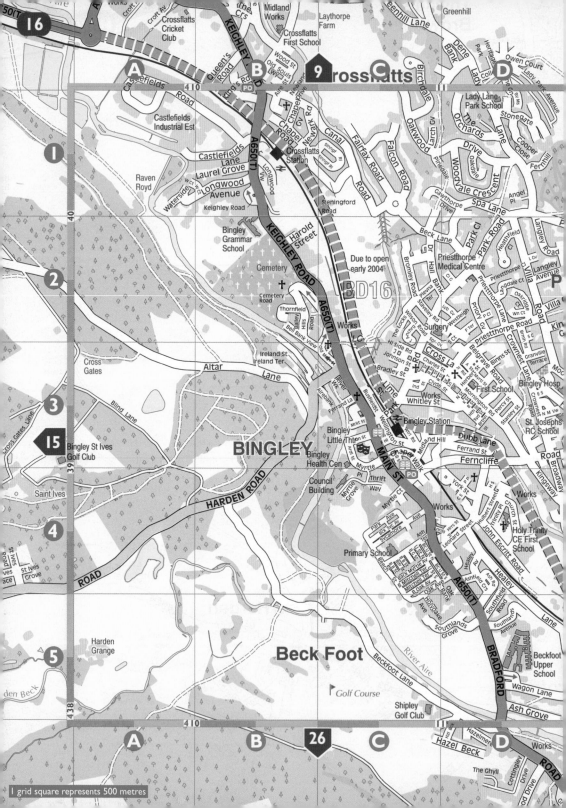

I grid square represents 500 metres

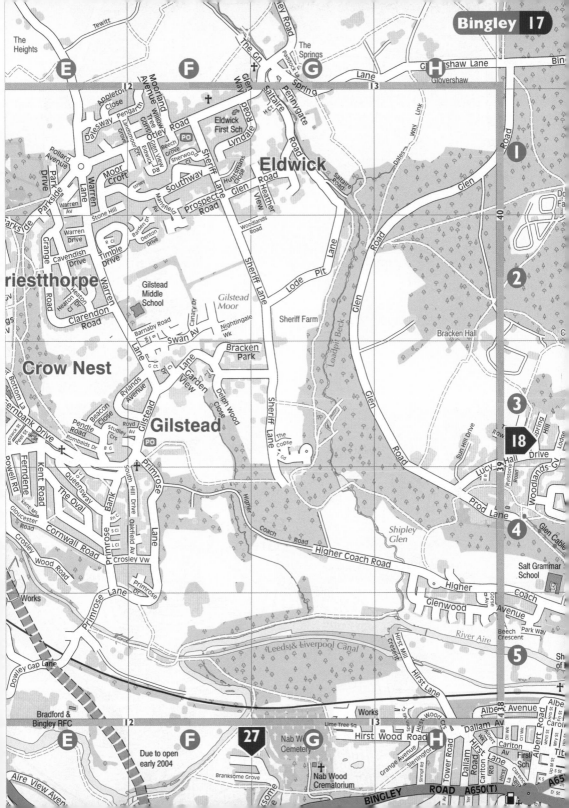

E F G H I

The Heights

Tewitt

The Gn

The Springs

Gloversham

shaw Lane

Bin

Gloversham

Moorland Avenue
Appleton Close
Pengarth
Willow Tree Gdns
Landsmoor Cft
Daleway
Otley Road
Eldwick Dr
Glen View Rd
Beech Grove
Sherwoo

Eldwick First Sch

Saltaire Road
Pennygate
Paddock La

Lane

Glen Way

Spring

Lyndale

Eldwick

Pollard Avenue
Park Drive
Parkside
Warren Lane
Moor Croft
Stone Hill
Southway
Mansfield
Prospect Road
Sheriff Lane
Glen
Heather View
Road

Hutchinans Close

Woodlands Road

Saltaire Road

Road

Dales Way

Link

Way

Glen

I

riestthorpe

Grange
Cavendish Drive
Warren Drive
R Cl
Barton Dr
Denton Drive
Timble Drive

Glen

40

Do
Fa

2

s

Heaton Cl
Heaton Cl
Clarendon Road
Warren Road

Gilstead Middle School

Gilstead Moor

Sheriff Lane

Lode Pit Lane

Sheriff Farm

Glen Road

Loadpit Beck

Bracken Hall

3

Crow Nest

Barnaby Road
WI
G Ct
Swan Av
Canary Dr
Nightingale Wk

Bracken Park

Rylands Avenue
Gilstead
Garden View
Lane
Delph Wood
Sheriff Lane

The Copse Gd

Spring Hill

Lodg

18

ernbank Drive
Beacon Close
Pendle Road
Studley Crs
Rombalds Dr
Royd Av
Gilstead
PO

Gilstead

Higher

Coach Road

Shipley Glen

Sun Hill Drive

Lucy La

Rylstone Ho

Hall

39

Woodlands Gr

4

Glen Cable

powell Rd
Ferndene
Kent Road
Queensway
The Oval
Primrose Bank
South Hill Drive
Oakfield La
Sn Cl
S Cl
LCl
Higher
Coach Road

Prod Lane

Salt Grammar School

Gloucester Road
Cornwall Road
Crosley Wood Road
Primrose Lane
Crosley Vw
Primrose Dr

Higher Glenwood

Higher Coach Avenue

Beech Crescent
Park Way

Sh of

5

Works

Bradford & Bingley RFC

Leeds & Liverpool Canal

River Aire

Hirst Mill Crescent

Albert Avenue
Albe
Carol

E F G H

27

Due to open early 2004

Nab W Cemetery

Hirst Wood Road

Works
Lime Tree Sq

Grange Avenue
Steningfor

Dallam Av
Carlton Av
Carlton Lane

Dallam Road

First Sch

Tower Road

Albert Road

Tit

Up St
MY St

Aire View Aven

Branksome Grove

Nab Wood Crematorium

BINGLEY

ROAD A650(T)

A65

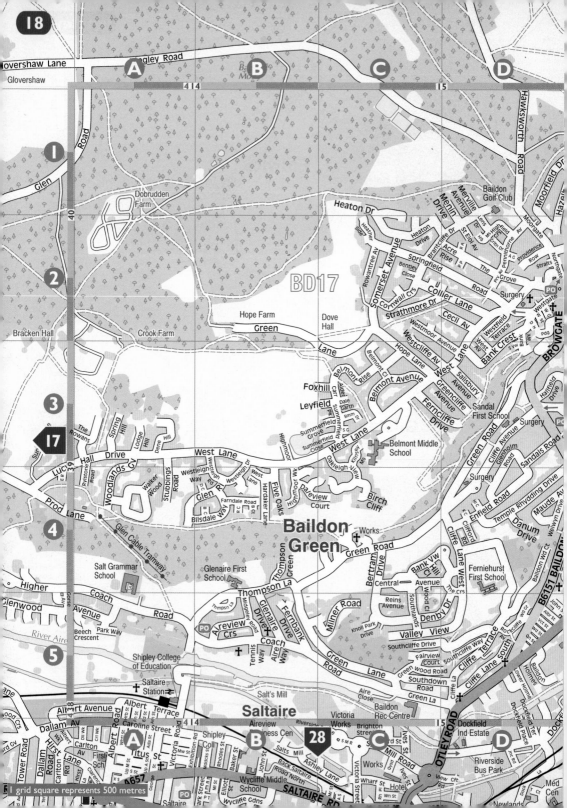

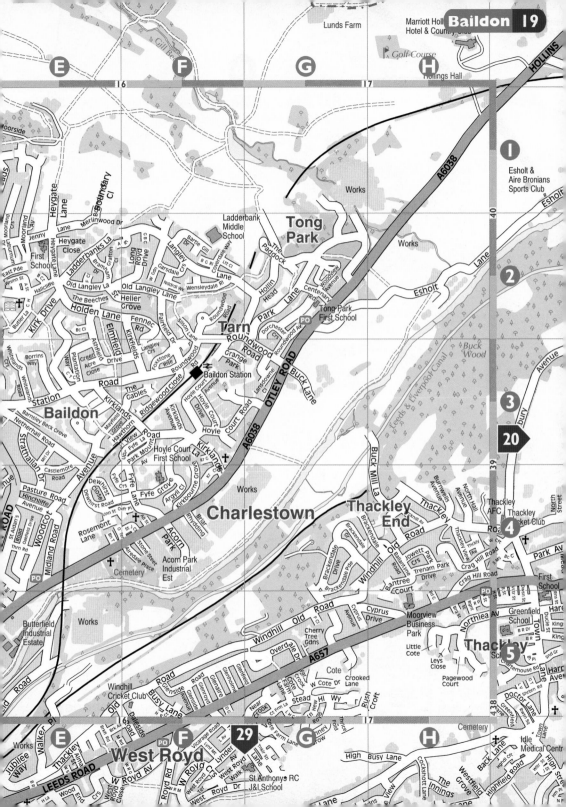

E   F   II   G   H   I

Old Whack House La
Westfield
Woodlea Approach
Greenlea Av
Woodlea Grove
Highlea Close
Thornlea Close
Woodlea Road
Woodlea Cl
Greenlea Rd
Gill Lane
Barfield Dr
St John's Way
Church St
Barfield
Parkland V
The Grove
Enfield
South View Junior School
Henshaw Oval
Rufford
Rufford Bank
Belfry
Moorland Av
Moorfield Ct
Moorfield
Dorchester Dr
Belmont Grove
HARROGATE Rd

Henshaw
YEADON
Works
Sizers Ct
Cnl Bldg
Rowan Ct
Works
A658
Windmill Lane
Aire
Bolton
Markham Av
Second Av
First
Hill Crescent
Markham Crs

Nether Yeadon
Warm Lane
Highfold
APPERLEY LA
Mawcroft Cl
Mawcroft Gra
NEW ROAD SIDE
Greenacre Park Avenue
Greenacre PK
Greenacre Rise
Quakers Lane
Benton Park School
Benton Park
Chrl L
B6152
Primary School
Canada Rd
Canada Crs
Canada Ter
Batter La
Larkfield Crs

2 Larkfiel

The Cha
Surgery
White Lands
Prs St
Bk Lbd
Lbd St
King St
London La
ULSt
Sall bury
The Gv
HARROGATE RD
Derby Rd
North St
James St
George St
John St
Park Rd
Crow Trees PK
Cleeve H
Larkfield Dr
Larkfield AV
Peasehill
Lakeside
Larkfield
Larkfield Rd
Rawdon Cricket Club
Billing View
Town

Little London
APPERLEY LANE
Springwood
Fulford Grange Hospital
Rawdon Golf & Lawn Tennis Club
MICKLEFIELD LANE
Micklefield Rd
MC
Crowtrees
Rawdon
Golf Course
A65
Over Lane
Well Cl
Well La
Henley
Henley Mt
PO

3

A658
Cliffe Dr
cragg
Buckstone
Rawdon Drive
High Close
Rawdon Hall Dr
Cliffe Lane
Low Gn
LEEDS
HARROGATE RD

Low Green

The Spinney
Acacia Park
Present
APPERLEY LANE
Acacia Park Dr
Bronte House School
Acacia Park Terrace
Fairway
Woodlands Drive
Cliffe Drive
Wood Drive
Drive
Woodlands Dr
Underwood Drive
Snaith Wd Dr
Snaith Wd Ms

4

Rawdon Carrs

Hotel
A658
Woodlands Dr
Woodlands Close
Woodhouse Grove School
Leeds Country Way
Leeds Country Way
Snaith Wd Ms
Leeds Way
Leeds Co

5

W

E   F   **31**   G   H

Calverley Wood
Thornhill Drive
Lodge Wood

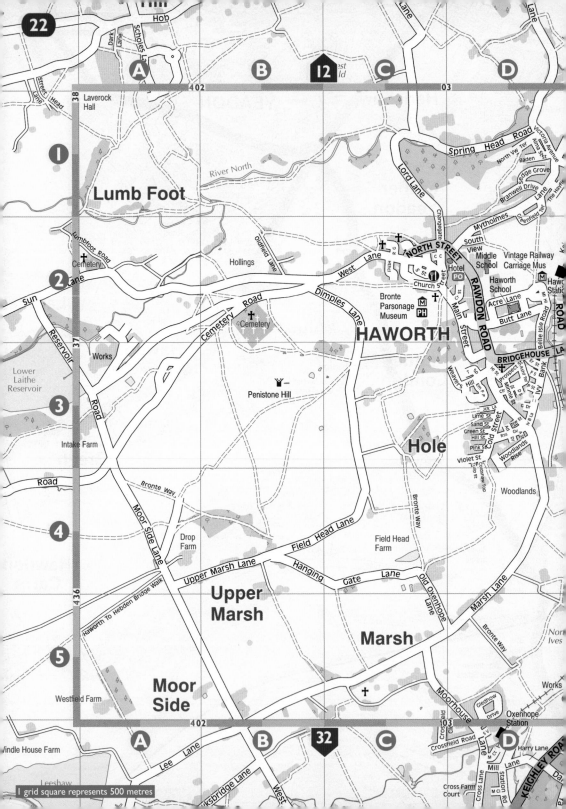

A   B   12   C   D

402   03

38   Laverock
Hall

I

River North

Lumb Foot

Lumbfoot Road
37
Cemetery
2   Sun   Lane
Reservoir   Road

West Lane
North View Ter   Alma St
Baden
Spring Head Road   Victoria Avenue
Lord Lane   Hedge Grove
Branwell Drive   The Hayfe
Mytholmes   Brentfield Ter   Greenfield Ter
Changegate   St R G
NORTH STREET
St C   Middle   South View
School   Vintage Railway
Hotel   Carriage Mus
PO   M   Haworth Station
Church Street   Haworth School
Acre Lane
HAWORTH   Butt Lane

Oldfield Lane
Hollings
Dimples Lane
Bronte
Parsonage   M
Museum   PH

Rawdon Road

Lower
Laithe
Reservoir
3
Intake Farm

Cemetery   Road
Cemetery

Works

Penistone Hill

BRIDGEHOUSE
Prospect St   Belle Isle Rd   Ivy Bank   North Road
Hill   Weaver's   Minie St   Myrtle
Lime St   Jck   RR
Sand St   Green St   D   Woodlands Rise
Hole   Hill St   R SS
Pink St
Violet St   Foldswar Top   Woodlands

Road   Bronte Way

4   Drop
Farm

Field Head Lane   Field Head
Farm   Bronte Way

Moor Side Lane

Upper Marsh Lane   Hanging   Gate   Lane   Old Oxenhope Lane
Haworth To Hebden Bridge Walk

436   Upper
Marsh   Marsh

Marsh Lane   Bronte Way   Nor
Ives

5

Moor
Side   Westfield Farm   Gledhow Drive
Moorhouse   Oxenhope
Station   Works

A   B   32   C   D   Harry Lane
402   03   Crossfield Road   Mill Lane   Station Rd
Lee Lane   Clough Lane   Cross Lane
Windle House Farm   ksbridge Lane   West   Crossfield   Cross Farm Court   Da

Leeshaw

Keighley Road

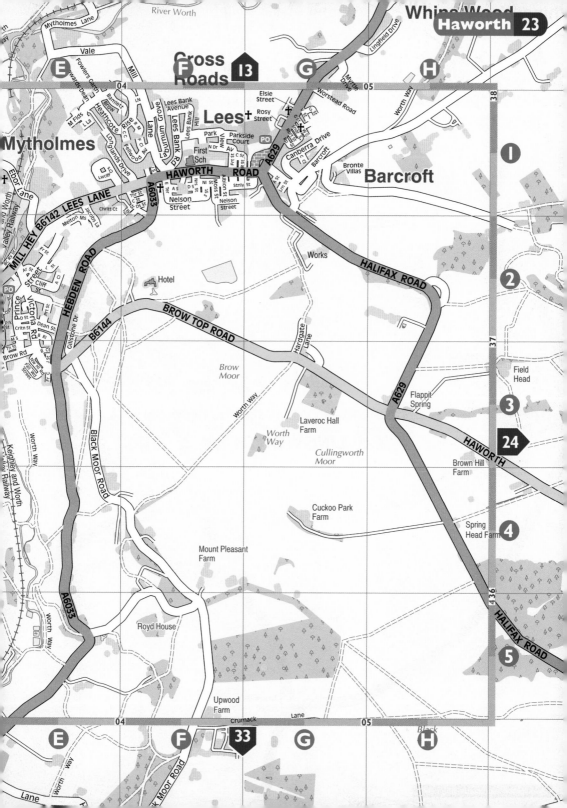

26

Harden Grange

Beck Foot

River Aire

BRADFOR

Beckfoot Upper School

Beckfoot Lane

Wagon Lane

A 410 **B** 16 Golf Cou **C** Shipley Golf Club **D** Ash Grove

38

Hazel Beck

Hazelmere Av

Works

Harden Beck

Ghyll Wood Drive

ROAD

Cottingley Drive

The Ghyll

1 Bank Top

Cottingley Wood Estate

Manor

Lee Lane

Beckfield Road

Northfield Crs

Staybrite Avenue

Fair Del

2

Cross Lane

March Cote Farm

37

Coplowe Lane

Cottingley Clinic

Beckfield Road

Hope Hill View

Cottingley

Woodside View

Woodside Crs

Woodside Avenue

Woodside Drive

Langlands Road

Little

Chapwell Springs

Moorview Drive

elands

PO T Pde

3 Coplowe Hall

Airedale Avenue

Rycroft Av

Cottingley Moor

March Cote Lane

25

House oad

Spring Park Road

Norr

Lee Lane

Cottingley

Nor

4 Tweedy Street

Wilsden Primary School

Cemetery

Crack Lane

Main Street

Albion

Stocka House Farm

COTTINGLEY ROAD

Lingfield Road

Lingfield Grove

Tilly Hall Gdns

Simms Dene

whirst St

Mrs Rd

Peel St

Florida Rd

Syringa Avenue

5 Albert St

Victoria St

Queen St

Laurel Pk

Crooke Lane

LOW WOOD

Meadow Green

Lingbob

Shay Gate

Acacia Dr

Hornbeam Cl

Sandymoor

Sandy Lane First School

B6144

Shay Lane

Back Lane

WILSDEN

PO

A 410 **B** **36** **C** **Sandy Lane** **D** B6144

ROAD

Prune

Gazeby Hall

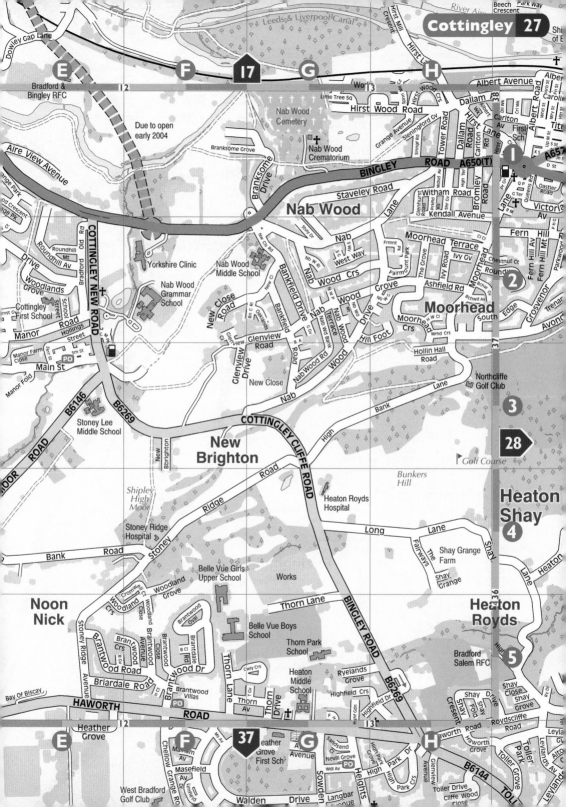

I grid square represents 500 metres

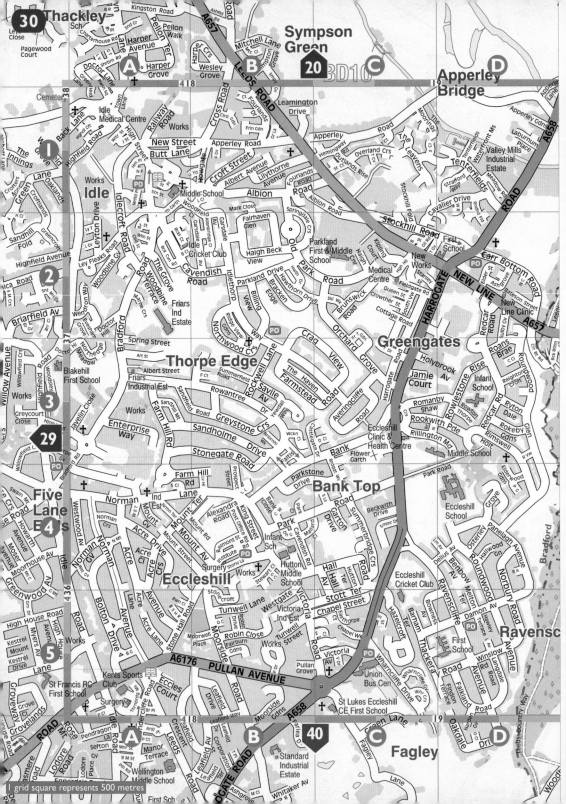

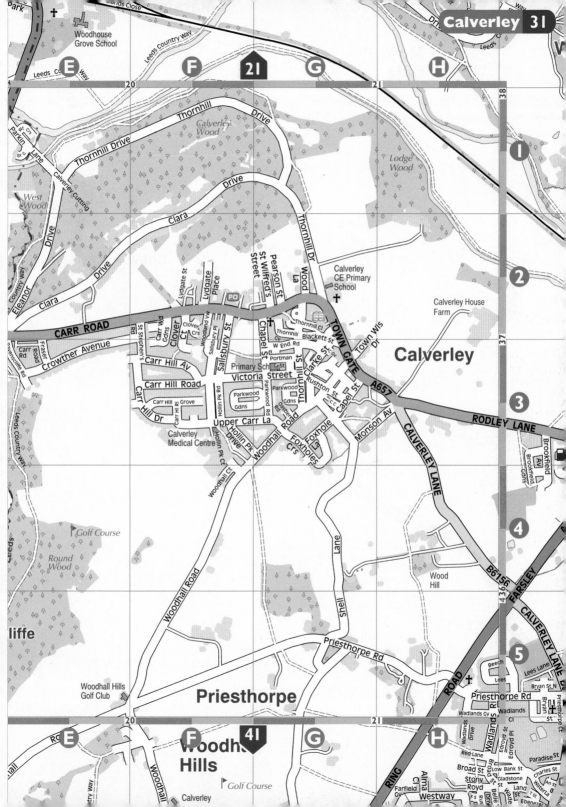

Woodhouse Grove School

Leeds Country Way

E F 21 G H

Leeds Co Way

20 21 38

I

Thornhill Drive

Parkin Lane

Calverley Wood

Thornhill Drive

Calverley Cutting

Clara Drive

Drive

Lodge Wood

West Wood

Clara

Drive

Thornhill Dr

Wood La

Calverley CE Primary School

Calverley House Farm

2

37

Eleanor Drive

Country Way

Clara

Lydgate St

St Wilfred's Street

Lydgate Place

Pearson St

PO

CARR ROAD

St Stephen's Rd

Carr Wd Gdns

Clover Ct

Clover Crs

Woodland Vw

Salisbury Pl

Chapel St

Thornhill

W End Rd

Portman

Blackett St

Town Wls

Clarke St

Town Ga Dr

Calverley

Crowther Avenue

Fraser Road

Carr Rd

Clover

Salisbury St

Primary Sch

Victoria Street

Post St

Rushton St

Capel St

A657

3

RODLEY LANE

Carr Hill Av

Carr Hill Road

Carr Hill Grove

Parkwood Gdns

Parkwood Rd

Parkwood Gdns

Thornhill St

CCC

Monson Av

CALVERLEY LANE

Brookfield AV

Brookfield Gdns

Carr Hill Dr

Carr Hl Rd

Hollin Pk Rd

Upper Carr La

Calverley Medical Centre

Hollin Pk Drive

Woodhall Rd

Foxhole La

Foxholes Crs

4

B6156

FARSLEY

436

CALVERLEY LANE DR

Golf Course

Round Wood

Woodhall Ct

Woodhall Road

Shell Lane

Wood Hill

5

Beech Lees

Lees Lane

Bryan St N

liffe

Priesthorpe Rd

Priesthorpe Rd

Wadlands Ri

Bryan St

Priesthorpe St

Woodhall Hills Golf Club

Priesthorpe

Wadlands Gv

Wadlands Cl

RING ROAD

20 21

E F 41 G H

Woodhs Hills

Golf Course

Calverley

Red Lane

Edroyd Pl

Ectroyd Pl

Paradise St

Broad St

Low Bank St

Charles St

Stony Royd

Gladstone St

Belle Vue

Land St

Wade

WaterLa

Farfield Gv

Alma St

Broad Dr

WESTWAY

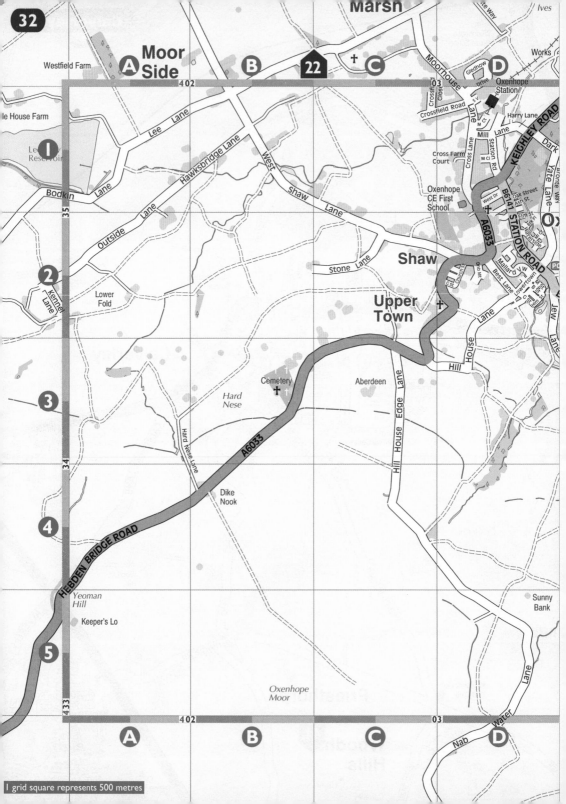

32

Marsh

Ives

Westfield Farm

Moor Side

A **B** **22** † **C** **D**

le House Farm

Works

Moorhouse Lane

te Way

Oxenhope Station

Glednow Drive

Crossfield Close

Crossfield Road

Harry Lane

KEIGHLEY ROAD

Lee Lane

Hawksbridge Lane

Outside Lane

West shaw Lane

I Leeshaw Reservoir

Bodkin

Station Rd

Mill Lane

Cross Farm Court

Cross Lane

Oxenhope CE First School

West Dr

B6141

Ach St

Dark

Yate Lane

A6033

2 Kennel Lane

Lower Fold

Stone Lane

Shaw

STATION ROAD

Elm St

Church

Mallard

Best Lane

Jew Lane

Upper Town

†

Powertown

3 Hard Nese

Cemetery †

Aberdeen

Hill House Lane

Hill House Edge Lane

34

Hard Nese Lane

A6033

Hill

4

Dike Nook

HEBDEN BRIDGE ROAD

Yeoman Hill

Keeper's Lo

Sunny Bank

5

Water Lane

Oxenhope Moor

433 **402** 03

A **B** **C** **D**

Nab

I grid square represents 500 metres

E F **23** G H

Upw... Farm

Crumack Lane

Black Moor

04 05 35

I

Lan... Bott...

2

Worth Lane

High Binns Lane

Black Moor Road

...xenhope

Height Lane

Lower Town

B6141

Back Leeming

Leeming

Black Moor Road

DENHOLME ROAD

Leeming Reservoir

Bronte Way

Trough Lane

3

34 LONG CAUSEWAY B6141

Sawood Lane

Sawood

4

Cobling Farm

Nan Scar

Bronte Way

Sawood Lane

Works

Thornton Moor Road

5

White Moor

Thornton Moor Reservoir

433

04 05

E F G H

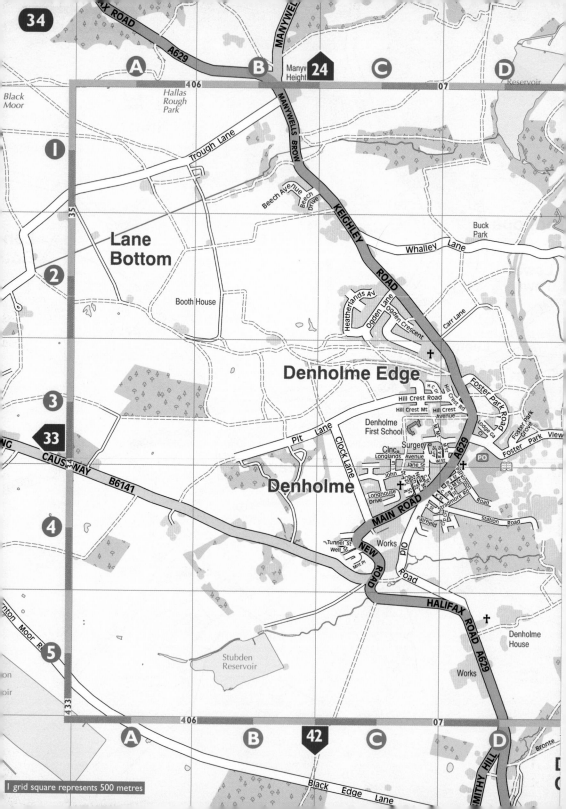

34

A   B   C   D

HALIFAX ROAD
A629

MANYWELLS

24
Manyw
Height

Reservoir

406

07

Black
Moor

Hallas
Rough
Park

Trough Lane

MANYWELLS BROW

Beech Avenue

Beech Drive

KEIGHLEY ROAD

Whalley Lane

Buck
Park

1

35

**Lane
Bottom**

Heatherlands Av

Ogden Lane

Ogden Crescent

Carr Lane

2

Booth House

Denholme Edge

Hill Crest Road

Hill Crest Rd

Foster Park Road

3

Pit Lane

Clock Lane

Hill Crest Mt

Hill Crest
Avenue

Denholme
First School

Lodge Ca
Cl

Foster Park
Grove

Foster Park View

33

NG

CAUSEWAY

B6141

Surgery

Clnc

Longlands Avenue

Jane St

John St

A629

PO

4

Longhouse
Drive

MAIN ROAD

Stradmore Rd

Fairfield

Station Road

Road

Tunnel St

Well St

Mite Pl

NEW ROAD

Works

PIO Road

HALIFAX ROAD A629

Denholme
House

5

tton Moor Rd

433

Stubden
Reservoir

Works

406

07

A   B   C   D

42

Bronte

SMITHY HILL

Black Edge Lane

1 grid square represents 500 metres

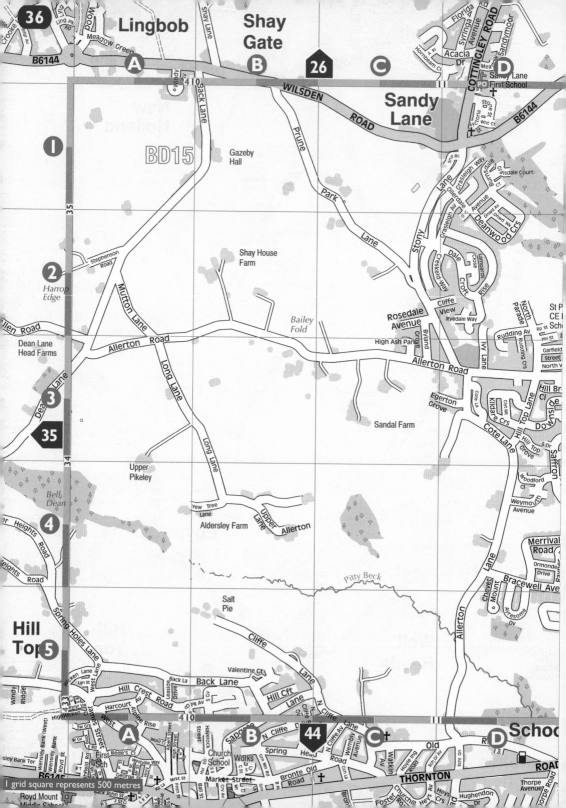

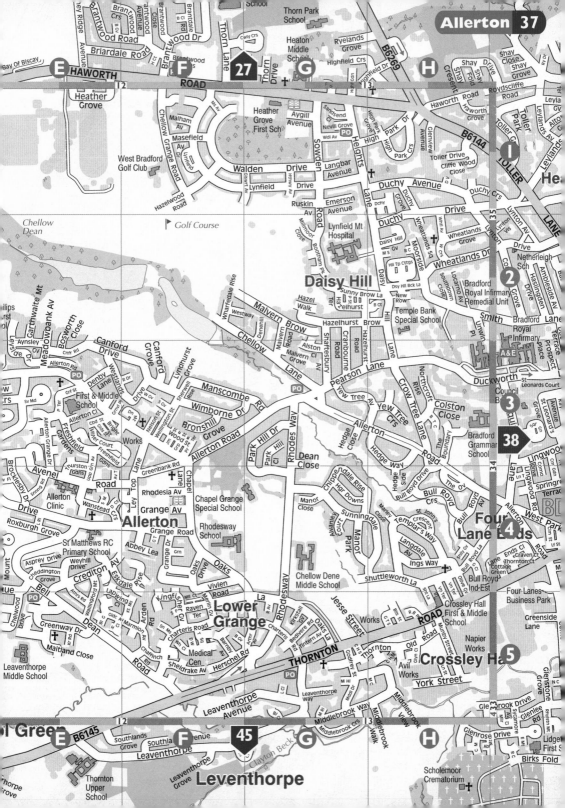

I grid square represents 500 metres

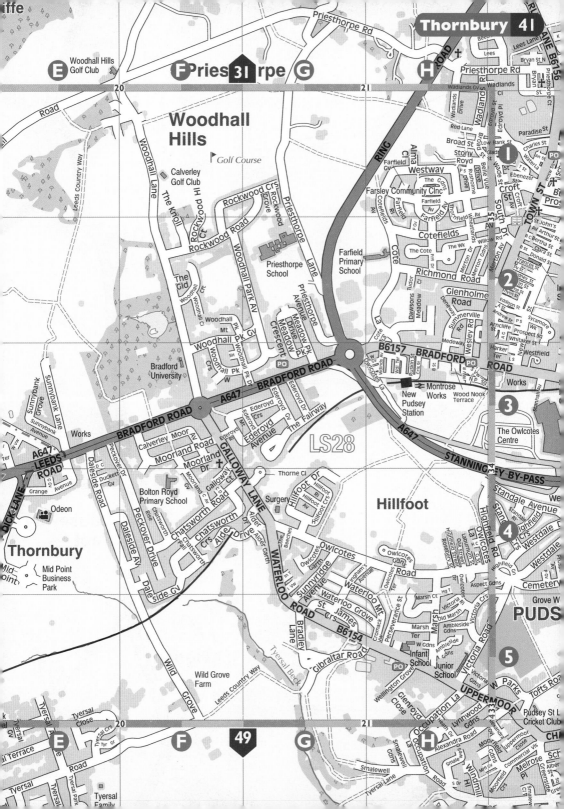

42

A

34

B

C

406

07

D

33

I

Thornton
Moor

Black Edge Lane

Smithy Hill

BRIGHOUS

Works

Denholme
House

Bronte

Cragg Lane

Denholme Gate †

Cragg Tp

Foreside Lane

2

Foreside Lane

Foreside

32

Foreside Bottom Lane

Halifax Road A629

B6145

3

Bradford
Calderdale

Coal Lane

Works

4

Ogden
Plantation

431

Ogden
Reservoir

**Causeway
Foot**

Ogden Lane

Syke Lane

Ned Hill

5

Ogden

Hill Gate

406

07

A

B

50

C

A629

D

Golf Course

I grid square represents 500 metres

44

Thornton

Chat Hill

West Scholes

BD14

36

52

43

Royd Mount Middle School

Golf Course

Headley Golf Club

Foxhill First School

Med Centre

Church School

Market Street

Baths

THORNTON

Headley Lane

Cockin Lane

Marley Lane

Brewery Lane

Brow Lane

Carter Lane

Bridle Stile Lane

Lane Side

Corn Mill Lane

Westminster Crs
Westminster Drive
Westminster Avenue

Ferndal Avenue

Broomfield

Baldwin Lane

Chat Hill

Low

Old Dolp

SCARLET HEIG

CALDER

SAND BEDS

BRIGHOUSE

HIGH ST

The Willows Medical Cen

Mosstree Close

Works

Lane End

A644

Chapel Street

Chapel Lane

Foxhill Grove

Foxhill Drive

Parkway

Fleet Avenue

Glazier Road

ALBERT ROAD

Station Road

Nelson St

Naseby Rise

Crooned Close

Littlemoor

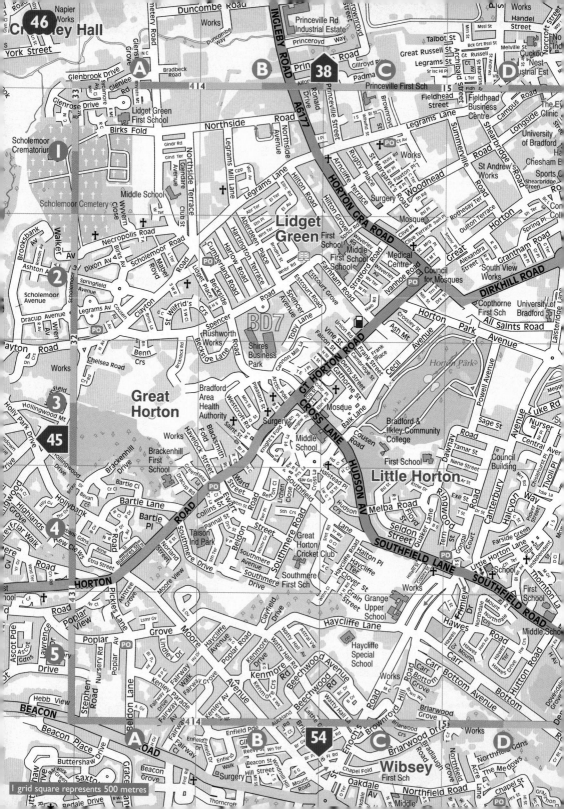

E

F

`41`

G

H

UPPERMOOR

W Parks

Tofts Road

Pudsey St L
Cricket Club

Wild Grove
Farm

Leeds Country Way

Tyersal Beck

Gibraltar Road

Wellington Grove

Glenroyd

Occupation La

New Occupation

Lynwood
Gdns

Alexandra Road

Moor Field

Uppermoor
Close

CHA

Melrose
Pl

Greenside

Albert
St

Sch

I

Tyersal Avenue

Tyersal
Close

Tyersal
Road

`20`

Tyersal Crs

Tyr Gr

Tyersal Terrace

Tyersal

Tyersal Walk

Tyersal Park

Tyersal
Green

Tyersal Drive

Tyersal Court

Tyersal
Family
Clinic

Pudsey Tyersal
Primary School

Tyersal

`21`

Smalewell
Gdns

Smalewell

Road

Tyersal Lane

Tyersal Lane

Windmill Hl

Westroyd
Gdns

Westroyd Crs

Westroyd

West Royd
Crs

Westroyd Av

Wheatfield

Green La

Greentop

`33`

`32`

2

Bankhouse

Bankhouse

Lwr Ba

Scholebrook
Lane

Black Hey
Farm

Tyersal
Lane

Tyersal
Hall

Leeds
Bradford

Black
Carr

Leeds Country Way

Lane

3

Works

Harper
Gate

Tyersal
Gate

Ned

Lane

Holmefield
First
School

VW

Holme

BD4

Golf Course

Scholebrook

**Holme
Wood**

Heysham

Heysham
Drive

Drive

Wbrgh La

scent

Maythorne Farm

Scholebrook Farm

Park
Wood

4

First
Sch

Kstv

Road

Thorn Royd
Drive

Holme La

Westvew

WK

Avenue

Eggleston
Drive

Argent

Way

Daniel Court

Ar Cl

Sm

Bt

Ln Ct

Bn

Raikes Lane

New Lane

`431`

5

n Cl

Howden
Close

Chilver

Ryecroft Farm

Goosedale
Ct

Denbrook Wk

Denbrook
Walk

Denbrook Av

Road

`20`

`21`

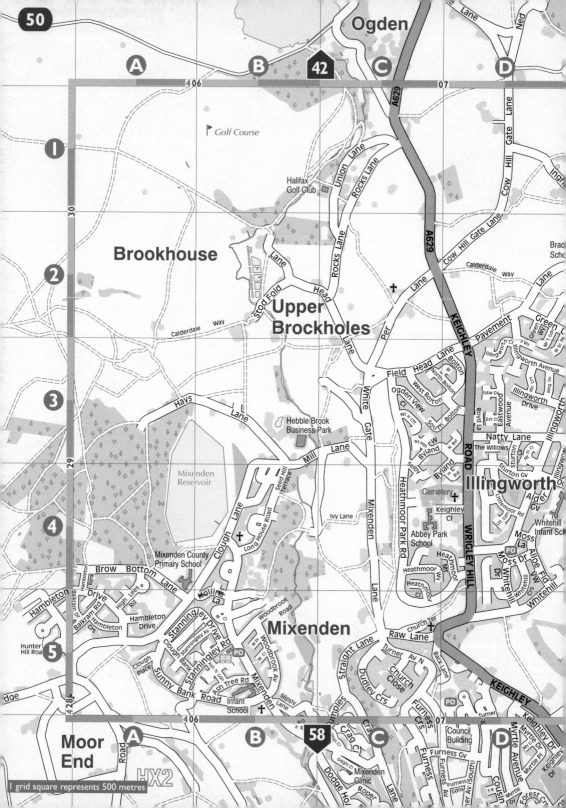

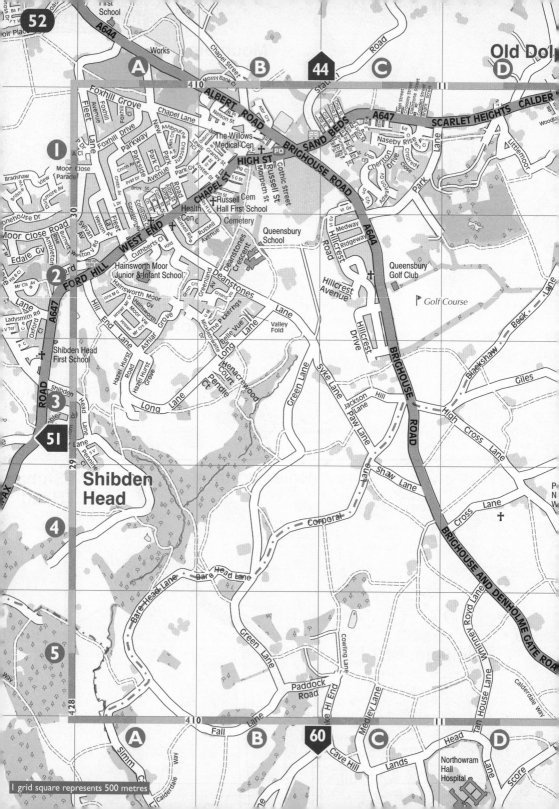

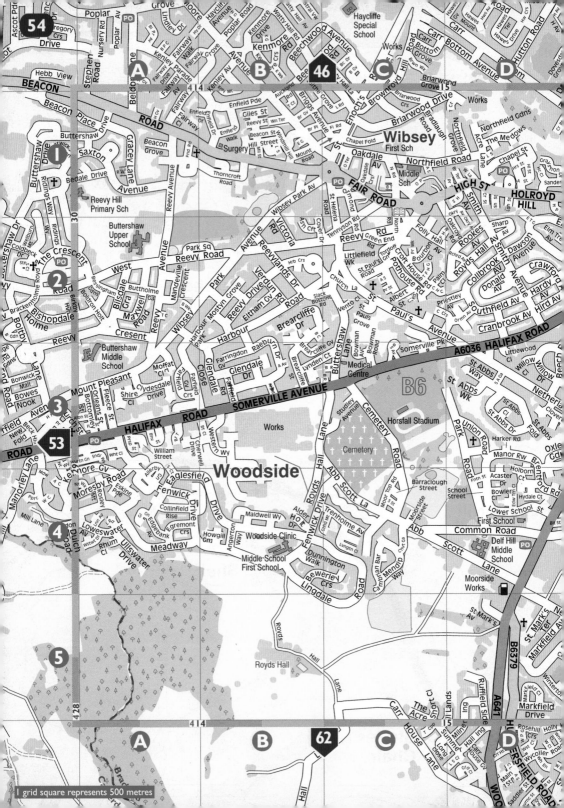

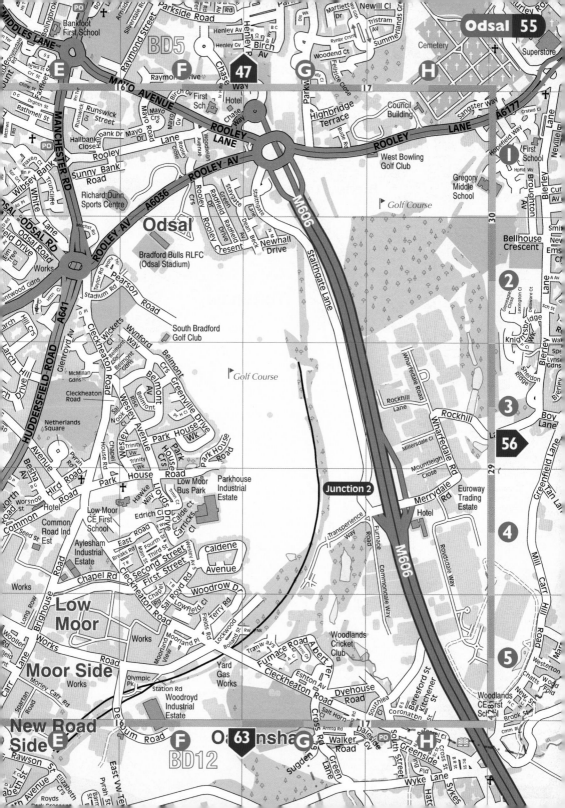

E   F   **53**   G   H

Stone Chair

A644

HALIFAX ROAD

BRIGHOUSE AND DENHOLME GATE ROAD

Bridle

Bridle

Stile

Belle Vue Road

Shelf

Beechwood Avenue

Spring

West Cross St

Sun Wood Avenue

Westcroft Avenue

PH

A644

ORD ROAD

Hud Hill

Queen Victoria St

Victoria Dr

ands Av

ness Park

Westercroft

Greencroft AV

Westercroft Lane

Top Lane

Northowram

Bird Lane

Holme

Wood Lane

Caythorn Terrace

Southfield Terrace

Gate

Denholme

Dominion Industrial Park

Garden Fold

Gardener's Sq

Grove Lane

Groveville

Bradley C

Brodley C

The Grove

Northedge Park

Northedge Park

Hipperholme

Hipperholme Grammar School

Towngate

Kirk Lane

Lane Ends Green

Road

Gate

Coley Road

Coley

Coley

Hall Lane

Soaper House Lane

Bogart Lane

Ash Close

Bramley Lane

Craiglands

Bramley

The Drive

Astral

Amisfield

The Cresnt

Astral

Whitehall Street

Smt

Astral Road

AV

Priestley Green

Northedge Lane

Syke Lane

Leyburn

Holly Bank Dr

The Avenue

Shutts Lane

Norwood Green

Queen's Rd

Norwood Green Hill

Norwood

Bronte Way

Green Lane

Bradford

derdale

I

2

3

62

4

Flowerlands

Leeds Rd

Mountfields

Bramley View

Sutherland Av

Sutherland

Upper Sutherland Road

LEEDS ROAD

Golf Course

Lightcliffe Gf Club

Cecil Avenue

Knowle Top Drive

Knowle Top

5

PO

Lig

Co-Operative Shopping Parade

PO

Hipperholme Clinic

Lightcliffe Preparatory School

Highand Vile

Ludgate Park

Lightcliffe CE Primary School

WAKE

E   F   **70**   G   H

8(T)

LC

Halifax

Old

HALIFAX ROAD

Rd(2)

Tanhouse Hill

Station Road

Badger Lane

Barfield Rd

Southedge

Welburn Av

Sandholme Crcs

Gl Gv

George

Westfield

Westfield Drive

W Gdn

Park Cl

Park Place

Park Place

Coach

Southedge

62

A 414 **B** **54** **C** **D**

Royds Hall

Markfield
Drive

1

Bradford Calderdale

28

HUDDERSFIELD ROAD

WOODSIDE ROAD

B6379

B6379

The Acre

Carr House Lane

Hall Ing

Summer

Milner

Wycoller

Rosehill Crs

Holly

West

Main

Saddler St

Crown

Fernley

Royds

Hall

Lane

High Fernley First School

Wyke Middle School

Grove Works

Hannah Ct
The Hudson

Carr Hall

Huddersfield Rd

Wo Hea

Brick St

Surgery

Gard

Acomb Ter

High   Fernley   Road

West

Hind St

Oakenshaw Court

2

Watford Avenue

27

orwood Green

Queen's Rd

Green Hill

Village

Street

Hill End Close

Norwood

Norwood Business Park

HUDDERSFIELD ROAD

Clare Rd

Hanson Mt

Vicarage

St Mary's Dr

Green Lane

TOWNGATE

Wyk

3

Shutt Lane

Rookes Lane

Station   Road

St Mary's Crs Close

St Mary's

Griffe Head Road

Blackstone

Tofts

Griffe Road

Ashley Rd

61

Shirley Crs

Whitehall Av

Crest Av

Angus Av

Shirley Pl

Griffe Dr

Villa Mt

Paddock Cl

4

Syke Lane

A641

Shirley   Avenue

Meadow

A58(T)

Flowerlands Lane

Leeds Rd

26

Golf Course

Lwr Wyke Green

Wyke

Lower

Lower Wyk

5

tcliffe Golf Club

Cecil Avenue

Knowle Top Road

Knowle Top Drive

Valley Av

Till Carr Lane

PO

Lightcliffe CE Primary School

Park Cl

Coach

Lightcliffe

A FIELD

ROAD

A649

West Av

414

R Street

B

Acacia Drive

East Street

Bailiff Bridge

71

Victoria Road

A641

Mayfield Gv

Royds Old Lane

Highfield Av

Wyke Old Lane

C

Branxholme Industrial Estate

Bailiff Bridge Primary School

D

1 grid square represents 500 metres

64

Woodlands
CE First
School

A

B

56 Spen Valley Heritage Trail

C

Copley House
Farm
Lower Lane

D

418

19

I

M606

2

Kirklees Way

Woodlands Pk

Bradford Road

Cleckheaton &
District Golf Club

Junction 1/26

27

3

Golf Course

63

Hotel

4

M62

426

BD19

Whitechapel
Middle
School

Whitechapel Road

Snelsins Road

Snelsins

Bradford Rd

Cleckheaton
Sports Club

Spenborough
Moorend
CE School

BRADFORD ROAD

Willow St
Kelloe St

Savile St

Exchange Street

HUNSWORTH LANE

Riverside Drive

Stubs Beck Lane

Hang Ing Wood

Dyehouse Dr

Little Wood

Mill Lane

Oak Rise

Savile Park Road

Hunsworth La

Westroyd Avenue

Greenroyd Av

Green Lane

A58

Whitehall Rd W

PO

Whitehall Rd E

Kilroyd Dr

Kilroyd Avenue

WHITEHALL ROAD

Mazebrook Crs

Mazebrook Avenue

Drub Lane

Hunsworth
Lodge Farm

Hunsworth

Links AV

Spen Valley Heritage Trail

**Merchant
Fields**

Brookfield Ter

Brookfield Av

Brookfield View

Kestre IVW

Cliffe

APEL ROAD

5

M62

418

TURNSTEADS AVENUE

Church View

Turnsteads Dr

Turnsteads Mt

Turnsteads Crs

Kenmore Road

Kenmore View

Kenmore Way

Kenmore Crs

Kenmore Dr

Vine Crs

Vine AV

Milton Ter

Mount Gdns

A638

Heaton St

Victoria St

Mount Crs

Mount St

Booth Street

High St

Turnsteads Street

Farfield St

John William St

Balme Rd

Brook Ln

Brooklyn Rd

Brook Hill Road

Fairfield St

Cavan Rd

Moorlands
Small
Business
Centre

Law Lane

Cleckheaton

Wesley St

York St

SCOTT LANE

Valley Road

The Nook

Chapel st

Spenborough
Whitcliffe
Mount School

Park View

W **A** **t End**

West End
Middle School

St Lukes
CE First
School

B

Westcliffe Road

Heaton AV

Heaton Grove Rise

Highfield Road

Grange Rd

Bramhope Road

B6120

Ash St

WHITCLIFFE ROAD

Cemetery

Stanley St

Prospect St

Prospect Street

Holdsworth St

73

Hotel

Bath Pl
Bath Rd
Upp Rd

C

Serpentine Rd

Albion Works

Gr St

Walker St

King St

Sickle St

Northgate

Works

D

Town
Hall

Church
Street

St Peg Lane

MARKET

PARKSIDE

DEWSBURY

Brooke Street

ST PEG LANE

WESTGATE

A643

Surgery lo

PO

1 grid square represents 500 metres

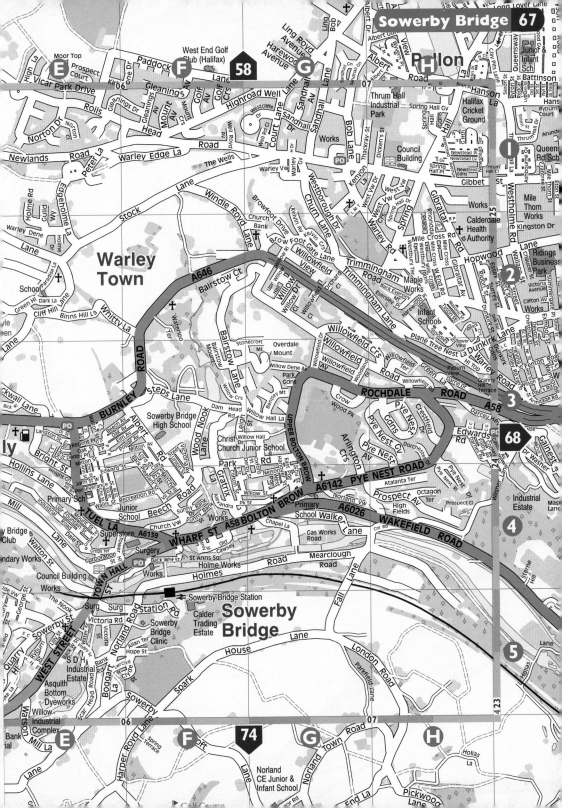

Warley Town

Sowerby Bridge

Pellon

West End Golf Club (Halifax)

Thrum Hall Industrial Park

Halifax Cricket Ground

Council Building

Calderdale Health Authority

Ridings Business Park

Sowerby Bridge High School

Christ Church Junior School

Sowerby Bridge Station

Calder Trading Estate

Sowerby Bridge Clinic

Norland CE Junior & Infant School

58   E   F   G   H   I

2

3

68

4

5

74   E   F   G   H

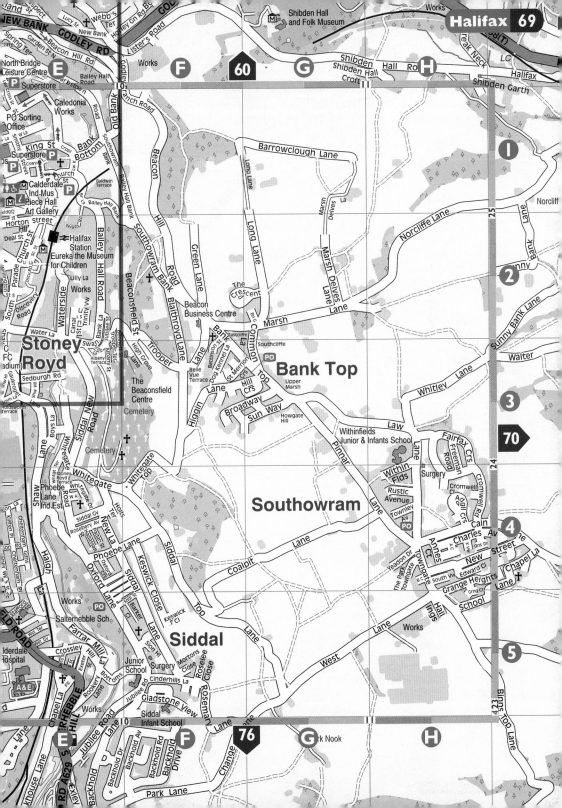

A   B   63   C   Scholes   D

416

Oddfellows St   Wellands Lane

New
Hoplewell
Lane

SCHOLES LANE

Field   Hillcrest   Mt St

BIRKBY

LANE

A649   HALIFAX ROAD

Hartshead
Moor Top

Moorfield
AV

Sunnybank
Close

Copse

B6120

Manor
Street

Works

Hartshead
Moor Side

East Vw

MOOR

Thornton
Street

New Lane

A643

Storefield
Street

1

Whitwood Lane

Birkhouse La

25

Birkhouse Lane

Pits Lane

Brier Hill Cl

Highmoor Lane

Hartshead
Moor Side

2

Birkhouse

WALTON LANE

A643

Clough Lane

House   Lane

Jay

3

71

24

Bronte Way

Highmoor

Lane

Willow Valley Golf
& Country Club

Hotel

M62

i   Hartshead Moor Service Area

4

Thornhills

Bronte Way

Golf Course

Linden Close

5

Victoria
St

Edward St

Kiln Folg

CLIFTON COMMON

A643

Rowan Dr

Towngate
AV

Bramwell
AV

Highmoor
crescent

Savile Ct

Blake Law Drive

Highley Hall Ct

Cliftonhills

Cam Lane

HIGHMOOR

LANE

416

17

Calderdale
Kirklees

A   B   79   C   D

Vine earth

New
Vine
Court

Towngate

Vine
Street

Cannon Hall Dr

Vine
Grove

Cemetery

Primary
School

Highley Hall
Park

Park Rd

Hood Way

Robin
Towngate

Grange La

Well Lane

Green Lane

Blake   Law

Lane

Clifton

Station
Rd

America
Lane

Britannia
Works

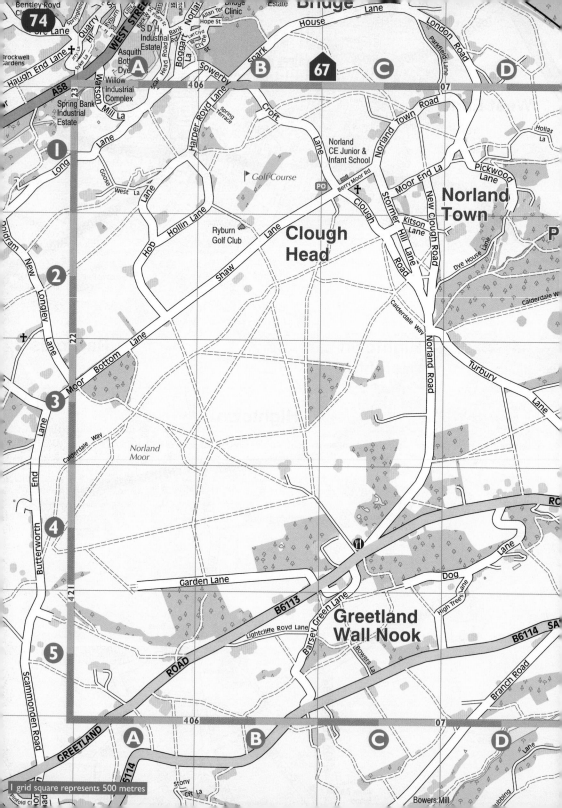

E F 70 G H

Ashday Hall

Brookfoot Works

Brookfoot

Vine Industrial Estate

Binns Top Lane

12 13

Ashday Lane

Wood Lane

Brier Lane

Calderdale Way

Carr Cut

23

Brookfoot Industrial Estate

I

BR

Lilland

Oak

River Calder

Ash Grove Works

Works

ELLAND ROAD

A6025

Cromwell Bottom

Calder & Hebble Navigation Canal

2

Ridge Hill

Foxcroft Dr

Rdg Lea

H Su

Wood Crt

Foxcroft Dr

Lowfields Way

LC

William Henry Smith School

Reins Road

Ascot Gv

Hanson

Holly Bank

Linton

Bedale Av

Highfield Road

Thornton Road

Malham Av

Grove

Field

Castl

3 Rastr

Lowfields Business Park

Calder Works

Booth Royd Lane

Sherburn

Arncliffe Crs

Road

Burnsall Road

Malham

Smith Crs

Mayster Rd

Tofts Gv

Grove

Crowtrees Pk

78

Mdw

Football Club

Old Earth

PO

Grasmere Dr

Thirlmere Av

Elland Old Earth School

Shaw Lane

Lower Edge Road

Carlton Grove

Lodge Dr

Lodge Av

Church La

Arnold Royd

Lower Edge Road

Shannon Road

Mayster Rd

Tofts Gv Gdns

Tofts

Chap

Whitwell Gv

Ennerdale Dr

Alexandra Dr

Bracken La

New Hall Works

Elland Lower Edge

Shannon Close

Delf Hill

The Hoods

Oak Green

4

Carr La

Carr Gre

Wentwo court

Springfield Rd

ve Rd

Whitwell Drive

Whitwell Green Lane

Beverley Close

Elland Upper Edge

Common Road

Bean Street

Banks End Road

Mount La

Croft Works

Spout Hill

Carr Green

Carr Green Av

Lower Fold

Carr Green Dr

HX5

DEWSBURY

ROAD

B6114

A643

Badger Hill

Garlick St

CROWTREES LANE

Grind La

F C

Slade Lane

Clough Lane

5

C

12

E F

Hey Lane

G

Pinfold Lane

ROAD

M H

13

Crof

A629

Road

NEW HEY ROAD

Kirklees Way

Cote Lane

CLO

Fix

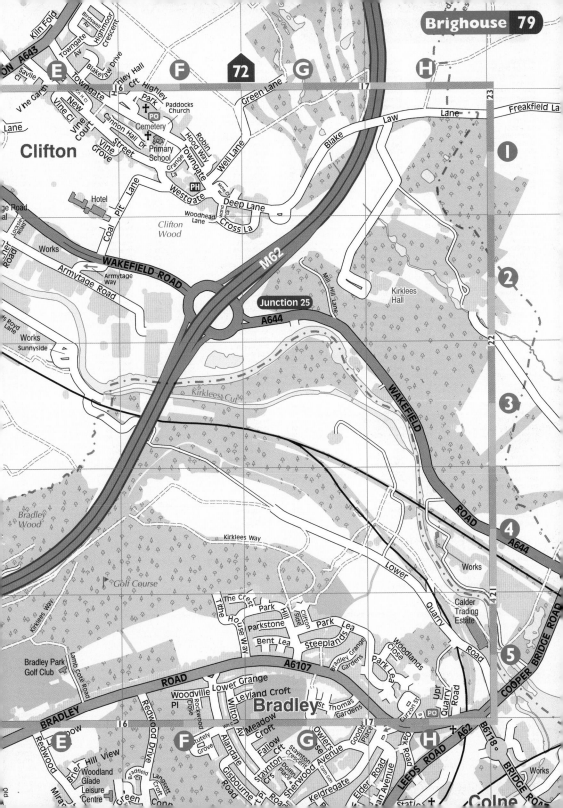

Allerton	37 F4	East Morton	9 F2	Leeming	33 E3	Sandy Lane	36 C1

Allerton ... 37 F4
Ambler Thorn ... 51 G2
Apperley Bridge ... 20 D5
Baildon ... 19 E3
Baildon Green ... 18 B4
Bailiff Bridge ... 62 B5
Bank Top ... 30 B4
Bank Top ... 69 G3
Barcroft ... 23 G1
Beck Foot ... 16 B5
Beechcliffe ... 7 G2
Bierley ... 56 A1
Bingley ... 16 B3
Birkenshaw ... 57 G4
Birkenshaw Bottoms ... 65 H1
Birkhouse ... 71 H2
Black Hill ... 6 C2
Bogthorn ... 13 F2
Bolton ... 29 G5
Bolton Woods ... 29 F5
Boothtown ... 59 F3
Bowling ... 48 A3
Bracken Bank ... 13 G3
Bradford ... 2 B5
Bradley ... 79 G5
Bradshaw ... 51 E1
Braithwaite ... 6 A3
Brighouse ... 78 A1
Brookfoot ... 70 D5
Brookhouse ... 50 A2
Buttershaw ... 53 G2
Cackleshaw ... 13 E4
Calverley ... 31 H3
Catherine Slack ... 51 H4
Causeway Foot ... 42 D4
Charlestown ... 19 F4
Chat Hill ... 44 D2
Claremount ... 5 H1
Clayton ... 45 F3
Clayton Heights ... 45 F5
Cleckheaton ... 64 D5
Clifton ... 79 E1
Clough Head ... 74 B2
Coley ... 61 G3
Copley ... 75 F1
Cottingley ... 26 D2
Cromwell Bottom ... 77 F2
Crossflatts ... 9 G5
Crossley Hall ... 37 H5
Cross Roads ... 13 F5
Crow Nest ... 17 E3
Cullingworth ... 24 A3
Daisy Hill ... 37 G2
Damems ... 13 G4
Dam Head ... 60 C2
Denholme ... 34 B4
Denholme Clough ... 42 D1
Denholme Edge ... 34 B3
Denholme Gate ... 42 C2
Dockroyd ... 12 D5
Drub ... 65 E3
Dudley Hill ... 48 B5
East Bierley ... 57 E3

East Morton ... 9 F2
Eccleshill ... 30 A4
Egypt ... 35 G4
Eldwick ... 17 G1
Elland ... 76 D5
Elland Lower Edge ... 77 F4
Elland Upper Edge ... 77 E5
Esholt ... 20 B1
Exley ... 75 H1
Exley Head ... 13 G1
Fagley ... 40 C1
Fell Lane ... 6 B5
Five Lane Ends ... 29 H4
Four Lane Ends ... 37 H4
Friendly ... 66 D3
Frizinghall ... 28 B4
Gilstead ... 17 F3
Girlington ... 38 B3
Gomersal ... 65 H5
Great Horton ... 46 A3
Green Clough ... 43 G2
Greengates ... 30 C3
Greetland ... 75 F3
Greetland Wall Nook ... 74 C5
Guard House ... 6 B4
Guiseley ... 10 B3
Hainworth ... 14 B3
Hainworth Shaw ... 14 C3
Halifax ... 5 H5
Harden ... 15 G5
Hare Croft ... 25 E5
Harewood Hill ... 13 F4
Hartshead Moor Side ... 72 D2
Hartshead Moor Top ... 72 B1
Haworth ... 22 C2
Heaton ... 38 A1
Heaton Royds ... 27 H5
Heaton Shay ... 28 A4
Henshaw ... 21 F1
Highroad Well Moor ... 58 A4
Hightown ... 73 G3
Hightown Heights ... 73 F3
Hillfoot ... 41 H4
Hill Top ... 35 H5
Hipperholme ... 61 E5
Holdsworth ... 51 G4
Hole ... 22 C3
Holme ... 49 E3
Holme Wood ... 49 E4
Holmfield ... 51 E5
Hove Edge ... 70 D3
Hunsworth ... 64 D2
Idle ... 30 A1
Idle Moor ... 29 G3
Illingworth ... 50 D4
Ingrow ... 13 H3
Keelham ... 43 E2
Keighley ... 7 F3
Kelcliffe ... 10 C1
Knowle Park ... 14 A1
Laisterdyke ... 48 C1
Lane Bottom ... 34 A2
Lane End ... 12 B4

Leeming ... 33 E3
Lees ... 23 F1
Leventhorpe ... 45 F1
Lidget Green ... 46 B2
Lightcliffe ... 71 E1
Lindwell ... 75 H3
Lingbob ... 26 A5
Little Horton ... 46 C4
Little London ... 21 F3
Long Lee ... 7 H5
Lower Grange ... 37 F5
Lower Town ... 33 E2
Lower Wyke ... 62 D5
Low Green ... 21 H3
Low Moor ... 55 E5
Lumb Foot ... 22 A1
Manningham ... 38 D2
Marsh ... 22 C5
Merchant Fields ... 64 D4
Micklethwaite ... 9 F4
Mixenden ... 50 B5
Moorhead ... 27 H2
Moor Side ... 22 A5
Moor Side ... 55 E5
Mountain ... 43 G5
Mytholmes ... 23 E1
Nab Wood ... 27 G1
Nether Yeadon ... 21 F1
New Brighton ... 27 F3
New Holland ... 35 H1
New Road Side ... 63 E1
Newsholme ... 12 B2
Noon Nick ... 27 E5
Norland Town ... 74 C1
Norr ... 26 A4
Northowram ... 61 E3
Norwood Green ... 61 H2
Oakenshaw ... 63 F1
Oakworth ... 12 C5
Odsal ... 55 F2
Ogden ... 42 C5
Old Dolphin ... 44 D5
Ousel Hole ... 9 F1
Ovenden ... 59 E3
Owlet ... 28 D4
Oxenhope ... 32 D2
Peas Acre ... 9 F3
Pellon ... 58 D5
Pepper Hill ... 53 E4
Pickles Hill ... 12 A5
Pickwood Scar ... 74 D2
Priesthorpe ... 31 F5
Priestley Green ... 61 G4
Priestthorpe ... 16 D2
Pule Hill ... 59 H2
Queensbury ... 51 H1
Rastrick ... 78 A3
Ravenscliffe ... 30 D5
Rawdon ... 21 H3
Rawfolds ... 73 H3
Riddlesden ... 8 B2
Ryecroft ... 14 D5
Saltaire ... 18 B5

Leeming ... 33 E3
Sandy Lane ... 36 C1
Sawood ... 33 G4
Scholemoor ... 45 H2
Scholes ... 63 G5
School Green ... 44 D1
Shaw ... 32 C2
Shay Gate ... 26 B5
Shelf ... 53 G4
Shibden Head ... 52 A4
Shipley ... 28 B2
Siddal ... 69 F5
Southowram ... 69 G4
Sowerby Bridge ... 67 F5
Stockbridge ... 7 G1
Stone Chair ... 61 F1
Stoney Royd ... 5 H6
Stump Cross ... 60 B4
Swain House ... 29 G4
Swincliffe ... 65 F1
Sympson Green ... 20 B5
Tarn ... 19 F2
Thackley ... 19 H5
Thackley End ... 19 G4
Thornbury ... 41 E4
Thornhills ... 71 H4
Thornton ... 44 B1
Thorpe Edge ... 30 A3
Thwaites ... 8 A4
Thwaites Brow ... 8 A5
Toftshaw ... 56 B2
Tong Park ... 19 G2
Tong Street ... 56 C1
Toothill ... 78 B5
Tyersal ... 49 E2
Undercliffe ... 39 H2
Upper Brockholes ... 50 B2
Upper Marsh ... 22 B5
Upper Town ... 32 C2
Utley ... 7 E1
Warley Town ... 67 E2
Well Heads ... 35 F5
West Bowling ... 47 G4
West End ... 73 E1
Westfield ... 20 D1
Westgate Hill ... 57 F2
West Morton ... 8 B1
West Royd ... 29 E1
West Scholes ... 44 A4
West Vale ... 76 A5
Wheatley ... 58 C3
Whins Wood ... 13 H5
Wibsey ... 54 C1
Wilsden ... 25 G4
Windhill ... 29 E2
Woodhall Hills ... 41 F1
Woodhouse ... 14 C1
Woodhouse ... 78 D3
Woodlands ... 59 H3
Woodside ... 54 B4
Wrose ... 29 F3
Wyke ... 62 D3
Yeadon ... 21 G1

USING THE STREET INDEX

Street names are listed alphabetically. Each street name is followed by its postal town or area locality, the Postcode District, the page number, and the reference to the square in which the name is found.

Standard index entries are shown as follows:

Aachen Wy *HFAX* HX1 ....**4** C7

Street names and selected addresses not shown on the map due to scale restrictions are shown in the index with an asterisk:

Ackroyd Ct *CUL/QBY* * BD13 ....**44** A1

GENERAL ABBREVIATIONS

ACC	ACCESS	CEN	CENTRE	CP	CAPE	DRY	DRIVEWAY
ALY	ALLEY	CFT	CROFT	CPS	COPSE	DWGS	DWELLINGS
AP	APPROACH	CH	CHURCH	CR	CREEK	E	EAST
AR	ARCADE	CHA	CHASE	CREM	CREMATORIUM	EMB	EMBANKMENT
ASS	ASSOCIATION	CHYD	CHURCHYARD	CRS	CRESCENT	EMBY	EMBASSY
AV	AVENUE	CIR	CIRCLE	CSWY	CAUSEWAY	ESP	ESPLANADE
BCH	BEACH	CIRC	CIRCUS	CT	COURT	EST	ESTATE
BLDS	BUILDINGS	CL	CLOSE	CTRL	CENTRAL	EX	EXCHANGE
BND	BEND	CLFS	CLIFFS	CTS	COURTS	EXPY	EXPRESSWAY
BNK	BANK	CMP	CAMP	CTYD	COURTYARD	EXT	EXTENSION
BR	BRIDGE	CNR	CORNER	CUTT	CUTTINGS	F/O	FLYOVER
BRK	BROOK	CO	COUNTY	CV	COVE	FC	FOOTBALL CLUB
BTM	BOTTOM	COLL	COLLEGE	CYN	CANYON	FK	FORK
BUS	BUSINESS	COM	COMMON	DEPT	DEPARTMENT	FLD	FIELD
BVD	BOULEVARD	COMM	COMMISSION	DL	DALE	FLDS	FIELDS
BY	BYPASS	CON	CONVENT	DM	DAM	FLS	FALLS
CATH	CATHEDRAL	COT	COTTAGE	DR	DRIVE	FLS	FLATS
CEM	CEMETERY	COTS	COTTAGES	DRO	DROVE	FM	FARM

FT....FORT	L....LAKE	PK....PARK	SOC....SOCIETY
FWY....FREEWAY	LA....LANE	PKWY....PARKWAY	SP....SPUR
FY....FERRY	LDG....LODGE	PL....PLACE	SPR....SPRING
GA....GATE	LGT....LIGHT	PLN....PLAIN	SQ....SQUARE
GAL....GALLERY	LK....LOCK	PLNS....PLAINS	ST....STREET
GDN....GARDEN	LKS....LAKES	PLZ....PLAZA	STN....STATION
GDNS....GARDENS	LNDG....LANDING	POL....POLICE STATION	STR....STREAM
GLD....GLADE	LTL....LITTLE	PR....PRINCE	STRD....STRAND
GLN....GLEN	LWR....LOWER	PREC....PRECINCT	SW....SOUTH WEST
GN....GREEN	MAG....MAGISTRATE	PREP....PREPARATORY	TDG....TRADING
GND....GROUND	MAN....MANSIONS	PRIM....PRIMARY	TER....TERRACE
GRA....GRANGE	MD....MEAD	PROM....PROMENADE	THWY....THROUGHWAY
GRG....GARAGE	MDW....MEADOWS	PRS....PRINCESS	TNL....TUNNEL
GT....GREAT	MEM....MEMORIAL	PRT....PORT	TOLL....TOLLWAY
GTWY....GATEWAY	MKT....MARKET	PT....POINT	TPK....TURNPIKE
GV....GROVE	MKTS....MARKETS	PTH....PATH	TR....TRACK
HGR....HIGHER	ML....MALL	PZ....PIAZZA	TRL....TRAIL
HL....HILL	ML....MILL	QD....QUADRANT	TWR....TOWER
HLS....HILLS	MNR....MANOR	QU....QUEEN	U/P....UNDERPASS
HO....HOUSE	MS....MEWS	QY....QUAY	UNI....UNIVERSITY
HOL....HOLLOW	MSN....MISSION	R....RIVER	UPR....UPPER
HOSP....HOSPITAL	MT....MOUNT	RBT....ROUNDABOUT	V....VALE
HRB....HARBOUR	MTN....MOUNTAIN	RD....ROAD	VA....VALLEY
HTH....HEATH	MTS....MOUNTAINS	RDG....RIDGE	VIAD....VIADUCT
HTS....HEIGHTS	MUS....MUSEUM	REP....REPUBLIC	VIL....VILLA
HVN....HAVEN	MWY....MOTORWAY	RES....RESERVOIR	VIS....VISTA
HWY....HIGHWAY	N....NORTH	RFC....RUGBY FOOTBALL CLUB	VLG....VILLAGE
IMP....IMPERIAL	NE....NORTH EAST	RI....RISE	VLS....VILLAS
IN....INLET	NW....NORTH WEST	RP....RAMP	VW....VIEW
IND EST....INDUSTRIAL ESTATE	O/P....OVERPASS	RW....ROW	W....WEST
INF....INFIRMARY	OFF....OFFICE	S....SOUTH	WD....WOOD
INFO....INFORMATION	ORCH....ORCHARD	SCH....SCHOOL	WHF....WHARF
INT....INTERCHANGE	OV....OVAL	SE....SOUTH EAST	WK....WALK
IS....ISLAND	PAL....PALACE	SER....SERVICE AREA	WKS....WALKS
JCT....JUNCTION	PAS....PASSAGE	SH....SHORE	WLS....WELLS
JTY....JETTY	PAV....PAVILION	SHOP....SHOPPING	WY....WAY
KG....KING	PDE....PARADE	SKWY....SKYWAY	YD....YARD
KNL....KNOLL	PH....PUBLIC HOUSE	SMT....SUMMIT	YHA....YOUTH HOSTEL

POSTCODE TOWNS AND AREA ABBREVIATIONS

AIRE....Airedale	CLAY....Clayton	HFAX....Halifax	LVSG....Liversedge
BAIL....Baildon	CLECK....Cleckheaton	HIPP....Hipperholme	MIRF....Mirfield
BFD....Bradford	CUL/QBY....Cullingworth/Queensbury	HTON....Heaton	PDSY/CALV....Pudsey/Calverley
BFDE....Bradford east	ECHL....Eccleshill	HUDN....Huddersfield north	RPDN/SBR....Ripponden/Sowerby Bridge
BGLY....Bingley	ELL....Elland	HWTH....Haworth	SHPY....Shipley
BIRK/DRI....Birkenshaw/Drighlington	GIR....Girlington	IDLE....Idle	WBOW....West Bowling
BOW....Bowling	GSLY....Guiseley	LM/WK....Low Moor/Wyke	WBSY....Wibsey
BRIG....Brighouse	GTHN....Great Horton	LUD/ILL....Luddenden/Illingworth	WIL/AL....Wilsden/Allerton
BTLY....Batley	GTL/HWG....Greetland/Holywell Green		YEA....Yeadon

Index - streets

A

Aachen Wy *HFAX* HX1 ....4 C7
Abaseen Cl *BFDE* BD3 ....3 K5
Abbey La *LUD/ILL* HX2 ....66 C1
Abbey Lea *WIL/AL* BD15 ....37 F4
Abbey Wk *HIPP* HX3 ....68 D4
Abbey Wk South *HIPP* HX3 ....68 D4
Abbotside Cl *IDLE* * BD10 ....30 B3
Abbotts Ter *HFAX* HX1 ....4 C4
Abb Scott La *LM/WK* BD12 ....54 C4
Abelia Mt *GTHN* BD7 ....45 H1
Abel St *LM/WK* BD12 ....62 D1
Aberdeen Pl *GTHN* BD7 ....46 B2
Aberdeen Ter *CLAY* BD14 ....45 G3
  GTHN BD7 ....46 B1
Aberford Rd *GIR* BD8 ....38 C3
Abingdon St *GIR* BD8 ....38 C3
Acacia Dr *BRIG* HD6 ....71 F1
  WIL/AL BD15 ....26 D5
Acacia Park Crs *IDLE* BD10 ....21 E4
Acacia Park Dr *IDLE* BD10 ....21 E4
Acacia Park Ter *IDLE* BD10 ....21 E4
Acaster St *LM/WK* BD12 ....54 D4
Acer Wy *CLECK* BD19 ....63 C5
Ackroyd Ct *CUL/QBY* * BD13 ....44 A1
Ackworth Av *YEA* LS19 ....11 H5
Ackworth Crs *YEA* LS19 ....11 H5
Ackworth Dr *YEA* LS19 ....11 H5
Ackworth St *WBOW* BD5 ....47 F3
Acomb Ter *LM/WK* BD12 ....62 D2
Acorn Cl *WBSY* BD6 ....53 H4
Acorn Pk *BAIL* BD17 ....19 F4
Acorn St *HFAX* HX1 ....4 C3
The Acre *LM/WK* BD12 ....54 C5
Acre Av *ECHL* BD2 ....30 A4
Acre Cl *ECHL* BD2 ....30 A4
Acre Crs *ECHL* BD2 ....30 A4
Acre Dr *ECHL* BD2 ....30 A4

Acre Gv *ECHL* * BD2 ....30 A4
Acrehowe Ri *BAIL* BD17 ....19 E2
Acre La *ECHL* BD2 ....30 A5
  HWTH BD22 ....22 D2
  WBSY BD6 ....54 D1
Acre Ri *BAIL* BD17 ....18 D2
Acres St *KGHY* BD21 ....7 E5
Acton St *BFDE* BD3 ....40 B5
Adam Cft *CUL/QBY* BD13 ....24 C3
Adam St *WBSY* BD6 ....54 C1
Ada St *BAIL* BD17 ....19 F4
  CUL/QBY BD13 ....52 A1
  HIPP HX3 ....59 H4
  KGHY BD21 ....6 D4
  SHPY BD18 ....28 A1
Addison Av *BFDE* BD3 ....40 C3
Addison Dr *HWTH* BD22 ....22 D3
Addi St *BOW* BD4 ....48 B4
Adelaide St *HFAX* HX1 ....4 B4
  WBOW BD5 ....47 F2
Adgil Crs *HIPP* HX3 ....69 H4
Adolphus St *BFD* BD1 ....3 F6
Adwalton Gv *CUL/QBY* BD13 ....52 C1
Agar St *GIR* BD8 ....38 A4
Agar Ter *GIR* BD8 ....38 A4
Agnes St *KGHY* BD21 ....7 F2
Ainley St *ELL* HX5 ....76 C5
Ainsbury Av *IDLE* BD10 ....20 A3
Ainsdale Gv *CUL/QBY* BD13 ....24 D3
Airebank *BGLY* BD16 ....16 B3
Aire Cl *BAIL* BD17 ....18 C5
Airedale Av *BGLY* BD16 ....26 D3
Airedale College Mt *BFDE* BD3 ....39 H3
Airedale College Rd *BFDE* BD3 ....39 H3
Airedale College Ter *BFDE* BD3 ....39 H3
Airedale Crs *BFDE* BD3 ....39 H3
Airedale Dr *HIPP* HX3 ....53 E5
Airedale Mt *AIRE* BD20 ....8 D3
Airedale Pl *BAIL* BD17 ....19 F4
Airedale Rd *BFDE* BD3 ....39 G3
  KGHY BD21 ....8 A3

Airedale St *BGLY* BD16 ....16 C3
  ECHL BD2 ....40 A1
  KGHY BD21 ....7 H3
Aire Gv *YEA* LS19 ....11 H5
Aire St *KGHY* BD16 ....16 B1
  BRIG HD6 ....78 C2
  HWTH BD22 ....23 E2
  IDLE BD10 ....19 H5
  KGHY BD21 ....7 G3
Airevalley Rd *KGHY* BD21 ....7 H3
Aire Vw *AIRE* BD20 ....8 A1
  YEA LS19 ....11 H5
Aire View Av *BGLY* BD16 ....27 E1
  SHPY BD18 ....28 B1
Aireview Crs *BAIL* BD17 ....18 B5
Aire View Dr *AIRE* BD20 ....8 D4
Aire View Ter *KGHY* BD21 ....7 H5
Aireville Av *SHPY* BD18 ....28 C5
  SHPY BD18 ....28 C4
Aireville Cl *AIRE* BD20 ....6 D1
  SHPY BD18 ....28 C4
Aireville Crs *HTON* BD9 ....28 C4
Aireville Dr *HTON* BD9 ....28 C4
Aireville Gra *SHPY* BD18 ....28 C5
Aireville Gv *HTON* BD9 ....28 C4
Aireville Mt *AIRE* BD20 ....8 D4
Aireville Ri *HTON* BD9 ....28 C5
Aireville Rd *HTON* BD9 ....28 C4
Aireville St *AIRE* BD20 ....6 D1
Aire Wy *BAIL* BD17 ....18 B5
Aireworth Cl *KGHY* BD21 ....7 H3
Aireworth Gv *KGHY* BD21 ....7 H3
Aireworth Rd *KGHY* BD21 ....7 H2
Aireworth St *KGHY* BD21 ....7 E5
Airey St *KGHY* BD21 ....6 D4
Akam Rd *BFD* BD1 ....2 A4
Aked's Rd *HFAX* HX1 ....4 E5
Aked St *BFD* * BD1 ....3 F5
Akroyd Ct *HIPP* HX3 ....5 G1
Akroyd Pl *HFAX* HX1 ....5 G2
Akroyd Ter *LUD/ILL* HX2 ....68 A3
Alabama St *HFAX* HX1 ....4 B3

Aac - Alb

Alban St *BOW* BD4 ....48 A3
Albany Ct *KGHY* BD21 ....6 D3
Albany St *HIPP* HX3 ....5 K7
  WBOW * BD5 ....47 F3
  WBSY BD6 ....54 D1
Albany Ter *HIPP* HX3 ....5 K7
Albert Av *IDLE* BD10 ....30 B1
  LUD/ILL HX2 ....58 D5
  SHPY BD18 ....17 H5
Albert Ct *LUD/ILL* HX2 ....58 D5
Albert Crs *BIRK/DRI* BD11 ....65 C1
  CUL/QBY BD13 ....52 B1
Albert Dr *LUD/ILL* HX2 ....58 C5
Albert Gdns *LUD/ILL* HX2 ....58 D5
Albert Pl *BFDE* BD3 ....40 D4
Albert Prom *HIPP* HX3 ....68 B4
Albert Rd *CUL/QBY* BD13 ....44 A5
  LUD/ILL HX2 ....58 D5
  RPDN/SBR HX6 ....67 F3
  SHPY BD18 ....28 A1
Albert St *BAIL* BD17 ....18 D5
  BRIG HD6 ....71 H5
  CLECK * BD19 ....64 C5
  CUL/QBY BD13 ....44 A1
  CUL/QBY BD13 ....52 C1
  ELL HX5 ....76 C5
  HFAX HX1 ....4 E3
  HWTH BD22 ....23 G1
  IDLE BD10 ....30 A3
  ....7 E4
  LM/WK BD12 ....62 D3
  WBSY BD6 ....54 C2
  WIL/AL BD15 ....25 H5
Albert Ter *LM/WK* BD12 ....55 G5
  SHPY BD18 ....18 A5
Albert Vw *LUD/ILL* HX2 ....58 D5
Albert Wy *BIRK/DRI* BD11 ....65 G1
Albion Ct *HFAX* HX1 ....5 G3
Albion Fold *WIL/AL* BD15 ....25 H4
Albion Rd *IDLE* BD10 ....30 B1

Albion St *BRIG* HD6 ....71 F5
CLECK BD19 ....73 H1
CUL/QBY BD13 ....34 C4
CUL/QBY BD13 ....52 A1
ELL HX5 ....76 D5
HFAX HX1 ....5 H4
HWTH BD22 ....23 F1
WBSY BD6 ....53 H3
Alcester Garth *BFDE* BD3 ....3 J3
Alder Av *KGHY* BD21 ....14 C1
Alder Carr *BAIL* BD17 ....18 C3
Alder Dr *PDSY/CALV* LS28 ......41 G4
Alder Garth *PDSY/CALV* LS28 ..41 G4
Alder Gv *LUD/ILL* HX2 ....50 D4
Alder Holt Dr *WBSY* BD6 ....54 B4
Aldermanbury *BFD* BD1 ....2 C6
Alderscholes Cl *CUL/QBY* BD13 ..44 A1
Alderscholes La *CUL/QBY* BD13 ..43 H2
Alderson St *WBSY* BD6 ....53 H3
Alegar St *BRIG* HD6 ....78 D1
Alexander Sq *CLAY* BD14 ....45 E3
Alexander St *WBSY* BD6 ....54 C2
Alexander Ter *HFAX* HX1 ....4 B3
Alexandra Cl *RPDN/SBR* HX6 ....67 F4
Alexandra Crs *ELL* HX5 ....77 E4
Alexandra Gv *PDSY/CALV* LS28 ..41 H5
Alexandra Rd *ECHL* BD2 ....30 B4
PDSY/CALV LS28 ....49 H1
SHPY BD18 ....28 B2
Alexandra St *CUL/QBY* * BD13 ..52 B1
GTHN BD7 ....46 D2
HFAX HX1 ....5 G5
Alexandra Ter *ECHL* BD2 ....40 B2
YEA LS19 ....11 H4
Alford Ter *GTHN* BD7 ....38 B5
Alfred St East *HFAX* * HX1 ....5 J4
Alfred St *BRIG* HD6 ....71 G5
GTL/HWG HX4 ....76 A4
HFAX HX1 ....4 B3
Alice St *CLECK* BD19 ....64 C5
GIR BD8 ....2 A2
HWTH BD22 ....22 D3
KGHY BD21 ....7 F4
Alkincote St *KGHY* BD21 ....7 E5
Allanbridge Cl *IDLE* BD10 ....30 D2
Allandale Av *WBSY* BD6 ....54 B3
Allandale Rd *WBSY* BD6 ....54 B3
Allan St *BFDE* BD3 ....3 J6
Allan Ter *RPDN/SBR* HX6 ....67 F5
Allen Cft *BIRK/DRI* BD11 ....57 F5
Allerby Gn *WBSY* BD6 ....54 A4
Allerton Cl *WIL/AL* BD15 ....37 E3
Allerton Grange Dr
WIL/AL BD15 ....37 E3
Allerton La *WIL/AL* BD15 ....36 D5
Allerton Pl *HFAX* HX1 ....4 C4
Allerton Rd *GIR* BD8 ....37 G3
WIL/AL BD15 ....36 A3
WIL/AL BD15 ....37 E3
Allison La *ECHL* BD2 ....29 E5
Alloe Field Vw *LUD/ILL* HX2 ....50 D4
All Saints Cl *KGHY* BD21 ....7 E4
All Saints Rd *GTHN* BD7 ....46 D2
All Saints Ter *KGHY* BD21 ....7 E4
All Souls' Rd *HIPP* HX3 ....59 H4
All Souls' St *HIPP* HX3 ....59 H4
All Souls' Ter *HIPP* HX3 ....59 H4
Alma Cl *PDSY/CALV* LS28 ......41 H1
Alma Pl *BFDE* BD3 ....40 C4
KGHY BD21 ....14 B1
Alma St *BOW* BD4 ....48 B2
CUL/QBY BD13 ....52 A1
HWTH BD22 ....22 D1
KGHY BD21 ....14 B2
SHPY BD18 ....28 E1
YEA LS19 ....11 H4
Alma Ter *KGHY* BD21 ....14 B2
Almond St *BFDE* BD3 ....48 C1
Alpha St *KGHY* BD21 ....7 G4
Alpine Ri *CUL/QBY* BD13 ....36 A5
Alston Cl *HTON* BD9 ....37 G3
Alston Rd *KGHY* BD21 ....7 G2
Altar Dr *AIRE* BD20 ....8 B2
HTON BD9 ....38 B1
Altar La *BGLY* BD16 ....15 F2
Althorpe Gv *IDLE* BD10 ....29 H3
Alton Gv *HTON* BD9 ....38 A1
SHPY BD18 ....28 C4
Alum Ct *HTON* BD9 ....38 B1
Alum Dr *HTON* BD9 ....38 B1
Alvanley Ct *GIR* BD8 ....37 G4
Amberley Ct *BFDE* * BD3 ....40 B5
Amberley Rd *BFDE* BD3 ....40 B5
Ambler Gv *LUD/ILL* HX2 ....51 E4
Amblers Cft *IDLE* BD10 ....20 A4
Amblers Ter *HIPP* HX3 ....59 H4
Ambler St *GIR* BD8 ....38 D2

KGHY BD21 ....7 G4
Ambler Wy *CUL/QBY* BD13 ....51 H3
Ambleside Av *HTON* BD9 ....38 A2
Ambleside Gdns *PDSY/CALV* LS28 ..41 H5
Ambleton Wy *CUL/QBY* BD13 ..51 H2
Amelia St *SHPY* BD18 ....28 A1
America La *BRIG* HD6 ....78 D1
Amisfield Rd *HIPP* HX3 ....61 G5
Amos St *HFAX* HX1 ....4 B3
Amport Cl *BFDE* HD6 ....78 C2
Amundsen Av *ECHL* BD2 ......29 H4
Amyroyce Dr *SHPY* BD18 ......29 F2
Amy St *BGLY* BD16 ....16 D3
HIPP HX3 ....59 F3
The Anchorage *BGLY* BD16 ....16 C2
Anderson St *GIR* * BD8 ....38 D3
Andover Gn *BOW* BD4 ....48 D3
Andrew Cl *HIPP* HX3 ....69 H4
Angel Pl *BGLY* BD16 ....16 D1
Angel Rd *HFAX* HX1 ....4 D2
Angel St *BAIL* BD17 ....19 E2
Angel Wy *BFD* BD1 ....2 A5
Angerton Wy *WBSY* BD6 ....54 B4
Angus Av *LM/WK* BD12 ....62 D4
Anlaby St *BOW* BD4 ....48 C2
Anne Ga *BFDE* BD3 ....3 F4
Annes Ct *HIPP* HX3 ....69 H4
Anne St *GTHN* BD7 ....46 A4
Annie St *KGHY* * BD21 ....7 F2
RPDN/SBR HX6 ....67 E3
SHPY BD18 ....28 D3
Annison St *BFDE* BD3 ....3 G5
Ann Pl *WBSY* BD5 ....47 F2
Ann St *CUL/QBY* BD13 ....34 C3
KGHY BD21 ....7 E5
Anson Gv *GTHN* BD7 ....46 A5
Anthony La *BGLY* BD16 ....15 G4
Anvil Ct *GIR* BD8 ....38 C3
Anvil St *BRIG* BD6 ....71 F5
GIR BD8 ....38 C3
Apperley Gdns *IDLE* BD10 ......30 D1
Apperley La *IDLE* BD10 ....30 C1
Apperley Rd *IDLE* BD10 ....30 C1
Appleby Cl *CUL/QBY* BD13 ....51 H1
Apple St *HWTH* BD22 ....13 H3
HWTH * BD22 ....32 D2
Appleton Cl *BGLY* BD16 ....17 E1
LM/WK BD12 ....55 G5
Apsley Crs *GIR* BD8 ....38 D3
Apsley St *HWTH* BD22 ....13 E3
KGHY BD21 ....14 A1
Apsley Vls *GIR* BD8 ....38 D3
Aquila Wy *LVSG* WF15 ....73 G3
Arcadia St *KGHY* BD21 ....14 A1
Archbell Av *BRIG* HD6 ....78 C3
Archer Rd *BRIG* HD6 ....79 E2
The Arches *HIPP* * HX3 ....59 H4
Arches St *HFAX* HX1 ....5 F5
Archibald St *GTHN* BD7 ....38 D5
Arctic Pde *GTHN* BD7 ....46 B3
Arctic St *HWTH* BD22 ....23 F1
KGHY BD21 ....7 F2
Ardennes Cl *BRIG* HD6 ....29 G5
Arden Rd *GIR* BD8 ....37 F5
HFAX HX1 ....4 C7
Ardsley Cl *BOW* BD4 ....49 E5
Argent Wy *BOW* BD4 ....49 E5
Argyle St *BOW* BD4 ....48 A3
KGHY BD21 ....7 E4
SHPY BD18 ....28 C3
Argyll Cl *BAIL* BD17 ....19 F4
Arkendale Ms *HFAX* * BD7 ....45 H4
Arkwright St *BOW* BD4 ....48 C1
CLAY BD14 ....45 E3
Arlesford Rd *BOW* BD4 ....48 D5
Arlington Crs *LUD/ILL* HX2 ....67 G3
Arlington St *BFDE* BD3 ....3 J6
Armadale Av *BOW* BD4 ....56 A2
Armgill La *SHPY* BD18 ....29 E5
Armidale Wy *ECHL* BD2 ....39 G1
Armitage Av *BRIG* HD6 ....78 C3
Armitage Rd *HFAX* HX1 ....4 A7
LM/WK BD12 ....63 G1
Armstrong St *BOW* BD4 ....48 C1
Armytage Rd *BRIG* HD6 ....78 D1
Armytage Wy *BRIG* HD6 ....79 E2
Arncliffe Crs *BRIG* HD6 ....77 H3
Arncliffe Crs *BRIG* HD6 ....77 H3
Arncliffe Pl *HWTH* * BD22 ....6 D5
Arncliffe Rd *HWTH* BD22 ....13 H1
Arncliffe Ter *GTHN* BD7 ....46 C1
Arnford Cl *BFDE* BD3 ....3 F2
Arnold Pl *GIR* BD8 ....38 C4
Arnold Royd *BRIG* HD6 ....77 H4
Arnold St *GIR* BD8 ....38 C3
HFAX HX1 ....4 C4
RPDN/SBR HX6 ....67 E4

Arnside Av *AIRE* BD20 ....7 H2
Arnside Rd *WBOW* BD5 ....47 E5
Arthington St *GIR* BD8 ....38 D4
Arthur Av *GIR* BD8 ....37 G5
Arthur St *BGLY* * BD16 ....16 C3
BRIG HD6 ....78 D1
HWTH BD22 ....12 C4
IDLE BD10 ....30 A3
Arum St *WBOW* BD5 ....46 D4
Ascot Av *GTHN* BD7 ....45 H5
Ascot Dr *WBSY* BD6 ....45 H5
Ascot Gdns *GTHN* BD7 ....45 H5
Ascot Gv *BRIG* HD6 ....77 H3
Ascot Pde *GTHN* BD7 ....45 H5
Ashbourne Av *CLECK* BD19 ....73 G2
ECHL BD2 ....39 G1
Ashbourne Bank *ECHL* BD2 ....39 G1
Ashbourne Cl *ECHL* BD2 ....39 G1
Ashbourne Crs *CUL/QBY* BD13 ..52 A1
ECHL BD2 ....39 G1
Ashbourne Cft *CLECK* BD19 ....73 G2
Ashbourne Dr *CLECK* BD19 ....73 G2
ECHL BD2 ....39 G1
Ashbourne Gdns *CLECK* BD19 ..73 G1
ECHL BD2 ....39 G1
Ashbourne Garth *ECHL* BD2 ....29 H5
Ashbourne Gv *ECHL* BD2 ....39 G1
HFAX HX1 ....4 A4
Ashbourne Hvn *ECHL* BD2 ......39 G1
Ashbourne Mt *ECHL* BD2 ....39 G1
Ashbourne Ov *ECHL* BD2 ....39 G1
Ashbourne Ri *ECHL* BD2 ....39 G1
Ashbourne Rd *ECHL* BD2 ....39 G1
HWTH BD22 ....13 H2
Ashbourne Vw *CLECK* BD19 ....73 G2
Ashbourne Wy *CLECK* BD19 ....73 G2
ECHL BD2 ....39 G1
Ashburn Gv *BAIL* BD17 ....18 D2
Ashburnham Gv *HTON* BD9 ....38 A3
Ashby St *BOW* BD4 ....47 H3
Ash Cl *HIPP* HX3 ....61 G5
Ash Ct *CLECK* BD19 ....63 G5
Ash Cft *WBSY* BD6 ....54 B4
Ashday La *HIPP* HX3 ....77 F1
Ashdene Ct *CUL/QBY* BD13 ....24 C3
Ashfield *BOW* BD4 ....56 C1
Ashfield Av *WBSY* BD18 ....28 C4
Ashfield Cl *HIPP* HX3 ....59 E3
Ashfield Crs *BGLY* BD16 ....16 B4
Ashfield Dr *BAIL* BD17 ....19 E2
HIPP HX3 ....59 F3
SHPY BD18 ....28 B4
Ashfield Gv *SHPY* BD18 ....28 B4
Ashfield Pl *ECHL* BD2 ....40 C2
Ashfield Rd *CUL/QBY* BD13 ....44 A1
GTL/HWG HX4 ....75 G4
IDLE BD10 ....20 B5
SHPY BD18 ....27 H2
Ashfield Ter *GTL/HWG* HX4 ....75 G3
HWTH BD22 ....22 D3
Ash Ford Gn *WBSY* * BD6 ......54 A1
Ash Ghyll Gdns *BGLY* * BD16 ..16 C4
Ash Gv *BGLY* BD16 ....16 D5
BIRK/DRI BD11 ....57 F3
BRIG HD6 ....78 D1
CLECK BD19 ....65 F4
KGHY BD21 ....13 H2
Ashgrove *ECHL* BD2 ....40 B1
GTHN BD7 ....2 A7
IDLE BD10 ....30 D2
Ashgrove Av *HIPP* * HX3 ....69 F5
Ashgrove Rd *AIRE* BD20 ....6 D1
Ashington Cl *ECHL* BD2 ....40 C1
Ashlar Cl *HWTH* BD22 ....23 E2
Ashlar Gv *CUL/QBY* BD13 ......52 A3
Ashlea Av *BRIG* HD6 ....78 C3
Ashlea Cl *BRIG* HD6 ....78 C3
Ashlea Dr *BRIG* HD6 ....78 C3
Ashleigh St *KGHY* BD21 ....7 G4
Ashley Cl *CLECK* BD19 ....65 F3
Ashley La *BAIL* BD17 ....28 B1
Ashley Rd *BGLY* BD16 ....16 D4
LM/WK BD12 ....62 D3
Ashley St *HFAX* HX1 ....4 C4
SHPY BD18 ....28 C1
Ashmews *IDLE* * BD10 ....30 D2
Ashmore Gdns *BOW* * BD4 ....56 A2
Ashmount *CLAY* BD14 ....45 E3
Ash Mt *GTHN* BD7 ....46 C2
KGHY BD21 ....13 H1
Ash St *CLECK* BD19 ....73 F1
HWTH BD22 ....22 D3
Ash Ter *BGLY* BD16 ....16 C4
Ashtofts Mt *GSLY* LS20 ....16 D1
Ashton Av *GTHN* BD7 ....45 H2
Ashton St *BFD* BD1 ....2 A4
Ashton Wk *IDLE* BD10 ....29 H2

Ash Tree Av *CUL/QBY* BD13 ....43 G1
Ash Tree Gdns *LUD/ILL* HX2 ....50 B5
Ashtree Gv *GTHN* BD7 ....46 A5
Ash Tree Rd *LUD/ILL* HX2 ......50 B5
Ashville Cft *LUD/ILL* HX2 ....58 C4
Ashville Gdns *LUD/ILL* HX2 ....58 C4
Ashville Gv *LUD/ILL* HX2 ....58 C4
Ashville St *HIPP* * HX3 ....59 F4
Ashwell Rd *GIR* BD8 ....38 C3
HTON BD9 ....28 B5
Ashwell St *GIR* BD8 ....38 C3
Ashwood Dr *AIRE* BD20 ....8 B2
Ashwood St *BOW* BD4 ....56 C1
Ashworth Pl *WBSY* BD6 ....54 E1
Aspect Gdns *PDSY/CALV* LS28 ..41 H4
Aspen Cl *KGHY* BD21 ....14 C1
Aspen Ri *WIL/AL* BD15 ....26 C5
Aspinall St *HFAX* HX1 ....4 B6
Asprey Dr *WIL/AL* BD15 ....37 E4
Asquith Ct *LUD/ILL* * HX2 ......67 G1
Aston Rd *WBOW* BD5 ....47 F4
Astral Av *HIPP* HX3 ....61 G5
Astral Cl *HIPP* HX3 ....61 G5
Astral Vw *WBSY* BD6 ....46 B5
Atalanta Ter *WIL/AL* HX2 ....67 H4
Atherstone Rd *WIL/AL* BD15 ..37 E4
Atherton La *BRIG* HD6 ....78 C3
Athol Gdns *HIPP* HX3 ....59 F2
Athol Gn *HIPP* HX3 ....59 F2
Athol Rd *HIPP* HX3 ....59 F2
HTON BD9 ....38 C2
Athol St *HIPP* HX3 ....59 F2
KGHY BD21 ....7 F3
Atkinson St *SHPY* BD18 ....28 C1
Atlas Mill Rd *BRIG* HD6 ....78 B1
Atlas St *GIR* BD8 ....38 C3
Atlas Works *KGHY* * BD21 ......7 G4
Auckland Rd *WBSY* BD6 ....54 B1
Austin Av *BRIG* HD6 ....71 G4
Austin St *KGHY* BD21 ....7 G3
Autumn St *HFAX* * HX1 ....4 D7
Avenel Rd *WIL/AL* BD15 ....37 E4
Avenel Ter *WIL/AL* BD15 ....37 E4
Avenham Wy *BFDE* BD3 ....3 G3
The Avenue *BGLY* * BD16 ......27 E1
CLAY BD14 ....45 E3
HIPP HX3 ....61 G5
IDLE BD10 ....20 D3
Avenue No 2 *BRIG* HD6 ....78 D2
Avenue Rd *WBOW* BD5 ....47 G4
Avenue St *BOW* BD4 ....56 C1
Averingcliffe Rd *IDLE* BD10 ....30 C4
Avondale *KGHY* BD21 ....6 D3
Avondale Crs *SHPY* BD18 ......28 B2
Avondale Gv *SHPY* BD18 ......28 B2
Avondale Mt *SHPY* BD18 ......28 B2
Avondale Pl *HIPP* HX3 ....68 C4
Avondale Rd *SHPY* BD18 ......28 A2
Aydon Wy *WBSY* BD6 ....53 H3
Aygill Av *HTON* BD9 ....37 G3
Aylesbury St *KGHY* BD21 ......13 H2
Aynsley Gv *WIL/AL* BD15 ......37 E3
Ayresome Gv *WIL/AL* BD15 ....36 D5
Aysgarth Av *BRIG* HD6 ....71 F2
Aysgarth Cl *LM/WK* BD12 ......62 D3
Ayton Cl *BFDE* BD3 ....3 H3
Azalea Ct *BFDE* BD3 ....3 J3

B

Back Ada St *KGHY* BD21 ....6 D4
Back Aireview Ter *KGHY* * BD21 ..7 H5
Back Aireville St *AIRE* BD20 ......6 D1
Back Ann St *CUL/QBY* BD13 ....34 D3
Back Ashgrove West *GTHN* BD7 ..2 A7
Back Aylesbury St *HWTH* BD22 ..13 H2
Back Baker St *SHPY* BD18 ......28 B1
Back Balfour St *BGLY* BD16 ....16 C4
KGHY * BD21 ....7 H5
Back Beech St *BGLY* BD16 ......16 C4
Back Blackwood Gv *HFAX* HX1 ..4 A1
Back Blenheim Mt *GIR* * BD8 ..38 D2
Back Bower Rd *ELL* HX5 ....76 D4
Back Broomfield Rd
KGHY BD21 ....7 E4
Back Broomfield St *KGHY* * BD21 ..7 E4
Back Buxton St *KGHY* BD21 ......7 G4
Back Byrl St *KGHY* * BD21 ....7 F2
Back Caister St *KGHY* BD21 ....14 A2
Back Caledonia Rd *KGHY* * BD21..7 F2
Back Cartmel Rd *KGHY* BD21 ....6 D4
Back Castle Rd *KGHY* BD21 ......7 E3
Back Cavendish Rd *IDLE* BD10 ..30 A2
Back Cavendish St *KGHY* BD21 ..7 F2
Back Cavendish Ter *HFAX* HX1 ..4 D3
Back Charles St *BRIG* HD6 ......71 F5

Back Clarence St HFAX HX1 .....4 E4
Back Clarendon Pl HFAX HX1 .....4 C4
Back Clock View St KGHY * BD21 ...7 E1
Back Close Lea BRIG HD6 .....78 B4
Back Close Lea Dr BRIG * HD6 ...78 B2
Back Clough HIPP HX3 .....60 D3
Back Colenso Rd KGHY BD21 .....7 H2
Back Croft House La AIRE BD20 ...6 D1
Back Cromer St KGHY * BD21 ...14 A2
Back Cromer Gv KGHY * BD21 ...14 A1
Back Cromwell Ter HFAX HX1 .....4 E3
Back Cross La ELL HX5 .....76 B5
Back Dudley Hill Rd ECHL * BD2 ...40 A2
Back Eaton St KGHY BD21 .....13 H2
Back Edensor Rd KGHY BD21 .....6 D4
Back Elizabeth St WBOW BD5 ...47 F2
Back Elmfield Ter HFAX HX1 .....68 B3
Back Emily St KGHY BD21 .....7 G3
Back Eric St KGHY BD21 .....7 F3
Back Eversley Mt LUD/ILL HX2 ...67 H2
Back Ferguson St HFAX * HX1 .....5 G5
Back Field Ct CUL/OBY * BD13 ...44 A1
Back Florist St KGHY BD21 .....7 H2
Back Fold CLAY BD14 .....45 E2
Back Foster Rd KGHY BD21 .....14 A2
Back Foster St KGHY BD21 .....14 A1
Back Gerrard St HFAX HX1 .....4 E4
Back Giles St North
 WBOW * BD5 .....47 E2
Back Giles St South WBOW BD5 ...47 E2
Back Girlington Rd GIR BD8 .....38 B3
Back Gladstone St BGLY BD16 ...16 C4
Back Gooder La BRIG * HD6 .....78 C2
Back Grant St HWTH BD22 .....6 D4
Back Great Russell St GTHN BD7 ...38 D5
Back Greaves St WBOW BD5 .....47 E4
Back Grosvenor St HFAX HX1 .....4 A4
Back Grouse St KGHY BD21 .....7 G3
Back Heights Rd CUL/OBY BD13 ...35 G5
Back High St CUL/OBY BD13 .....44 A1
Back Hird St KGHY * BD21 .....7 E5
Backhold Av HIPP HX3 .....76 B1
Backhold Dr HIPP HX3 .....76 B1
Backhold La HIPP HX3 .....76 A1
Backhold Rd HIPP HX3 .....76 B1
Back Hyde Gv KGHY * BD21 .....7 G3
Back Irwell St BOW BD4 .....47 H2
Back John St CUL/OBY BD13 .....44 A1
Back Kensington St GIR BD8 .....38 B3
Back Kirby St KGHY * BD21 .....7 G3
Back Kirkgate SHPY * BD18 .....28 D2
Back Laisteridge La GTHN BD7 ...46 D1
Back La AIRE BD20 .....9 E2
 CUL/OBY BD13 .....36 B5
 CUL/OBY BD13 .....45 E5
 GSLY LS20 .....10 C2
 HTON BD9 .....28 B5
 IDLE BD10 .....29 H1
 LUD/ILL HX2 .....50 C5
 WIL/AL BD15 .....26 B5
 YEA LS19 .....21 F1
Back Leeming HWTH BD22 .....33 E3
Back Lime St KGHY * BD21 .....14 A3
Back Lindum St GIR BD8 .....38 D2
Back Lombard St YEA LS19 .....21 F2
Back Lord St HFAX * HX1 .....5 F4
Back Lyon St CUL/OBY BD13 .....52 C1
Back Malt St HWTH * BD22 .....13 H2
Back Mannville Rd KGHY BD21 ...6 D5
Back Manor St ECHL BD2 .....40 A1
Back Market St WBSY * BD6 .....54 D1
Back Minnie St KGHY * BD21 .....7 E5
Back Mitchell Ter BGLY BD16 .....16 C4
Back Moorfield St HFAX HX1 .....4 C7
Back Morning St KGHY * BD21...14 A2
Back Muff St BOW BD4 .....48 A2
Back Myrtle Av BGLY BD16 .....16 C4
Back North St LM/WK * BD12 .....63 H1
Back Oak Av BGLY BD16 .....16 C4
Back O' the Ml BGLY BD16 .....15 F5
Back Otterburn St KGHY * BD21 ...7 F3
Back Paget St KGHY BD21 .....6 D4
Back Park Ter HFAX HX1 .....4 C4
Back Pleasant St
 RPDN/SBR HX6 .....67 F3
Back Prospect St KGHY BD21 .....7 F5
Back Queen St GTL/HWG HX4 ...75 H5
Back Rhodes St HFAX HX1 .....4 E4
Back Ribble St KGHY BD21 .....8 A3
Back Richardson St
 LM/WK BD12 .....63 H1
Back Ripley St AIRE BD20 .....8 A2
Back Ripon Ter HIPP HX3 .....59 G4
Back River St HWTH BD22 .....23 E2
Back Rd LM/WK BD12 .....62 D1
Back Rowsley St KGHY BD21 .....7 G4
Back Rupert St KGHY BD21 .....7 F3
Back Russell St WBOW BD5 .....47 E2

Back Rydal St KGHY * BD21 .....6 D5
Back Rylstone St KGHY BD21.....7 H3
Back St Paul's Rd SHPY * BD18 ...28 B2
Back Saltaire Rd North
 SHPY BD18.....28 B1
Back Savile Pde HFAX HX1 .....68 C3
Back Shaw La KGHY BD21 .....14 C3
Back Simpson St KGHY BD21 .....6 D4
Back Sladen St KGHY BD21 .....6 D5
Back Smith Rw WBOW * BD5.....46 D4
Back Springfield St ELL * HX5...77 E4
Back Stone Hall Rd ECHL BD2 ...30 A5
Back Swinton St HFAX HX1 .....4 A6
Back Sycamore Av BGLY BD16 ...16 C4
Back Tamworth St BOW BD4.....48 D1
Back Thornhill St
 PDSY/CALV * LS28 .....31 G3
Back Trinity Ter WBOW BD5.....47 E2
Back Unity St North BGLY BD16 ...16 C4
Back Unity St South BGLY BD16 ...16 C4
Back Victoria St HFAX HX1 .....5 G3
Back Victor Ter HFAX * HX1 .....5 G3
Back Walnut St KGHY * BD21 ...14 A3
Back West St RPDN/SBR HX6 ...77 E4
Back Wharf St RPDN/SBR HX6 ...67 F4
Back Winterburn St KGHY * BD21 ...7 F3
Back Wood St GIR BD8 .....38 D4
Back Wright Av HWTH BD22 .....13 E3
Bacon St GSLY LS20 .....11 E3
Baddeley Gdns IDLE BD10 .....19 H5
Baden St HWTH BD22 .....22 D1
Badgergate Av WIL/AL BD15 ...25 H5
Badger Hl BRIG HD6 .....77 C5
Badger La HIPP HX3 .....70 A1
Badgers Wy ECHL BD2 .....29 F5
Bagnall Ter WBSY BD6 .....54 C1
Baildon Holmes BAIL BD17.....18 D5
Baildon Rd BAIL BD17 .....18 D4
Baildon Stoop BAIL BD17.....18 D4
Bailey Hall Bank HIPP HX3 .....5 K4
Bailey Hall Rd HIPP HX3 .....5 K3
Bailey Hills Rd BGLY BD16.....16 K2
Bailey St BOW BD4.....47 G2
Bailey Wells Av WBOW BD5 ...46 D4
Baines St HFAX HX1 .....4 C5
Baird St WBOW BD5.....47 F3
Bairstow Ct LUD/ILL HX2 .....67 F2
Bairstow La LUD/ILL HX2 .....67 F2
Bairstow Mt LUD/ILL HX2 .....67 F2
Bairstow St WIL/AL BD15 .....36 D1
Baker Fold HFAX HX1 .....4 D3
Baker St ECHL BD2 .....40 A2
 SHPY BD18 .....28 B1
Baker St North LUD/ILL HX2 ...51 F5
Bakes St GTHN BD7 .....46 B3
Baldwin La CLAY BD14 .....44 D4
Baldwin Ter HIPP HX3 .....5 K4
Balfour St BGLY BD16 .....16 C4
 BOW BD4.....47 H3
 KGHY BD21 .....7 E5
Balk La GTHN BD7 .....46 C2
Balkram Rd LUD/ILL HX2 .....50 A5
Ballantyne Rd IDLE BD10 .....19 H4
Ball St CUL/OBY BD13 .....44 B1
Balme Rd CLECK BD19 .....64 C5
Balme St BFD BD1 .....2 E4
 LM/WK BD12 .....62 D2
Balme Ter HWTH * BD22 .....22 D3
Balmoral Pl HFAX HX1 .....5 F5
Bamlett Brow HWTH BD22.....23 E1
Bank IDLE BD10 .....30 C3
Bank Bottom HFAX HX1 .....5 K4
Bank Cl IDLE BD10 .....30 C3
Bank Crest BAIL BD17 .....18 D5
Bank Crest Ri SHPY BD18 .....27 G2
Bank Dr WBSY BD6 .....55 E2
Bank Edge Gdns LUD/ILL HX2 ...58 D2
Bank Edge Rd LUD/ILL HX2 .....58 C2
Bankfield Av SHPY BD18 .....27 G3
Bankfield Dr HWTH BD22 .....6 B4
 SHPY BD18 .....27 G2
Bankfield Gdns HIPP HX3 .....69 G2
Bank Field Gra GTL/HWG HX4 ...75 H4
Bankfield Mt HWTH BD22 .....6 B3
Bankfield Rd HWTH BD22 .....6 B3
 SHPY BD18.....27 G2
Bankfield St HWTH BD22 .....6 B3
Bankfield Ter BAIL BD17 .....19 E4
Bankfield Vw HWTH HX3 .....59 G4
Bankfield Wk HWTH BD22 .....6 B3
Bankfield Yd HIPP * HX3 .....59 G4
Bankholme Ct BOW BD4.....49 E5
Bankhouse La HIPP HX3.....76 A1
Bank Rd RPDN/SBR HX6 .....67 E5
Banks End Rd ELL HX5 .....77 F5
Banksfield Av YEA LS19 .....11 G3
Banksfield Cl YEA LS19 .....11 G3

Banksfield Crs YEA LS19 .....11 G3
Banksfield Gv YEA LS19 .....11 G3
Banksfield Mt YEA LS19 .....11 G3
Banksfield Ri YEA LS19 .....11 G3
Banks La AIRE BD20.....8 A1
Bank St BFD BD1 .....2 D5
 BRIG HD6 .....78 B1
 CLECK BD19 .....73 F1
 SHPY BD18 .....28 C1
 WBSY * BD6 .....54 D1
Bank Top HIPP HX3 .....69 F2
Bank Top Dr AIRE BD20.....8 A1
Bank Top Wy KGHY BD21 .....8 A5
Bank Vw BAIL BD17 .....18 C4
Bank Wk BAIL BD17 .....18 D3
Bankwell Fold WBSY BD6 .....55 E1
Bannerman St LM/WK BD12 ...55 H5
Banner St BFDE BD3 .....3 H6
Bannockburn Ct BOW * BD4 ...55 H1
Bantree Ct IDLE BD10 .....19 H5
Baptist Fold CUL/OBY BD13 ...52 B1
Baptist Pl BFD BD1 .....2 B4
Barberry Av BFDE BD3 .....40 C5
Barber St BRIG HD6 .....71 F4
Barclay Cl CUL/OBY BD13 .....24 D4
Barcroft HWTH BD22 .....23 C1
Barcroft Gv YEA LS19 .....11 F5
Barden Av WBSY BD6 .....53 G1
Barden Dr BGLY BD16 .....17 F2
Barden St GIR BD8 .....38 C3
Bardsey Crs BFDE BD3 .....3 H5
Bare Head La HIPP HX3 .....52 A5
Barfield Av YEA LS19 .....11 F5
Barfield Dr YEA LS19 .....11 F5
Barfield Rd HIPP HX3 .....70 B1
Bargrange Av SHPY BD18 .....28 C3
Barham Ter IDLE BD10 .....30 C5
Baring Av BFDE BD3 .....40 C4
Barker Cl HIPP HX3 .....69 F5
Barkerend Rd BFDE BD3 .....3 G2
Bar La AIRE BD20 .....8 A2
Barley Cote Av AIRE BD20 .....8 A1
Barley Cote Gv AIRE BD20 .....8 B1
Barley Cote Rd AIRE BD20 .....8 A1
Barley St HWTH * BD22 .....13 H2
Barlow Rd KGHY BD21 .....7 E5
Barlow St BFDE BD3 .....3 J4
Barmby Pl ECHL BD2 .....40 A3
Barmby Rd ECHL BD2 .....40 A3
Barmby St LM/WK BD12 .....63 E1
Barmouth Ter BFDE BD3 .....39 G3
The Barn LM/WK BD12 .....55 F4
Barnaby Rd BGLY BD16 .....17 F2
Barnard Rd BOW BD4 .....47 H2
Barnby Av BGLY BD8 .....37 F5
Barnes Rd GIR BD8 .....38 A4
Barnsley Beck Gv BAIL BD17 ...19 E3
Barn St HWTH * BD22 .....32 D2
Barraclough Sq LM/WK BD12 ...62 D1
Barraclough St LM/WK BD12 ...54 C4
Barran St BGLY BD16 .....16 D3
Barrington Cl HIPP HX3 .....69 H4
Barrington Pde CLECK BD19 ...65 F5
Barrowclough La HIPP HX3 ...69 G1
Barr Ter GIR BD8 .....38 A4
Barry St BFD BD1 .....2 C4
Barsey Green La GTL/HWG HX4 ...74 B5
Barthorpe Cl BOW BD4 .....49 E5
Bartle Cl GTHN BD7 .....46 A4
Bartle Fold GTHN BD7 .....46 B3
Bartle Gill Dr BAIL BD17 .....19 F2
Bartle Gill Ri BAIL BD17 .....19 F2
Bartle Gill Vw BAIL * BD17 .....19 F2
Bartle Gv GTHN BD7 .....46 A4
Bartle La GTHN BD7 .....46 A4
Bartle Pl GTHN BD7 .....46 A4
Bartle Sq GTHN BD7 .....46 B3
Barton Ter BRIG * HD6 .....71 F5
 WBOW BD5 .....46 C4
Barwick Gn WBSY BD6 .....53 H1
Basil St WBOW BD5 .....46 C4
Baslow Gv HTON BD9 .....38 A2
Bateman St GIR BD8 .....39 E3
Bates Av RPDN/SBR HX6 .....66 C5
Bateson St IDLE BD10 .....30 D2
Bath Pl CLECK BD19 .....73 G1
 HIPP HX3 .....59 G4
Bath Rd CLECK BD19 .....73 G1
 HIPP HX3 .....68 D3
Bath St BFDE BD3 .....3 G5
 ELL HX5 .....76 C5
 HFAX * HX1 .....5 J5
 KGHY BD21 .....7 E4
Batley Cl BAIL BD17 .....19 E2
Batley St HIPP HX3 .....59 F4
Batter La YEA LS19.....21 H2
Battinson Rd HFAX HX1 .....4 A2
Battinson St HIPP HX3 .....69 F3

Battye St BOW BD4 .....48 B1
Bavaria Pl GIR BD8 .....38 C3
Bawson Ct CLECK BD19 .....65 F4
Baxandall St WBOW BD5 .....47 E4
Baxter La HIPP HX3 .....60 D2
Bayne Dr BOW BD4 .....56 A2
Bay of Biscay WIL/AL BD15 ...27 E5
Bayswater Gv ECHL BD2.....40 C2
Bayswater Ter HIPP HX3 .....40 D5
Beacon Brow WBSY BD6 .....45 G5
Beacon Cl BGLY BD16 .....17 E3
Beacon Gv WBSY BD6 .....54 A1
Beacon Hill Rd HIPP HX3 .....5 J2
Beacon Pl WBSY BD6.....53 H1
Beacon Rd WBSY BD6.....54 A1
Beaconsfield Rd CLAY BD14 ...45 H5
Beaconsfield St HIPP HX3 .....69 F2
Beacon St GTHN * BD7 .....45 H5
 WBSY BD6 .....54 B1
Beamsley Gv BGLY BD16 .....17 E3
Beamsley Rd HTON BD9 .....28 C4
 HTON BD9 .....38 C2
Beamsley Wk HTON BD9 .....38 B2
Bean St ELL HX5 .....77 F5
Beatrice St CLECK BD19 .....64 C5
 HWTH BD22 .....32 D2
 KGHY BD21 .....7 F2
Beaufort Gv ECHL BD2 .....39 H1
Beaumont Rd GIR BD8 .....38 C3
Beck Bottom PDSY/CALV LS28 ...30 D3
Beckenham Pl HFAX HX1 .....58 D5
Beckfield Rd BGLY BD16 .....26 D2
Beckfoot La BGLY BD16 .....16 C2
Beck Hl WBSY BD6 .....53 H3
Beck La AIRE BD20 .....8 A1
Beck Rd BGLY BD16 .....9 F3
Beck Side KGHY BD21 .....7 F3
Beckside La GTHN BD7 .....46 A2
Beckside Rd GTHN BD7 .....46 A2
Becks Rd HWTH BD22 .....6 D5
Beck St KGHY BD21 .....7 F2
Beckwith Dr IDLE BD10 .....30 C4
Bedale Av BRIG HD6 .....77 H3
Bedale Dr WBSY BD6 .....53 H1
Bede's Cl CUL/OBY BD13 .....44 A1
Bedford St BOW BD4.....2 E7
 ELL HX5 .....76 C5
 HFAX HX1 .....7 E4
 KGHY BD21 .....7 E4
Bedford St North HFAX HX1 ...7 E4
Bedivere Rd GIR BD8 .....37 G5
Beech Av CUL/OBY BD13 .....34 B1
 RPDN/SBR HX6 .....67 E3
Beech Cl HIPP HX3 .....53 G4
 IDLE BD10 .....20 A4
Beech Crs BAIL BD17 .....18 A5
 BFDE BD3 .....3 K1
Beech Dr CUL/OBY BD13.....34 B1
Beecher St HIPP HX3 .....59 G3
 KGHY BD21 .....7 H2
The Beeches BAIL BD17 .....19 E2
 GSLY LS20 .....10 C4
 PDSY/CALV LS28 .....41 G4
Beeches Rd KGHY BD21 .....7 H3
Beech Gv BFDE BD3 .....3 J1
 BGLY BD16 .....17 E3
 CLAY BD14 .....45 E5
 CLECK BD19 .....65 F4
 HIPP HX3 .....59 F4
Beech Lees PDSY/CALV LS28 ...31 H5
Beechmount Cl BAIL BD17 .....19 E2
Beech Rd RPDN/SBR HX6 .....67 F4
 WBSY BD6 .....54 D3
Beech Sq CLAY BD14 .....45 F4
Beech St BGLY BD16 .....16 C5
 ELL HX5 .....76 C5
 HFAX * HX1 .....4 E3
 KGHY BD21 .....7 H3
Beech Ter BFDE BD3 .....3 J2
Beechtree Ct BAIL BD17 .....18 B4
Beech Vw RPDN/SBR * HX6 ...67 E3
Beech Wk CLECK BD19 .....65 C5
Beechwood Av AIRE BD20.....8 A2
 HIPP HX3 .....53 E5
 LUD/ILL HX2 .....51 F5
 RPDN/SBR HX6 .....27 H2
 SHPY BD18 .....27 H2
 WBSY BD6 .....46 C5
Beechwood Cl LUD/ILL HX2 ...59 E1
Beechwood Crs RPDN/SBR HX6 ...66 C5
Beechwood Dr LUD/ILL HX2 ...59 E1
 RPDN/SBR HX6 .....66 C5
 WBSY BD6 .....46 C5
Beechwood Gv LUD/ILL * HX2 ...59 E1
 SHPY BD18 .....27 H2
 WBSY BD6 .....46 C5
Beechwood Rd LUD/ILL HX2 ...59 E1
 WBSY BD6 .....46 B5

Beechwood St *PDSY/CALV* LS28 ....41 H3
Beecroft St *KGHY* BD21 ....7 G4
Beehive St *WBSY* BD6 ....54 A3
Beehive Yd *WBSY* BD6 ....54 A3
Bela Av *BOW* BD4 ....48 B4
Belcross Dr *HIPP* HX3 ....5 J1
Beldon La *WBSY* BD6 ....54 A1
Beldon Park Av *GTHN* BD7 ....46 A5
Beldon Park Cl *GTHN* BD7 ....46 A5
Beldon Pl *ECHL* BD2 ....40 A2
Beldon Rd *GTHN* BD7 ....46 B4
Belfast St *HFAX* HX1 ....4 B6
The Belfry *YEA* LS19 ....11 H5
Belgrave Av *HIPP* HX3 ....5 K1
Belgrave Cl *HIPP* HX3 ....5 K1
Belgrave Crs *HIPP* HX3 ....60 B5
Belgrave Dr *HIPP* HX3 ....60 B5
Belgrave Gdns *HIPP* HX3 ....5 K1
Belgrave Ms *YEA* * LS19 ....21 F2
Belgrave Mt *HIPP* HX3 ....60 A4
Belgrave Pk *HIPP* HX3 ....5 K1
Belgrave Rd *BGLY* BD16 ....16 D3
   KGHY BD21 ....7 E3
Belgrave St *RPDN/SBR* HX6 ....67 E4
Bell Bank Vw *BGLY* BD16 ....16 B2
Bell Dean Rd *WIL/AL* BD15 ....37 E4
Belle Isle Rd *HWTH* BD22 ....22 D3
Bellerby Brow *WBSY* BD6 ....53 G1
Belle View Ri *HIPP* HX3 ....53 E5
Belle Vue *CUL/QBY* BD13 ....52 B3
   GIR BD8 ....2 A1
Belle Vue Crs *HIPP* HX3 ....5 K1
Belle Vue Dr *PDSY/CALV* LS28 .....41 H1
Belle Vue Pk *HFAX* * HX1 ....4 D4
Belle Vue Ri *HIPP* HX3 ....53 E5
Belle Vue Ter *HIPP* HX3 ....69 F3
   KGHY * BD21 ....7 G5
Bell Hall Mt *HFAX* HX1 ....68 B3
Bell Hall Ter *HFAX* HX1 ....68 B3
Bell House Av *BOW* BD4 ....56 A1
Bellhouse Crs *BOW* BD4 ....56 A2
Belloe St *WBOW* BD5 ....47 E3
Bellshaw St *GIR* BD8 ....37 H5
Bell St *HIPP* HX3 ....5 J1
   LM/WK BD12 ....62 D1
Belmont Av *BAIL* BD17 ....18 C3
   LM/WK BD12 ....55 F3
Belmont Cl *BAIL* BD17 ....18 C3
Belmont Crs *LM/WK* BD12 ....55 F3
   SHPY BD18 ....28 B1
Belmont Gdns *WBSY* BD6 ....55 E3
Belmont Gv *WBSY* BD6 ....55 E3
   YEA LS19 ....21 H1
Belmont Pl *HFAX* HX1 ....4 C6
Belmont Ri *BAIL* BD17 ....18 C3
   LM/WK BD12 ....55 F3
Belmont St *ECHL* BD2 ....30 B4
   HIPP HX3 ....60 B5
   RPDN/SBR * HX6 ....67 F4
Belmont Ter *LUD/ILL* HX2 ....66 B3
   SHPY BD18 ....28 B1
Belton Cl *GTHN* BD7 ....46 B4
Belvedere Ter *GIR* BD8 ....38 C4
Belvoir Gdns *HIPP* HX3 ....68 D5
Bempton Ct *GTHN* * BD7 ....46 C3
Bempton Pl *GTHN* * BD7 ....46 C3
Benbow Av *IDLE* BD10 ....30 D4
Benn Av *GTHN* BD7 ....46 A3
Benn Crs *GTHN* BD7 ....46 A3
Bennett St *HIPP* HX3 ....5 K6
Bentfield Cottages *CLAY* BD14 .....45 F2
Bent Lea *HUDN* HD2 ....79 G5
Bentley Av *BRIG* HD6 ....71 F1
Bentley Cl *BAIL* BD17 ....18 C2
Bentley Mt *RPDN/SBR* HX6 ....67 C3
Bentley Royd Cl *RPDN/SBR* HX6 ..66 D5
Bentley St *LM/WK* BD12 ....63 E2
Benton Park Av *YEA* LS19 ....21 H1
Benton Park Crs *YEA* LS19 ....21 H1
Benton Park Dr *YEA* LS19 ....21 H1
Benton Park Rd *YEA* LS19 ....21 H1
Bents La *WIL/AL* BD15 ....25 F3
Beresford Rd *WBSY* BD6 ....54 C3
Beresford St *LM/WK* BD12 ....55 H5
Berrington Wy *HWTH* BD22 ....12 C3
Berry La *HFAX* HX1 ....5 K4
   KGHY BD21 ....14 A1
Berry Moor Rd *RPDN/SBR* HX6 ...74 C1
Berry St *KGHY* BD21 ....7 G4
Bertie St *BOW* BD4 ....48 B4
Bertram Dr *BAIL* BD17 ....18 C4
Bertram Rd *GIR* BD8 ....38 D2
Berwick St *HFAX* HX1 ....5 J4
Bescaby Gv *BAIL* * BD17 ....19 F3
Besha Av *LM/WK* BD12 ....55 E4
Besha Gv *LM/WK* BD12 ....55 E4
Bessingham Gdns *WBSY* BD6 .....54 A2

Best La *HWTH* BD22 ....32 D2
Beswick Cl *BFDE* BD3 ....40 C5
Bethel Rd *SHPY* BD18 ....29 E1
Bethel St *AIRE* BD20 ....9 E3
   BRIG HD6 ....78 C1
   HIPP HX3 ....59 F3
Beulah St *LUD/ILL* HX2 ....66 B3
Bevan Ct *GTHN* BD7 ....46 A4
Beverley Av *LM/WK* BD12 ....63 E3
Beverley Cl *ELL* HX5 ....77 E5
Beverley Dr *LM/WK* BD12 ....63 E3
Beverley St *BOW* BD4 ....48 C2
Beverley Ter *HIPP* HX3 ....59 G4
Bewerley Crs *LM/WK* BD12 ....54 B4
Bewick Ct *CUL/QBY* BD13 ....45 E5
Bierley Hall Gv *BOW* BD4 ....56 A3
Bierley La *BOW* BD4 ....56 A1
Bierley Vw *BOW* BD4 ....56 B1
Bilberry Cl *CLAY* BD14 ....45 F4
Bilberry Ri *HWTH* BD22 ....23 E3
Billing Vw *BAIL* BD10 ....30 B2
Bilsdale Gra *WBSY* BD6 ....54 A2
Bilsdale Wy *BAIL* BD17 ....18 A4
Bilton Pl *GIR* BD8 ....38 D4
Binbrook Vw *WIL/AL* * BD15 .....37 E3
Bingley Rd *CUL/QBY* BD13 ....24 D2
   HTON BD9 ....27 C5
   KGHY BD21 ....14 A5
   SHPY BD18 ....27 G1
Bingley St *GIR* BD8 ....38 B5
Binks Fold *LM/WK* BD12 ....63 E3
Binnie St *BFDE* BD3 ....3 J4
Binns Hill La *LUD/ILL* HX2 ....67 E2
Binns La *GTHN* BD7 ....46 A2
Binns St *BGLY* BD16 ....16 D3
Binns Top La *HIPP* HX3 ....70 A5
Birch Av *WBOW* BD5 ....47 C5
Birch Cliff *BAIL* BD17 ....18 C4
Birch Cl *BRIG* HD6 ....71 H3
   WBOW BD5 ....47 C5
Birchdale *BGLY* BD16 ....9 C5
The Birches *GSLY* LS20 ....10 D1
Birch Gv *HWTH* BD22 ....13 H2
   WBOW BD5 ....55 F1
Birchlands Av *WIL/AL* BD15 ......25 C3
Birchlands Gv *WIL/AL* BD15 ......25 C3
Birch La *WBOW* BD5 ....47 G4
Birch St *GIR* BD8 ....38 B4
Birch Tree Gdns *KGHY* BD21 ......7 H5
Birch Wy *WBOW* BD5 ....47 G5
Birchwood Av *AIRE* BD20 ....7 E1
Birchwood Dr *AIRE* BD20 ....6 D1
Birchwood Rd *AIRE* BD20 ....6 D1
Birdcage Hl *HIPP* HX3 ....68 B5
Birdcage La *HIPP* HX3 ....68 B5
Bird Holme La *HIPP* HX3 ....61 E4
Birds Royd La *BRIG* HD6 ....78 D2
Birdswell Av *BRIG* HD6 ....72 A5
The Birdwalk *CUL/QBY* BD13 .....45 F5
Birkby Hvn *WBSY* BD6 ....53 H2
Birkby La *BRIG* HD6 ....71 H1
Birkby St *LM/WK* BD12 ....63 E1
Birkdale Cl *CUL/QBY* BD13 ....24 D3
Birkdale Gv *LUD/ILL* HX2 ....51 E3
Birkenshaw La *BIRK/DRI* BD11 ...57 C5
Birkett St *CLECK* BD19 ....64 C5
Birkhill Crs *BIRK/DRI* BD11 ......57 C5
Birkhouse La *BRIG* HD6 ....72 A2
Birkhouse Rd *BRIG* HD6 ....71 H1
Birklands Moor *CLECK* BD19 .....65 G2
Birklands Rd *SHPY* BD18 ....28 B2
Birklands Ter *SHPY* BD18 ....28 C2
Birk Lea St *WBOW* BD5 ....47 F5
Birks Av *GTHN* BD7 ....46 A2
Birks Fold *GTHN* BD7 ....46 A1
Birkshall La *BFDE* BD3 ....3 K7
Birks Hall St *HFAX* HX1 ....4 D2
Birks Hall Ter *HFAX* HX1 ....4 D2
Birksland St *BOW* BD4 ....48 A2
Birnam Gv *BOW* BD4 ....47 H3
Birr Rd *HTON* BD9 ....38 C1
Bishopdale Holme *WBSY* BD6 ....53 H2
Bishop St *HTON* BD9 ....38 C1
Bitterne Ct *CUL/QBY* BD13 ....45 F5
Blackberry Wy *CLAY* BD14 ....45 E4
Blackbird Gdns *GIR* BD8 ....37 E5
Black Brook Wy *GTL/HWG* HX4 ..75 H5
Blackburn Cl *GIR* BD8 ....37 G5
   HIPP HX3 ....59 E2
Blackburn Rd *BRIG* HD6 ....71 E4
Black Dyke La *CUL/QBY* BD13 ....35 G3
Black Edge La *CUL/QBY* BD13 ....42 B1
Blackett St *PDSY/CALV* LS28 .....31 G2
Black Hill La *AIRE* BD20 ....6 A2
Blackledge *HFAX* HX1 ....5 J5
Blackmires *LUD/ILL* HX2 ....51 F5
Black Moor Rd *HWTH* BD22 ......23 E3

Blackshaw Beck La *HIPP* HX3 ....52 D3
Blackshaw Dr *WBSY* BD6 ....53 G2
Blacksmith *GTHN* BD7 ....46 B3
Blacksmith Fold *GTHN* BD7 ......46 B3
Blackstone Av *LM/WK* BD12 .....62 D3
Blackwall *HFAX* HX1 ....5 F5
Blackwall La *RPDN/SBR* HX6 .....66 C3
Blackwall Ri *RPDN/SBR* HX6 .....67 E3
Blackwood Gv *HFAX* HX1 ....4 A2
Blacup Moor Vw *CLECK* BD19 ...73 G1
Blaithroyd La *HIPP* HX3 ....69 F2
Blake Crs *GSLY* LS20 ....11 E3
Blake Hl *HIPP* HX3 ....60 B2
Blakehill Av *ECHL* BD2 ....40 B3
Blake Hill End *HIPP* HX3 ....60 C1
Blakehill Ter *ECHL* BD2 ....40 B3
Blakelaw Dr *BRIG* HD6 ....72 A5
Blake Law La *BRIG* HD6 ....79 G1
Blamires Pl *GTHN* BD7 ....46 A4
Blamires St *GTHN* BD7 ....46 A4
Blanche St *BOW* BD4 ....48 C1
Bland St *HFAX* * HX1 ....5 F4
Blantyre Ct *CUL/QBY* BD13 ......24 C3
Bleak St *CLECK* BD19 ....65 H5
Bleak St Lower *CLECK* BD19 .....65 H5
Blenheim Ct *HFAX* * HX1 ....5 F2
Blenheim Mt *GIR* BD8 ....38 D2
Blenheim Pl *IDLE* BD10 ....20 A5
Blenheim Rd *GIR* BD8 ....38 D3
Blind La *BGLY* BD16 ....16 A3
Blucher St *BOW* BD4 ....48 C1
Bluebell Cl *SHPY* BD18 ....29 E4
   WIL/AL * BD15 ....37 E4
Bluebird Wk *BGLY* BD16 ....17 F2
Blythe Av *GIR* BD8 ....38 B4
Blythe St *GTHN* BD7 ....38 D5
Bob La *LUD/ILL* HX2 ....67 G1
Bodmin Av *SHPY* BD18 ....29 F2
Boggart La *HIPP* HX3 ....75 C1
   RPDN/SBR HX6 ....67 E5
Bogthorn *HWTH* BD22 ....13 F2
Boland Crs *HWTH* BD22 ....13 F3
Boldron Holt *WBSY* BD6 ....54 A2
Boldshay St *BFDE* BD3 ....3 J3
Bolehill Pk *BRIG* HD6 ....70 D2
Bolingbroke St *WBOW* BD5 ......47 F5
Bolland St *LM/WK* BD12 ....55 F5
Bolling Rd *BOW* BD4 ....53 F7
Boltby La *WBSY* BD6 ....53 H2
Bolton *LUD/ILL* HX2 ....59 E4
Bolton Brow *RPDN/SBR* HX6 .....67 F4
Bolton Dr *ECHL* BD2 ....30 A5
Bolton Gra *YEA* LS19 ....11 H5
Bolton Gv *ECHL* BD2 ....30 A5
Bolton Hall Rd *SHPY* BD18 ....29 E4
Bolton La *ECHL* BD2 ....39 G1
Bolton Rd *BFD* BD1 ....2 E4
   BFDE BD3 ....39 G2
   YEA LS19 ....11 H5
Bolton St *BFDE* BD3 ....3 G4
   BOW BD4 ....54 D4
Bond St *BRIG* HD6 ....71 F5
   HFAX * HX1 ....5 F5
Bonegate Av *BRIG* HD6 ....71 G5
Bonegate Rd *BRIG* HD6 ....71 F5
Bonn Rd *HTON* BD9 ....38 B2
Bonwick Ml *WBSY* BD6 ....53 H3
Bootham Pk *HTON* BD9 ....37 G2
Bootham Wk *KGHY* BD21 ....13 H1
Booth Royd *IDLE* BD10 ....20 A5
Booth Royd Dr *IDLE* BD10 ....20 A5
Booth Royd La *BRIG* HD6 ....77 G3
Booth St *CLECK* BD19 ....64 C5
   CUL/QBY BD13 ....52 A1
   IDLE BD10 ....30 A2
   SHPY BD18 ....29 E2
Boothtown Rd *HIPP* HX3 ....59 G2
Borough Market *HFAX* * HX1 ....5 H4
Borrins Wy *BAIL* BD17 ....19 E3
Borrowdale Cft *YEA* LS19 ....11 F4
Boston St *HFAX* HX1 ....4 B4
   RPDN/SBR HX6 ....66 D5
Boston Wk *WBSY* BD6 ....54 A2
Bosworth Cl *WIL/AL* BD15 ....37 E3
Botany Av *ECHL* BD2 ....29 G5
Botany Dr *AIRE* BD20 ....9 F1
Bottomley St *BRIG* HD6 ....71 G4
   WBOW BD5 ....47 E3
   WBSY BD6 ....54 A3
Bottoms *HIPP* HX3 ....69 E5
Bottoms La *BIRK/DRI* BD11 ......65 G3
The Boundary *GIR* BD8 ....37 H3
Boundary Cl *BAIL* BD17 ....19 E2
Bourbon Cl *WBSY* BD6 ....54 C2
Bourne St *IDLE* BD10 ....20 A4
Bowater Ct *BOW* BD4 ....49 E5
Bow Beck *BOW* BD4 ....47 H2
Bowbridge Rd *WBOW* * BD5 .....47 F4

Bower Gn *BFDE* * BD3 ....40 B5
Bowers La *GTL/HWG* HX4 ....74 C5
Bower St *WBOW* * BD5 ....47 F2
Bowes Nook *WBSY* BD6 ....53 H3
Bow Gn *CLAY* BD14 ....45 G3
Bowland St *GIR* BD8 ....2 A2
Bowler Cl *LM/WK* BD12 ....54 D4
Bowling Aly *BRIG* HD6 ....78 B3
Bowling Back La *BOW* BD4 ....47 H2
Bowling Ct *BRIG* HD6 ....71 E5
Bowling Dyke *HFAX* HX1 ....5 H2
Bowling Hall Rd *BOW* BD4 ....47 H4
Bowling Old La *WBOW* BD5 ......47 E5
Bowling Park Cl *BOW* BD4 ....47 G3
Bowling Park Dr *WBOW* BD5 .....47 G4
Bowman Av *WBSY* BD6 ....54 C3
Bowman Gv *HFAX* HX1 ....4 C3
Bowman Pl *HFAX* * HX1 ....4 C3
Bowman Rd *WBSY* BD6 ....54 C3
Bowman St *HFAX* * HX1 ....4 C3
Bowman Ter *HFAX* HX1 ....4 D3
Bowness Av *IDLE* BD10 ....30 C5
Bow St *KGHY* BD21 ....7 F3
Bowwood Dr *AIRE* BD20 ....8 C3
Boxhill Rd *ELL* HX5 ....76 C4
Box Tree Cl *GIR* BD8 ....37 H3
Box Tree Gv *KGHY* * BD21 ....7 H5
Box Trees La *LUD/ILL* HX2 ....58 C2
Boyd Av *BFDE* BD3 ....40 D3
Boy La *BOW* BD4 ....56 A3
   HIPP HX3 ....58 C3
Boyne St *HFAX* HX1 ....5 F4
Boynton St *WBOW* BD5 ....47 E4
Boynton Ter *WBOW* BD5 ....47 E4
Boys La *HIPP* HX3 ....69 E3
Bracewell Av *WIL/AL* BD15 ....36 D4
Bracewell Bank *HIPP* HX3 ....59 F3
Bracewell Dr *HIPP* HX3 ....59 F3
Bracewell Gv *HIPP* HX3 ....59 F4
Bracewell St *KGHY* BD21 ....7 H4
Bracken Av *BRIG* HD6 ....71 H3
Bracken Bank Av *HWTH* BD22 ...13 G3
Bracken Bank Crs *HWTH* BD22 ..13 G3
Bracken Bank Gv *HWTH* BD22 ...13 G3
Bracken Bank Wk *HWTH* BD22 ..13 G3
Bracken Bank Wy *HWTH* BD22 ..13 G3
Brackenbeck Rd *GTHN* BD7 ......46 A3
Brackenbed Gra *LUD/ILL* HX2 ...58 D4
Brackenbed La *HFAX* HX1 ....59 E4
Bracken Cl *BRIG* HD6 ....71 F3
   ELL HX5 ....77 E4
Brackendale *IDLE* BD10 ....19 G4
Brackendale Av *IDLE* BD10 ....19 H4
Brackendale Dr *IDLE* BD10 ....19 G4
Brackendale Gv *IDLE* BD10 ....19 G4
Brackendale Pde *IDLE* BD10 .....19 G4
Bracken Edge *IDLE* BD10 ....30 B2
Brackenhill Dr *GTHN* BD7 ....45 H4
Brackenholme Royd *WBSY* BD6 ..53 H2
Bracken Pk *BGLY* BD16 ....17 F3
Bracken Rd *BRIG* HD6 ....71 F3
   HWTH BD22 ....13 H2
Brackens La *HIPP* HX3 ....53 E3
Bracken St *KGHY* BD21 ....14 A2
Bradbeck Rd *GTHN* BD7 ....38 A5
Bradford & Wakefield Rd
   BOW BD4 ....57 H3
Bradford La *BFDE* BD3 ....40 C5
Bradford Old Rd *BGLY* BD16 .....27 E2
   HIPP HX3 ....59 H2
Bradford Rd *BGLY* BD16 ....16 D5
   BIRK/DRI BD11 ....65 F1
   BRIG HD6 ....71 G4
   CLAY BD14 ....45 G2
   CLECK BD19 ....64 A2
   GSLY LS20 ....10 B2
   HIPP HX3 ....60 C4
   IDLE BD10 ....29 H4
   KGHY BD21 ....7 G3
   PDSY/CALV LS28 ....41 E3
   SHPY BD18 ....28 B1
Bradford St *KGHY* BD21 ....7 F3
Bradlaugh Rd *WBSY* BD6 ....54 C1
Bradlaugh Ter *WBSY* BD6 ....54 D1
Bradley Grange Gdns
   HUDN HD2 ....79 G5
Bradley La *GTL/HWG* HX4 ....75 G5
   PDSY/CALV LS28 ....41 G5
Bradley Quarry Cl *HUDN* * HD2 ..79 H5
Bradley St *BGLY* BD16 ....16 C3
   HTON BD9 ....28 D5
Bradshaw La *LUD/ILL* HX2 ....51 E2
Bradshaw Vw *CUL/QBY* BD13 ....51 H1
Brae Av *ECHL* BD2 ....39 G1
Brafferton Arbor *WBSY* BD6 ......53 H2
Braithwaite Av *HWTH* BD22 ....6 C4
Braithwaite Crs *HWTH* BD22 ......6 C4
Braithwaite Dr *HWTH* BD22 ....6 C4

Braithwaite Edge Rd
HWTH BD22 6 A3
Braithwaite Gv HWTH BD22 6 C4
Braithwaite Rd HWTH BD22 6 A4
Braithwaite Wk HWTH BD22 6 C4
Braithwaite Wy HWTH BD22 6 C4
Bramble Cl CLAY BD14 45 E4
Bramble Ct HWTH BD22 23 E3
Brambling Dr CUL/QBY BD13 45 F5
Bramham Dr BAIL BD17 19 E2
Bramham Rd BGLY BD16 16 D2
Bramhope Rd CLECK BD19 64 B5
Bramley Cl HWTH BD22 12 C3
Bramley Fold HIPP HX3 61 G5
Bramley La HIPP HX3 61 G5
Bramley St WBOW BD5 47 F3
Bramley Vw HIPP HX3 61 H5
Bramston Gdns BRIG HD6 78 B3
Bramston St BRIG HD6 78 B2
Branch Rd CLECK BD19 63 G4
GTL/HWG HX4 74 D5
Brandfort St GTHN BD7 46 B2
Branksome Ct HTON * BD9 38 A2
Branksome Crs HTON BD9 38 A2
Branksome Dr SHPY BD18 27 G1
Branksome Gv BGLY BD16 27 F1
Bransdale Av GSLY LS20 10 D3
Bransdale Cl BAIL BD17 18 B4
GSLY LS20 10 D3
Bransdale Clough WBSY BD6 53 H1
Bransdale Garth GSLY LS20 10 D3
Branshaw Dr HWTH BD22 13 F1
Branshaw Gv HWTH BD22 13 F1
Branshaw Mt HWTH BD22 13 F1
Bran St HWTH BD22 13 H2
Brant Av LUD/ILL HX2 59 E1
Brantcliffe Dr BAIL BD17 18 C2
Brantdale Cl HTON BD9 27 F5
Brantdale Rd HTON BD9 27 F5
Brantwood Av HTON BD9 27 F5
Brantwood Cl HTON BD9 27 F5
Brantwood Crs HTON BD9 27 E5
Brantwood Dr HTON BD9 27 F5
Brantwood Gv HTON BD9 27 E5
Brantwood Ov HTON BD9 27 F5
Brantwood Rd HTON BD9 27 E5
Brantwood Vls HTON BD9 27 F5
Branwell Ct HTON BD9 37 H2
Branwell Dr HWTH BD22 22 D1
Brassey Rd BOW BD4 47 H3
Brassey St HFAX HX1 5 F6
Brassey Ter BOW BD4 47 H3
Braybrook Ct GIR BD8 38 D1
Bray Cl WBSY * BD6 45 G5
Brayshaw Dr GTHN BD7 45 G5
Break Neck HIPP HX3 60 D5
Breaks Rd LM/WK BD12 55 E4
Brearcliffe Cl WBSY BD6 54 B2
Brearcliffe Dr WBSY BD6 54 B2
Brearcliffe Gv WBSY BD6 54 B3
Brearcliffe Rd WBSY BD6 54 C3
Brearcliffe St WBSY BD6 54 B3
Brearton St BFD BD1 2 C2
Brecks Rd CLAY BD14 45 G2
Brecon Cl IDLE BD10 30 A2
Bredon Av SHPY BD18 29 G2
Breighton Adown WBSY BD6 53 G2
Brendon Ct BOW BD4 48 C4
Brendon Wk BOW * BD4 48 C5
Brentford Rd WBSY BD6 54 D3
Brentwood Gdns WBSY BD6 54 D2
Bretton Ct WBSY * BD6 54 A2
Brewery La CUL/QBY BD13 44 A4
CUL/QBY BD13 51 H3
Brewery Rd HWTH BD22 13 H3
Brewery St HIPP HX3 59 H3
KGHY BD21 7 G4
Brian Royd La GTL/HWG HX4 75 E4
Briardale Rd HTON BD9 27 E5
Briarfield Av IDLE BD10 29 H2
Briarfield Cl IDLE BD10 29 H2
Briarfield Gdns SHPY BD18 28 C3
Briarfield Gv IDLE BD10 29 H2
Briarfield Rd SHPY BD18 28 D3
Briarlea Cl YEA LS19 11 E5
Briar Rhydding BAIL BD17 19 F4
Briar Wd SHPY BD18 29 F2
Briarwood Av KGHY BD21 8 A2
Briarwood Crs WBSY BD6 54 C1
Briarwood Dr WBSY BD6 54 C1
Briarwood Gv WBSY BD6 46 C5
Brick & Tile Ter BRIG HD6 78 B2
Brickfield Gv LUD/ILL HX2 51 F5
Brickfield La LUD/ILL HX2 51 F5
Brickfield Ter LUD/ILL HX2 51 F5
Brick Rw LM/WK BD12 62 D2
Brick St CLECK BD19 73 F1
Brick Ter BRIG HD6 78 C2
Bridge End BRIG HD6 78 B2
Bridgegate Wy IDLE BD10 30 C3
Bridgehouse La HWTH BD22 22 D3
Bridge La HIPP HX3 53 E3
Bridge Rd BRIG HD6 78 B1
Bridge St BFD BD1 2 C5
HWTH BD22 12 C4
KGHY BD21 7 E5
Bridgeway BOW BD4 48 B5
Bridgwater Rd HTON BD9 38 B2
Bridle Dene HIPP HX3 53 F5
Bridle Stile HIPP HX3 53 F5
Bridle Stile La CUL/QBY BD13 44 B5
Brier Hill Cl CLECK BD19 72 D2
Brier La ELL HX5 77 G1
Brierley Cl SHPY BD18 28 D3
Brier St HIPP HX3 59 G3
KGHY BD21 14 A2
Briery Fld SHPY BD18 28 C4
Briggate BAIL BD17 28 C1
BRIG HD6 78 B1
ELL HX5 76 C4
Brigg Gdns HWTH BD22 6 C4
Briggland Ct WIL/AL BD15 25 H4
Brigglands WIL/AL * BD15 25 H4
Briggs Av WBSY BD6 54 B1
Briggs Gv WBSY BD6 54 B1
Briggs Pl WBSY BD6 54 B1
Briggs St CUL/QBY * BD13 52 B1
Brighouse & Denholme Gate Rd
HIPP HX3 52 D4
Brighouse & Denholme Rd
CUL/QBY BD13 43 F3
Brighouse Rd CUL/QBY BD13 42 D1
CUL/QBY BD13 52 B1
HIPP HX3 70 B1
LM/WK BD12 55 E5
Brighouse Wood La BRIG HD6 71 E5
Brighouse Wood Rw BRIG HD6 71 E5
Brighton Gv HFAX HX1 4 C2
Brighton St BAIL BD17 28 C1
HIPP HX3 59 F4
IDLE BD10 19 H5
Brighton Ter CLECK BD19 63 G5
Bright St CLAY * BD14 45 E3
CUL/QBY BD13 52 C1
RPDN/SBR HX6 67 E3
WIL/AL BD15 37 E3
Brindley Gv GIR BD8 37 F5
Brisbane Av ECHL BD2 39 F1
Briscoe La GTL/HWG HX4 75 G4
Bristol Av AIRE BD20 8 C3
Bristol St HIPP HX3 69 E5
Britannia St BGLY BD16 16 D3
WBOW BD5 2 E7
Britannia Ter CLECK BD19 64 C5
Broadfield Cl BOW BD4 56 D1
Broadfolds CLAY BD14 45 F3
Broad Ings Wy HIPP HX3 53 F5
Broadlands KGHY BD21 6 C3
Broadlands St BOW BD4 48 C3
Broad La BOW BD4 48 C2
Broadlea Crs WBOW BD5 47 G4
Broadley Av LUD/ILL HX2 58 A4
Broadley Cl LUD/ILL HX2 58 B4
Broadley Gv LUD/ILL HX2 58 B4
Broadley Rd LUD/ILL HX2 58 A4
Broad Oak La HIPP HX3 70 C2
Broad Oak St HIPP HX3 70 C2
Broadstones Pk BGLY * BD16 17 G3
Broadstone Wy BOW BD4 48 D3
Broad St BFD BD1 2 D4
HFAX HX1 5 H3
PDSY/CALV LS28 41 H1
Broad Tree Rd HIPP HX3 59 F3
Broadway BFD BD1 2 D5
BGLY BD16 16 D3
GSLY LS20 10 B3
HIPP HX3 69 F3
RPDN/SBR HX6 66 A5
Broadway Av WBOW BD5 47 E5
Broadway Cl WBOW BD5 47 E5
Broadwood Av LUD/ILL HX2 58 B4
Brocklesby Dr WIL/AL BD15 37 E3
Brockstones GTL/HWG * HX4 75 E4
Brockwell Gdns RPDN/SBR HX6 66 D5
Brodley Cl HIPP HX3 61 F5
Broken Wy WBOW * BD5 47 E5
Bromet Pl ECHL BD2 30 A5
Bromford Rd BOW BD4 47 H3
Bromley Gv HWTH BD22 13 F1
Bromley Rd BGLY BD16 16 C2
SHPY BD18 27 H1
Brompton Av BOW BD4 47 H4
Brompton Rd BOW BD4 47 H3
Bronshill Gv WIL/AL BD15 37 F3
Bronte Cl CLECK BD19 65 G4
HTON BD9 37 H2
Bronte Dr HWTH BD22 13 F3
Bronte Old Rd CUL/QBY BD13 44 B1
Bronte Pl CUL/QBY BD13 44 B1
Bronte St HWTH * BD22 22 C2
KGHY BD21 7 G3
Bronte Vls HWTH BD22 23 G1
Bronte Wy BRIG HD6 62 C5
BRIG HD6 72 A4
CUL/QBY BD13 44 C1
CUL/QBY BD13 53 E1
HWTH BD22 22 A4
Brooke St BRIG HD6 78 B2
CLECK BD19 73 H1
Brookeville Av HIPP HX3 70 B1
Brookfield Av CLECK BD19 64 C4
SHPY BD18 29 E1
Brookfield Rd BFDE BD3 3 H3
SHPY BD18 29 E1
Brookfields Av CLECK BD19 63 F5
Brookfields Rd LM/WK BD12 63 E4
Brookfield Ter CLECK BD19 64 C4
Brookfield Vw CLECK BD19 64 D4
Brookfoot Av BIRK/DRI BD11 57 F5
Brookfoot La HIPP HX3 70 D5
Brook Grain Hl BRIG HD6 78 B3
Brookhouse Gdns IDLE BD10 31 E1
Brooklands Crs YEA LS19 11 G5
Brooklands Dr YEA LS19 11 G5
Brook La LVSG WF15 73 F4
Brooklyn Ct CLECK BD19 64 C5
Brooklyn Dr CLECK BD19 64 C5
Brooklyn Rd CLECK BD19 64 D5
Brooklyn Ter BRIG HD6 70 D3
Brook Rw GTL/HWG * HX4 75 E4
Brookroyd Av BRIG HD6 71 G2
Brooksbank Av GTHN BD7 45 H2
Brooksbank Gdns ELL HX5 76 C4
Brookside Fold HWTH BD22 32 D2
Brooks Ter CUL/QBY BD13 45 E5
Brook St ELL HX5 76 D5
KGHY BD21 14 A1
LM/WK BD12 64 A1
Brooks Yd HUDN HD2 79 H5
Broomcroft CLAY BD14 45 E3
Broome Av ECHL BD2 39 F1
Broomfield CLAY BD14 44 D4
GTL/HWG HX4 76 A5
Broomfield Av HIPP HX3 68 C5
Broomfield Pl CLAY BD14 44 D4
KGHY BD21 7 E4
Broomfield Rd KGHY BD21 7 E4
Broomfield St CUL/QBY BD13 52 B1
KGHY * BD21 7 E4
Broomfield Ter CLECK BD19 73 E2
Broomhill Av KGHY BD21 13 H2
Broomhill Dr KGHY BD21 13 H1
Broomhill Gv KGHY BD21 13 H1
Broomhill Mt KGHY BD21 13 H1
Broomhill St KGHY BD21 13 H2
Broomhill Wk KGHY BD21 13 H1
Broomhill Wy KGHY BD21 14 A1
Broom St BOW BD4 2 E7
CLECK BD19 73 E2
KGHY BD21 7 F5
Broster Av HWTH BD22 6 C4
Brougham Rd HIPP HX3 59 H4
Brougham St HIPP HX3 59 H4
Brougham Ter HIPP HX3 59 H4
Broughton Av BOW BD4 56 A1
Brow Bottom La LUD/ILL HX2 50 A4
Browfield Vw HWTH BD22 13 F1
Browfoot SHPY BD18 29 E2
Browfoot Dr LUD/ILL HX2 67 G1
Brow Foot Gate La LUD/ILL HX2 67 G2
Browgate BAIL BD17 18 D3
Brow La CLAY BD14 44 D4
HIPP HX3 53 G4
HIPP HX3 60 B2
LUD/ILL HX2 51 F4
Brownberry Gv HIPP HX3 53 G3
Brown Hill Cl BIRK/DRI BD11 57 F3
Brown Hill Dr BIRK/DRI BD11 57 F4
Browning Av HIPP * HX3 69 E5
Browning St BFDE BD3 3 J5
Brown Lee La WIL/AL BD15 25 F5
Brownroyd Hill Rd WBSY BD6 54 C1
Brownroyd St GIR BD8 38 C5
GTHN BD7 46 C1
Brownroyd Wk WBSY BD6 46 C5
Brown St KGHY * BD21 7 G3
Brow Rd HWTH BD22 23 E3
Browsholme St KGHY * BD21 7 E5
Brow St KGHY BD21 7 G5
Brow Top Rd HWTH BD22 23 F2
Brow Wood Crs ECHL BD2 39 F1
Brow Wood Ri HIPP HX3 53 G4
Brow Wood Rd HIPP HX3 53 G4
Browwood Ter WBSY BD6 54 A3
Bruce St HFAX HX1 4 B6
Brunel Cl HTON BD9 38 B2
Brunel Ct HIPP HX3 59 G3
Brunswick Gdns HFAX HX1 5 F4
Brunswick Pl IDLE BD10 30 C2
Brunswick Rd IDLE BD10 30 C2
Brunswick St BGLY BD16 17 E3
CUL/QBY BD13 24 D3
CUL/QBY BD13 52 C1
Bryan Rd GTL/HWG HX4 76 A5
Bryanstone Rd BOW BD4 48 C2
Bryan St BRIG HD6 78 B2
Bubwith Gv LUD/ILL * HX2 67 H2
Buckfast Ct IDLE BD10 30 A2
Buckingham Crs CLAY BD14 45 G2
Buckland Pl HFAX HX1 67 H2
Buck La BAIL BD17 19 G3
Buckley La LUD/ILL HX2 58 B3
Buck Mill La IDLE BD10 19 H3
Buck Pk CUL/QBY * BD13 34 D2
Buckstone Dr YEA LS19 21 F3
Buckstone Garth AIRE BD20 9 E2
Buck St BFDE BD3 3 H7
CUL/QBY BD13 34 D4
Bude Rd WBOW BD5 55 G1
Bullace Trees La LVSG WF15 73 H5
Bull Close La HFAX HX1 5 F5
Buller St BOW BD4 48 B2
The Bullfield BGLY BD16 15 G5
Bull Gn HFAX HX1 5 G5
Bull Royd Av GIR BD8 37 H4
Bull Royd Crs GIR BD8 37 H4
Bull Royd Dr GIR BD8 37 H4
Bull Royd La GIR BD8 37 H4
Bundria Ct GIR BD8 38 D2
The Bungalows HIPP * HX3 76 B1
LUD/ILL * HX2 58 C4
RPDN/SBR * HX6 66 D4
Bunker's Hill La HWTH BD22 13 E1
Bunting Dr CUL/QBY BD13 45 F5
Burberry Cl BOW BD4 56 B2
Burdale Pl GTHN BD7 46 C1
Burdock Wy HFAX HX1 5 F4
Burleigh St HFAX HX1 4 B7
Burley St ECHL BD2 29 E5
ELL HX5 76 C5
Burlington Av BFDE BD3 40 D3
Burlington St GIR BD8 2 B1
HFAX HX1 4 B3
Burned Gv HIPP HX3 53 F3
Burned Rd HIPP HX3 53 G3
Burneston Gdns WBSY BD6 53 H2
Burnett Av WBOW BD5 47 E4
Burnett Pl WBOW BD5 47 E4
Burnett Ri CUL/QBY BD13 51 H2
Burnett St BFD BD1 3 F5
Burnham Av BOW BD4 56 A1
Burniston Cl WIL/AL BD15 25 H5
Burnley Rd RPDN/SBR HX6 67 E3
Burnleyville CLECK BD19 65 G4
Burnsall Rd BFDE BD3 3 K3
BRIG HD6 77 G3
Burnsdale WIL/AL BD15 36 D1
Burns St HIPP HX3 59 F1
Burnup Gv CLECK BD19 73 F1
Burnwells Av IDLE BD10 19 H4
Burrage St BGLY BD16 16 C3
Burras Rd BOW BD4 48 A5
Burrow St WBOW BD5 2 C7
Burton St BOW BD4 47 H3
KGHY BD21 7 E2
LUD/ILL HX2 51 F5
Busfield St BGLY BD16 16 C3
BOW BD4 48 A4
Bushill Fold CUL/QBY BD13 43 H5
Busy La SHPY BD18 19 F5
Butcher St BFD BD1 2 A6
Bute Av BRIG HD6 71 F3
Bute St SHPY BD18 29 E5
Butler La BAIL BD17 19 E2
Butler St BFDE BD3 3 G3
Butler St East BFDE BD3 3 H3
Butler St West BFDE BD3 3 G3
Butterfield Homes BAIL * BD17 18 D2
BGLY * BD16 27 E3
Buttermeade Cl WBSY BD6 54 B3
Buttershaw Dr WBSY BD6 53 H2
Buttershaw La LVSG WF15 73 E3
WBSY BD6 54 C3
Buttholme Ga WBSY BD6 54 A2
Butt La HWTH BD22 22 D2
IDLE BD10 30 A1
Butts Green La LUD/ILL HX2 66 C1
Butts Green Rd LUD/ILL HX2 66 C1
Butts Hl CLECK BD19 65 F5
Butts Yd CLECK BD19 73 G1
Buxton Av HTON * BD9 28 D5
Buxton La HTON BD9 28 D5

Buxton St *HIPP* HX3 ....59 F4
HTON BD9 ....38 C2
KGHY BD21 ....7 G4
Buxton Wy *HIPP* HX3 ....59 F4
Byeway *LSG* LS20 ....10 B2
Byland *LUD/ILL* HX2 ....50 C4
Byland Gv *WIL/AL* BD15 ....36 C2
Byrl St *KGHY* BD21 ....7 G3
Byron Av *RPDN/SBR* * HX6 ....67 E3
Byron Ms *BGLY* BD16 ....16 D1
Byron St *BFDE* BD3 ....3 J3
RPDN/SBR HX6 ....67 E3

C

Cadney Cft *HFAX* HX1 ....5 G5
Cain La *HIPP* HX3 ....69 H4
Cairn Cl *AIRE* BD20 ....6 D1
Cairns Cl *ECHL* BD2 ....39 G1
Caister Gv *KGHY* * BD21 ....13 H2
Caister St *KGHY* BD21 ....14 A2
Caister Wy *KGHY* BD21 ....14 A2
Calde Ct *LM/WK* BD12 ....55 F4
Caldene Av *LM/WK* BD12 ....55 F4
Calder Av *LUD/ILL* HX2 ....68 A3
Calder Banks *CUL/QBY* BD13 ....52 D1
Caldercroft *ELL* HX5 ....76 D5
Calderdale Av *BRIG* HD6 ....71 H3
ELL HX5 ....76 B4
GTL/HWG HX4 ....75 H5
HIPP HX3 ....52 D5
Calderstone Av *WBSY* BD6 ....53 G2
Calder St *BRIG* HD6 ....78 A2
GTL/HWG HX4 ....76 A4
Calder Ter *HIPP* HX3 ....52 D5
GTL/HWG HX4 ....76 A4
Calder Vw *BRIG* HD6 ....78 A2
Caledonia Rd *KGHY* BD21 ....7 G3
Caledonia St *WBOW* BD5 ....47 G2
Calpin Cl *IDLE* * BD10 ....30 A1
Calton Gv *KGHY* BD21 ....8 A5
Calton Rd *KGHY* BD21 ....7 H5
Calton St *KGHY* BD21 ....14 A1
Calver Av *KGHY* BD21 ....6 C3
Calver Gv *KGHY* BD21 ....6 C3
Calverley Av *BFDE* BD3 ....40 C4
Calverley Cutting *IDLE* BD10 ....31 E1
Calverley La *PDSY/CALV* LS28 ....31 H3
Calverley Moor Av
PDSY/CALV LS28 ....41 F3
Calver Rd *KGHY* BD21 ....6 D4
Calversyke St *HWTH* BD22 ....6 D4
Camargue Fold *ECHL* BD2 ....29 G5
Camberley Mt *BOW* BD4 ....48 D3
Camborne Wy *HWTH* BD22 ....13 F1
Cambrian Bar *LM/WK* BD12 ....54 C4
Cambridge Pl *BFDE* BD3 ....3 F2
CUL/QBY BD13 ....52 B1
Cambridge St *CLAY* * BD14 ....45 E3
CUL/QBY BD13 ....52 C1
GTHN BD7 ....46 C3
Camden Ter *GIR* BD8 ....2 A1
Camellia Ct *SHPY* BD18 ....29 E4
Camellia Mt *HFAX* HX1 ....45 H1
Cameron Av *LM/WK* BD12 ....62 C4
Cameronian Ct *KGHY* * BD21 ....7 F4
Cam La *BRIG* HD6 ....72 A5
Camm St *BRIG* HD6 ....71 F5
KGHY BD21 ....7 F4
Campbell St *CUL/QBY* BD13 ....52 D1
KGHY BD21 ....7 F4
Campus Rd *GTHN* BD7 ....46 D1
Canada Crs *YEA* LS19 ....21 H2
Canada Dr *YEA* LS19 ....21 H1
Canada Rd *YEA* LS19 ....21 H1
Canada Ter *YEA* LS19 ....21 H1
Canal Rd *AIRE* BD20 ....7 H1
BFDE BD3 ....3 G2
BGLY BD16 ....16 C1
ECHL BD2 ....28 D5
RPDN/SBR HX6 ....67 H4
Canal St *BRIG* HD6 ....71 F4
HIPP HX3 ....5 K6
Canary Dr *BGLY* BD16 ....17 F2
Canary St *CLECK* BD19 ....64 C5
Canberra Cl *HWTH* BD22 ....23 G1
Canberra Dr *HWTH* BD22 ....23 G1
Canford Dr *WIL/AL* BD15 ....37 E3
Canford Gv *WIL/AL* BD15 ....37 F3
Canford Rd *WIL/AL* BD15 ....37 E3
Canker La *HIPP* HX3 ....69 E4
Cannon Hall Cl *BRIG* HD6 ....79 E1
Cannon Hall Dr *BRIG* HD6 ....79 E1
Cannon Mill La *GTHN* BD7 ....46 B3
Cannon St *BGLY* BD16 ....16 C4
HFAX * HX1 ....4 B7
Canterbury Av *WBOW* BD5 ....46 D4
Canterbury Crs *HIPP* HX3 ....59 G4

Capel Ct *PDSY/CALV* LS28 ....31 G3
Capel St *BRIG* HD6 ....78 B2
PDSY/CALV LS28 ....31 G3
Cape St *BFD* BD1 ....2 D2
Captain St *BFD* BD1 ....2 E4
Carden Rd *BOW* BD4 ....48 D2
Cardigan St *CUL/QBY* BD13 ....52 C1
Carisbrooke Crs *WBSY* BD6 ....54 C2
Cark Rd *KGHY* BD21 ....7 F3
Carlby Gv *HWTH* BD22 ....6 D5
Carlby St *HWTH* BD22 ....6 D5
Carleton St *KGHY* BD21 ....7 F2
Carling Cl *GTHN* BD7 ....46 A4
Carlisle Av *YEA* LS19 ....11 H5
Carlisle Pl *GIR* BD8 ....38 D3
Carlisle Rd *GIR* BD8 ....38 C3
Carlisle St *GIR* BD8 ....38 C3
KGHY BD21 ....7 G5
LUD/ILL HX2 ....58 D5
PDSY/CALV LS28 ....41 H3
Carlisle Ter *GIR* BD8 ....38 C3
Carlton Av *SHPY* BD18 ....28 A1
Carlton Dr *BAIL* BD17 ....18 D2
GSLY LS20 ....11 E1
HTON BD9 ....28 B5
Carlton Gv *ELL* HX5 ....77 E4
SHPY BD18 ....28 C4
WBOW BD5 ....47 E4
Carlton House Ter *HFAX* HX1 ....4 D7
Carlton La *GSLY* LS20 ....11 E1
Carlton Mt *YEA* LS19 ....11 H5
Carlton Pl *HFAX* HX1 ....5 G5
Carlton Rd *SHPY* BD18 ....27 H1
Carlton St *GTHN* BD7 ....2 B6
HFAX HX1 ....5 G5
HWTH BD22 ....23 E2
Carlton Ter *HFAX* HX1 ....5 G5
Carlton Wk *SHPY* BD18 ....28 A1
Carmel Rd *HIPP* HX3 ....59 G3
Carmona Av *SHPY* BD18 ....28 C4
Carmona Gdns *SHPY* BD18 ....28 C4
Carnaby Rd *GTHN* BD7 ....45 H5
Carnegie Dr *SHPY* BD18 ....28 D1
Carnoustie Gv *BGLY* BD16 ....26 D2
Caroline St *CLECK* BD19 ....64 C5
SHPY BD18 ....28 A1
Carperley Crs *CUL/QBY* BD13 ....34 D4
Carr Bank *AIRE* BD20 ....8 C2
Carr Bottom Av *WBOW* BD5 ....46 C5
Carr Bottom Fold *WBSY* BD6 ....54 D1
Carr Bottom Gv *WBSY* BD6 ....46 C5
Carr Bottom Rd *IDLE* BD10 ....30 D3
WBOW BD5 ....46 D5
Carr Green Av *BRIG* HD6 ....78 A5
Carr Green Cl *BRIG* HD6 ....78 A5
Carr Green Dr *BRIG* HD6 ....78 A5
Carr Green La *BRIG* HD6 ....78 A4
Carr Gv *AIRE* BD20 ....8 B2
Carr Hall Rd *LM/WK* BD12 ....62 D2
Carr Hill Av *PDSY/CALV* LS28 ....31 H3
Carr Hill Dr *PDSY/CALV* LS28 ....31 H3
Carr Hill Gv *PDSY/CALV* LS28 ....31 H3
Carr Hill Nook *PDSY/CALV* LS28 ....31 H3
Carr Hill Ri *PDSY/CALV* LS28 ....31 H3
Carr Hill Rd *PDSY/CALV* LS28 ....31 H3
Carr House Gv *LM/WK* BD12 ....62 D1
Carr House La *HIPP* HX3 ....53 H3
LM/WK BD12 ....54 C5
Carr House Mt *LM/WK* * BD12 ....62 D1
Carr House Rd *HIPP* HX3 ....53 G4
The Carriage Dr *GTL/HWG* HX4 ....75 H3
Carriage Dr *CLECK* BD19 ....65 G3
Carricks Cl *LM/WK* BD12 ....55 F4
Carrington St *BFDE* BD3 ....40 B5
Carrington Ter *GSLY* LS20 ....10 C3
Carr La *AIRE* BD20 ....8 B2
CUL/QBY BD13 ....34 D2
LM/WK BD12 ....55 E5
SHPY BD18 ....29 E2
Carroll St *BFDE* BD3 ....3 G6
Carr Rd *LM/WK* * BD12 ....62 D2
PDSY/CALV LS28 ....31 E3
Carr St *BRIG* HD6 ....71 F4
CLECK BD19 ....73 G1
KGHY BD21 ....7 F4
WBOW BD5 ....47 E5
Carr Wood Gdns
PDSY/CALV LS28 ....31 F3
Carter La *CUL/QBY* BD13 ....44 A4
Carter St *BFD* BD1 ....3 H7
Cartmel Rd *KGHY* BD21 ....6 D4
Carver St *CLECK* BD19 ....64 C5
Caryl Rd *BOW* BD4 ....47 H4
Cashmere St *HWTH* BD22 ....6 D4
Castle Av *BRIG* HD6 ....78 A3
Castle Cft *BGLY* BD16 ....15 F5
Castlefields Crs *BRIG* HD6 ....78 A3
Castlefields Dr *BRIG* HD6 ....78 A3

Castlefields La *BGLY* BD16 ....16 B1
Castlefields Rd *BGLY* BD16 ....16 A1
BRIG HD6 ....78 A3
Castlegate Dr *IDLE* BD10 ....30 B3
Castle Gv *BGLY* BD16 ....15 F5
Castle Hl *BRIG* HD6 ....78 A3
Castle Hill Ct *HWTH* * BD22 ....6 D5
Castlemore Rd *BAIL* BD17 ....19 E4
Castle Rd *KGHY* BD21 ....7 E5
SHPY BD18 ....28 B2
Castle St *WBOW* BD5 ....47 F2
Cater St *BFD* BD1 ....3 F5
Cathcart St *HIPP* HX3 ....59 G3
Catherine Slack *BRIG* HD6 ....71 E2
Catherine St *BRIG* HD6 ....71 F5
ELL HX5 ....76 C5
KGHY BD21 ....14 A1
Cat La *GTL/HWG* HX4 ....74 D4
Cauldwell Gdns *WBOW* * BD5 ....47 F3
Causeway *HFAX* HX1 ....5 J4
Cavalier Dr *IDLE* BD10 ....30 C2
Cave Hl *HIPP* HX3 ....60 C1
Cavendish Ct *KGHY* * BD21 ....7 F4
Cavendish Dr *BGLY* BD16 ....17 E2
GSLY LS20 ....10 C3
Cavendish Gv *GSLY* LS20 ....10 C3
Cavendish Rd *GSLY* LS20 ....10 C3
IDLE BD10 ....30 A2
Cavendish St *HFAX* HX1 ....4 D3
KGHY BD21 ....7 F4
YEA LS19 ....11 H4
Cavendish Ter *HFAX* * HX1 ....4 D4
Cawcliffe Dr *BRIG* HD6 ....71 F4
Cawcliffe Rd *BRIG* HD6 ....71 F4
Cawood Hvn *WBSY* * BD6 ....53 H2
Caygill Ter *HFAX* HX1 ....5 G7
Caythorne Wk *IDLE* BD10 ....30 B4
Cecil Av *BAIL* BD17 ....18 D2
GTHN BD7 ....46 C3
Cecil Gv *GTHN* BD7 ....46 C3
HIPP HX3 ....61 H5
Cecil St *HWTH* BD22 ....23 F1
Cedar Dr *LM/WK* BD12 ....63 F1
Cedar Gv *GTL/HWG* HX4 ....75 E2
KGHY BD21 ....14 A2
Cedar Wy *CLECK* BD19 ....65 F5
Cemetery La *AIRE* BD20 ....7 E1
RPDN/SBR HX6 ....66 D4
Cemetery Rd *BGLY* BD16 ....16 B3
GIR BD8 ....38 A5
HWTH BD22 ....22 B2
WBSY BD6 ....54 C3
YEA LS19 ....11 H4
Centenary Rd *BAIL* BD17 ....19 G2
Central Av *BAIL* BD17 ....18 C4
HWTH BD22 ....13 C3
LVSG WF15 ....73 E3
SHPY BD18 ....28 C2
WBOW BD5 ....46 D3
Central Av East *LVSG* WF15 ....73 E3
Central Dr *HWTH* BD22 ....13 C3
Central Pk *HFAX* HX1 ....5 F5
Central St *HFAX* HX1 ....5 G4
Centre St *WBOW* * BD5 ....46 D4
Century Pl *GIR* BD8 ....38 D3
Century Rd *ELL* HX5 ....76 C4
Century St *KGHY* * BD21 ....14 A2
Chadwell Springs *BGLY* BD16 ....26 D2
Chaffinch Rd *GIR* BD8 ....37 F5
Chain St *BFD* BD1 ....2 B4
Challenge Wy *BOW* BD4 ....48 C3
Challis Gv *WBOW* BD5 ....47 F4
Chandos St *BOW* BD4 ....2 E7
Changegate *HWTH* BD22 ....22 C1
Changegate Ct *HWTH* BD22 ....22 C2
Change La *HIPP* HX3 ....76 B1
Channing Wy *BFD* BD1 ....2 C6
Chapel Cft *BRIG* HD6 ....78 A4
WBSY BD6 ....54 C1
Chapel Gv *BGLY* BD16 ....16 B1
Chapel Hl *YEA* LS19 ....11 G4
Chapel House Rd *LM/WK* BD12 ....55 E3
Chapel La *BAIL* BD17 ....20 A1
CUL/QBY BD13 ....45 G5
CUL/QBY BD13 ....52 A1
HIPP HX3 ....70 A4
HIPP HX3 ....76 A1
KGHY BD21 ....7 E4
RPDN/SBR HX6 ....67 G4
WIL/AL BD15 ....37 F4
YEA LS19 ....11 G4
Chapel Ms *GIR* * BD8 ....37 F4
Chapel Rd *BGLY* BD16 ....16 B1
LM/WK BD12 ....55 E4
Chapel Rw *WIL/AL* BD15 ....25 H3
Chapel St *BFD* BD1 ....3 F5
BRIG HD6 ....70 D3

CLECK BD19 ....64 D5
CUL/QBY BD13 ....34 C4
CUL/QBY BD13 ....44 A1
CUL/QBY BD13 ....52 A1
ECHL BD2 ....30 C5
LUD/ILL * HX2 ....58 D5
LVSG WF15 ....73 F3
PDSY/CALV LS28 ....31 G2
WBOW * BD5 ....47 E3
WBSY BD6 ....54 D1
YEA LS19 ....21 G2
YEA * LS19 ....21 G2
Chapel St North *LUD/ILL* HX2 ....59 E2
Chapel Ter *WIL/AL* * BD15 ....37 E3
Chapeltown *HFAX* HX1 ....5 F3
Chapel Wk *BGLY* BD16 ....16 C3
ECHL BD2 ....30 C5
Chapman St *BOW* BD4 ....48 C1
Charles Av *BFDE* BD3 ....40 C5
HIPP HX3 ....69 H4
Charles Ct *HWTH* * BD22 ....32 D2
Charles St *BAIL* BD17 ....28 C1
BFD BD1 ....2 D5
BGLY BD16 ....16 C3
CLECK BD19 ....65 G5
CUL/QBY BD13 ....52 A1
ELL HX5 ....76 C5
HFAX HX1 ....5 J4
RPDN/SBR HX6 ....67 E3
Charlestown Rd *HIPP* HX3 ....5 J2
Charlesworth Gv *LUD/ILL* HX2 ....58 D5
Charlesworth Sq *CLECK* BD19 ....65 F5
Charlesworth Ter *LUD/ILL* HX2 ....58 D5
Charlotte Ct *HWTH* BD22 ....23 E1
Charnwood Cl *ECHL* * BD2 ....40 B2
Charnwood Gv *ECHL* BD2 ....40 B2
Charnwood Rd *ECHL* BD2 ....40 B2
Charterhouse Rd *IDLE* BD10 ....20 A5
Charteris Rd *GIR* BD8 ....37 G5
The Chase *KGHY* BD21 ....6 C3
YEA LS19 ....21 F2
Chase Wy *WBOW* BD5 ....47 F5
Chassum Gv *HTON* BD9 ....38 B2
Chatham St *BFDE* BD3 ....39 G3
HFAX HX1 ....4 E3
RPDN/SBR HX6 ....67 E3
Chat Hill Rd *CUL/QBY* BD13 ....44 C2
Chatsworth Av *PDSY/CALV* LS28 ....41 F4
Chatsworth Crs
PDSY/CALV LS28 ....41 F4
Chatsworth Dr *PDSY/CALV* LS28 ....41 F4
Chatsworth Fall
PDSY/CALV LS28 ....41 F4
Chatsworth Pl *GIR* BD8 ....38 C2
Chatsworth Ri *PDSY/CALV* LS28 ....41 F4
Chatsworth Rd *PDSY/CALV* LS28 ....41 F4
Chatsworth St *KGHY* BD21 ....7 F4
Chatts Wood Fold *LM/WK* BD12 ....56 A5
Chaucer St *HFAX* HX1 ....4 E3
Cheapside *BFD* BD1 ....2 D4
CLECK BD19 ....73 H1
HFAX * HX1 ....5 H4
HIPP HX3 ....53 F4
Cheddington Gv *WIL/AL* BD15 ....37 E4
Chellow Gdns *WIL/AL* HX2 ....36 D2
Chellow Grange Rd *HTON* BD9 ....37 F1
Chellow La *HTON* BD9 ....37 F2
Chellow St *WBOW* BD5 ....47 E5
Chelmsford Rd *BFDE* * BD3 ....40 B4
Chelmsford Ter *BFDE* BD3 ....40 B5
Chelsea Man *HIPP* HX3 ....60 D3
Chelsea Rd *GTHN* BD7 ....46 A3
Chelsea St *KGHY* BD21 ....14 A1
Cheltenham Ct *HIPP* * HX3 ....69 E4
Cheltenham Gdns *HIPP* HX3 ....69 E4
Cheltenham Pl *HIPP* HX3 ....69 E4
Cheltenham Rd *ECHL* BD2 ....29 G4
Chelwood Dr *WIL/AL* BD15 ....37 E3
Cheriton Dr *CUL/QBY* BD13 ....52 C1
Cherry Ct *HFAX* * HX1 ....4 D5
Cherry Flds *ECHL* BD2 ....29 F5
Cherry Lea Ct *YEA* LS19 ....21 G2
Cherry St *HWTH* BD22 ....23 F1
KGHY BD21 ....7 H3
Cherry Tree Av *IDLE* * BD10 ....30 C3
Cherry Tree Dr *GTL/HWG* HX4 ....75 G4
Cherry Tree Gdns *SHPY* BD18 ....19 G5
Cherry Tree Ri *KGHY* BD21 ....14 C1
Cherry Tree Rw *BGLY* BD16 ....25 G2
Chervana Ct *BOW* BD4 ....48 D3
Cherwell Dr *WBSY* BD6 ....54 A3
Chesham St *GTHN* BD7 ....46 D1
KGHY BD21 ....7 G5
Chester Cl *HIPP* HX3 ....59 G4
Chester Gv *HIPP* HX3 ....59 G4
Chester Pl *HIPP* HX3 ....59 G4
Chester Rd *HIPP* HX3 ....59 G4
Chester St *GTHN* BD7 ....2 B6

HIPP HX3 ....59 G4
RPDN/SBR HX6 ....67 E4
Chester Ter HIPP HX3 .....59 G4
Chestnut Cl GTL/HWG HX4 ..75 G3
HWTH BD22 ....6 C5
Chestnut Ct SHPY BD18 ....27 H2
Chestnut Gv ECHL BD2 .....29 E5
PDSY/CALV LS28 ....31 G3
Chestnut St HFAX HX1 ......4 A6
Chevet Mt WIL/AL BD15 ....36 D5
Chevington Ct YEA * LS19 .21 F3
Cheviot Ga LM/WK BD12 ....54 C4
Cheyne Wk KGHY BD21 ....6 D5
Childs La SHPY BD18 ......29 F3
Chiltern Wy LVSG WF15 ....73 G3
Chilver Dr BOW BD4 ....49 F5
Chippendale Ri GIR BD8 ...37 G4
Chislehurst Pl WBOW BD5 ..46 A4
Chrisharben Pk CLAY BD14 .45 F3
Chrismoor IDLE BD10 ......29 H2
Christopher St WBOW * BD5 46 B4
Christopher Ter WBOW BD5 .46 A4
Church Bank BFD BD1 ....2 E5
LUD/ILL HX2 ....67 G2
Church Cl LUD/ILL HX2 ....50 C5
Church Ct GTHN * BD7 .....46 A2
YEA LS19 ....11 G5
Church Crs YEA LS19 ......11 G4
Church Flds ECHL BD2 .....40 C2
Churchfields Rd BRIG HD6 .71 F5
Church Gn GIR BD8 ....38 C3
LUD/ILL * HX2 ....58 D4
Church Hl BAIL BD17 ......19 E2
Churchill Rd CUL/QBY BD13 44 C1
Church La BAIL BD17 ......20 B1
BRIG HD6 ....71 F5
CLECK BD19 ....65 H5
ELL HX5 ....77 C4
HIPP HX3 ....59 D4
LUD/ILL HX2 ....58 D4
LVSG WF15 ....73 E5
WBSY BD6 ....54 C2
Church Pl HFAX HX1 ....4 E5
Church Rd WBSY BD6 ....54 C3
Church Side Cl HIPP HX3 ..59 H4
Church Side Dr HIPP HX3 ..59 H4
Church St BGLY BD16 ......16 D4
BRIG HD6 ....78 A3
CLECK BD19 ....73 H1
CUL/QBY * BD13 ....24 C3
ELL HX5 ....76 C4
GIR BD8 ....38 D3
GSLY LS20 ....10 D2
GTL/HWG HX4 ....5 J5
HWTH BD22 ....22 C2
HWTH BD22 ....32 D2
KGHY BD21 ....7 E5
KGHY BD21 ....7 E5
LVSG WF15 ....73 F3
SHPY BD18 ....29 E1
WBSY BD6 ....53 H3
YEA LS19 ....11 F5
Church Ter LUD/ILL HX2 ...50 C5
Church Vw CLECK BD19 .....64 A5
RPDN/SBR HX6 ....67 F4
Church Wk HIPP HX3 ....60 D3
Church Wy KGHY BD21 ....7 F5
Churn La LUD/ILL HX2 .....67 G1
Churn Milk La HIPP HX3 ...59 F1
Cinderhills La HIPP HX3 ..59 F1
City La HIPP HX3 ....58 D4
City Rd GIR BD8 ....38 C4
Clapham St CUL/QBY BD13 ..34 D4
Clapton Av HFAX HX1 ....4 D6
Clara Dr PDSY/CALV LS28 ..31 G2
Clara Rd ECHL BD2 ....29 G4
Clara St BRIG HD6 ....78 B2
Clare Crs LM/WK BD12 .....62 D3
Clare Hall La HFAX HX1 ....5 H6
Claremont Av SHPY BD18 ...29 F3
Claremont Crs SHPY BD18 ..29 F3
Claremont Gdns BGLY BD16 .16 D2
Claremont Rd SHPY BD18 ...29 F3
Claremont St CLECK BD19 ..64 A5
ELL HX5 ....76 D5
RPDN/SBR * HX6 ....67 F4
Claremont Ter GTHN BD7 ....2 A7
Claremount Rd HIPP HX3 ...59 H3
Claremount Ter HIPP HX3 ..59 H3
Clarence Rd SHPY BD18 ....28 A1
Clarence St CLECK BD19 ...73 C1
HFAX HX1 ....5 F4
Clarendon Pl CUL/QBY BD13 44 C1
HFAX * HX1 ....4 C5
Clarendon Rd BGLY BD16 ...17 E2
Clarendon St HWTH BD22 ...22 D3

KGHY BD21 ....14 A1
Clare Rd CLECK BD19 ......73 F1
HFAX HX1 ....5 H5
LM/WK BD12 ....62 D3
Clare Rd Flats HFAX HX1 ...5 H6
Clare St HFAX HX1 ....5 H5
Clarges St WBOW BD5 ......46 D4
Clarke St PDSY/CALV LS28 .31 G4
Clayborn Vw CLECK BD19 ...73 G2
Clayfield Dr GTHN BD7 ....46 B3
Clay Hill Dr LM/WK BD12 ..63 E2
Clay House La GTL/HWG HX4 76 A4
Clay Pits La HFAX HX1 .....4 C1
Clay St HFAX HX1 ....4 B3
RPDN/SBR HX6 ....67 F4
Clayton Gv YEA LS19 ......11 G4
Clayton La CLAY BD14 .....45 E4
WBOW BD5 ....47 F3
Clayton Ri KGHY BD21 ......6 D3
Clayton Rd GTHN BD7 ......45 H3
Cleckheaton Rd WBSY BD6 ..55 E3
Cleeve Hl YEA LS19 ....21 G2
Clegg La GTL/HWG HX4 .....75 E4
Clement St GIR BD8 ....38 A4
RPDN/SBR * HX6 ....67 E4
Clevedon Pl HIPP HX3 .....59 F3
Cleveland Av HIPP * HX3 ..69 F4
Cleveland Rd HTON BD9 ....38 C1
Cliff Crs LUD/ILL HX2 ....67 H3
Cliffe Av BAIL BD17 ......18 D3
BGLY BD16 ....15 F5
HIPP HX3 ....71 F1
Cliffe Crs AIRE BD20 ......8 C3
Cliffe Dr YEA LS19 ....21 F3
Cliffe La BAIL BD17 ......18 D5
CLECK BD19 ....64 D4
CUL/QBY BD13 ....36 B5
YEA LS19 ....21 F3
Cliffe La South BAIL BD17 18 D5
Cliffe La West BAIL BD17 .18 D4
Cliffe Mill Fold AIRE BD20 9 F3
Cliffe Mt CLECK BD19 .....65 F4
Cliffe Rd BFDE BD3 ....39 G2
BRIG HD6 ....78 B1
KGHY BD21 ....14 A2
Cliffestone Dr AIRE BD20 ..9 E3
Cliffe St CUL/QBY BD13 ...36 A5
KGHY BD21 ....7 E3
Cliffe Ter BAIL BD17 .....18 D5
GIR BD8 ....39 E3
KGHY BD21 ....14 B2
RPDN/SBR HX6 ....66 D3
Cliffe Vw WIL/AL BD15 ....36 C2
Cliffe Wood Cl HTON BD9 ..37 H1
Cliff Gdns LUD/ILL HX2 ...67 H3
Cliff Hill La LUD/ILL HX2 67 E2
Cliff Hollins La LM/WK BD12 56 C4
Clifford Rd BAIL BD17 ....18 D4
Clifford St WBOW BD5 .....47 F2
Cliff St HWTH BD22 ....23 E2
Cliff Vale Rd SHPY BD18 ..28 C4
Cliff Wood Av SHPY BD18 ..28 C3
Clifton Av HFAX HX1 ....4 A6
Clifton Common BRIG HD6 ..78 D1
Clifton Pl SHPY BD18 .....28 C3
Clifton Rd HIPP HX3 ......68 D4
Clifton Side HUDN HD2 ....79 G5
Clifton St GIR BD8 ....39 E3
HIPP HX3 ....59 F4
HWTH BD22 ....6 D5
RPDN/SBR HX6 ....67 F4
Clifton Vls GIR BD8 ......39 E3
Clipstone St WBOW BD5 ....47 F5
Clive Pl GTHN BD7 ....46 C2
Clive Ter GTHN BD7 ....46 C2
Clock La CUL/QBY BD13 ....34 C3
Clock View St KGHY BD21 ...7 E2
Clog Sole Rd BRIG HD6 ....71 E4
The Cloisters HFAX HX1 ....4 C7
The Close GSLY LS20 ......10 B3
Close Head Dr CUL/QBY BD13 43 F1
Close Head La CUL/QBY BD13 35 C5
Close Lea BRIG HD6 ....78 A2
Close Lea Av BRIG HD6 ....78 A2
Close Lea Dr BRIG HD6 ....78 A3
Close Lea Wy BRIG HD6 ....78 A2
Closes Rd BRIG HD6 ....78 A2
Cloudsdale Av WBOW BD5 ...47 F3
Clough Bank LUD/ILL HX2 ..50 A5
Clough Ga HWTH BD22 ......13 G4
Clough La BRIG HD6 ....72 A3
BRIC HD6 ....78 A4
HWTH BD22 ....12 D3
LUD/ILL HX2 ....50 B4
LVSG WF15 ....73 G4
Clough Pl LUD/ILL HX2 ....50 A5
Clough Rd RPDN/SBR HX6 ...74 C1
Clough St WBOW BD5 ....47 F4

Clover Ct PDSY/CALV LS28 .31 F3
Clover Crs PDSY/CALV LS28 31 F2
Cloverdale HIPP HX3 ......53 G3
Clover Hill LVSG WF15 ....73 G3
Clover Hill Cl HFAX HX1 ...5 F6
Clover Hill Rd HFAX HX1 ..68 C3
Clover Hill Ter HFAX HX1 .68 C3
Clover Hill Vw HFAX * HX1 68 C3
Clover Ri KGHY BD21 ....7 H4
Clover St GTHN BD7 ....46 C4
Cloverville Ap WBSY BD6 ..54 D3
Club La LUD/ILL HX2 ......59 E2
Club Rw YEA LS19 ....11 H4
Club St GTHN BD7 ....46 A1
Clydesdale Dr WBSY BD6 ...54 A3
Clyde St BGLY BD16 ....16 C3
RPDN/SBR HX6 ....67 E5
Coach La CLECK * BD19 ....64 D5
Coach Rd BAIL BD17 ....18 B5
GSLY LS20 ....10 C4
HIPP HX3 ....71 E1
Coal La LUD/ILL HX2 ......42 D4
Coal Pit La HIPP HX3 .....79 E2
Coalpit La HIPP HX3 ......69 F4
Coates St WBOW BD5 ....47 E3
Coates Ter WBOW BD5 ......47 E3
Cobden Ct HFAX HX1 ....5 F2
Cobden St CLAY BD14 ......45 E3
CUL/QBY BD13 ....52 C1
IDLE BD10 ....30 A2
WIL/AL BD15 ....37 E3
Cock Hill La HIPP HX3 ....52 D4
Cockin La CLAY BD14 ......44 B4
Cockroft Gv BFDE BD3 ......3 H4
Cockshott La IDLE BD10 ...29 H1
Coldbeck Dr WBSY BD6 .....53 H2
Cold St HWTH BD22 ....22 D3
Coleman St BFDE BD3 ....2 E1
Colenso Rd CUL/QBY * BD21 7 H2
Colenso Wk KGHY * BD21 ....7 H2
Coleridge Gdns IDLE BD10 .30 B1
Coleridge St HFAX HX1 .....5 H5
Coles Wy AIRE BD20 ....1 G3
Coley Hall La HIPP HX3 ...61 G3
Coley Rd HIPP HX3 ....61 F2
Coley Vw HIPP HX3 ....60 D2
Colbrook Av WBSY BD6 .....54 D2
College Rd BGLY BD16 ......9 F5
College Ter HFAX * HX1 ...68 A3
Collier La BAIL BD17 .....18 C2
Colliers Cl SHPY BD18 ....27 H2
Collindale Cl IDLE BD10 ..30 D3
Collinfield Rd WBSY BD6 ..54 A4
Collingham Av WBSY BD6 ...53 C2
Collin Moor La GTL/HWG HX4 75 H3
Collins Cl HWTH BD22 .....23 F1
Collinson St CLECK BD19 ..64 C5
Collins St BOW BD4 ....48 A2
GTHN BD7 ....46 B4
Colne Rd Goodley HWTH BD22 12 C4
Colston Cl GIR BD8 ....37 H3
Columbus St HIPP * HX3 ...59 H4
Colyton Mt WIL/AL BD15 ...36 D3
Commerce Ct BOW BD4 ......48 C3
Commercial Buildings
LM/WK BD12 ....64 A1
BRIG HD6 ....78 B1
CLECK BD19 ....73 H1
CUL/QBY BD13 ....34 C4
CUL/QBY * BD13 ....44 B1
CUL/QBY BD13 ....52 A1
HFAX HX1 ....5 G2
SHPY BD18 ....28 C1
Commondale Wy BOW BD4 ....55 H4
Common La HIPP HX3 ....69 G2
Common Rd ELL HX5 ....77 F5
LM/WK BD12 ....54 D4
Como Dr GIR BD8 ....38 A3
Como Gdns GIR BD8 ....38 A3
Como Gv GIR BD8 ....38 A3
Compeigne Av AIRE BD20 ....8 A2
Compton St BOW BD4 ....48 B5
KGHY BD21 ....7 G3
Concrete St HIPP * HX3 ...59 H4
Condor Cl WBSY BD6 ....53 F1
Conduit St GIR BD8 ....2 B7
Coney La KGHY BD21 ....7 F4
Coniston Av CUL/QBY BD13 .52 A1
Coniston Cl CUL/QBY BD13 .52 A1
ELL HX5 ....77 E4
Coniston Gv HTON BD9 .....38 A2
Coniston Rd GTHN BD7 .....45 H4
Constance St SHPY * BD18 .28 A1

Constitutional St HFAX HX1 .4 B7
Conway St HFAX HX1 ....4 C5
Cooke Crs CLECK BD19 .....65 F5
Cooke St KGHY BD21 ....7 F4
Cookson St BRIG HD6 ......71 E5
Coombe Hl CUL/QBY BD13 ...45 E5
Co-operative Buildings
BRIG HD6 ....71 G1
HIPP HX3 ....59 E3
Cooper Cl BGLY BD16 ......16 D1
Cooperfields LUD/ILL HX2 .66 B3
Cooper Gv WBSY BD6 ....54 C3
Cooper La HIPP HX3 ....53 G2
Copeland St WBOW BD4 .....48 C2
Copgrove Cl BOW BD4 ......48 D4
Copgrove Ct BOW BD4 ......48 D4
Copgrove Rd BOW BD4 ......48 D4
Copley Av LUD/ILL HX2 ....67 H3
Copley Gln HIPP HX3 ......75 G1
Copley Gv HIPP HX3 ....75 G1
Copley Hall St HIPP * HX3 75 G1
Copley La HIPP HX3 ....75 G1
Copley Mt HIPP HX3 ....75 G1
Copley St WBOW BD5 ....46 C4
Copley Ter HIPP HX3 ......75 G1
Coplowe La WIL/AL BD15 ...26 A2
Copperas Rw GTL/HWG * HX4 74 D4
The Coppice HFAX * HX1 ....4 E7
YEA LS19 ....21 E1
Coppice Gra YEA LS19 .....11 G3
Coppice Vw IDLE BD10 .....29 H1
Coppice Wood Av GSLY LS20 11 F2
GTHN BD7 ....46 B1
Coppice Wood Cl GSLY LS20 11 F3
Coppice Wood Crs YEA LS19 11 F3
Coppice Wood Gv GSLY LS20 11 F3
GTHN * BD7 ....46 B1
Coppice Wood Ri YEA LS19 .11 F3
The Coppies LM/WK BD12 ...62 C1
Coppy Cl BGLY BD16 ....26 D3
The Copse BGLY BD16 ......17 G3
CLECK BD19 ....72 C1
Copt Royd Gv YEA LS19 ....11 F4
Corban St BOW BD4 ....48 B4
Cordingley Cl BOW BD4 ....56 D1
Cordingley St BOW BD4 ....56 D1
Corn Market HFAX HX1 ......5 H4
Corn Mill La CLAY BD14 ...44 C2
Corn St HWTH BD22 ....13 H2
Cornwall Crs BAIL BD17 ...18 C2
BRIG HD6 ....71 G2
Cornwall Pl GIR BD8 ....2 B1
Cornwall Rd BGLY BD16 ....17 E4
GIR BD8 ....2 B1
KGHY BD21 ....7 E2
Cornwall Ter GIR BD8 ......2 B1
Coronation Av IDLE BD10 ..20 C2
Coronation Mt HWTH BD22 ...6 C4
Coronation Rd HIPP HX3 ...68 D2
Coronation St ELL HX5 ....76 C5
GTL/HWG HX4 ....76 A3
LM/WK BD12 ....55 H5
Coronation Wk HWTH BD22 ...6 C3
Coronation Wy HWTH BD22 ...6 B3
Corporal La CUL/QBY BD13 .52 B4
Corporation St ECHL BD2 ..40 B1
HFAX HX1 ....5 G2
RPDN/SBR HX6 ....67 E4
Corrance Rd LM/WK BD12 ...63 E4
Corrie St CUL/QBY BD13 ...44 B1
The Cote PDSY/CALV LS28 ..41 H2
Cote Farm La SHPY BD18 ...19 G5
Cotefields Av PDSY/CALV LS28 41 H2
Cote Gap CUL/QBY * BD13 ..36 B5
Cote La PDSY/CALV LS28 ...41 H2
WIL/AL BD15 ....36 D3
Cotewall Rd WBOW BD5 .....47 E4
Cotswold Av SHPY BD18 ....29 F3
Cotswold Dr LVSG WF15 ....73 G3
Cottage Gn GIR BD8 ....38 A4
Cottage Ms HWTH * BD22 ...22 C2
Cottage Rd IDLE BD10 .....30 C2
Cottam Av GTHN BD7 ....46 C1
Cottam Ter GTHN BD7 ......46 C1
Cotterdale WIL/AL BD15 ...36 D3
Cottingley Cliffe Rd BGLY BD16 27 F3
Cottingley Dr BGLY BD16 ..26 D1
Cottingley Manor Pk
BGLY BD16 ....26 D4
Cottingley Moor Rd BGLY BD16 26 D4
Cottingley New Rd BGLY BD16 27 E2
Cottingley Rd WIL/AL BD15 36 D1
Cottingley Ter GIR * BD8 ..2 B1
Courtenay Cl BFDE BD3 ....40 D5
The Court LVSG WF15 ......73 H4
SHPY * BD18 ....27 H2
Court La LUD/ILL HX2 .....67 G1

Courts Leet *LM/WK* BD12 ....62 D1
Cousen Av *GTHN* BD7 ....46 A2
Cousen Rd *GTHN* BD7 ....46 C3
Cousin La *LUD/ILL* HX2 ....58 D1
Coventry St *BOW* BD4 ....48 A3
HFAX * HX1 ....67 H1
Coverdale Wy *BAIL* BD17 ....19 F2
Cover Dr *WBSY* BD6 ....54 B2
Coverley Ri *YEA* LS19 ....11 E4
The Covet *IDLE* BD10 ....30 C1
Cow Close La *LM/WK* BD12 ....63 F3
Cowdray Dr *CLECK* BD19 ....63 G5
Cowgill St *GIR* BD8 ....38 D3
Cow Gn *HFAX* HX1 ....5 G4
Cow Hill Gate La *LUD/ILL* HX2 .....50 D2
Cow La *HIPP* HX3 ....70 C4
HIPP HX3 ....75 H1
Cowley Crs *HTON* BD9 ....27 F5
Cowling La *HIPP* HX3 ....52 C5
Cowroyd Pl *HFAX* HX1 ....5 J1
Crabtree Pl *GTHN* BD7 ....46 B3
Crabtree St *GTHN* BD7 ....46 B3
HFAX HX1 ....4 A4
Crack La *WIL/AL* BD15 ....26 A4
Cracoe Rd *BFDE* BD3 ....3 K6
Crag Cl *LUD/ILL* HX2 ....58 C1
Cragg La *CUL/QBY* BD13 ....42 D2
GTHN BD7 ....46 B4
Cragg Ter *GTHN* BD7 ....46 B4
Cragg Top *CUL/QBY* BD13 ....42 D2
Cragg Wood Dr *YEA* LS19 ....21 F3
Crag Hill Rd *IDLE* BD10 ....19 H4
Crag La *LUD/ILL* HX2 ....58 C1
Crag Pl *KGHY* BD21 ....14 B2
Crag Rd *SHPY* BD18 ....28 D3
Crag Vw *IDLE* BD10 ....30 D2
Craiglands *HIPP* HX3 ....61 G5
Craiglea Dr *LM/WK* BD12 ....63 E3
Craigmore Ct *BOW* BD4 ....49 E5
Cranbourne Rd *HTON* BD9 ....37 G2
Cranbrook Av *WBSY* BD6 ....54 D2
Cranbrook Rl *WBOW* BD5 ....47 F4
Cranbrook St *CLAY* BD14 ....45 E3
WBOW BD5 ....47 F4
Cranford Pl *WIL/AL* BD15 ....25 H4
Cranleigh Mt *KGHY* BD21 ....13 H1
Cranmer Rd *BFDE* BD3 ....39 G3
Craven Av *CUL/QBY* BD13 ....44 B1
Craven Cl *CLECK* BD19 ....65 H5
Craven Ct *GIR* BD8 ....38 A4
HFAX HX1 ....4 C4
Craven Dr *CLECK* BD19 ....65 H5
Craven La *CLECK* BD19 ....65 H5
Craven Rd *KGHY* BD21 ....7 H2
Craven St *BFDE* * BD3 ....3 F3
Craven Ter *HFAX* HX1 ....4 C5
Crawford Av *WBSY* BD6 ....54 D2
Crawford St *BOW* BD4 ....47 H3
Crediton Av *WIL/AL* BD15 ....37 E4
The Crescent *BAIL* BD17 ....18 D4
BGLY BD16 ....9 F5
BIRK/DRI BD11 ....57 F3
GSLY LS20 ....10 B3
HIPP HX3 ....69 F2
LVSG WF15 ....73 G3
WBSY BD6 ....53 H2
The Cresent *HIPP* HX3 ....61 G5
Crescent Vw *HWTH* BD22 ....13 H3
Crescent Wk *CLAY* BD14 ....45 E4
Creskeld Wy *WIL/AL* BD15 ....36 C2
Cresswell Mt *GTHN* BD7 ....45 H5
Cresswell Pl *GTHN* BD7 ....45 H5
Cresswell Ter *GTHN* BD7 ....45 H5
The Crest *HUDN* HD2 ....79 F5
Crest Av *LM/WK* BD12 ....62 D4
Crestfield Av *ELL* HX5 ....76 B5
Crestfield Dr *LUD/ILL* HX2 ....67 H3
Crestville Cl *CLAY* BD14 ....45 F2
Crestville Rd *CLAY* BD14 ....45 F2
Crestville Ter *CLAY* BD14 ....45 E2
Crestwood Cl *BOW* BD4 ....56 A1
Crib La *HFAX* HX1 ....5 G2
Cricketers Gn *YEA* LS19 ....11 G5
Crimshaw La *SHPY* BD18 ....29 E3
Cripplegate *HFAX* HX1 ....5 K3
Croft Av *ELL* HX5 ....9 E5
Crofters Gn *IDLE* BD10 ....29 H1
Crofters Lea *YEA* LS19 ....11 E4
Croft Fold *HIPP* HX3 ....59 G1
Croft House Cl *WBSY* BD6 ....54 C2
Croft House Rd *WBSY* BD6 ....54 C4
Croftlands *IDLE* BD10 ....29 H1
Crofton Rd *HTON* BD9 ....38 B1
Croft Pl *BRIG* HD6 ....71 G4
Croft Ri *HIPP* HX3 ....59 E3
Croft Rd *AIRE* BD20 ....9 E3

Croft St *BFD* BD1 ....2 E7
BIRK/DRI BD11 ....57 F5
BRIG HD6 ....78 B1
HWTH BD22 ....22 D2
IDLE BD10 ....30 B1
KGHY BD21 ....7 E5
RPDN/SBR * HX6 ....67 F4
SHPY BD18 ....28 C2
WBSY BD6 ....54 D1
Croisdale Cl *LVSG* WF15 ....73 H4
Cromack Vw *PDSY/CALV* LS28 ....41 H5
Cromer Av *KGHY* BD21 ....14 A1
Cromer Gv *KGHY* BD21 ....14 A1
Cromer Rd *KGHY* BD21 ....14 A1
Cromer St *HFAX* HX1 ....4 A7
KGHY BD21 ....14 A1
Cromwell Bottom Dr
BRIG * HD6 ....71 F4
Cromwell Cl *HIPP* HX3 ....69 H4
Cromwell Ct *BGLY* BD16 ....27 E5
Cromwell Rd *HIPP* HX3 ....69 H4
Cromwell Ter *HFAX* * HX1 ....4 E4
Crooked La *HIPP* HX3 ....51 G4
IDLE BD10 ....19 G5
Crooke La *WIL/AL* BD15 ....25 H5
Cropredy Cl *CUL/QBY* BD13 ....52 C1
Crosby St *KGHY* BD21 ....7 E3
Croscombe Wk *WBOW* BD5 ....47 F2
Crosley Vw *BGLY* BD16 ....17 E4
Crosley Wood Rd *BGLY* BD16 ....17 E4
Cross Banks *SHPY* BD18 ....28 C2
Cross Crown St *CLECK* BD19 ....73 G1
Crossdale Av *WBSY* BD6 ....53 G2
Cross Emily St *KGHY* * BD21 ....7 E5
Cross Farm Ct *HWTH* BD22 ....32 C1
Crossfield Cl *HWTH* BD22 ....32 C1
Crossfield Rd *HWTH* BD22 ....32 C1
Cross Gates La *BGLY* BD16 ....15 H3
Cross HI *GTL/HWG* HX4 ....75 H4
HFAX HX1 ....5 H2
Cross Hills *HFAX* HX1 ....5 H2
Crosshills Mt *GTL/HWG* HX4 ....75 H4
Cross House Ct *LM/WK* * BD12 .....63 H1
Cross La *BGLY* BD16 ....16 C3
BIRK/DRI BD11 ....57 G3
BRIG HD6 ....79 F2
CUL/QBY BD13 ....51 H2
ELL HX5 ....76 B5
GTHN BD7 ....46 B4
HIPP HX3 ....52 D4
HIPP HX3 ....61 E1
HWTH BD22 ....32 D1
WIL/AL BD15 ....26 A2
Cross Leeds St *KGHY* BD21 ....7 E4
Crossley Gdns *HFAX* HX1 ....4 D2
Crossley Hall Ms *GIR* BD8 ....37 H5
Crossley Hall St *GIR* BD8 ....37 G5
Crossley HI *HIPP* HX3 ....69 E5
Crossley St *BRIG* HD6 ....78 C2
CUL/QBY BD13 ....52 C1
GTHN BD7 ....46 C2
HFAX HX1 ....5 G3
Crossley Ter North *LUD/ILL* HX2 ..59 F1
Crossley Ter South *LUD/ILL* HX2 ..59 F1
Cross River St *KGHY* * BD21 ....7 H2
Cross Rd *GIR* BD8 ....38 C3
IDLE BD10 ....30 B1
LM/WK BD12 ....55 G5
Cross Rosse St *SHPY* * BD18 ....28 C1
Cross Rydal St *KGHY* * BD21 ....6 D5
Cross St *BRIG* HD6 ....71 F4
CLAY BD14 ....45 F3
GTL/HWG HX4 ....76 A4
HFAX HX1 ....5 H2
HFAX * HX1 ....5 J5
LM/WK BD12 ....63 H1
WBSY * BD6 ....54 A3
Cross St West *LUD/ILL* * HX2 ....58 D5
Cross Sun St *BFD* BD1 ....2 E5
Crossway *BGLY* BD16 ....26 C2
Crowgill Rd *SHPY* BD18 ....28 C1
Crown Dr *LM/WK* BD12 ....62 D1
Crownest La *BGLY* BD16 ....16 D2
Crownest Rd *BGLY* BD16 ....16 D3
Crown Rd *HIPP* HX3 ....59 G3
Crown St *BFD* BD1 ....2 D5
BRIG HD6 ....71 F5
CLECK BD19 ....73 G1
ELL HX5 ....76 C5
HFAX HX1 ....5 G4
LM/WK BD12 ....62 D1
Crowther Av *PDSY/CALV* LS28 .....31 E3
Crowther Fold *BGLY* BD16 ....15 G5
Crowther St *CLECK* BD19 ....64 C5
IDLE BD10 ....30 C2
LM/WK BD12 ....62 D1
Crowther Wk *WBOW* * BD5 ....47 F2
Crow Tree Cl *BAIL* BD17 ....19 E3

Crow Tree La *GIR* BD8 ....37 H3
Crowtrees Ct *YEA* LS19 ....21 G3
Crowtrees Crs *BRIG* HD6 ....78 A3
Crowtrees La *BRIG* HD6 ....77 H5
Crowtrees Pk *BRIG* HD6 ....78 A4
Crow Trees Pk *YEA* LS19 ....21 G2
Crow Wood Pk *LUD/ILL* HX2 ....67 G2
Croydon Rd *GTHN* BD7 ....46 A3
Crumack La *HWTH* BD22 ....33 F1
Crystal Ter *BOW* BD4 ....48 B4
Cullingworth Rd *CUL/QBY* BD13 ..24 C4
Culver St *HFAX* HX1 ....5 G3
Cumberland Cl *LUD/ILL* HX2 ....58 D1
Cumberland Rd *GTHN* BD7 ....46 B2
Cunliffe La *BAIL* BD17 ....20 A1
Cunliffe Rd *GIR* BD8 ....38 C2
Cunliffe Ter *GIR* BD8 ....39 E1
Cunliffe Vls *HTON* BD9 ....39 E1
Cure HI *HWTH* BD22 ....12 C3
Curlew St *WBOW* BD5 ....46 D4
Currer Av *BOW* BD4 ....56 A1
Currer St *BFD* BD1 ....2 E5
Curtis Ct *CUL/QBY* * BD13 ....24 C3
Curzon Rd *BFDE* BD3 ....3 K5
Cuthberts Cl *CUL/QBY* BD13 ....52 A2
Cutler Heights La *BOW* BD4 ....48 B4
Cutler Pl *BOW* BD4 ....48 C3
Cyprus Av *IDLE* BD10 ....19 G5
Cyprus Dr *IDLE* BD10 ....19 G5

D

Daffels Wood Cl *BOW* BD4 ....56 A2
Daffodil Ct *WIL/AL* BD15 ....37 E4
Dagenham Rd *BOW* BD4 ....48 B4
Daisy Bank *HFAX* HX1 ....5 F7
Daisy HI *LM/WK* BD12 ....62 D2
Daisy Hill Back La *HTON* BD9 ......37 H2
Daisy Hill Gv *HTON* BD9 ....37 H2
Daisy Hill La *HTON* BD9 ....37 H2
Daisy Mt *RPDN/SBR* HX6 ....66 D3
Daisy St *BRIG* HD6 ....78 B1
GTHN BD7 ....46 B4
HFAX HX1 ....4 E5
HWTH BD22 ....23 F1
Dalby Av *BFDE* BD3 ....40 C3
Dalby St *BFDE* * BD3 ....40 B4
Dalcross Gv *WBOW* BD5 ....47 G3
Dalcross St *WBOW* BD5 ....47 F3
Dale Cl *GSLY* LS20 ....10 A3
Dale Croft Ri *WIL/AL* BD15 ....36 D2
Dale Garth *BAIL* BD17 ....18 C3
Dale Gv *SHPY* BD18 ....19 F5
Dales Dr *GSLY* LS20 ....10 A3
Daleside *GTL/HWG* HX4 ....75 F4
Daleside Cl *PDSY/CALV* LS28 ....41 F4
Daleside Gv *LM/WK* BD12 ....63 G1
PDSY/CALV LS28 ....41 F4
Daleside Rd *AIRE* BD20 ....8 B2
BFDE BD3 ....38 B5
SHPY BD18 ....19 F5
Daleside Wk *WBOW* BD5 ....47 G5
Daleson Cl *HIPP* HX3 ....60 D2
Dale St *BFD* BD1 ....2 D4
KGHY BD21 ....7 H2
RPDN/SBR HX6 ....67 E4
SHPY BD18 ....28 C2
Dalesway *BGLY* BD16 ....17 E1
Dale Wy *GSLY* LS20 ....10 A3
Dale View Ct *BAIL* BD17 ....18 B4
Dale View Gv *KGHY* BD21 ....7 H5
Dale View Rd *KGHY* BD21 ....14 D1
Dallam Av *SHPY* BD18 ....27 H1
Dallam Rd *SHPY* BD18 ....27 H1
Dallam Wk *SHPY* BD18 ....28 A1
Dalton La *KGHY* BD21 ....7 G4
Dalton Rd *KGHY* BD21 ....7 H4
Dalton St *RPDN/SBR* HX6 ....67 E3
Dalton Ter *GIR* BD8 ....38 C4
KGHY BD21 ....7 G5
Damask St *HFAX* * HX1 ....5 F2
Damems La *HWTH* BD22 ....13 H4
Damems Rd *HWTH* BD22 ....13 H4
Dames La *HWTH* BD22 ....13 H4
Dam Head Rd *RPDN/SBR* HX6 ......67 F3
Dam La *YEA* LS19 ....11 H4
Damon Av *IDLE* BD10 ....30 D5
Damside *KGHY* BD21 ....7 E5
Damson Ct *CLAY* BD14 ....45 F4
Danby Av *BOW* BD4 ....56 A2
Danebury Rd *BRIG* HD6 ....78 C2

Danecourt Rd *BOW* BD4 ....48 D4
Dane Hill Dr *BOW* BD4 ....48 D3
Daniel Ct *BOW* BD4 ....49 E5
Dan La *CUL/QBY* BD13 ....53 F1
Danny La *LUD/ILL* HX2 ....66 A1
Danum Dr *BAIL* BD17 ....18 D4
Darcey Hey La *LUD/ILL* HX2 ....67 H3
Darfield St *GIR* BD8 ....2 B3
Dark La *HWTH* BD22 ....12 A5
HWTH BD22 ....32 D1
LUD/ILL HX2 ....67 E2
Darley St *BFD* BD1 ....2 D4
KGHY BD21 ....7 E2
Darnes Av *LUD/ILL* HX2 ....67 H3
Darren St *BOW* BD4 ....48 D3
Darryl Dr *LUD/ILL* HX2 ....67 H3
Dartmouth Ter *GIR* BD8 ....38 C2
Darwin St *WBOW* BD5 ....46 D4
Dawnay Rd *WBOW* BD5 ....46 D3
Dawson Av *WBSY* BD6 ....54 D2
Dawson La *BOW* BD4 ....56 B1
Dawson Mt *BOW* BD4 ....56 B1
Dawson Pl *BOW* BD4 ....56 B1
KGHY BD21 ....14 B1
Dawson Rd *KGHY* BD21 ....14 B1
Dawsons Meadow
PDSY/CALV LS28 ....41 H2
Dawson St *BOW* BD4 ....48 B5
IDLE BD10 ....20 A4
Dawson Ter *BOW* BD4 ....56 B1
Dawson Wy *KGHY* BD21 ....14 B1
Deacon Cl *BFDE* * BD3 ....40 C2
Dealburn Rd *LM/WK* BD12 ....55 E5
Deal St *HFAX* HX1 ....5 J5
KGHY BD21 ....7 H3
Dean Beck Av *WBSY* BD6 ....55 F3
Dean Beck Ct *WBSY* * BD6 ....55 G2
Dean Cl *GIR* BD8 ....37 G3
Dean Clough *HFAX* HX1 ....5 G2
Dean Ct *HIPP* HX3 ....75 F1
Dean End *GTL/HWG* HX4 ....76 A3
Deanery Gdns *IDLE* BD10 ....30 B4
Dean La *CUL/QBY* BD13 ....35 H3
Dean La Head *CUL/QBY* * BD13 ....36 A3
Dean Rd *WBSY* BD6 ....55 E2
Deanstones Crs *CUL/QBY* BD13 ...52 B2
Deanstones La *CUL/QBY* BD13 .....52 B2
Dean St *GTL/HWG* HX4 ....76 A4
HWTH BD22 ....23 F1
Deanwood Av *WIL/AL* BD15 ....36 D2
Deanwood Crs *WIL/AL* BD15 ....36 D2
Deanwood Wk *WIL/AL* BD15 ....36 D2
Dearden St *RPDN/SBR* HX6 ....67 E3
Dee Ct *HWTH* BD22 ....12 D4
Deepdale Cl *BAIL* BD17 ....18 B4
Deep La *BRIG* HD6 ....79 F1
CLAY BD14 ....45 F2
CUL/QBY BD13 ....43 F3
LUD/ILL HX2 ....66 C1
Defarge Ct *WBOW* BD5 ....47 F4
De Lacey Ms *BOW* BD4 ....48 B5
De Lacy Av *BOW* * BD4 ....56 A2
Delamere St *WBOW* BD5 ....47 E5
Delaware Ct *BOW* BD4 ....56 A2
Delf HI *BRIG* HD6 ....77 H4
Delius Av *IDLE* BD10 ....30 C4
The Dell *CUL/QBY* BD13 ....24 D3
Dellside Fold *CUL/QBY* BD13 ....24 C3
Delph Crs *CLAY* BD14 ....45 E3
Delph Croft Vw *KGHY* BD21 ....7 G5
Delph Dr *CLAY* BD14 ....44 D3
Delph Gv *CLAY* BD14 ....45 E3
Delph HI *BAIL* BD17 ....18 D2
Delph Hill Castle *LUD/ILL* * HX2 ...67 G2
Delph Hill Rd *LUD/ILL* HX2 ....68 A4
Delph Hill Ter *LUD/ILL* HX2 ....68 A4
Delph St *HFAX* HX1 ....5 F5
Delph Ter *CLAY* BD14 ....45 E3
Delph Wood Cl *BGLY* BD16 ....17 F3
Delverne Gv *ECHL* BD2 ....40 B1
Denbrook Av *BOW* BD4 ....57 E2
Denbrook Cl *BOW* BD4 ....57 E1
Denbrook Crs *BOW* BD4 ....57 E1
Denbrook Wk *BOW* BD4 ....57 E1
Denbrook Wy *BOW* BD4 ....57 E1
Denbury Mt *BOW* BD4 ....48 D5
Denby Ct *HWTH* BD22 ....12 C5
Denby Dr *BAIL* BD17 ....18 C5
Denby Hill Rd *HWTH* BD22 ....12 C4
Denby La *WIL/AL* BD15 ....37 E3
Denby Mt *HWTH* BD22 ....32 D2
Denby Pl *RPDN/SBR* HX6 ....67 E3
Denby Rd *KGHY* BD21 ....14 B1
Denby St *GIR* BD8 ....38 C4
Dence Gn *BOW* * BD4 ....48 D2
Dendrum Cl *HWTH* BD22 ....12 D3
Dene Bank *BGLY* BD16 ....9 H5
Dene Crs *GTHN* BD7 ....45 H3

Dene HI BAIL BD17 ...... 18 A3
Denehill HTON BD9 ...... 37 G2
Dene Mt WIL/AL BD15 ...... 37 G2
Dene PI HFAX HX1 ...... 5 F2
Dene Rd WBSY BD6 ...... 53 G1
Deneside Mt WBOW BD5 ...... 54 D1
Deneside Ter WBOW BD5 ...... 47 E5
Deneway PDSY/CALV LS28 ...... 41 H2
Denfield Av HIPP HX3 ...... 58 D3
Denfield Crs HIPP HX3 ...... 59 E3
Denfield Edge HIPP HX3 ...... 59 E3
Denfield Gdns HIPP HX3 ...... 59 E3
Denfield La HIPP HX3 ...... 58 D3
Denfield Sq HIPP HX3 ...... 59 E3
Denham St BRIG HD6 ...... 78 B2
Denholme Gate Rd HIPP HX3 ...... 61 F4
Denholme Rd HWTH BD22 ...... 33 F3
Denison St YEA LS19 ...... 11 G4
Dennison Fold BOW BD4 ...... 48 D2
Denton Dr BCLY BD16 ...... 17 F2
Derby PI BFDE * BD3 ...... 40 C5
Derby Rd BFDE BD3 ...... 40 D5
  YEA LS19 ...... 21 G3
Derby St CLAY * BD14 ...... 45 E3
  CUL/QBY BD13 ...... 52 A1
  GTHN BD7 ...... 46 C3
  RPDN/SBR HX6 ...... 67 F3
Derwent Av WIL/AL BD15 ...... 25 H5
Derwent Rd ECHL BD2 ...... 39 H1
Derwent St KGHY BD21 ...... 7 H3
Devonshire St KGHY BD21 ...... 7 H3
Devonshire St West KGHY BD21 ...... 6 D4
Devonshire Ter GIR BD8 ...... 38 D2
Devon St HFAX HX1 ...... 4 A6
Devon Wy BRIG HD6 ...... 71 G2
Dewhirst CI BAIL BD17 ...... 19 E4
Dewhirst Rd BAIL BD17 ...... 19 E4
  BRIG HD6 ...... 71 G2
Dewhirst St WIL/AL BD15 ...... 25 H4
Dewsbury Rd CLECK BD19 ...... 65 G3
  CLECK BD19 ...... 73 H1
  ELL HX5 ...... 77 F5
Diamond St BFD BD1 ...... 2 E6
  HFAX HX1 ...... 4 C2
  HWTH BD22 ...... 13 H2
Diamond Ter HFAX HX1 ...... 4 C1
Dibb La YEA LS19 ...... 11 E4
Dicken's St LUD/ILL HX2 ...... 67 H1
  WBOW BD5 ...... 5 F4
Dick La BFDE BD3 ...... 41 E4
  BOW BD4 ...... 48 D2
Dimples La AIRE BD20 ...... 9 E3
  HWTH BD22 ...... 8 D2
Dirkhill Rd GTHN BD7 ...... 46 D2
Dirkhill St GTHN BD7 ...... 46 C2
Discovery Rd HFAX HX1 ...... 5 J4
Dispensary Wk HFAX HX1 ...... 5 J4
Dixon Av HFAX HX1 ...... 4 A2
Dixon CI GTL/HWG HX4 ...... 75 F3
Dob La RPDN/SBR HX6 ...... 66 A5
Dockfield PI BAIL BD17 ...... 18 D5
Dockfield Rd BAIL BD17 ...... 28 D1
Dockfield Ter BAIL BD17 ...... 18 D5
Dock La BAIL BD17 ...... 28 D1
Dockroyd La HWTH BD22 ...... 12 C3
Doctor HI IDLE BD10 ...... 29 H3
  LUD/ILL HX2 ...... 58 C4
Doctor La IDLE BD10 ...... 20 A5
Dodgeholme CI LUD/ILL HX2 ...... 58 C1
Dodge Holme Gdns LUD/ILL HX2 ...... 58 C1
Dodge Holme Rd LUD/ILL HX2 ...... 58 C1
Dog Kennel La HIPP HX3 ...... 69 F2
Dog La GTL/HWG HX4 ...... 74 D4
Dole St CUL/QBY BD13 ...... 51 B1
Doll La CUL/QBY BD13 ...... 24 D4
Dombey St HFAX HX1 ...... 4 A4
Donald Av WBSY BD6 ...... 54 D2
Doncaster St HIPP HX3 ...... 69 E5
Donisthorpe St WBOW BD5 ...... 47 F4
Don St KGHY BD21 ...... 7 E3
Dorchester Ct BOW * BD4 ...... 48 D4
Dorchester Crs BAIL BD17 ...... 19 G2
  BOW BD4 ...... 48 D4
Dorchester Dr LUD/ILL HX2 ...... 67 H3
  YEA LS19 ...... 11 H5
Dorian CI IDLE BD10 ...... 30 C3
Dorothy St KGHY BD21 ...... 13 H3
Dorset CI WBOW BD5 ...... 46 D4
Dorset St WBOW BD5 ...... 47 E4
Douglas Dr BOW * BD4 ...... 48 D3
Douglas Rd BOW BD4 ...... 48 D3
Douglas St HIPP HX3 ...... 59 E3
Dovedale CI HIPP HX3 ...... 53 E4
Dover St BFDE BD3 ...... 3 F1
Dovesdale Gv WBOW BD5 ...... 46 D5

Dovesdale Rd WBOW BD5 ...... 47 E5
Dove St SHPY BD18 ...... 28 A1
Dowker St HFAX HX1 ...... 4 B7
Dowley Gap La BCLY BD16 ...... 17 G5
Downham St BFDE BD3 ...... 3 H6
Downing CI BFDE BD3 ...... 3 J4
Downside Crs WIL/AL BD15 ...... 36 D3
Dracup Av GTHN BD7 ...... 45 H2
Dracup Rd GTHN BD7 ...... 46 A4
Drake St KGHY BD21 ...... 7 F3
Draughton Gv WBOW BD5 ...... 55 E1
Draughton St WBOW BD5 ...... 55 E1
Drewry Rd KGHY BD21 ...... 7 E4
Drewton Rd BFD BD1 ...... 2 B4
Drill Pde GIR BD8 ...... 2 A1
Drill St HWTH BD22 ...... 22 D3
  KGHY BD21 ...... 7 F4
The Drive BCLY BD16 ...... 9 F5
  HIPP HX3 ...... 61 G5
  IDLE BD10 ...... 30 C3
Drovers Wy ECHL BD2 ...... 39 F1
Drub La CLECK BD19 ...... 64 D3
Druids St CLAY BD14 ...... 45 E3
Drummond Rd GIR BD8 ...... 38 D3
Dryclough CI HIPP HX3 ...... 68 D5
Dryclough La HIPP HX3 ...... 68 D5
Dryden St BFD BD1 ...... 3 F7
  BCLY * BD16 ...... 16 C3
Dubb La BCLY BD16 ...... 16 D3
Duchy Av HTON BD9 ...... 37 H1
Duchy Crs HTON BD9 ...... 37 H1
Duchy Dr HTON BD9 ...... 37 H2
Duchy Gv HTON BD9 ...... 37 H1
Duchy Vls HTON BD9 ...... 37 H1
Duchywood HTON BD9 ...... 37 H1
Ducie St IDLE BD10 ...... 20 A3
Duckett Gv PDSY/CALV LS28 ...... 41 E4
Duckworth Gv HTON BD9 ...... 38 A2
Duckworth La HTON BD9 ...... 37 H3
Duckworth Ter HTON BD9 ...... 38 A2
Dudley Crs LUD/ILL HX2 ...... 50 C3
Dudley Gv BOW BD4 ...... 48 D2
Dudley Hill Rd ECHL BD2 ...... 40 A1
Dudley St BOW BD4 ...... 48 B5
  BOW BD4 ...... 48 D2
Dudwell Av HIPP * HX3 ...... 76 A1
Dudwell Gv HIPP HX3 ...... 75 H1
Dudwell La HIPP HX3 ...... 75 H1
Duich Rd WBSY BD6 ...... 53 H4
Duinen St WBOW BD5 ...... 47 G2
Duke St BFD BD1 ...... 2 C4
  ELL HX5 ...... 76 C5
  HWTH BD22 ...... 23 E2
  KGHY BD21 ...... 7 E2
Dulverton Gv BOW BD4 ...... 48 C4
Dunbar Cft CUL/QBY BD13 ...... 52 C1
Duncan St WBOW BD5 ...... 47 F5
Duncombe Rd GIR BD8 ...... 38 A5
Duncombe St GIR BD8 ...... 38 B5
Duncombe Wy GTHN BD7 ...... 38 B5
Dundas St HFAX HX1 ...... 5 J1
  KGHY BD21 ...... 7 G5
Dunkhill Cft IDLE * BD10 ...... 30 A2
Dunkirk Crs HFAX HX1 ...... 67 H3
Dunkirk La HFAX HX1 ...... 67 H3
Dunkirk Ri AIRE BD20 ...... 7 H1
Dunkirk St HFAX HX1 ...... 67 H2
Dunkirk Ter HFAX HX1 ...... 4 A6
Dunlin Wy GIR BD8 ...... 37 F5
Dunmore Av CUL/QBY BD13 ...... 51 H1
Dunnington Av LM/WK BD12 ...... 54 A4
Dunsford Av BOW BD4 ...... 56 A2
Durham Rd GIR BD8 ...... 38 B3
Durham St LUD/ILL HX2 ...... 58 D5
Durham Ter GIR BD8 ...... 38 B3
Durkheim Ct BFDE * BD3 ...... 40 B5
Durley Av HTON BD9 ...... 38 A1
Durling Dr SHPY BD18 ...... 29 F2
Durlston Gv LM/WK BD12 ...... 63 E1
Durlston Ter LM/WK BD12 ...... 63 E1
Durrance St HWTH BD22 ...... 6 C5
Dyehouse Dr CLECK BD19 ...... 64 B3
Dyehouse La BRIG HD6 ...... 78 D2
Dye House La RPDN/SBR HX6 ...... 74 D2
  WIL/AL BD15 ...... 25 G4
Dyehouse Rd LM/WK BD12 ...... 55 G5
Dyer La HIPP HX3 ...... 59 E4
Dyson PI HIPP * HX3 ...... 69 E5
Dyson Rd HFAX HX1 ...... 4 B7
Dyson St BFD BD1 ...... 2 A4
  BRIG HD6 ...... 71 F5
  HTON BD9 ...... 28 B5

E

Eaglesfield Dr WBSY BD6 ...... 54 A4

Eagle St HWTH BD22 ...... 23 F2
  KGHY BD21 ...... 7 E4
Earls Ter HIPP HX3 ...... 59 F3
Earl St HWTH BD22 ...... 22 D3
  KGHY BD21 ...... 7 E3
  WBOW BD5 ...... 47 F2
Earlswood LM/WK * BD12 ...... 63 E2
Earl Ter HIPP HX3 ...... 59 F3
Easby Rd WBOW BD5 ...... 47 E2
East Av KGHY BD21 ...... 7 F3
East Bolton LUD/ILL HX2 ...... 50 C3
Eastbourne Rd HTON BD9 ...... 28 C4
Eastbury Av WBSY BD6 ...... 53 G1
East Byland LUD/ILL HX2 ...... 50 D4
Eastcliffe HIPP HX3 ...... 69 F2
Eastfield Gdns BOW BD4 ...... 48 D4
Eastgate ELL HX5 ...... 76 C4
Easthorpe Ct ECHL BD2 ...... 30 C5
Eastleigh Gv WBOW BD5 ...... 47 E4
East Mt BRIG HD6 ...... 71 F5
East Pde BAIL BD17 ...... 19 E2
  BFD BD1 ...... 3 F5
  KGHY BD21 ...... 7 F4
  RPDN/SBR HX6 ...... 67 G3
East Park Rd HIPP * HX3 ...... 59 F4
East Rd LM/WK BD12 ...... 55 E4
East Royd HWTH BD22 ...... 13 E4
East Squire La GIR BD8 ...... 38 D2
East St BRIG HD6 ...... 78 B2
  HIPP HX3 ...... 71 F1
East Ter HWTH BD22 ...... 23 F1
East Vw CLECK BD19 ...... 72 D2
  WBSY BD6 ...... 45 F5
  YEA LS19 ...... 11 H5
East View Rd YEA LS19 ...... 11 H5
East View Ter LM/WK BD12 ...... 63 E1
Eastwick Vw WIL/AL * BD15 ...... 37 E3
Eastwood Av LUD/ILL HX2 ...... 50 D3
  RPDN/SBR HX6 ...... 66 C5
Eastwood CI LUD/ILL HX2 ...... 50 D3
Eastwood Gv LUD/ILL HX2 ...... 50 D3
Eastwood Gdns BOW BD4 ...... 47 G2
  BRIG HD6 ...... 71 G5
East Wood St HIPP HX3 ...... 59 F3
Eaton St KGHY BD21 ...... 13 H2
Ebenezer PI GTHN BD7 ...... 46 B3
Ebenezer St BFD BD1 ...... 2 E6
Ebor La HWTH BD22 ...... 23 E1
Eccles Ct ECHL BD2 ...... 30 A5
Edale Gv LUD/ILL HX2 ...... 51 H2
Edderthorpe St BFDE BD3 ...... 3 H6
Eden CI LM/WK BD12 ...... 63 E2
Edensor Rd KGHY BD21 ...... 6 D4
Ederoyd Av PDSY/CALV LS28 ...... 41 H3
Ederoyd Crs PDSY/CALV LS28 ...... 41 G3
Ederoyd Dr PDSY/CALV LS28 ...... 41 G3
Ederoyd Gv PDSY/CALV LS28 ...... 41 G3
Ederoyd Mt PDSY/CALV LS28 ...... 41 H3
Ederoyd Ri PDSY/CALV LS28 ...... 41 F3
Edgar St CLAY BD14 ...... 45 E3
Edgebank Av WBSY BD6 ...... 54 A4
Edge End Gdns WBSY BD6 ...... 53 H3
Edge End Rd WBSY BD6 ...... 53 H3
Edgehill CI CUL/QBY BD13 ...... 52 C1
Edgeholme La LUD/ILL HX2 ...... 67 E1
Edgemoor CI BOW BD4 ...... 56 D2
  HIPP HX3 ...... 68 C4
Edlington CI BOW BD4 ...... 48 D4
Edmund St BFD BD1 ...... 2 B7
Edrich CI LM/WK BD12 ...... 55 F4
Edward CI HIPP HX3 ...... 69 H4
Edward Rd LUD/ILL HX2 ...... 67 H3
Edward St BOW BD4 ...... 2 E7
  BOW BD4 ...... 56 D1
  BRIG HD6 ...... 71 F5
  RPDN/SBR HX6 ...... 67 E4
  SHPY BD18 ...... 28 A1
Edward Turner CI LM/WK BD12 ...... 54 A4
Eel Holme View St AIRE BD20 ...... 7 H1
Effingham Rd BCLY BD16 ...... 15 F5
Egerton Gv WIL/AL BD15 ...... 36 C3
Egerton St RPDN/SBR HX6 ...... 67 E4
Eggleston Dr BOW BD4 ...... 49 E5
Egremont Crs WBSY BD6 ...... 54 A4
Egremont St RPDN/SBR HX6 ...... 66 C5
Egypt Rd CUL/QBY BD13 ...... 35 H4
Eighth Av LVSG WF15 ...... 73 G3
Elbow La ECHL BD2 ...... 40 A2
Elder St AIRE BD20 ...... 9 D1
  IDLE BD10 ...... 30 C2
Elderwood Gdns IDLE BD10 ...... 30 D4
  CLECK BD19 ...... 73 H1
Eldon PI BFD BD1 ...... 2 B3
Eldon St HIPP HX3 ...... 5 H1
Eldroth Mt HFAX HX1 ...... 68 B3
Eldroth Rd HFAX HX1 ...... 68 B3
Eldwick Cft BCLY BD16 ...... 17 F1
Eleanor Dr PDSY/CALV LS28 ...... 31 E2

Eleanor St BRIG HD6 ...... 78 B2
Eleventh Av LVSG WF15 ...... 73 F3
Elia St KGHY BD21 ...... 7 G3
Eliot Gv GSLY LS20 ...... 11 E3
Eli St WBOW BD5 ...... 47 G4
Elizabeth Av LM/WK BD12 ...... 62 D1
Elizabeth CI LM/WK BD12 ...... 63 E1
Elizabeth Crs LM/WK BD12 ...... 63 E1
Elizabeth Dr LM/WK BD12 ...... 63 E1
Elizabeth Frances St ELL HX5 ...... 76 C5
Elizabeth St BGLY * BD16 ...... 16 D3
  ELL HX5 ...... 76 C5
  GTL/HWG HX4 ...... 76 A4
  KGHY BD21 ...... 8 A4
  LM/WK BD12 ...... 62 D1
  LVSG WF15 ...... 73 H4
  WBOW BD5 ...... 47 F2
Elland Br ELL HX5 ...... 76 D4
Elland La ELL HX5 ...... 76 D4
Elland Riorges Link ELL HX5 ...... 76 D4
Elland Rd ELL HX5 ...... 77 F2
Elland Wood Bottom ELL HX5 ...... 76 D4
  IDLE BD10 ...... 20 B4
Ellar Carr Rd CUL/QBY BD13 ...... 24 B2
Ellen Royd St HIPP HX3 ...... 5 H1
Ellen St BGLY BD16 ...... 16 D3
Ellenthorpe Rd BAIL BD17 ...... 17 H4
Ellercroft Av GTHN BD7 ...... 46 B1
Ellercroft Rd GTHN BD7 ...... 46 B1
Ellercroft Ter GTHN BD7 ...... 46 B1
Ellerton St BFDE BD3 ...... 40 B3
Ellinthorpe St BOW BD4 ...... 48 A2
Elliott St SHPY BD18 ...... 28 B1
Ellis St WBOW BD5 ...... 47 E4
Ellistones Gdns GTL/HWG HX4 ...... 75 F5
Ellistones La GTL/HWG HX4 ...... 75 F5
Ellistones PI GTL/HWG HX4 ...... 75 F5
Elliton Gv WBSY BD6 ...... 54 B1
Elm Av RPDN/SBR HX6 ...... 67 E3
Elm Ct CLECK BD19 ...... 65 G1
Elm Crs AIRE BD20 ...... 9 E3
Elmfield BAIL BD17 ...... 19 E2
Elmfield Ct BIRK/DRI BD11 ...... 65 F1
Elmfield Dr WBSY BD6 ...... 54 D2
Elmfield Ter HFAX HX1 ...... 68 C3
Elm Gdns HFAX HX1 ...... 68 C3
Elm Gv AIRE BD20 ...... 9 E3
  CLECK BD19 ...... 65 F5
  HIPP HX3 ...... 53 G4
  HWTH BD22 ...... 13 H2
  SHPY BD18 ...... 29 F2
Elm PI RPDN/SBR HX6 ...... 67 E3
Elm Rd SHPY BD18 ...... 29 E2
Elmsall St GIR BD8 ...... 2 B2
The Elms GSLY LS20 ...... 10 D3
Elm St WBOW BD5 ...... 32 D2
Elm Tree Av WBSY BD6 ...... 54 D2
Elm Tree CI KGHY BD21 ...... 7 G5
  WBSY BD6 ...... 55 E2
Elm Tree Gdns WBSY BD6 ...... 54 D2
Elm Vw HIPP HX3 ...... 68 D4
Elmwood Dr BRIG HD6 ...... 71 E5
  HWTH BD22 ...... 13 G2
Elmwood PI BFDE BD3 ...... 40 B3
Elmwood Rd HWTH BD22 ...... 13 G2
Elm Wood St BRIG HD6 ...... 71 G4
Elmwood Ter HWTH BD22 ...... 13 G2
Elsdon Gv WBOW BD5 ...... 47 F2
Elsie St HWTH BD22 ...... 23 G1
  KGHY BD21 ...... 7 E1
Elsinore Av ELL HX5 ...... 76 B5
Elsinore Ct ELL HX5 ...... 76 B5
Elsworth Av BFDE BD3 ...... 40 C3
Eltham Gv WBSY BD6 ...... 54 B2
Elvey CI ECHL BD2 ...... 30 C5
Elwell St WBSY BD6 ...... 53 G3
Elwyn Gv WBOW BD5 ...... 47 G4
Elwyn Rd WBOW BD5 ...... 47 G4
Ely St GTL/HWG HX4 ...... 76 A5
Emerald St HWTH BD22 ...... 13 H2
Emerson Av HTON BD9 ...... 37 F3
Emily Hall Gdns WIL/AL BD15 ...... 25 H4
Emily St KGHY BD21 ...... 7 F3
Emmeline CI IDLE * BD10 ...... 30 A1
Emmfield Dr HTON BD9 ...... 28 B5
Emm La HTON BD9 ...... 38 B1
Emmott Farm Fold HWTH BD22 ...... 22 D3
Emscote Av HFAX HX1 ...... 4 D7
Emscote Gdns HFAX HX1 ...... 4 D7
Emscote PI HFAX HX1 ...... 4 D7
Emscote St South HFAX HX1 ...... 4 D7
Emsley CI BOW BD4 ...... 56 A2
Enderby CI HIPP HX3 ...... 59 E2
Enderley Rd CUL/QBY BD13 ...... 44 A1
Endsleigh PI CLAY * BD14 ...... 45 E3
Enfield YEA LS19 ...... 11 G5

Enfield Dr *GTHN* BD7 ....54 A1
Enfield Pde *WBSY* BD6 ....54 B1
Enfield Rd *BAIL* BD17 ....18 D4
Enfield St *KGHY* BD21 ....7 E4
Enfield Wk *WBSY* BD6 ....54 B1
Engleheld Cl *BOW* BD4 ....48 D5
Englefield Crs *BOW* BD4 ....48 D5
Ennerdale Dr *ECHL* BD2 ....40 A1
  ELL HX5 ....77 E4
Ennerdale Rd *ECHL* BD2 ....39 H1
Enterprise Wy *IDLE* BD10 ....30 A3
Epworth Pl *HWTH* BD22 ....12 C3
Eric St *KGHY* BD21 ....7 F3
Escroft Cl *LM/WK* BD12 ....63 E4
Esholt Av *GSLY* LS20 ....10 C4
Esholt La *BAIL* BD17 ....19 H2
Eshton Av *LM/WK* BD12 ....55 G5
Eskdale Av *HIPP* HX3 ....53 E5
Eskdale Ri *WIL/AL* BD15 ....37 E4
Eskine Pde *WBSY* BD6 ....54 B1
Esmond St *GTHN* BD7 ....46 A4
Essex St *BFDE* BD3 ....3 H7
  BOW BD4 ....47 H1
  HFAX HX1 ....4 A5
Estcourt Gv *GTHN* BD7 ....46 B2
Estcourt Rd *GTHN* BD7 ....46 B2
Ethel St *KGHY* BD21 ....7 E2
Etna St *GTHN* BD7 ....46 A4
Eton St *HFAX* HX1 ....4 B4
Evelyn Av *BFDE* BD3 ....40 A4
Evens Ter *WBOW* BD5 ....47 F5
Everest Av *SHPY* BD18 ....29 F3
Eversley Dr *BOW* BD4 ....48 D3
Eversley Ldg *LUD/ILL* * HX2 ....67 H2
Eversley Mt *LUD/ILL* HX2 ....67 H2
Eversley Pl *LUD/ILL* HX2 ....67 H2
Evesham Gv *IDLE* BD10 ....30 A2
Ewart Pl *GTHN* BD7 ....46 B4
Ewart St *CUL/QBY* * BD13 ....52 B1
  GTHN BD7 ....46 B4
Exchange Sq *BFD* * BD1 ....2 E6
Exchange St *CLECK* BD19 ....64 C4
  GTL/HWG HX4 ....76 A5
Exe St *WBOW* BD5 ....46 D4
Exeter St *HIPP* HX3 ....69 E5
  RPDN/SBR HX6 ....67 F4
Exhibition Rd *SHPY* BD18 ....28 A1
Exley Av *KGHY* BD21 ....13 H2
Exley Bank *HIPP* HX3 ....76 A1
Exley Bank Top *HIPP* HX3 ....76 A1
Exley Crs *KGHY* BD21 ....13 H1
Exley Dr *KGHY* * BD21 ....13 H1
Exley Gdns *ELL* HX5 ....76 A2
Exley Gv *KGHY* BD21 ....13 H2
Exley Head *KGHY* BD21 ....13 G1
Exley Head Vw *HWTH* BD22 ....6 B3
Exley La *ELL* HX5 ....76 B2
Exley Mt *GTHN* BD7 ....46 A1
  KGHY BD21 ....13 H1
Exley Rd *KGHY* BD21 ....13 H1
Exley St *KGHY* BD21 ....13 H2
Exley Wy *KGHY* * BD21 ....13 H2
Exmoor St *HFAX* HX1 ....4 A6
Exmouth Pl *BFDE* BD3 ....39 G1

F

Factory La *BOW* BD4 ....48 A5
Factory St *BOW* BD4 ....48 B5
Fagley Crs *ECHL* BD2 ....40 C2
Fagley Cft *ECHL* BD2 ....40 C2
Fagley Dr *ECHL* BD2 ....40 B2
Fagley La *ECHL* BD2 ....40 B3
Fagley Pl *ECHL* BD2 ....40 B3
Fagley Rd *ECHL* BD2 ....40 C2
Fagley Ter *ECHL* BD2 ....40 B3
Fair Bank *SHPY* BD18 ....28 D3
Fairbank Rd *GIR* BD8 ....38 B3
Fairbank Ter *GIR* BD8 ....38 B3
Fairburn Ct *HIPP* * HX3 ....69 H4
Fairburn Gdns *ECHL* BD2 ....30 D5
Fairclough Gv *LUD/ILL* HX2 ....59 E2
Fairfax Av *BOW* BD4 ....56 B1
Fairfax Crs *BOW* BD4 ....56 B1
  HIPP HX3 ....69 H3
Fairfax Rd *BGLY* BD16 ....16 C1
  CUL/QBY BD13 ....24 C2
Fairfax St *BOW* BD4 ....47 G2
  HWTH BD22 ....23 C4
Fairfield Cl *CUL/QBY* BD13 ....34 C4
Fairfield Dr *BAIL* BD17 ....19 F2
Fairfield Rd *GIR* BD8 ....38 C3
  LM/WK BD12 ....63 H2
Fairfield St *BOW* BD4 ....56 C1
Fairhaven Gn *IDLE* BD10 ....30 B2

Fair Isle Ct *KGHY* BD21 ....7 F4
Fairless Av *HIPP* HX3 ....71 F1
Fairmount *HTON* BD9 ....38 D2
Fairmount Pk *SHPY* BD18 ....27 H2
Fairmount Ter *KGHY* BD21 ....8 A5
Fair Rd *WBSY* BD6 ....54 C1
Fairview Ct *BAIL* BD17 ....18 C5
Fairview Ter *HIPP* HX3 ....59 F4
The Fairway *LUD/ILL* HX2 ....51 E3
  PDSY/CALV LS28 ....41 C3
Fairway *GSLY* LS20 ....10 B2
  IDLE BD10 ....21 E5
  SHPY BD18 ....28 A2
  WBSY BD6 ....54 A1
Fairway Av *GTHN* BD7 ....54 A1
Fairway Cl *GSLY* LS20 ....10 B3
  WBSY BD6 ....54 A1
Fairway Crs *HWTH* BD22 ....23 E3
Fairway Dr *GTHN* BD7 ....46 A5
Fairway Gra *GTHN* BD7 ....46 A5
The Fairways *HTON* BD9 ....27 H4
Fairway Wk *GTHN* BD7 ....46 A5
Fairweather Ms *GIR* * BD8 ....37 H5
Fairy Dell *BGLY* BD16 ....26 D2
Falcon Ms *GIR* * BD8 ....37 F4
Falcon Rd *BGLY* BD16 ....16 C1
Falcon St *GTHN* BD7 ....46 B2
  HIPP HX3 ....69 E5
Falkland Rd *IDLE* BD10 ....30 D5
Fall Brow Cl *CLAY* BD14 ....44 D4
Fall La *HIPP* HX3 ....60 B1
  RPDN/SBR HX6 ....67 G5
Fallowfield Cl *BOW* BD4 ....56 B2
Fallowfield Dr *BOW* BD4 ....56 B1
Fallowfield Gdns *BOW* BD4 ....56 B1
Fall Wood St *HWTH* BD22 ....23 E4
Falmouth Av *BFDE* BD3 ....3 F1
Falsgrave Av *ECHL* BD2 ....40 C2
Faltis *IDLE* BD10 ....30 B4
Fanny St *KGHY* BD21 ....7 E5
  SHPY BD18 ....28 A1
Farcliffe Pl *GIR* BD8 ....38 C3
Farcliffe Rd *GIR* BD8 ....38 C3
Farcliffe Ter *GIR* BD8 ....38 C3
Far Crook *IDLE* BD10 ....19 C5
Farfield Av *PDSY/CALV* LS28 ....41 H1
  WBSY BD6 ....53 H3
Farfield Crs *WBSY* BD6 ....54 A3
Farfield Dr *PDSY/CALV* LS28 ....41 H2
Farfield Gv *PDSY/CALV* LS28 ....41 H1
  WBSY BD6 ....54 A3
Farfield Ri *PDSY/CALV* LS28 ....41 H1
Farfield Rd *BAIL* BD17 ....19 E5
  SHPY BD18 ....28 B2
  WBSY BD6 ....54 B3
Farfield St *CLECK* BD19 ....64 C4
  HTON BD9 ....38 B2
Farfield Ter *HTON* BD9 ....38 B2
Farlea Dr *ECHL* BD2 ....40 B1
Farleton Dr *ECHL* BD2 ....40 C2
Farley Crs *HWTH* BD22 ....12 C3
Farm Hill Rd *IDLE* BD10 ....30 A4
Farm Pond Dr *BRIG* HD6 ....70 D2
Farmstead Rd *IDLE* BD10 ....30 B3
Farndale Rd *BAIL* BD17 ....18 B4
  WIL/AL BD15 ....25 H5
Farnham Cl *BAIL* BD17 ....19 E2
Farnham Rd *GTHN* BD7 ....46 B2
Farrar Mill La *HIPP* HX3 ....69 E5
Farriers Cft *ECHL* BD2 ....29 C5
Farringdon Cl *ECHL* BD2 ....48 C3
Farringdon Dr *BOW* BD4 ....48 C4
Farringdon Gv *WBSY* BD6 ....54 B3
Farside Gn *WBOW* BD5 ....46 D4
Farway *BOW* BD4 ....48 D3
Faversham Wk *BOW* * BD4 ....48 D3
Fawcett Pl *BOW* BD4 ....56 B2
Faxfleet St *WBOW* BD5 ....55 E1
Faye Gdns *BOW* BD4 ....56 B2
Fearnsides St *GIR* BD8 ....38 C4
Fearnsides Ter *GIR* BD8 ....38 C4
Fearnville Dr *BOW* BD4 ....48 C2
Featherbed Cl *GTL/HWG* HX4 ....76 A5
Feather Bed La *ELL* HX5 ....76 A5
Feather Rd *BFDE* BD3 ....3 J4
Federation St *WBOW* BD5 ....47 G5
Felbrigg Av *HWTH* BD22 ....6 C5
Felcourt Dr *BOW* BD4 ....48 C5
Felcourt Fold *BOW* BD4 ....48 D5
Fell Crs *HWTH* BD22 ....13 F1
Fell Gv *HWTH* BD22 ....6 C5
Fell La *HWTH* BD22 ....6 B5
Fellside Cl *WBOW* BD5 ....47 G5
Fellwood Av *HWTH* BD22 ....23 F1
Fellwood Cl *HWTH* BD22 ....23 F1
Fenby Av *BOW* BD4 ....48 A3
Fenby Cl *BOW* BD4 ....48 B4
Fenby Gv *BOW* BD4 ....48 B3

Fencote Crs *ECHL* BD2 ....40 C1
Fender Rd *WBSY* BD6 ....54 A1
Fennec Rd *BAIL* BD17 ....19 F2
Fenton Rd *HFAX* HX1 ....4 A7
Fenwick Dr *WBSY* BD6 ....54 A4
Ferguson St *HFAX* HX1 ....5 G5
Fernbank Av *HWTH* BD22 ....13 G2
Fernbank Dr *BAIL* BD17 ....18 B5
  BGLY BD16 ....16 D3
Fernbank Rd *BFDE* BD3 ....3 J1
Ferncliffe Dr *AIRE* BD20 ....6 C1
  BAIL BD17 ....18 C3
Ferncliffe Rd *BGLY* BD16 ....16 D3
  SHPY * BD18 ....28 A1
Fern Ct *AIRE* BD20 ....6 D1
Fern Cft *LVSG* WF15 ....73 F4
Ferndale Av *CLAY* BD14 ....44 D4
Ferndale Gv *HTON* BD9 ....38 B1
Ferndene *BGLY* BD16 ....17 E3
Ferndown Gn *WBOW* BD5 ....47 E4
Fernhill *BGLY* BD16 ....16 D1
Fern Hill Av *SHPY* BD18 ....28 A2
Fern Hill Gv *SHPY* BD18 ....28 A2
Fern Hill Mt *SHPY* BD18 ....28 A2
Fern Hill Rd *SHPY* BD18 ....28 A2
Fern Lea St *RPDN/SBR* HX6 ....67 E3
Fernley Gdns *LM/WK* BD12 ....62 D1
Fern St *BOW* BD4 ....48 C4
  HIPP HX3 ....59 G3
  KGHY BD21 ....7 F3
Fern Ter *AIRE* BD20 ....8 A2
  GIR BD8 ....38 D2
Ferrand Av *BOW* BD4 ....56 B2
Ferrand La *BGLY* BD16 ....16 C3
  CLECK BD19 ....65 F4
Ferrands Cl *BGLY* BD16 ....15 G5
Ferrands Park Wy *BGLY* BD16 ....15 G5
Ferrand St *BGLY* BD16 ....16 D3
Ferriby Cl *ECHL* BD2 ....40 C1
Festival Av *SHPY* BD18 ....29 E3
Feversham St *BFDE* BD3 ....3 G6
Field Cl *HIPP* HX3 ....59 F4
Fieldedge La *AIRE* BD20 ....8 B1
Fieldgate Rd *IDLE* BD10 ....30 C3
Fieldhead Dr *GSLY* LS20 ....10 C3
Field Head La *HWTH* BD22 ....22 B4
  LUD/ILL HX2 ....66 C2
Fieldhead Rd *GSLY* LS20 ....10 B3
Fieldhead St *GTHN* BD7 ....38 B5
Fieldhouse Gv *PDSY/CALV* LS28 ....41 H2
Field Hurst *CLECK* BD19 ....72 C1
Fieldhurst Ct *BOW* BD4 ....56 A2
Field La *BRIG* HD6 ....78 A3
Fieldside *CUL/QBY* BD13 ....24 C3
Field Side *HFAX* HX1 ....4 A1
Fields Rd *LM/WK* BD12 ....55 F5
Field St *BFD* BD1 ....2 E5
Field Top Rd *BRIG* HD6 ....78 A3
Field Vw *HIPP* HX3 ....59 E3
Fieldway *CLAY* BD14 ....45 E3
Fifth Av *BFDE* BD3 ....40 B3
Fifth Av West *LVSG* WF15 ....73 E4
Filey St *BFD* BD1 ....3 F6
Filley Royd *CLECK* BD19 ....73 G2
Finchley St *WBOW* BD5 ....47 E4
Finch St *WBOW* BD5 ....47 E3
Findon Ter *IDLE* BD10 ....30 D5
Finkil St *BRIG* HD6 ....70 D3
Finkle St *LUD/ILL* HX2 ....66 A4
Finsbury Dr *ECHL* BD2 ....29 G3
Firbank Gn *ECHL* * BD2 ....40 C2
Firbeck *BGLY* BD16 ....25 G1
Firethorn Cl *GIR* * BD8 ....38 B4
First Av *BFDE* BD3 ....40 B3
  HIPP HX3 ....68 C4
  KGHY BD21 ....7 E5
  LVSG WF15 ....73 F3
  YEA LS19 ....21 H1
Fir St *HWTH* BD22 ....22 D3
  KGHY BD21 ....14 A2
First St *LM/WK* BD12 ....55 F4
Firth Av *BRIG* HD6 ....71 F5
Firth House La *BRIG* HD6 ....78 C4
Firth La *WIL/AL* BD15 ....25 H4
Firth Rd *HTON* BD9 ....38 B1
Firth St *BRIG* HD6 ....78 B2
  CUL/QBY BD13 ....44 A1
Fir Tree Gdns *IDLE* BD10 ....30 C3
Fitzgerald St *WBOW* BD5 ....47 E2
Fitzroy Rd *BFDE* BD3 ....3 K5
Fitzwilliam St *BOW* BD4 ....47 G2
Five Oaks *BAIL* BD17 ....18 B4
Fixby La *LUD/ILL* HX2 ....67 H3
Flasby St *WBOW* BD5 ....7 F3
Flat Nook *BGLY* * BD16 ....17 E3
Flawith Dr *ECHL* BD2 ....40 C2
Flaxen Ct *WBSY* BD6 ....55 E1

Flaxton Gn *ECHL* BD2 ....40 C2
Flaxton Pl *GTHN* BD7 ....46 C1
Fleece St *KGHY* BD21 ....7 F4
  WBSY BD6 ....54 A3
Fleet La *CUL/QBY* BD13 ....52 A2
Fletcher Crs *BRIG* HD6 ....77 H5
Fletcher La *SHPY* BD18 ....29 E4
Fletcher Rd *WBSY* BD6 ....54 C1
Fletton Ter *ECHL* BD2 ....40 A2
Flinton Gv *ECHL* BD2 ....40 C1
Flockton Av *BOW* BD4 ....47 H3
Flockton Cl *BOW* BD4 ....47 H3
Flockton Crs *BOW* BD4 ....47 H3
Flockton Dr *BOW* BD4 ....47 H3
Flockton Gv *BOW* BD4 ....47 H3
Flockton Rd *BOW* BD4 ....47 H3
Florence Av *WIL/AL* BD15 ....25 G3
Florence St *BFDE* BD3 ....48 B1
  HFAX HX1 ....4 D3
Florida Rd *WIL/AL* BD15 ....26 D5
Florist St *KGHY* BD21 ....7 H2
Flower Acre *ELL* HX5 ....76 C5
Flower Bank *ECHL* BD2 ....29 G5
  RPDN/SBR HX6 ....66 C5
Flower Cl *YEA* LS19 ....11 F4
Flower Ct *ECHL* * BD2 ....40 B1
Flower Cft *HWTH* BD22 ....13 C1
Flower Garth *IDLE* BD10 ....30 C3
Flower Hvn *HTON* BD9 ....27 G5
Flower Hl *HTON* BD9 ....28 A5
Flowerlands *HIPP* HX3 ....61 H4
Floyd St *WBOW* BD5 ....46 C4
Foldings Cl *CLECK* BD19 ....63 G5
Foldings Cl *CLECK* BD19 ....63 F5
Foldings Gv *CLECK* BD19 ....63 F5
Foldings Pde *CLECK* BD19 ....63 F5
Foldings Rd *CLECK* BD19 ....63 F5
Folkestone St *BFDE* BD3 ....3 K4
Folkton Holme *ECHL* BD2 ....40 C2
Folly Hall Av *WBSY* BD6 ....54 C2
The Folly Hall Gdns *WBSY* BD6 ....54 C2
Folly Hall Wk *WBSY* BD6 ....54 C2
Folly View Rd *HWTH* * BD22 ....23 E3
Fontmell Cl *BOW* BD4 ....48 D5
Football *YEA* LS19 ....11 H5
Forber Gv *BOW* BD4 ....48 D3
Ford *CUL/QBY* BD13 ....51 H2
Ford Hl *CUL/QBY* BD13 ....51 H2
Ford Houses *BAIL* * BD17 ....19 G3
Ford St *KGHY* BD21 ....7 H2
Fore La *RPDN/SBR* HX6 ....66 D5
Fore Lane Av *RPDN/SBR* HX6 ....66 C5
Foreside Bottom La
  CUL/QBY BD13 ....42 C3
Foreside La *CUL/QBY* BD13 ....42 A2
Forest Av *LUD/ILL* HX2 ....58 D2
Forest Crs *LUD/ILL* HX2 ....58 D1
Forest Gn *LUD/ILL* HX2 ....58 D2
Forster Ct *BFD* BD1 ....2 D4
Forster Sq *BFD* BD1 ....2 E5
Foster Av *CUL/QBY* BD13 ....44 C3
Foster Gdns *HWTH* BD22 ....6 C4
Foster Park Gv *CUL/QBY* BD13 ....34 D3
Foster Park Rd *CUL/QBY* BD13 ....34 D3
Foster Park Vw *CUL/QBY* BD13 ....34 D3
Foster Rd *KGHY* BD21 ....14 A1
Foster St *CUL/QBY* BD13 ....52 A1
Foston Cl *ECHL* BD2 ....40 D2
Foston La *ECHL* BD2 ....40 D2
Foulds' Ter *BGLY* BD16 ....16 D2
Foundry Hl *BGLY* BD16 ....16 C3
Foundry La *BOW* BD4 ....48 A2
Foundry St *BRIG* HD6 ....78 D2
  CLECK BD19 ....64 C5
  HFAX HX1 ....5 H2
  RPDN/SBR HX6 ....67 E5
Foundry St North *LUD/ILL* HX2 ....59 E1
Fountain Ct *LUD/ILL* * HX2 ....58 D2
Fountain St *CUL/QBY* BD13 ....44 A1
  CUL/QBY BD13 ....52 B1
  HFAX HX1 ....5 G4
  LM/WK BD12 ....54 D2
Fountain Ter *LM/WK* BD12 ....63 E3
Fountain Wy *SHPY* BD18 ....28 D2
Fourlands Ct *IDLE* BD10 ....30 B1
Fourlands Crs *IDLE* * BD10 ....30 B1
Fourlands Dr *IDLE* BD10 ....30 B1
Fourlands Gdns *IDLE* BD10 ....30 B1
Fourlands Gv *IDLE* BD10 ....30 B1
Fourlands Rd *IDLE* BD10 ....30 B1
Fourth Av *BFDE* BD3 ....40 B3
  KGHY BD21 ....6 D5
  LVSG WF15 ....73 E3
Fourth St *LM/WK* BD12 ....55 F4
Fowlers Garth *HWTH* BD22 ....13 C5
Fowler St *BOW* * BD4 ....48 A2
Fox Ct *GTL/HWG* HX4 ....76 A4

Foxcroft Cl *CUL/QBY* BD13............**51** H3
Foxcroft Dr *BRIG* HD6..................**77** H3
Foxhill *BAIL* BD17 ....**18** B3
Foxhill Av *CUL/QBY* BD13...........**52** A1
Foxhill Cl *CUL/QBY* BD13.............**52** A1
Foxhill Dr *CUL/QBY* BD13............**52** A1
Foxhill Gv *CUL/QBY* BD13............**52** A1
Foxhole La *PDSY/CALV* LS28.......**31** G3
Foxholes Crs *PDSY/CALV* LS28....**31** G3
Foxstone Ri *BAIL* BD17 ....**19** F3
Fox St *BGLY* BD16..........................**16** C3
  CLECK BD19 ....**73** E1
  WBOW * BD5 ....**46** D4
Fraisthorpe Md *ECHL* BD2 ....**40** C2
Frances St *BRIG* * HD6 ....**71** F5
  KGHY BD21.............................**6** D3
Francis Cl *HFAX* HX1 ....**4** B4
Francis St *BFDE* BD3 ....**47** H2
  HFAX HX1...............................**4** C5
Franklin St *HFAX* HX1 ....**4** B4
Frank Pl *GTHN* BD7 ....**46** C3
Frank St *GTHN* BD7 ....**46** C3
  HFAX HX1...............................**4** C5
Fraser Rd *PDSY/CALV* LS28........**31** G3
Fraser St *GIR* BD8..........................**38** D4
Frederick Cl *IDLE* BD10 ....**19** G5
Frederick St *BFD* BD1 ....**3** F6
  KGHY BD21.............................**7** G4
  PDSY/CALV LS28..................**41** H1
Fred's Pl *BOW* BD4........................**48** B4
Fred St *KGHY* * BD21 ....**7** E5
Freeman Rd *HIPP* HX3 ....**69** H3
Free School La *HFAX* HX1............**68** B3
Fremantle Gv *BOW* BD4 ....**48** D2
Frensham Dr *GTHN* BD7 ....**45** G4
Frensham Gv *GTHN* BD7 ....**45** G5
Frensham Wy *GTHN* BD7 ....**45** G4
Freshfield Gdns *WIL/AL* BD15 ...**37** E3
Friar Ct *IDLE* BD10 ....**30** B3
Friendly Av *RPDN/SBR* HX6 ....**66** D3
Friendly Fold Rd *HIPP* HX3 ....**59** F3
Friendly St *CUL/QBY* BD13.........**44** A1
  HIPP HX3...............................**59** F3
Frimley Dr *WBOW* BD5 ....**46** D5
Frith St *HWTH* BD22......................**23** F1
Frizinghall Rd *ECHL* BD2 ....**28** D4
  HTON BD9 ....**38** D1
Frizley Gdns *HTON* BD9 ....**28** C2
Frodingham Vls *ECHL* BD2...........**40** C2
Frogmoor Av *LM/WK* * BD12 ......**55** G5
Fruit St *KGHY* BD21 ....**7** H3
Fulford Wk *KGHY* BD21..............**40** C2
Fullerton St *BFDE* BD3 ....**3** G6
Fulmar Ms *GIR* * BD8...................**37** F5
Fulton St *BFD* BD1...........................**2** B5
Furnace Gv *LM/WK* BD12 ....**55** C5
Furnace Inn St *BOW* BD4 ....**48** C2
Furnace Rd *BIRK/DRI* BD11........**57** F4
Furnace Rd *LM/WK* BD12.............**55** C5
Furness Av *LUD/ILL* HX2 ....**58** C1
Furness Crs *LUD/ILL* HX2 ....**50** C5
Furness Dr *LUD/ILL* HX2 ....**58** C1
Furness Gdns *LUD/ILL* HX2 ....**58** D1
Furness Pl *LUD/ILL* HX2...............**58** D1
Fusden La *CLECK* BD19 ....**65** F4
Fyfe Crs *BAIL* BD17 ....**19** E4
Fyfe Gv *BAIL* BD17 ....**19** F4
Fyfe La *BAIL* BD17 ....**19** F4

G

The Gables *BAIL* BD17 ....**19** F3
  HWTH BD22............................**6** D4
Gainest *LUD/ILL* HX2 ....**68** A3
Gain La *BFDE* BD3 ....**40** D3
Gainsborough Cl *BFDE* BD3 ....**39** H2
Gaisby La *ECHL* BD2....................**28** D5
Gaisby Mt *SHPY* BD18 ....**29** E4
Gaisby Pl *SHPY* BD18 ....**29** E3
Gaisby Ri *SHPY* BD18 ....**29** E3
Galefield Gn *WBSY* BD6 ....**54** A4
Gale St *KGHY* BD21.......................**7** F3
Galloway Ct *PDSY/CALV* LS28...**41** F4
Galloway La *PDSY/CALV* LS28 ...**41** F4
Galloway Rd *IDLE* BD10 ....**30** C2
Galsworthy Av *HTON* BD9 ....**37** G1
Gannerthorpe Cl *LM/WK* BD12 ..**62** D3
Ganny Rd *BRIG* HD6.....................**78** C1
Gaol La *HFAX* HX1 ....**5** H5
Garden Cl *LM/WK* BD12...............**62** D1
Gardener's Sq *HIPP* HX3 ....**61** F5
Garden Fold *HIPP* HX3 ....**61** F5
Garden La *HTON* BD9...................**38** A1
  RPDN/SBR HX6 ....**74** A4

The Gardens *BGLY* BD16 ....**17** G3
Garden Rd *BRIG* HD6 ....**71** E4
Gardens St *HTON* BD9 ....**28** B5
  HFAX HX1...............................**68** D3
  PDSY/CALV LS28..................**41** H1
Garden St *HWTH* BD22 ....**23** G1
Garden St North *HWTH* HX3..........**5** J2
Garden Ter *HTON* BD9 ....**38** B1
Garden Vw *BGLY* BD16 ....**17** F3
Gardiner Rw *BOW* BD4 ....**48** A5
Garfield Av *GIR* BD8 ....**38** C2
Garfield St *HIPP* HX3 ....**59** F4
  WIL/AL BD15 ....**36** D3
Garforth Rd *KGHY* BD21 ....**7** H3
Garforth St *WIL/AL* BD15 ....**37** E3
Gargrave St *BRIG* HD6 ....**77** G4
Garibaldi St *BFDE* BD3................**40** D5
Garlick St *BRIG* HD6 ....**77** H5
Garnett St *BFDE* BD3 ....**3** G5
Garsdale Av *IDLE* BD10 ....**30** B2
Garsdale Crs *BAIL* BD17 ....**19** F2
Garth Barn Cl *HTON* BD9 ....**38** B1
Garth Land Wy *BOW* BD4 ....**48** B4
Garth St *HWTH* * BD22...................**6** D4
Garthwaite Mt *WIL/AL* BD15 .....**37** E2
Garton Dr *IDLE* BD10...................**30** C4
Garvey Vw *WBOW* BD5 ....**47** F3
Garwick Ter *GTL/HWG* HX4 ....**76** A4
Gas St *HWTH* * BD22....................**23** E2
Gas Works La *ELL* HX5 ....**76** C4
Gas Works Rd *KGHY* BD21 ....**8** A4
  RPDN/SBR HX6 ....**67** G4
Gatefield Mt *LM/WK* BD12 ....**54** C4
Gate Head La *GTL/HWG* HX4 .....**75** E5
Gateway *BGLY* BD16 ....**15** F5
Gate Way Dr *YEA* LS19 ....**11** F5
Gathorne St *BRIG* HD6 ....**71** G5
  GTHN BD7 ....**46** C3
Gaukroger La *HFAX* HX1 ....**5** J7
Gavin Cl *BFDE* BD3 ....**40** D5
Gawthorpe Dr *BGLY* BD16 ....**16** C1
Gawthorpe St *WIL/AL* BD15 ....**25** G3
Gayle Cl *LM/WK* BD12 ....**62** D3
Gaynor St *BD1* **2** A4
Gaythorne Rd *ECHL* BD2 ....**40** B2
  WBOW BD5 ....**47** F4
Gaythorne Ter *CLAY* BD14 ....**45** F3
Gaythorn Ter *HIPP* HX3...............**61** F4
Geelong Cl *ECHL* BD2 ....**39** G1
George Sq *HFAX* HX1 ....**5** G4
George's Sq *CUL/QBY* BD13 ....**24** C3
  KGHY BD21.............................**7** E5
George's St *LUD/ILL* HX2 ....**59** E2
George St *BAIL* * BD17 ....**18** D5
  BFD BD1..................................**3** F6
  BRIG HD6 ....**78** B1
  CLECK BD19 ....**64** C5
  CUL/QBY * BD13 ....**34** D3
  CUL/QBY BD13 ....**44** A1
  GTL/HWG HX4 ....**76** A4
  HFAX HX1...............................**5** G4
  HIPP HX3...............................**70** C1
  RPDN/SBR HX6 ....**67** E5
  SHPY BD18.............................**28** A1
  YEA LS19...............................**21** G2
Geraldton Av *ECHL* BD2 ....**39** F1
Gerrard St *HFAX* HX1 ....**4** A4
The Ghyll *BGLY* BD16 ....**26** D1
Ghyll Dr *HWTH* BD22 ....**22** D3
Ghyll Mt *YEA* LS19 ....**11** E5
Ghyll Royd *GSLY* LS20 ....**10** D4
Ghyllroyd Av *BIRK/DRI* BD11 ....**57** G5
Ghyllroyd Dr *BIRK/DRI* BD11.....**57** G5
Ghyll Wood Dr *BGLY* BD16 ....**26** D1
Gibbet St *HFAX* HX1 ....**4** A4
Gibb La *LUD/ILL* HX2 ....**58** A2
Gibraltar Av *HFAX* HX1 ....**67** H1
Gibraltar Rd *HFAX* HX1 ....**67** H1
  PDSY/CALV LS28..................**41** G5
Gibson St *BFDE* BD3.......................**3** K6
Giles Hill La *HIPP* HX3 ....**52** D3
Giles St *WBOW* BD5 ....**47** E2
  WBSY BD6 ....**54** B1
Gill Beck Cl *BAIL* BD17 ....**19** F2
Gillingham Gn *BOW* BD4 ....**48** D4
Gill La *BAIL* BD17..........................**20** D2
  HWTH BD22............................**12** B2
Gillroyd Ri *GTHN* BD7..................**38** C5
Gillstone Dr *HWTH* BD22 ....**23** E3
Gilmour St *HIPP* HX3....................**59** F4
Gilpin St *BFDE* BD3 ....**3** K4
Gilstead Cl *BGLY* BD16 ....**17** F3
Gilstead Dr *BGLY* BD16 ....**17** F3
Gilstead La *BGLY* BD16 ....**17** F3
Glynda Cl *GIR* BD8.......................**38** C4
Gipsy St *BFDE* BD3 ....**40** D3
Girlington Rd *GIR* BD8 ....**38** A3
Gisburn St *KGHY* BD21 ....**7** E3

The Glade *PDSY/CALV* LS28........**41** F2
Gladstone Crs *YEA* LS19 ....**21** G1
Gladstone Rd *HFAX* * HX1..............**4** D3
Gladstone St *BFDE* BD3 ....**40** B5
  BGLY BD16 ....**16** C4
  CLECK BD19 ....**73** C1
  CUL/QBY BD13 ....**52** C1
  KGHY BD21.............................**7** E5
  PDSY/CALV LS28..................**41** H1
  WIL/AL BD15 ....**37** G3
Gladstone Vw *HIPP* HX3 ....**69** F5
Glaisdale Cl *WIL/AL* BD15 ....**36** D1
Glaisdale Gv *HIPP* HX3................**70** C1
Glazier Rd *CUL/QBY* BD13..........**43** H5
Gleanings Av *LUD/ILL* HX2 ....**58** B3
  LUD/ILL HX2 ....**67** F1
Gleanings Dr *LUD/ILL* HX2 ....**67** G1
Gledcliffe *HFAX* HX1.......................**5** H2
Gleddings Cl *HIPP* HX3 ....**68** B5
Gledhill Rd *BFDE* BD3 ....**3** K6
Gledhow Dr *HWTH* BD22............**22** D5
Glenaire *SHPY* BD18 ....**19** F5
Glenaire Dr *BAIL* BD17 ....**18** B5
Glenbrook Dr *GTHN* BD7 ....**37** H5
Glen Dl *BGLY* BD16 ....**26** C2
Glendale Cl *WBSY* BD6 ....**54** B3
Glendale Dr *WBSY* BD6 ....**54** B3
Glendare Av *GTHN* BD7 ....**46** A1
Glendare Rd *GTHN* BD7 ....**46** A1
Glendare Ter *GTHN* BD7 ....**46** A1
Glen Dene *BGLY* BD16 ....**26** C2
Gleneagles Cl *BOW* BD4 ....**56** A2
Glenfield *SHPY* BD18 ....**19** F5
Glenfield Av *WBSY* * BD6 ....**55** E2
Glen Garth *KGHY* BD21 ....**14** C1
Glenholme *SHPY* BD18 ....**19** F5
Glenholme Heath *HFAX* HX1 ......**67** H1
Glenholme Rd *GIR* BD8 ....**38** C3
  PDSY/CALV LS28..................**41** H2
Glenholm Rd *BAIL* BD17 ....**18** D3
Glenhurst *BOW* BD4 ....**56** C1
Glenhurst Av *KGHY* BD21 ....**14** C1
Glenhurst Dr *KGHY* BD21 ....**14** C1
Glenhurst Gv *KGHY* BD21...........**14** C1
Glenhurst Rd *SHPY* BD18 ....**27** H1
Glen Lee La *KGHY* BD21 ....**14** C2
Glenlee Rd *GTHN* BD7 ....**46** A1
Glenlyon Av *KGHY* BD21 ....**6** D2
Glenlyon Dr *KGHY* BD21 ....**6** D2
Glenmore Cl *ECHL* BD2 ....**40** B3
Glen Mt *BGLY* BD16 ....**26** C2
  HIPP HX3...............................**58** D3
Glenmount Cl *HIPP* HX3 ....**58** D3
Glen Ri *BAIL* BD17 ....**18** A4
Glen Rd *BGLY* BD16 ....**17** F3
Glenrose Dr *GTHN* BD7 ....**45** H1
Glenroyal Buildings *BAIL* * BD17 ..**28** C1
Glenroyd Av *WBSY* BD6 ....**55** E3
Glenroyd Rd *SHPY* BD18 ....**19** F5
Glenroyd Cl *PDSY/CALV* LS28 ...**41** H5
Glenside Av *SHPY* BD18 ....**19** F5
Glenside Rd *SHPY* BD18 ....**19** F5
Glenstone Gv *GIR* BD8 ....**38** A5
Glen Ter *HFAX* HX1 ....**68** C3
Glenton Sq *HTON* BD9 ....**38** B2
Glen Vw *BGLY* BD16 ....**15** G3
  HFAX HX1...............................**5** F7
Glenview Av *HTON* BD9 ....**37** H1
Glenview Cl *SHPY* BD18 ....**27** F2
Glenview Dr *BGLY* BD16 ....**27** F2
Glenview Gv *SHPY* BD18 ....**27** F2
Glen View Rd *BGLY* BD16 ....**17** F1
Glenview Rd *SHPY* BD18 ....**27** G2
Glenview Ter *SHPY* BD18 ....**28** A1
Glenwood Av *BAIL* BD17 ....**17** H5
Globe Fold *GIR* BD8 ....**38** D4
Gloucester Av *BFDE* BD3 ....**40** C3
Gloucester Rd *BGLY* BD16 ....**17** E4
Glover Ct *WBOW* BD5 ....**47** F3
Glydegate *WBOW* BD5 ....**2** C1
Glyndon Ct *BRIG* HD6 ....**78** C3
Glynn Ter *GIR* BD8 ....**38** C4
Gobind Marg *BFDE* BD3 ....**3** G5
Godfrey Rd *HIPP* HX3 ....**75** H1
Godfrey St *GIR* BD8 ....**37** G5
Godley Branch Rd *HIPP* HX3 ....**60** B5
Godley Gdns *HIPP* HX3 ....**60** C4
Godley La *HIPP* HX3.....................**60** B5
Godley Rd *HIPP* HX3......................**5** H3
Godwin St *BFD* BD1........................**2** D1
Goff Well La *KGHY* BD21 ....**14** B4
Goit Stock La *BGLY* BD16 ....**25** G1
Goit Stock Ter *BGLY* BD16 ....**25** G1
Goldcrest Av *GIR* BD8 ....**37** E5
Golden View Dr *KGHY* BD21 ....**8** A5
Goldfields Av *GTL/HWG* HX4 .....**75** G3
Goldfields Cl *GTL/HWG* HX4 ......**75** G3
Goldfields Vw *GTL/HWG* HX4 ....**75** G3

Goldfields Wy *GTL/HWG* HX4 ....**75** G3
Golf Av *LUD/ILL* HX2 ....**67** F1
Golf Crs *LUD/ILL* HX2 ....**67** F1
Gondal Ct *WBOW* BD5 ....**46** D4
Gooder La *BRIG* HD6 ....**78** B2
Gooder St *BRIG* HD6 ....**78** B1
Goose Cote La *HWTH* BD22 ....**13** F4
Goose Cote Wy *HWTH* BD22 ......**13** F3
Goosedale Ct *BOW* BD4 ....**57** F1
Goosegate *LUD/ILL* * HX2 ....**51** E4
Goose West La *RPDN/SBR* HX6 ..**74** A1
Gordon St *CLAY* * BD14 ....**45** E3
  ELL HX5 ....**76** C5
  HIPP HX3...............................**59** G3
  HWTH * BD22........................**23** F1
  KGHY BD21.............................**7** E4
  RPDN/SBR HX6 ....**66** D5
  WBOW BD5 ....**47** G2
Gordon Ter *IDLE* BD10 ....**20** A5
Gorse Av *BAIL* BD17 ....**17** H4
Gothic St *CUL/QBY* BD13............**52** B1
Gott's Ter *AIRE* BD20 ....**7** H5
Gott St *HWTH* BD22 ....**23** G1
Goulbourne St *KGHY* BD21 ....**7** E5
Gower St *WBOW* BD5 ....**47** F3
Gracechurch St *GIR* BD8 ....**2** A3
Grace St *KGHY* BD21......................**7** F3
Gracey La *WBSY* BD6 ....**54** A1
Grafton Cl *BAIL* BD17 ....**19** E2
Grafton Pl *HIPP* HX3 ....**59** F2
Grafton Rd *KGHY* BD21 ....**13** H1
Grafton St *KGHY* BD21 ....**14** A1
  WBOW BD5 ....**47** G2
Graham St *HTON* BD9 ....**38** B2
Grain St *WBOW* BD5.....................**47** G2
Grammar School St *BFD* BD1 ....**2** C3
Granary Ct *ECHL* BD2 ....**30** B4
Granby Dr *AIRE* BD20 ....**8** A2
Granby La *AIRE* BD20 ....**8** A2
Granby St *BOW* * BD4 ....**47** G2
  CUL/QBY BD13 ....**52** B1
Grandage Ter *GIR* BD8 ....**38** C4
Grandsmere Pl *HIPP* HX3 ....**68** C4
Grange Av *BFDE* BD3 ....**41** E4
  BOW BD4.............................**57** F2
  LUD/ILL HX2 ....**51** E5
  SHPY BD18.............................**27** H1
  WIL/AL BD15 ....**37** H4
  YEA LS19...............................**11** H5
Grange Bank *HIPP* HX3 ....**53** F4
Grange Ct *BGLY* BD16 ....**26** D3
  HIPP HX3...............................**69** H5
Grange Crs *AIRE* BD20 ....**7** H2
  YEA LS19...............................**11** H5
Grange Dr *GIR* BD8 ....**38** F4
Grange Gv *AIRE* BD20 ....**7** H2
  BFDE BD3.............................**41** E4
Grange Hts *HIPP* HX3...................**69** H5
Grange La *BRIG* HD6 ....**79** F1
  HWTH BD22..........................**12** A3
Grange Mt *YEA* LS19 ....**11** H5
Grange Pk *BAIL* BD17 ....**19** F3
  HIPP HX3...............................**69** C5
Grange Park Dr *BGLY* BD16 ....**26** D1
Grange Park Rd *BGLY* BD16 ....**26** D1
Grange Rd *AIRE* BD20 ....**7** H2
  BGLY BD16 ....**17** E2
  CLECK BD19 ....**64** B5
  WIL/AL BD15 ....**37** H4
  YEA LS19...............................**11** H5
Grange St *HIPP* HX3 ....**59** F4
  KGHY BD21.............................**7** F3
Grange Ter *SHPY* BD18................**28** C3
  WIL/AL BD15 ....**37** H4
Grange Vw *BFDE* * BD3................**41** E4
Grangeway *GIR* BD8 ....**37** F4
Granny Hall Gv *BRIG* HD6 ....**71** E4
Granny Hall La *BRIG* HD6 ....**71** E4
Granny Hall Pk *BRIG* HD6 ....**71** E3
Granny Hill Ter *HFAX* HX1 ....**68** C1
Grantham Pl *GTHN* BD7 ....**46** D2
  HIPP HX3...............................**59** G3
Grantham Rd *GTHN* BD7 ....**46** D2
Granton St *BFDE* BD3 ....**40** B5
Grant St *BFDE* BD3..........................**3** H4
  HWTH BD22............................**6** D4
  KGHY BD21...........................**32** D2
Granville Pl *WIL/AL* BD15 ....**37** E3
Granville Rd *HTON* BD9 ....**38** B2
Granville St *CLAY* BD14 ....**45** F3
  ELL * HX5 ....**76** C5
  KGHY * BD21...........................**7** E4
  PDSY/CALV LS28..................**41** H1
Granville Ter *BGLY* BD16 ....**16** D3
  SHPY BD18.............................**28** C4
  YEA LS19...............................**11** H4

Grape St *HFAX* HX1 ....4 E4
 KGHY BD21 ....7 H3
 WIL/AL BD15 ....37 F3
Grasleigh Av *WIL/AL* BD15 ....36 D2
Grasleigh Wy *WIL/AL* BD15 ....36 D1
Grasmere Dr *ELL* HX5 ....77 E4
Grasmere Rd *ECHL* BD2 ....39 H1
 LM/WK BD12 ....63 F4
Gratrix La *RPDN/SBR* HX6 ....67 F4
Grattan Rd *BFD* BD1 ....2 B5
Gray Av *SHPY* BD18 ....29 E4
Grayshon Dr *WBSY* BD6 ....54 D1
Gray St *LVSG* WF15 ....73 H4
Grayswood Crs *BOW* BD4 ....48 C4
Grayswood Dr *BOW* BD4 ....48 C3
Great Albion St *HFAX* HX1 ....5 G3
Great Cross St *BFD* BD1 ....2 E6
Great Edge Rd *LUD/ILL* HX2 ....66 C2
Great Horton Rd *GTHN* BD7 ....45 H5
Great Northern Rd *KGHY* BD21 .....7 F5
Great Russell Ct *GTHN* BD7 ....38 D5
Great Russell St *GTHN* BD7 ....38 C5
Greave House Dr *LUD/ILL* HX2 ...66 A1
Greave House Pk *LUD/ILL* HX2 ...66 A1
Greaves St *WBOW* BD5 ....47 E4
The Green *BGLY* BD16 ....9 F4
 BGLY BD16 ....11 H5
 BGLY * BD16 ....17 H5
 BOW BD4 ....57 E3
 GSLY LS20 ....10 D3
Greenacre Av *LM/WK* BD12 ....63 E3
Green Acre Cl *BAIL* BD17 ....19 E3
Greenacre Cl *LM/WK* BD12 ....63 E3
Greenacre Dr *LM/WK* BD12 ....63 E3
Greenacre Pk *YEA* LS19 ....21 G1
Greenacre Park Av *YEA* LS19 ......21 G1
Greenacre Park Ms *YEA* LS19 .....21 H1
Greenacre Park Ri *YEA* LS19 ....21 G1
Greenacres *HIPP* HX3 ....53 G4
Greenacres Av *HIPP* HX3 ....53 G4
Greenacres Dr *HIPP* HX3 ....53 G4
 KGHY BD21 ....6 C2
Greenacre Gv *HIPP* HX3 ....53 G4
Greenacre Wy *LM/WK* BD12 ....63 E3
Greenbank Rd *WIL/AL* BD15 ....37 F4
Greencliffe Av *BAIL* BD17 ....18 C3
Green Cl *GIR* BD8 ....37 H4
Green Ct *CLECK* BD19 ....63 C5
 GTHN BD7 ....46 A2
Greencroft Av *HWTH* BD22 ....6 D5
Greencroft Cl *IDLE* BD10 ....29 H2
Green End *BRIG* HD6 ....78 B2
 CLAY BD14 ....45 E3
Green End Rd *AIRE* BD20 ....9 F2
 WBSY BD6 ....54 C2
Greenfell Cl *HWTH* BD22 ....6 D5
Greenfield Av *GSLY* LS20 ....10 A4
 HIPP HX3 ....71 F1
 SHPY BD18 ....28 D3
Greenfield Cl *HIPP* HX3 ....60 D2
Greenfield Ct *HWTH* BD22 ....6 D4
Greenfield Crs *CUL/QBY* BD13 ....24 C3
Greenfield Rd *CLECK* BD19 ....63 C5
Greenfield La *BOW* BD4 ....56 A4
 GTHN BD7 ....46 A3
 IDLE BD10 ....20 A5
Greenfield Pl *GIR* * BD8 ....38 D3
 HIPP HX3 ....71 F1
Greenfield Ter *HWTH* BD22 ....22 D1
Greengate Rd *KGHY* BD21 ....7 F5
Greengates Av *LM/WK* BD12 ......62 D4
Green Hall Pk *HIPP* HX3 ....53 C5
Green Head Av *AIRE* BD20 ....6 D1
Green Head Dr *AIRE* BD20 ....6 D1
Green Head La *AIRE* BD20 ....6 D1
Greenhead La *BRIG* HD6 ....77 H5
Green Head Rd *AIRE* BD20 ....7 E1
Green Hl *LUD/ILL* HX2 ....67 E2
Greenhill Dr *BGLY* BD16 ....9 F4
Greenhill La *BFDE* BD3 ....40 B5
 BGLY BD16 ....9 C5
Greenhills *YEA* LS19 ....21 H3
Greenhill St *BFDE* BD3 ....48 B1
Greenholme Ct *BOW* BD4 ....49 E5
Greenland *CUL/QBY* BD13 ....44 C5
Greenland Av *CUL/QBY* BD13 .....52 B2
Greenland Vls *CUL/QBY* BD13 ....52 B2
Green La *BAIL* BD17 ....18 B2
 BAIL BD17 ....18 C5
 BRIG HD6 ....70 D3
 BRIG HD6 ....79 C1
 CLECK BD19 ....64 C3
 CUL/QBY BD13 ....43 G4
 CUL/QBY BD13 ....44 B2
 CUL/QBY BD13 ....52 B3
 ECHL BD2 ....40 C1
 GIR BD8 ....38 D4
 GTHN * BD7 ....46 B2

GTL/HWG HX4 ....75 H5
 HIPP HX3 ....52 B5
 HIPP HX3 ....53 H5
 HIPP HX3 ....69 F2
 HWTH BD22 ....12 A2
 HWTH BD22 ....13 E4
 IDLE BD10 ....29 H1
 IDLE BD10 ....30 B1
 LM/WK BD12 ....62 D3
 LM/WK BD12 ....63 G1
 LUD/ILL HX2 ....50 D2
 LUD/ILL HX2 ....67 H3
 LVSG WF15 ....73 G5
 YEA LS19 ....21 H1
Greenlea Av *YEA* LS19 ....11 E5
Greenlea Cl *YEA* LS19 ....21 E1
Greenlea Mt *YEA* LS19 ....11 E5
Greenlea Rd *YEA* LS19 ....11 E5
Green Meadow *WIL/AL* BD15 ......26 A5
Green Mt *BOW* * BD4 ....48 C4
Green Mount Rd *CUL/QBY* BD13 .44 B1
Green Park Av *HIPP* HX3 ....75 H1
Green Park Dr *HIPP* HX3 ....75 H1
Green Park Rd *HIPP* HX3 ....75 H1
Green Park St *HIPP* HX3 ....68 D5
Green Pl *ECHL* * BD2 ....40 A2
Green Rd *BAIL* BD17 ....18 C4
Green Royd *GTL/HWG* HX4 ....75 H5
 HIPP HX3 ....68 C5
Greenroyd Av *CLECK* BD19 ....64 C3
Greenroyd Cl *HIPP* HX3 ....75 C1
Greenroyd Crs *HFAX* * HX1 ....59 E4
Greenroyd La *LUD/ILL* HX2 ....58 D4
Greenside *CLECK* BD19 ....73 H1
 LM/WK BD12 ....63 H1
Greenside La *CUL/QBY* BD13 .....24 C3
 GIR BD8 ....38 A5
Green's Sq *LUD/ILL* HX2 ....58 D5
Green St *BFD* BD1 ....3 F5
 HWTH BD22 ....22 D3
 HWTH BD22 ....32 D2
Green Ter *ECHL* BD2 ....40 A2
Green Terrace Sq *HFAX* HX1 ....68 B3
Greenthwaite Cl *KGHY* BD21 ....6 D2
Greenton Av *CLECK* BD19 ....63 F4
Greenton Crs *CUL/QBY* BD13 .....52 A2
Green Top St *GIR* BD8 ....37 H5
Greenups Ter *RPDN/SBR* HX6 ....67 E4
Greenville Dr *LM/WK* BD12 ....55 F3
The Greenway *BFDE* BD3 ....3 J2
Greenway *GSLY* LS20 ....10 B4
Green Vw *LUD/ILL* HX2 ....50 D2
Greenway Dr *WIL/AL* BD15 ....37 E5
Greenway Rd *WBOW* BD5 ....47 F5
Greenwell Rw *CLAY* BD14 ....45 E3
Greenwood Av *ECHL* BD2 ....29 H4
Greenwood Dr *ECHL* BD2 ....29 H5
Greenwood Mt *ECHL* BD2 ....29 H5
Greenwood Rd *BAIL* BD17 ....18 C5
Gregory Ct *CLAY* BD14 ....45 E3
Gregory Crs *GTHN* BD7 ....45 H5
Grenfell Dr *BFDE* BD3 ....40 C4
Grenfell Ct *BFDE* BD3 ....40 C4
Grenfell Ter *BFDE* BD3 ....40 C4
Gresham Av *ECHL* BD2 ....29 C5
Gresley Rd *KGHY* BD21 ....7 F4
Greycourt Cl *ECHL* BD2 ....29 H3
 HFAX HX1 ....4 C6
Greyfriar Wk *GTHN* BD7 ....45 H4
Grey Scar Rd *HWTH* BD22 ....12 B4
Greystone Ct *BRIG* HD6 ....78 B4
Greystone Crs *IDLE* BD10 ....30 B3
Greystones Dr *HWTH* BD22 ....13 G3
Greystones Mt *HWTH* BD22 ....13 G4
Greystones Ri *HWTH* BD22 ....13 G3
Griffe Dr *LM/WK* BD12 ....62 D4
Griffe Gdns *HWTH* BD22 ....12 C4
Griffe Head Crs *LM/WK* * BD12 ..62 D3
Griffe Head Rd *LM/WK* BD12 ......62 D3
Griffe Rd *LM/WK* BD12 ....62 D3
The Grove *BAIL* BD17 ....18 D2
 BGLY BD16 ....11 C5
 HIPP HX3 ....61 F5
 IDLE BD10 ....30 A2
 IDLE BD10 ....30 C2
 SHPY BD18 ....27 H2
 YEA LS19 ....11 G5
 YEA LS19 ....21 F2
Grosvenor Av *SHPY* BD18 ....28 A1
Grosvenor Rd *GIR* BD8 ....2 A1
 SHPY BD18 ....28 A2
Grosvenor St *ELL* HX5 ....76 C5
Grosvenor Ter *GIR* BD8 ....2 A1
 HFAX * HX1 ....4 D4
Grouse Moor La *CUL/QBY* BD13 .43 H5
Grouse St *KGHY* * BD21 ....7 F3
Grove Av *HIPP* HX3 ....59 E3

SHPY BD18 ....28 C4
Grove Cl *CLECK* BD19 ....65 G4
 ECHL BD2 ....29 H5
Grove Ct *HIPP* HX3 ....59 F3
Grove Crs *LUD/ILL* HX2 ....66 A1
Grove Cft *HIPP* HX3 ....59 E3
Grove Dr *HIPP* HX3 ....59 E2
Grove Edge *HIPP* HX3 ....59 F3
Grove Gdns *HIPP* HX3 ....59 F3
Grove House Crs *ECHL* BD2 ....39 H1
Grove House Dr *ECHL* BD2 ....39 H1
Grove House Rd *ECHL* BD2 ....39 H1
Grovelands *ECHL* BD2 ....39 H1
Grove La *CLECK* BD19 ....65 G4
Grove Pk *HIPP* HX3 ....59 E2
Grove Rd *ELL* HX5 ....76 D4
 SHPY BD18 ....28 C4
Grove Royd *HIPP* HX3 ....59 F3
Grove Sq *CLECK* * BD19 ....65 G4
Grove St *BRIG* HD6 ....78 C1
 RPDN/SBR HX6 ....67 G4
Grove St South *HFAX* * HX1 ....4 B4
Grove Ter *GTHN* * BD7 ....2 B6
Groveville *HIPP* HX3 ....61 F4
Groveway *ECHL* BD2 ....29 H5
Guard House Av *HWTH* BD22 ....6 D4
Guard House Dr *HWTH* BD22 ....6 D4
Guard House Gv *HWTH* BD22 ....6 D4
Guard House Rd *HWTH* BD22 ....6 D4
Guild Wy *LUD/ILL* HX2 ....67 E2
Guiseley Dr *ILK* LS29 ....10 A1
Gurbax St *BFDE* BD3 ....40 D5
Gurney Cl *WBOW* BD5 ....47 E4
Guy St *BOW* BD4 ....2 E7
Gwynne Av *BFDE* BD3 ....40 D3

H

Hadassah St *HIPP* HX3 ....69 E4
Haddon Av *HIPP* HX3 ....68 D5
Haddon Cl *CLECK* BD19 ....65 G5
Hag La *HIPP* HX3 ....59 H2
Haigh Beck Vw *IDLE* BD10 ....30 B2
Haigh Cnr *IDLE* BD10 ....30 C2
Haigh Fold *ECHL* BD2 ....40 B1
Haigh Hall *IDLE* BD10 ....30 C2
Haigh La *HIPP* HX3 ....59 H2
Haigh St *BOW* BD4 ....48 A4
 BRIG HD6 ....71 F5
 GTL/HWG HX4 ....75 F4
 HFAX HX1 ....4 B2
Haincliffe Rd *KGHY* BD21 ....14 A2
Hainsworth Moor Crs
 CUL/QBY BD13 ....52 A2
Hainsworth Moor Dr
 CUL/QBY BD13 ....52 A2
Hainsworth Moor Garth
 CUL/QBY BD13 ....52 A2
Hainsworth Moor Gv
 CUL/QBY BD13 ....52 A2
Hainsworth Moor Vw
 CUL/QBY BD13 ....52 A2
Hainworth Crag Rd
 KGHY BD21 ....13 H4
Hainworth La *KGHY* BD21 ....14 A3
Hainworth Rd *KGHY* BD21 ....14 A3
Hainworth Wood Rd
 KGHY BD21 ....14 A2
Hainworth Wood Rd North
 KGHY BD21 ....14 B1
Halcyon Wy *WBOW* BD5 ....46 D4
Halesworth Crs *BOW* BD4 ....48 D4
Haley Ct *HIPP* HX3 ....5 G1
Haley Hl *HFAX* HX1 ....5 G1
 HIPP HX3 ....59 H4
Half Acre Rd *CUL/QBY* BD13 ......35 C5
Half House La *BRIG* HD6 ....70 C3
Half St *KGHY* BD21 ....7 E3
Halifax Old Rd *HIPP* HX3 ....46 A1
Halifax Rd *BRIG* HD6 ....78 B1
 CLECK BD19 ....72 B1
 CUL/QBY BD13 ....34 C5
 CUL/QBY BD13 ....51 H4
 ELL HX5 ....76 B4
 HIPP HX3 ....61 E1
 HWTH BD22 ....23 G2
 LUD/ILL HX2 ....42 C3
 LVSG WF15 ....73 E5
 WBSY BD6 ....54 A3
Hallas La *CUL/QBY* BD13 ....25 C5
Hall Av *IDLE* BD10 ....30 C4
Hallbank Cl *WBOW* BD5 ....55 E1
Hall Bank Dr *BGLY* BD16 ....16 C2
Hallbank Dr *WBOW* BD5 ....55 E1
Hallcliffe *BAIL* BD17 ....19 E2

Hall Cl *HIPP* HX3 ....60 D2
Hallfield Dr *BAIL* BD17 ....18 D3
Hallfield Pl *BFD* BD1 ....2 C2
Hallfield Rd *GIR* BD8 ....2 B3
Hallfield St *BFD* BD1 ....2 C2
Hall Ings *BFD* BD1 ....2 D6
 HIPP HX3 ....69 H5
Hall La *BOW* BD4 ....47 G2
 HIPP HX3 ....60 C1
 SHPY BD18 ....28 D1
Hallowes Gv *CUL/QBY* BD13 ......24 C4
Hallowes Park Rd
 CUL/QBY BD13 ....24 C4
The Hallows *KGHY* BD21 ....6 D3
Hallows Rd *KGHY* BD21 ....7 H2
Hall Rd *IDLE* BD10 ....30 C4
Hall Royd *SHPY* BD18 ....28 C2
Halls La *LUD/ILL* HX2 ....24 D4
Hall Stone Ct *HIPP* * HX3 ....53 F5
Hall St *BRIG* HD6 ....78 C1
 HFAX HX1 ....5 C1
 HWTH BD22 ....13 E3
 HWTH BD22 ....22 D3
 WBSY BD6 ....54 D1
Hall St North *HIPP* HX3 ....59 G3
Hall Ter *AIRE* * BD20 ....8 A2
Hallwood Gn *IDLE* BD10 ....30 D4
Halstead Pl *GTHN* BD7 ....46 B4
Halton Pl *GTHN* BD7 ....46 C4
Hambledon Av *BOW* BD4 ....56 A1
Hambleton Bank *LUD/ILL* HX2 ....22 B4
Hambleton Crs *LUD/ILL* HX2 ......50 A5
Hambleton Dr *LUD/ILL* HX2 ....50 A5
Hammerstones Rd *ELL* HX5 ....76 A5
Hammerton St *BFDE* BD3 ....3 C6
Hammond Pl *HTON* BD9 ....38 B1
Hammond St *HFAX* HX1 ....4 B5
Hamm Strasse *BFD* BD1 ....2 D3
Hampden Pl *HFAX* HX1 ....4 E4
 WBOW BD5 ....47 E3
Hampden St *WBOW* BD5 ....47 E3
Hampton Pl *IDLE* BD10 ....30 A1
Hampton St *HFAX* HX1 ....4 A7
Hamworth Dr *HWTH* BD22 ....13 E4
Handel St *GTHN* BD7 ....38 D5
Hanging Gate La *HWTH* BD22 .....22 B4
Hanging Wood Wy *CLECK* BD19 .64 B3
Hannah Ct *LM/WK* BD12 ....62 D2
Hanover Cl *GIR* BD8 ....38 B3
Hanover Gdns *WBOW* * BD5 ....47 E2
Hanover Sq *BFD* BD1 ....2 B2
Hanover St *HFAX* HX1 ....5 F5
 KGHY BD21 ....7 H4
 RPDN/SBR HX6 ....67 G3
Hanson Ct *LM/WK* BD12 ....62 C3
Hanson Fold *LM/WK* BD12 ....62 D2
Hanson La *HFAX* HX1 ....4 C3
Hanson Mt *LM/WK* BD12 ....62 D3
Hanson Rd *BRIG* HD6 ....77 H3
Hanworth Rd *LM/WK* BD12 ....54 C4
Harbeck Dr *BGLY* BD16 ....25 G1
Harbour Crs *WBSY* BD6 ....54 B2
Harbour Pk *WBSY* BD6 ....54 A3
Harbour Rd *WBSY* BD6 ....54 B3
Harclo Rd *KGHY* BD21 ....7 H3
Harcourt Av *CUL/QBY* BD13 ....36 A5
Harcourt St *BOW* BD4 ....48 A4
Hardaker La *BAIL* BD17 ....18 B4
Hardaker St *GIR* * BD8 ....2 A3
Harden Brow La *BGLY* BD16 ....15 F5
Harden Gv *IDLE* BD10 ....40 D1
 KGHY BD21 ....14 D1
Harden La *BGLY* BD16 ....25 G1
Harden Rd *BGLY* BD16 ....15 H5
 KGHY BD21 ....15 E2
Hardgate La *HWTH* BD22 ....23 G3
Hard Ings Rd *KGHY* BD21 ....7 F2
Hardknot Cl *GTHN* BD7 ....45 H4
Hard Nese La *HWTH* BD22 ....32 A3
Hardwick St *KGHY* BD21 ....6 D5
Hardy Av *WBSY* BD6 ....54 D2
Hardy Pl *BRIG* HD6 ....70 D3
Hardy St *BOW* BD4 ....2 E7
 BRIG HD6 ....71 G5
Harehill Cl *IDLE* BD10 ....20 A5
Harehill Rd *IDLE* BD10 ....20 A5
Hare Park Av *LVSG* WF15 ....73 F4
Harepark Dr *LVSG* WF15 ....73 F4
Hare Park La *LVSG* WF15 ....73 F4
Hare St *HFAX* HX1 ....4 B4
Harewood Av *LUD/ILL* HX2 ....58 C5
Harewood Crs *HWTH* BD22 ....13 F3
Harewood Pl *LUD/ILL* HX2 ....67 H2
Harewood Ri *HWTH* BD22 ....13 G3
Harewood Rd *HWTH* BD22 ....13 F4
Harewood St *BFDE* BD3 ....3 J4
Harker Rd *WBSY* BD6 ....54 D3

Harland Cl ECHL BD2.....39 F2
Harley St BRIG HD6.....78 B2
Harlow Rd GTHN BD7.....46 B2
Harmon Cl BOW BD4.....56 B2
Harold St BGLY BD16.....16 B2
Harper Av IDLE BD10.....20 A5
Harper Crs IDLE BD10.....20 B5
Harper Ga BOW BD4.....49 E3
Harper Gv IDLE BD10.....20 A5
Harper La YEA LS19.....11 G5
Harper Royd La RPDN/SBR HX6.....74 A1
Harrier Cl GIR BD8.....37 E5
Harriet St BRIG HD6.....71 F4
  GIR BD8.....38 C4
Harris Ct GTHN BD7.....46 B4
Harrison Rd HFAX HX1.....5 G5
Harrison St BGLY BD16.....16 D4
Harris St BFD BD1.....3 G5
  BGLY BD16.....16 D4
Harrogate Av BFDE BD3.....39 H2
Harrogate Pl BFDE BD3.....39 H2
Harrogate Rd ECHL BD2.....40 B1
  IDLE BD10.....30 C3
  YEA LS19.....21 G2
Harrogate St BFDE BD3.....39 H2
Harrogate Ter BFDE BD3.....39 H2
Harrop La WIL/AL BD15.....35 G1
Harrow St HFAX HX1.....4 B4
Harry La CLAY BD14.....45 E3
  HWTH BD22.....32 D1
Harry St BOW BD4.....48 B4
Hartington St KGHY BD21.....7 F3
Hartington Ter GTHN BD7.....46 B2
Hartland Rd BOW BD4.....48 D3
Hartley's Sq AIRE BD20.....9 E2
Hartley St BOW BD4.....47 H2
  HFAX HX1.....4 C2
Hartlington Cft BAIL * BD17.....19 F3
Hartman Pl HTON * BD9.....38 A2
Hart St GTHN BD7.....46 B3
Haslam Cl BFDE BD3.....3 H3
Haslam Gv SHPY BD18.....29 F3
Haslemere Cl BOW BD4.....48 C4
Haslingden Dr HTON BD9.....38 A2
Hastings Av WBOW BD5.....47 E5
Hastings Pl WBOW BD5.....47 E5
Hastings St WBOW BD5.....47 E5
Hastings Ter WBOW BD5.....47 E5
Hatchet La LM/WK BD12.....63 H1
Hatfield Rd ECHL BD2.....40 A2
Hathaway Av HTON BD9.....37 G1
Hatton Cl WBSY BD6.....55 E2
Haugh Shaw Cft HFAX HX1.....4 D7
Haugh Shaw Rd HFAX HX1.....4 C7
Haugh Shaw Rd West HFAX HX1....4 A3
Hauxwell Dr YEA LS19.....11 G5
Havelock Sq CUL/QBY BD13.....44 B1
Havelock St CUL/QBY BD13.....44 B1
  GTHN BD7.....46 A3
The Haven IDLE BD10.....30 B3
Haw Av YEA LS19.....11 H3
Hawes Av WBOW BD5.....46 D5
Hawes Crs WBOW BD5.....46 D5
Hawes Dr WBOW BD5.....46 D5
Hawes Gv WBOW BD5.....46 D5
Hawes Mt WBOW BD5.....46 D5
Hawes Rd WBOW BD5.....46 D5
Hawes Ter WBOW BD5.....46 D5
Hawke Wy LM/WK BD12.....55 F4
Hawkhill Av GSLY LS20.....10 C3
Hawksbridge La HWTH BD22.....32 A1
Hawkshead Cl WBOW BD5.....47 F2
Hawkshead Dr WBOW BD5.....47 F2
Hawkshead Wy WBOW * BD5.....47 F2
Hawkshead Wy WBOW BD5.....47 F2
Hawkstone Av GSLY LS20.....10 B4
Hawkstone Dr KGHY BD21.....6 D2
Hawkstone Vw GSLY LS20.....10 B4
Hawk St KGHY * BD21.....7 G3
Hawksworth Av GSLY LS20.....10 A4
Hawksworth Rd BAIL BD17.....18 D1
Haw La YEA LS19.....11 H3
Haworth Gv HTON BD9.....37 H1
Haworth La YEA LS19.....11 G4
Haworth Rd HTON BD9.....37 H1
  HWTH BD22.....23 H5
  WIL/AL BD15.....25 F5
Haworth to Hebden Bridge Wk
  HWTH BD22.....22 A5
  YEA LS19.....11 G4
Hawthorn Av BFDE BD3.....40 D4
  YEA LS19.....11 G4
Hawthorn Cl BRIG HD6.....71 H5
Hawthorn Crs YEA LS19.....11 G4
Hawthorn Dr IDLE BD10.....30 B2
  YEA LS19.....11 H3
Hawthorne Av SHPY BD18.....29 E4

Hawthorn Rd YEA LS19.....11 G4
Hawthorn St BFDE BD3.....40 D4
  HFAX * HX1.....4 C7
  HIPP * HX3.....61 G5
Hawthorn Ter HFAX * HX1.....4 C7
Hawthorn Vw BAIL BD17.....19 E3
Haycliffe Av GTHN BD7.....46 B5
Haycliffe Dr GTHN BD7.....46 A5
Haycliffe Gv GTHN BD7.....46 A5
Haycliffe Hill Rd WBOW BD5.....46 C5
Haycliffe La WBSY BD6.....46 C5
Haycliffe Rd GTHN BD7.....46 C4
Haycliffe Ter GTHN BD7.....46 C4
Hayden St BFDE BD3.....3 J7
The Hayfields HWTH BD22.....22 D1
Haynes St KGHY BD21.....7 G5
Hays La LUD/ILL HX2.....50 A3
Hazel Beck BGLY BD16.....26 D1
Hazel Cft SHPY BD18.....29 E2
Hazel Ct BIRK/DRI BD11.....57 F4
Hazelcroft IDLE BD10.....30 C5
Hazeldene CUL/QBY BD13.....52 A2
Hazelheads BAIL BD17.....18 D1
Hazelhurst Av BGLY BD16.....26 D1
Hazelhurst Brow HTON BD9.....37 G2
Hazelhurst Ct BFDE BD3.....40 B5
Hazel Hurst Gv CUL/QBY BD13.....52 A3
Hazel Hurst Rd CUL/QBY BD13.....52 A3
Hazelhurst Rd HTON BD9.....37 G2
Hazelhurst Ter HTON BD9.....37 G2
Hazelmere Av BGLY BD16.....26 D1
Hazel Mt SHPY BD18.....28 D2
Hazel Wk HTON BD9.....37 G2
Hazelwood Av AIRE BD20.....9 E3
Hazelwood Rd HTON BD9.....37 F1
Headland St WBSY BD6.....54 A1
Headley La CUL/QBY BD13.....44 B2
Healey Av BGLY BD16.....16 D4
Healey La BGLY BD16.....16 D4
Healey Wood Crs BRIG HD6.....78 B3
Healey Wood Gdns BRIG HD6.....78 B3
Healey Wood Gv BRIG HD6.....78 C3
Healey Wood Rd BRIG HD6.....78 B3
Heap La BFDE BD3.....3 G3
Heap St BFDE BD3.....3 G4
  HIPP HX3.....59 H3
Heath Av HIPP HX3.....68 C4
Heathcliff HWTH BD22.....22 C2
Heathcote Ri HWTH BD22.....23 E1
Heatherbank Av HWTH BD22.....13 G2
Heather Bank Cl CUL/QBY BD13....34 B4
Heather Gv HTON BD9.....37 E1
  KGHY BD21.....6 C3
Heatherlands Av CUL/QBY BD13....34 C2
Heather Rd BAIL * BD17.....19 E3
Heather Side BAIL BD17.....18 C2
Heatherstones HIPP HX3.....68 C4
Heather Vw BGLY BD16.....17 G1
Heathfield Av ELL HX5.....77 E4
Heathfield Cl BGLY BD16.....16 D2
Heathfield Gv GTHN BD7.....45 H3
  HIPP * HX3.....68 D4
Heathfield Pl HIPP * HX3.....68 D4
Heathfield St ELL HX5.....76 D5
Heathfield Ter HFAX HX1.....68 D3
Heath Gdns HIPP HX3.....68 D4
Heath Gv AIRE BD20.....9 E3
  PDSY/CALV LS28.....41 H5
Heath Hall HFAX HX1.....68 D3
Heath Hall Av BOW BD4.....56 A1
Heath La HIPP HX3.....68 D3
Heath Lea HFAX HX1.....5 G6
Heathmoor Cl IDLE BD10.....29 H2
  LUD/ILL HX2.....50 C4
Heathmoor Mt LUD/ILL HX2.....50 C4
Heathmoor Park Rd
  LUD/ILL HX2.....50 C4
Heathmoor Wy LUD/ILL HX2.....50 C4
Heath Mt HFAX HX1.....68 D3
Heath Mount Rd BRIG HD6.....78 B3
Heath Park Av HFAX HX1.....68 D3
Heath Rd BFDE BD3.....3 J1
  HFAX HX1.....68 D3
Heath Royd HIPP HX3.....68 D4
Heath St BFDE BD3.....40 B5
  BGLY BD16.....17 G1
  HIPP HX3.....68 D4
Heath Ter BFDE BD3.....3 K5
Heath Vw HFAX * HX1.....5 H6
Heath View St HFAX HX1.....5 H6
Heathy Av LUD/ILL HX2.....51 F5
Heathy La LUD/ILL HX2.....51 E4
Heaton Av AIRE BD20.....8 D4
  CLECK BD19.....73 F1
Heaton Cl BGLY BD16.....17 E2
Heaton Crs BGLY * BD16.....17 E2
Heaton Dr BAIL BD17.....18 C2

BGLY BD16.....17 E2
Heaton Gv CLECK BD19.....73 F1
  HTON BD9.....28 C5
  SHPY BD18.....28 D2
Heaton Hl WBSY BD6.....53 H5
Heaton Park Dr HTON BD9.....38 A1
Heaton Park Rd HTON BD9.....38 A1
Heaton Rd HTON BD9.....38 B1
Heaton Royds SHPY * BD18.....28 A4
Heaton Royds La SHPY BD18.....28 A4
Heaton St BOW BD4.....47 H2
  BRIG HD6.....78 B1
  CLECK BD19.....64 C5
Hebble Brook Cl LUD/ILL HX2.....58 B1
Hebble Gdns LUD/ILL HX2.....58 D4
Hebble La HFAX HX1.....59 E4
Hebble Vale Dr LUD/ILL HX2.....58 D3
Hebb Vw WBSY BD6.....45 H5
Hebden Rd HWTH BD22.....23 E2
Heber St KGHY BD21.....7 E5
Hector Cl WBSY BD6.....54 D1
Heddon Cl WBOW BD5.....47 F2
Heddon Gv WBOW BD5.....47 F2
Heddon Wk WBOW * BD5.....47 F2
Hedge Cl GIR BD8.....37 G3
Hedge Side GIR BD8.....37 H4
Hedge Top La HIPP HX3.....60 D2
Hedge Wy GIR BD8.....37 H3
Heidelberg Rd HTON BD9.....38 B2
Height Gn RPDN/SBR HX6.....67 E4
Height La HWTH BD22.....33 E2
Heights La BGLY BD16.....9 H4
  HTON BD9.....37 G1
Helena Wy BOW BD4.....56 B2
Helen Rose Ct SHPY BD18.....19 F5
Helen St SHPY BD18.....28 A1
Hellewell St WBSY BD6.....54 A3
Helmsley St BOW BD4.....47 H3
Hemingway Rd IDLE BD10.....30 C1
Hemsby Gv KGHY * BD21.....13 H2
Hemsby St KGHY BD21.....13 H2
Henacrewood Ct
  CUL/QBY BD13.....52 B3
Henderson Pl WBSY BD6.....54 D1
Hendford Dr BFDE BD3.....3 H4
Henley Av WBOW BD5.....47 F5
Henley Ct WBOW BD5.....47 F5
Henley Dr YEA LS19.....21 H3
Henley Gv WBOW BD5.....47 F5
Henley Hl YEA LS19.....21 H3
Henley Rd WBOW BD5.....47 F5
Henry St BRIG HD6.....71 F4
  CLAY BD14.....45 F3
  CUL/QBY BD13.....44 A1
  HFAX HX1.....5 F5
  KGHY BD21.....7 F4
Henry Ter YEA LS19.....11 E4
Henshaw Av YEA LS19.....11 G5
Henshaw Crs YEA LS19.....11 G5
Henshaw La YEA LS19.....11 G5
Henshaw Vw YEA LS19.....11 G5
Herbert Pl BFDE BD3.....40 D4
Herbert St BGLY BD16.....16 D3
  CLAY BD14.....45 F3
  HFAX HX1.....4 A5
  SHPY BD18.....28 A1
  WBOW BD5.....47 E3
Hereford Wy BOW * BD4.....47 H3
Heritage Ms HFAX * HX1.....5 J5
Heritage Pk BGLY BD16.....9 H4
Heritage Wy HWTH BD22.....12 D4
Hermit St HWTH BD22.....13 H4
Hermon Av HFAX HX1.....4 C5
Hermon Gv HFAX HX1.....4 C5
Heron Cl CUL/QBY BD13.....43 H5
Herschel Rd GIR BD8.....37 F5
Heshbon St BOW BD4.....48 B4
Hetton Dr BFDE BD3.....48 C1
Hew Clews GTHN BD7.....45 H4
Heybeck Wk BOW BD4.....49 E5
Heyford Ct ECHL BD2.....39 E1
Heygate Cl BAIL BD17.....19 E2
Heygate La BAIL BD17.....19 E2
Heys Av CUL/QBY BD13.....44 C1
Heys Crs CUL/QBY BD13.....44 C1
Heysham Dr BOW BD4.....49 E4
Hey St BRIG HD6.....71 G4
  GTHN BD7.....2 A5
Heywood Cl HIPP HX3.....60 D3
Heywood Pl HFAX HX1.....4 D3
Heywood St HFAX HX1.....4 D3
Hick St BFD * BD1.....3 F5
Higgin La HIPP HX3.....69 F3
High Ash SHPY BD18.....29 E1
High Ash Pk WIL/AL BD15.....36 C3
High Bank La SHPY BD18.....27 G5
High Banks Cl AIRE BD20.....8 A1
High Binns La HWTH BD22.....33 E1

Highbridge Ter WBOW BD5.....55 G1
High Bury Cl CUL/QBY BD13.....51 H2
High Busy La IDLE BD10.....29 G1
Highcliffe Dr LUD/ILL HX2.....67 G1
High Cl GSLY LS20.....10 A3
  YEA LS19.....21 G3
High Cft CUL/QBY BD13.....52 B1
  HIPP HX3.....59 E5
Highcroft Cl PDSY/CALV LS28.....41 H4
Highcroft Gdns KGHY BD21.....6 D3
High Cross La HIPP HX3.....52 D3
Highdale Cft IDLE BD10.....30 A1
Higher Brockwell
  RPDN/SBR HX6.....66 C5
Higher Coach Rd BGLY BD16.....17 F4
Higher Downs GIR BD8.....37 G5
Higher Intake Rd ECHL BD2.....40 B3
Higher School St SHPY * BD18.....28 A1
Higherwood Cl KGHY BD21.....7 H4
Highfell Ri HWTH BD22.....13 F1
High Fernley Ct LM/WK * BD12.....62 D1
High Fernley Rd LM/WK BD12.....62 B2
Highfield BOW BD4.....56 C1
  HIPP HX3.....53 E5
Highfield Av HIPP HX3.....62 C5
  GTL/HWG HX4.....75 G3
  IDLE BD10.....29 H2
Highfield Cl AIRE BD20.....8 D2
Highfield Crs BAIL BD17.....18 D1
  HTON BD9.....27 G5
  LVSG WF15.....73 H4
  YEA LS19.....21 H3
Highfield Gdns HTON BD9.....37 G1
Highfield Gv ELL HX5.....76 B3
  IDLE BD10.....29 H3
High Field La HWTH BD22.....12 D3
Highfield La BGLY BD16.....6 D3
Highfield Ms AIRE BD20.....8 D2
  BAIL BD17.....18 D1
Highfield Pl GIR BD8.....38 D3
  HFAX HX1.....4 B6
Highfield Rd BRIG HD6.....77 H3
  CLECK BD19.....73 F1
  ELL HX5.....76 C5
  HTON BD9.....29 H3
  IDLE BD10.....29 H3
  KGHY BD21.....6 D3
  PDSY/CALV LS28.....41 H4
High Flds LUD/ILL HX2.....67 H4
Highfield St KGHY BD21.....7 E4
  PDSY/CALV LS28.....41 H4
Highfield Ter HFAX * HX1.....4 B6
  PDSY/CALV LS28.....41 H4
  SHPY BD18.....27 H1
High Fold HWTH BD22.....13 G1
Highfold YEA LS19.....21 F1
High Fold La AIRE BD20.....6 D1
Highgate HTON BD9.....28 A5
Highgate Cl CUL/QBY BD13.....45 D5
Highgate Gdns LUD/ILL HX2.....58 D5
Highgate Gv CLAY BD14.....45 D5
Highgate Rd CUL/QBY BD13.....45 C5
  HTON BD9.....28 B5
High Grove La HIPP HX3.....69 F3
High Holly Garth KGHY BD21.....7 G5
High House Av ECHL BD2.....29 H5
High House Rd ECHL BD2.....29 H5
The Highlands LVSG WF15.....73 G3
Highlands Cl GTHN BD7.....45 H4
Highlands Gv GTHN BD7.....45 H4
Highlands La LUD/ILL HX2.....51 E4
Highland Ville HIPP HX3.....61 G5
High La LUD/ILL HX2.....50 B4
Highlea Cl YEA LS19.....21 E1
High Lees Rd LUD/ILL HX2.....50 A5
High Level Wy HFAX HX1.....4 B1
Highley Hall Cft BRIG HD6.....79 E1
Highley Pk BRIG HD6.....79 F1
High Meadow KGHY BD21.....6 D2
High Mdw GTL/HWG HX4.....75 G3
  WIL/AL BD15.....25 G4
Highmoor BAIL BD17.....18 B4
Highmoor Crs BRIG HD6.....72 A5
Highmoor La BRIG HD6.....72 A5
Highmoor Wk BAIL BD17.....18 B4
Highoak Garth HWTH BD22.....12 D4
High Park Crs HTON BD9.....37 H1
High Park Dr HTON BD9.....37 G1
High Park Gv HTON BD9.....37 H1
High Poplars ECHL BD2.....29 G5
Highroad Well La LUD/ILL HX2.....67 G1
High Spring Gardens La
  KGHY BD21.....6 D2
High Spring Rd KGHY BD21.....8 A5
High St BRIG HD6.....71 G5

CLECK BD19 .....64 C5
CUL/QBY BD13 .....44 A1
CUL/QBY BD13 .....52 B1
GTL/HWG * HX4 .....76 A4
HFAX HX1 .....5 F5
IDLE BD10 .....30 A1
KGHY BD21 .....7 E4
WBSY BD6 .....54 D1
YEA LS19 .....11 H4
High Sunderland La HIPP HX3 .....59 H4
Hightown Rd CLECK BD19 .....73 G5
Hightown Vw LVSG WF15 .....73 F3
High Trees La GTL/HWG HX4 .....74 C5
Highway GSLY LS20 .....10 A2
High Wicken Cl CUL/QBY BD13 .....43 H1
Hilda St HTON BD9 .....28 B5
Hillam Rd ECHL BD2 .....39 E1
Hillam St WBOW BD5 .....46 C4
Hillary Rd SHPY BD18 .....29 F2
Hillbro Ct BAIL * BD17 .....19 E2
Hill Brow Cl WIL/AL BD15 .....36 D3
Hill Cl BAIL BD17 .....18 C4
Hillcote Dr WBOW BD5 .....47 F3
YEA LS19 .....21 H1
Hill Crs HIPP HX3 .....69 F3
Hill Crest Av CUL/QBY BD13 .....34 C3
Hillcrest Crest Dr CUL/QBY BD13 .....52 C2
Hill Crest Dr CUL/QBY BD13 .....34 C3
Hillcrest Dr CUL/QBY BD13 .....52 C2
Hill Crest Mt CLECK BD19 .....72 C1
Hill Crest Mt CUL/QBY BD13 .....34 C3
Hillcrest Mt CUL/QBY BD13 .....34 C3
CUL/QBY BD13 .....36 A5
Hillcrest Rd CUL/QBY BD13 .....52 C2
Hill Cft CUL/QBY BD13 .....36 B5
Hill End Cl HIPP HX3 .....62 B3
Hill End Gv GTHN BD7 .....45 H4
Hill End La CUL/QBY BD13 .....24 D1
CUL/QBY BD13 .....52 A1
Hill Foot SHPY BD18 .....27 G2
Hillfoot Av PDSY/CALV LS28 .....41 G4
Hillfoot Crs PDSY/CALV LS28 .....41 G4
Hillfoot Dr PDSY/CALV LS28 .....41 G4
Hillfoot Ri PDSY/CALV LS28 .....41 G4
Hill House Edge La HWTH 32 C4
Hill House La HWTH BD22 .....32 D3
Hill Lands LM/WK BD12 .....62 C1
Hill Park Av HIPP HX3 .....59 E4
Hillside Av HWTH BD22 .....12 C4
LUD/ILL HX2 .....66 A1
Hillside Gv HWTH BD22 .....12 C4
Hillside Ri GSLY LS20 .....10 C1
Hill Side Rd BFDE BD3 .....3 G4
BGLY BD16 .....16 C3
Hillside Ter BAIL * BD17 .....18 D2
Hillside Vw RPDN/SBR HX6 .....66 D4
Hill St BOW BD4 .....48 A2
CLECK BD19 .....73 F1
HFAX HX1 .....5 F6
HWTH BD22 .....22 D3
WBSY BD6 .....54 B1
Hill Top HX1 .....67 H3
Hill Top Cottages HTON BD9 .....37 H2
Hill Top Gv WIL/AL BD15 .....36 D3
Hill Top La BGLY BD16 .....9 G3
WIL/AL BD15 .....36 D3
Hill Top Rd CUL/QBY BD13 .....35 G5
HWTH BD22 .....12 C4
KGHY BD21 .....13 H5
Hill Top Wk HWTH 6 A4
Hill Top Wy HWTH * BD22 .....6 A4
Hill Vw LUD/ILL HX2 .....51 E3
Hillview Gdns HIPP HX3 .....60 D4
Hillway GSLY LS20 .....10 A3
Hillworth Village KGHY * BD21 .....7 E5
Hilton Av SHPY BD18 .....28 C4
Hilton Crs BAIL BD17 .....18 D4
Hilton Dr SHPY BD18 .....28 C4
Hilton Gv GTHN BD7 .....28 C4
SHPY BD18 .....28 C4
Hilton Rd GTHN BD7 .....46 B1
SHPY BD18 .....28 C4
Hinchcliffe St BFDE BD3 .....3 J2
Hinchliffe Av BAIL BD17 .....19 E4
Hindley Wk GTHN BD7 .....45 G5
Hind St GIR BD8 .....38 D4
LM/WK BD12 .....62 D1
Hions Cl BRIG HD6 .....78 B3
Hipswell Pl BFDE BD3 .....40 B4
Hird Av WBSY BD6 .....54 D2
Hird Rd LM/WK BD12 .....55 E4
Hird St BAIL BD17 .....28 C1
KGHY BD21 .....14 A1
Hirst La SHPY BD18 .....17 H5
Hirst Lodge Ct ECHL BD2 .....29 C5
Hirst Mill Crs SHPY BD18 .....17 H5
Hirst Wood Crs SHPY BD18 .....27 H1

Hirst Wood Rd SHPY BD18 .....27 G1
Hive St HWTH BD22 .....6 D5
Hob Cote La HWTH BD22 .....12 A5
Hob La RPDN/SBR HX6 .....74 A2
Hockney Rd GIR BD8 .....38 C4
Hodgson Av BFDE BD3 .....40 C4
Hodgson La BIRK/DRI BD11 .....57 G3
Holborn Ct WBSY BD6 .....54 D4
Holden La BAIL BD17 .....19 E2
Holdsworth Ct CLECK BD19 .....73 G1
Holdsworth Rd LUD/ILL HX2 .....51 F3
Holdsworth St BFD1 BD1 .....2 E3
CLECK BD19 .....64 C5
SHPY BD18 .....28 D3
Holdsworth Ter HFAX HX1 .....69 E3
Holker St GIR BD8 .....38 C4
KGHY BD21 .....7 F3
Hollas La RPDN/SBR HX6 .....74 D1
Hollin Close La ECHL BD2 .....39 F1
Hollin Greaves La HIPP HX3 .....59 H4
Hollings HWTH * BD22 .....22 B2
Hollings Rd GIR BD8 .....38 C4
Hollings Sq GIR BD8 .....38 C4
Hollings St BGLY BD16 .....27 E2
GIR BD8 .....38 C4
Hollings Ter GIR BD8 .....38 C4
Hollingwood Av GTHN BD7 .....46 A3
Hollingwood Dr GTHN BD7 .....45 H3
Hollingwood La GTHN BD7 .....45 H4
Hollingwood Mt GTHN BD7 .....45 H3
Hollin Hall Rd SHPY BD18 .....27 H3
Hollin Head BAIL BD17 .....19 G2
SHPY BD18 .....29 E3
Hollin Park Av PDSY/CALV LS28 .....31 F3
Hollin Park Dr PDSY/CALV LS28 .....31 F3
Hollin Park Rd PDSY/CALV LS28 .....31 F3
Hollin Ri SHPY * BD18 .....28 D3
Hollin Park SHPY BD18 .....28 D3
Hollins Bank RPDN/SBR HX6 .....67 E4
Hollins Bungalows
RPDN/SBR * HX6 .....67 E3
Hollins Cl AIRE BD20 .....6 C1
Hollins Hl BAIL BD17 .....10 A5
Hollins La LUD/ILL HX2 .....50 B5
RPDN/SBR HX6 .....67 E3
Hollins Mill La RPDN/SBR HX6 .....66 D4
Hollin Ter SHPY * BD18 .....28 D3
Hollin Wood Cl SHPY BD18 .....27 H2
Hollinwood Vw AIRE BD20 .....9 E4
Hollowfield Cft LM/WK BD12 .....56 A5
Holly Bank Dr HIPP HX3 .....61 G5
Hollybank Gdns GTHN BD7 .....45 H4
Hollybank Gv GTHN BD7 .....45 H4
Holly Bank Pk BRIG HD6 .....78 A3
Holly Bank Rd BRIG HD6 .....77 H3
Holly Bank Rd GTHN BD7 .....45 H4
Holly Gv HFAX HX1 .....4 C5
Holly Hall La LM/WK BD12 .....62 D1
Hollynsmill GTL/HWG HX4 .....76 A4
Holly Park Dr GTHN BD7 .....45 H3
Holly Park Gv GTHN * BD7 .....45 H3
Holly Park Mills
PDSY/CALV * LS28 .....31 F3
Holly St WBSY BD6 .....54 C1
Holme Dr LUD/ILL HX2 .....67 E2
Holme Farm WBSY BD6 .....53 G1
Holmefield Vw BOW BD4 .....48 D3
Holme House La HWTH BD22 .....12 D1
Holme Mill La HWTH BD22 .....6 C5
Holme Rd LUD/ILL HX2 .....67 E2
Holmes Rd RPDN/SBR HX6 .....67 F4
Holmes St BGLY BD16 .....2 A3
Holmes Ter LUD/ILL HX2 .....58 C5
Holme St BRIG HD6 .....71 F1
HWTH BD22 .....32 D2
WBOW BD5 .....47 E3
Holme Top La WBOW BD5 .....47 E3
Holme Top St WBOW BD5 .....47 E3
Holme Wood Rd BOW BD4 .....48 C4
HWTH BD22 .....6 D1
Holroyd Hl WBSY BD6 .....54 C1
Holsworthy Rd BOW BD4 .....48 D4
The Holt SHPY BD18 .....28 D2
Holtby Gv BRIG HD6 .....71 F1
Holt Gdns IDLE BD10 .....29 G1
Holts La CLAY BD14 .....45 E2
Holts Ter HIPP HX3 .....69 E4
Holybrook Av IDLE BD10 .....30 C3
Holycroft St KGHY BD21 .....7 E5
Holyoake Av BGLY BD16 .....16 C5
Holywell Ash La GIR BD8 .....2 A2
Home View Ter GIR BD8 .....38 C3
Honey Pot La BAIL * BD17 .....18 C3
The Hoods BRIG HD6 .....78 A4
Hopbine Av WBOW BD5 .....47 F5
Hopbine Rd WBOW BD5 .....47 F5

Hope Av SHPY BD18 .....29 E1
WBOW BD5 .....46 D5
Hopefield Wy BOW BD4 .....56 A1
Hope Hall Ter HFAX HX1 .....5 H6
Hope Hall Ter HFAX HX1 .....5 H6
Hope Hill Vw BGLY BD16 .....26 D2
Hope La BAIL BD17 .....18 C3
Hope Pl KGHY * BD21 .....14 A1
Hope St HFAX HX1 .....4 E3
RPDN/SBR HX6 .....67 F5
Hope Vw SHPY BD18 .....28 D2
Hopkinson Dr BOW BD4 .....56 B2
Hopkinson St LUD/ILL HX2 .....59 E1
Hopkin St BOW BD4 .....56 D1
Hops La HIPP HX3 .....58 D3
Hopton Av BOW BD4 .....56 A1
Hopwood La HFAX HX1 .....4 A5
Horley Green La HIPP HX3 .....60 B4
Hornbeam Cl WIL/AL BD15 .....26 C5
Hornby St HFAX HX1 .....4 B6
Hornby Ter HFAX * HX1 .....4 B6
Horncastle St CLECK BD19 .....73 H1
Horne St HFAX HX1 .....4 E3
Hornsea Dr WIL/AL BD15 .....25 H5
Horsfall St HFAX HX1 .....68 B3
Horsham Ct HWTH BD22 .....13 F1
Horsham Rd BOW * BD4 .....48 D5
Horsley St WBSY BD6 .....54 D1
Horsman St BOW BD4 .....56 D1
Horton Grange Rd GTHN BD7 .....46 C1
Horton Hall Cl WBOW BD5 .....47 E2
Horton Park Av GTHN BD7 .....46 C2
Horton St HFAX HX1 .....5 H5
Hospital Rd AIRE BD20 .....8 B2
Hough HIPP HX3 .....69 G3
Houghton Pl BFD1 BD1 .....2 B3
Houghton St BRIG HD6 .....71 G5
Hoults La GTL/HWG HX4 .....75 G3
Howards Dean HWTH BD22 .....13 E5
Howard St HFAX HX1 .....5 H5
WBOW BD5 .....2 B7
Howarth Av ECHL BD2 .....29 H4
Howarth Crs ECHL * BD2 .....29 H4
Howbeck Av AIRE BD20 .....8 B2
Howbeck Dr AIRE BD20 .....8 B3
Howcans La HIPP HX3 .....59 F1
Howden Av AIRE BD20 .....6 D1
Howdenbrook HIPP HX3 .....53 G3
Howden Cl BOW BD4 .....49 E5
Howes La HIPP HX3 .....60 C2
Howgate IDLE BD10 .....30 B1
Howgate Hl HIPP HX3 .....69 G3
Howgill Gn WBSY BD6 .....54 B4
Howson Cl GSLY LS20 .....11 E3
Hoxton St GIR BD8 .....38 B4
Hoyle Court Av BAIL BD17 .....19 F3
Hoyle Court Dr BAIL BD17 .....19 F3
Hoyle Court Rd BAIL BD17 .....19 F3
Hoyle Fold HWTH BD22 .....13 G1
Hoyle Ing Rd CUL/QBY BD13 .....44 C1
Hubert St BFDE BD3 .....3 K7
LUD/ILL * HX2 .....67 G1
Huddersfield Rd BRIG HD6 .....78 C1
ELL HX5 .....76 A2
ELL HX5 .....76 C4
HFAX HX1 .....68 D3
LM/WK BD12 .....62 C3
Hud Hl HIPP HX3 .....61 E1
The Hudson LM/WK BD12 .....62 D2
Hudson Av GTHN BD7 .....46 C3
Hudson Cl GTHN BD7 .....46 C4
Hudson Crs GTHN BD7 .....46 C4
Hudson Gdns GTHN BD7 .....46 C3
Hudson St BFDE BD3 .....40 B4
Hughendon Dr CUL/QBY BD13 .....44 D1
Hughendon Wk CUL/QBY BD13 .....44 D1
Hugill St CUL/QBY BD13 .....44 A1
Hulbert St BGLY BD16 .....16 D4
Hullenedge Gdns ELL HX5 .....76 A5
Hullenedge La GTL/HWG HX4 .....76 A5
Hullenedge Rd ELL HX5 .....76 B5
Hullen Rd ELL HX5 .....76 A5
Humboldt St BFD1 BD1 .....3 G5
Hunger Hl HFAX HX1 .....5 H6
Hunsworth La BIRK/DRI BD11 .....56 D4
CLECK BD19 .....64 C1
Hunterscombe Ct BGLY BD16 .....17 G1
Hunters Ct HTON BD9 .....27 F5
Hunters Gn CUL/QBY BD13 .....24 C2
Hunters Park Av CLAY BD14 .....45 G2
Huntingdon Rd BRIG HD6 .....78 D2
Huntock Pl BRIG HD6 .....71 E3
Huntsmans Cl BGLY BD16 .....17 F1
KGHY BD21 .....6 D1
Hurstville Av BIRK/DRI BD11 .....57 E4
Hustlergate BFD1 BD1 .....2 D5
Hustler St BFDE BD3 .....3 H1
Hutson St WBOW BD5 .....47 E3

Hutton Rd WBOW BD5 .....46 D5
Hutton Ter IDLE BD10 .....30 C4
Hydale Cl KGHY BD21 .....14 C1
Hydale Ct LM/WK BD12 .....54 C4
Hyde Gv KGHY BD21 .....7 G3
Hyde Pk HFAX HX1 .....4 C6
Hyde Park Rd HFAX HX1 .....4 C7
Hyde Park St HFAX HX1 .....4 C6
Hyde St IDLE BD10 .....20 A5
Hyne Av BOW BD4 .....56 B1

I

Ida St WBOW BD5 .....46 D4
Iddesleigh St BOW BD4 .....48 B1
Idlecroft Rd IDLE BD10 .....30 A1
Idle Rd ECHL BD2 .....29 H4
Idlethorp Wy IDLE BD10 .....30 B2
Ilbert Av BOW BD4 .....56 B1
Ilkley Rd AIRE BD20 .....8 A1
Illingworth Av LUD/ILL HX2 .....50 D5
Illingworth Cl LUD/ILL HX2 .....50 D5
YEA LS19 .....21 H1
Illingworth Crs LUD/ILL HX2 .....50 D5
Illingworth Dr LUD/ILL HX2 .....50 D5
Illingworth Gdns LUD/ILL HX2 .....50 D4
Illingworth Gv LUD/ILL HX2 .....50 D5
Illingworth Rd LM/WK BD12 .....63 G1
LUD/ILL HX2 .....50 D5
Illingworth Wy LUD/ILL HX2 .....50 D5
The Incline HIPP HX3 .....5 K2
Independent St WBOW BD5 .....46 D5
Industrial Rd RPDN/SBR HX6 .....67 E4
Industrial St BGLY BD16 .....16 C3
BRIG HD6 .....71 G5
CLECK BD19 .....63 G5
HWTH BD22 .....6 D5
LVSG WF15 .....73 H4
Industrial Ter HFAX HX1 .....68 C3
Infirmary St BFD1 BD1 .....2 B4
Ing Fld LM/WK BD12 .....63 H1
Ingham Cl LUD/ILL HX2 .....51 E2
Ingham La LUD/ILL HX2 .....50 D1
Ingham's Av PDSY/CALV LS28 .....41 G4
Inghams Ct HIPP * HX3 .....59 F4
Inghams Ter PDSY/CALV LS28 .....41 G4
Ingham's Vw PDSY/CALV LS28 .....41 G4
Inghead Gdns HIPP HX3 .....61 G1
Ingleborough Cl BOW BD4 .....48 D4
Ingleby Pl GTHN BD7 .....46 B1
Ingleby Rd GIR BD8 .....38 B5
Ingleby St GIR BD8 .....38 B5
Ingram Sq HFAX * HX1 .....68 B3
Ingram St HFAX HX1 .....68 B3
KGHY BD21 .....14 A3
Ingrow Br KGHY * BD21 .....14 A2
Ingrow La HWTH BD22 .....13 G2
Ingrow St HWTH BD22 .....13 H2
The Ings BRIG HD6 .....71 F2
Ings Av GSLY LS20 .....10 C1
Ings Ct GSLY LS20 .....10 B1
Ings Crs GSLY LS20 .....10 B1
Ings La GSLY LS20 .....10 B1
Ing St BFDE BD3 .....48 C1
Ings Wy GIR BD8 .....37 H4
Ingwell Ter CLECK BD19 .....73 H1
Inkerman St BOW BD4 .....48 C3
ECHL BD2 .....30 C5
Inkersley Rd BFD1 BD1 .....2 C1
The Innings IDLE BD10 .....29 H1
Institute Rd ECHL BD2 .....30 B4
Intake Gv ECHL BD2 .....40 B2
Intake Rd ECHL BD2 .....40 B2
Intake Ter ECHL BD2 .....40 B2
Invertrees Av YEA LS19 .....21 H2
Iona St HIPP HX3 .....59 G3
Iona St HIPP HX3 .....59 G4
Iqbal Ct BFDE * BD3 .....48 C1
Ireland St BGLY BD16 .....16 B3
Ireland Ter BGLY BD16 .....16 B3
Ireton St GTHN BD7 .....46 C1
Iron St CLECK BD19 .....73 F1
Irving St HFAX HX1 .....4 A7
Irving Ter CLAY BD14 .....45 F4
Irwell St BOW BD4 .....47 H2
Isaac St GIR BD8 .....38 C4
Isles St GIR BD8 .....38 A4
Ivanhoe Rd GTHN BD7 .....46 C2
Ivegate BFD1 BD1 .....2 D5
YEA LS19 .....11 G5
Ives St SHPY BD18 .....28 B2
Ivy Bank La HWTH BD22 .....22 D3
Ivy Crs HIPP HX3 .....70 D1
Ivy Gv SHPY BD18 .....27 H2
Ivy House Rd WBOW BD5 .....55 F1

Ivy La *LUD/ILL* HX2 ......50 C4
  WIL/AL BD15 ......36 D3
Ivy Rd *KGHY* BD21 ......7 H5
  SHPY BD18 ......27 H2
Ivy St *BRIG* HD6 ......71 E5
  HFAX HX1 ......68 B3
  KGHY BD21 ......7 E3
Ivy Ter *BRIG* HD6 ......71 E5
  HIPP HX3 ......70 D1
  KGHY BD21 ......8 A5

J

Jacana Wy *CUL/QBY* BD13 ......53 F1
Jackie Smart Rd *WBOW* BD5 ......47 F3
Jackson Hill La *CUL/QBY* BD13 ......52 C3
Jackson St *BFDE* BD3 ......3 H7
Jacky La *HWTH* BD22 ......22 D3
Jacobs La *HWTH* BD22 ......23 E1
Jacob St *WBOW* BD5 ......47 E3
James Ga *BFD* BD1 ......2 C4
James St *BIRK/DRI* * BD11 ......57 F4
  BRIG HD6 ......71 F4
  CUL/QBY BD13 ......36 A5
  ELL HX5 ......76 D5
  HWTH BD22 ......12 C4
  WIL/AL BD15 ......37 F3
  YEA LS19 ......21 G2
Jamie St *IDLE* BD10 ......30 C3
Jane St *CUL/QBY* BD13 ......34 C3
  SHPY BD18 ......28 C1
Janet St *HWTH* BD22 ......23 F1
Jardine St *BGLY* BD16 ......16 D3
Jarratt St *GIR* BD8 ......38 C3
Jarratt St East *GIR* BD8 ......38 C3
Jarrom Cl *BOW* BD4 ......48 C3
Jasmin Ter *GIR* BD8 ......38 D4
Jasper St *HFAX* HX1 ......4 B4
  IDLE BD10 ......30 A1
Javelin Cl *IDLE* BD10 ......30 A3
Jay House La *BRIG* HD6 ......72 A3
Jay St *HWTH* BD22 ......23 E3
Jennings Pl *GTHN* BD7 ......46 B3
Jennings St *GTHN* BD7 ......46 B3
Jenny La *BAIL* BD17 ......19 E2
Jepson La *ELL* HX5 ......76 C5
Jer Gv *WBSY* BD6 ......45 H5
Jer La *WBSY* BD6 ......45 H5
Jermyn St *BFDE* BD3 ......2 E4
Jerry Fields Rd *LUD/ILL* HX2 ......66 A2
Jerry La *RPDN/SBR* HX6 ......66 D5
Jervaulx Crs *GIR* BD8 ......38 C4
Jerwood Hill Cl *HIPP* HX3 ......60 A4
Jerwood Hill Rd *HIPP* HX3 ......60 A4
Jesmond Av *HTON* BD9 ......38 A2
Jesmond Gv *HTON* BD9 ......38 A2
Jesse St *GIR* BD8 ......37 G5
  WBOW BD5 ......47 F2
Jew La *HWTH* BD22 ......32 D2
Jinnah Ct *GIR* BD8 ......2 A2
Joba Av *BFDE* BD3 ......3 K5
John Escritt Rd *BGLY* BD16 ......16 D4
John Naylor La *LUD/ILL* HX2 ......66 B3
  BGLY BD16 ......16 C3
Johnson St *BFDE* BD3 ......40 C5
John St *BAIL* BD17 ......18 D5
  BFD BD1 ......2 C4
  BOW BD4 ......56 D1
  BRIG HD6 ......71 F5
  CLAY BD14 ......45 F3
  CUL/QBY BD13 ......34 C4
  CUL/QBY BD13 ......44 A1
  ELL HX5 ......76 C5
  GTL/HWG HX4 ......5 G4
  HFAX HX1 ......5 G4
  HWTH BD22 ......13 G4
  SHPY BD18 ......28 B1
  YEA LS19 ......21 G2
John St West *RPDN/SBR* HX6 ......67 E4
John William St *CLECK* BD19 ......64 C5
  ELL HX5 ......76 C5
Joseph Av *HIPP* HX3 ......60 D3
Joseph St *BFD* BD1 ......3 G5
  BOW BD4 ......56 D1
Jowett Park Crs *IDLE* BD10 ......19 H4
Jowett St *BFD* BD1 ......3 B8
Jubilee Ct *SHPY* * BD18 ......28 C1
Jubilee Dr *KGHY* BD21 ......13 H1
Jubilee Rd *HIPP* HX3 ......76 A1
Jubilee St *GIR* BD8 ......2 B1
  HIPP HX3 ......5 K6
Jubilee St North *HIPP* HX3 ......59 F1
Jubilee Ter *HIPP* * HX3 ......5 K6
Jubilee Wy *SHPY* BD18 ......29 E1
Julian Dr *CUL/QBY* BD13 ......45 F5

Jumble Dyke *BRIG* HD6 ......78 A3
Jumples *LUD/ILL* HX2 ......58 C1
Jumples Cl *LUD/ILL* HX2 ......58 C1
Junction Rd *BAIL* BD17 ......28 D1
June St *KGHY* BD21 ......7 F3
Juniper Cl *GIR* * BD8 ......38 D4

K

Katherine St *SHPY* BD18 ......28 C1
Kaycell St *BOW* BD4 ......48 A5
Kay St *HTON* BD9 ......28 D4
Keeldar Cl *GTHN* BD7 ......46 C4
Keelham Dr *YEA* LS19 ......21 H2
Keelham La *AIRE* BD20 ......6 D1
Keighley Cl *LUD/ILL* HX2 ......50 C4
Keighley Dr *LUD/ILL* HX2 ......50 D5
Keighley Rd *BGLY* BD16 ......9 F5
  BGLY BD16 ......15 F3
  CUL/QBY BD13 ......24 C1
  CUL/QBY BD13 ......34 C1
  HTON BD9 ......38 D1
  HWTH BD22 ......13 F3
  HWTH BD22 ......32 A1
  LUD/ILL HX2 ......50 D5
Kelburn Gv *HWTH* BD22 ......12 C3
Kelcliffe Av *GSLY* LS20 ......10 D2
Kelcliffe La *GSLY* LS20 ......10 D1
Kell La *HIPP* HX3 ......60 C3
Kelloe St *CLECK* BD19 ......64 B4
Kell St *BGLY* BD16 ......16 D3
Kelmore Gv *WBSY* BD6 ......53 H4
Kelsey St *HFAX* HX1 ......4 B2
Kelvin Av *LUD/ILL* HX2 ......67 G1
Kelvin Crs *LUD/ILL* HX2 ......67 G2
Kelvin Rd *ELL* HX5 ......76 B5
Kelvin Wy *ECHL* BD2 ......40 D2
Kendall Av *SHPY* BD18 ......27 H1
Kendal Mellor Ct *KGHY* BD21 ......7 E4
Kendal St *BGLY* BD16 ......7 G5
Kenilworth Dr *BRIG* HD6 ......71 F2
Kenilworth St *BOW* BD4 ......47 H3
Kenley Av *WBSY* BD6 ......54 B1
Kenley Mt *WBSY* BD6 ......46 B5
Kenley Pde *GTHN* BD7 ......46 A5
Kenmore Av *CLECK* BD19 ......64 B5
Kenmore Cl *CLECK* BD19 ......64 B5
Kenmore Crs *CLECK* BD19 ......64 B5
  WBSY BD6 ......46 B5
Kenmore Dr *CLECK* BD19 ......64 B5
  WBSY BD6 ......46 B5
Kenmore Gv *CLECK* BD19 ......64 B5
  WBSY BD6 ......46 B5
Kenmore Rd *CLECK* BD19 ......64 B5
Kenmore Vw *CLECK* BD19 ......64 B5
Kenmore Wk *WBSY* BD6 ......46 B5
Kenmore Wy *CLECK* BD19 ......64 B5
Kennion St *WBOW* BD5 ......47 E2
Kensington Cl *HIPP* HX3 ......68 B4
Kensington Rd *HIPP* HX3 ......68 B4
Kensington St *GIR* BD8 ......38 B3
  KGHY BD21 ......7 E5
Kenstone Cres *IDLE* BD10 ......29 H2
Kentmere Av *LM/WK* BD12 ......63 F4
Kent Ms *BGLY* BD16 ......17 E4
Kenton Wy *BOW* * BD4 ......48 D4
Kent Rd *BGLY* BD16 ......17 E3
Kent St *HFAX* HX1 ......5 F5
Kenya Mt *HWTH* BD22 ......6 C3
Kenyon La *LUD/ILL* HX2 ......67 G1
Kershaw Crs *LUD/ILL* HX2 ......66 A1
Kershaw St *BFDE* BD3 ......40 C5
Kesteven Cl *BOW* BD4 ......49 E5
Kesteven Ct *BOW* BD4 ......49 E5
Kesteven Rd *BOW* BD4 ......48 E5
Kestrel Dr *ECHL* BD2 ......29 H5
Kestrel Mt *ECHL* BD2 ......29 H5
Kestrel Vw *CLECK* BD19 ......64 C4
Keswick Cl *HIPP* HX3 ......69 F5
Keswick St *BOW* BD4 ......48 C2
Kettlewell Dr *WBOW* BD5 ......46 C4
Khalaq St *BFDE* BD3 ......3 K3
Khus Wk *KGHY* BD21 ......14 A1
Kildare La *WIL/AL* BD15 ......36 D3
Killinghall Av *ECHL* BD2 ......40 A3
Killinghall Dr *ECHL* BD2 ......40 A3
Killinghall Gv *ECHL* BD2 ......40 A3
Killinghall Rd *BFDE* BD3 ......40 B3
Kilner Rd *WBSY* * BD6 ......54 B1
Kiln Fold *BRIG* HD6 ......72 A5
Kilnsea Mt *BOW* BD4 ......48 D4
Kilnsey Ms *BAIL* BD17 ......18 C3
Kilnsey Rd *BFDE* BD3 ......3 K6
Kilroyd Av *CLECK* BD19 ......64 C3
Kilroyd Dr *CLECK* BD19 ......64 D3

Kimberley Pl *HIPP* HX3 ......59 F1
Kimberley St *BFDE* BD3 ......48 B1
  BRIG HD6 ......71 G5
  HIPP HX3 ......59 F1
Kinara Cl *KGHY* BD21 ......8 A2
King Cross Rd *HFAX* HX1 ......4 B7
King Cross St *HFAX* HX1 ......4 C7
King Edward Rd *CUL/QBY* BD13 ......44 A1
King Edward St *HFAX* * HX1 ......5 H4
Kingfield *GSLY* LS20 ......11 E1
Kingfisher Ct *KGHY* * BD21 ......7 F4
Kingfisher Gv *GIR* BD8 ......37 F5
Kingsbury Pl *HFAX* HX1 ......4 A5
Kings Ct *HFAX* HX1 ......4 E5
Kingsdale Av *ECHL* BD2 ......39 H1
Kingsdale Crs *ECHL* BD2 ......39 H1
Kingsdale Dr *ECHL* BD2 ......39 H1
Kingsdale Gv *ECHL* BD2 ......39 G1
King's Dr *ECHL* BD2 ......29 G3
Kings Ga *BFDE* BD3 ......39 F3
Kings Gv *BGLY* BD16 ......16 D2
Kings Lea *HIPP* HX3 ......75 G1
Kingsley Av *BIRK/DRI* BD11 ......65 G1
  ECHL BD2 ......39 F1
  RPDN/SBR HX6 ......66 C5
Kingsley Cl *BIRK/DRI* BD11 ......65 G1
Kingsley Crs *BAIL* BD17 ......18 C4
  BIRK/DRI BD11 ......65 G1
Kingsley Dr *BIRK/DRI* BD11 ......65 G1
Kingsley Pl *HFAX* HX1 ......4 B6
King's Rd *BGLY* BD16 ......16 B1
  ECHL BD2 ......29 G4
  ECHL BD2 ......39 F2
Kingston Cl *HFAX* HX1 ......4 B5
  WIL/AL BD15 ......25 H5
Kingston Ct *HFAX* HX1 ......4 A6
Kingston Dr *HFAX* HX1 ......4 A5
Kingston Gv *IDLE* BD10 ......20 A5
Kingston Rd *IDLE* BD10 ......20 A5
Kingston St *HFAX* HX1 ......4 A5
King St *BRIG* HD6 ......78 C1
  CLECK BD19 ......64 D5
  HFAX HX1 ......5 J3
  IDLE BD10 ......30 B4
  KGHY BD21 ......7 E5
  RPDN/SBR * HX6 ......66 B5
  YEA LS19 ......11 H4
  YEA LS19 ......21 F2
Kings Vw *HIPP* HX3 ......69 H4
Kingsway *AIRE* BD20 ......8 B2
  BGLY BD16 ......16 D4
  ECHL BD2 ......29 G3
Kingswood Gn *HIPP* HX3 ......60 C4
Kingswood Pl *GTHN* BD7 ......46 B3
Kingswood St *GTHN* BD7 ......46 B3
Kingswood Ter *GTHN* * BD7 ......46 B3
Kinnaird Cl *ELL* HX5 ......76 C3
Kipling Ct *IDLE* BD10 ......30 C2
Kipping La *CUL/QBY* BD13 ......44 A1
Kipping Pl *CUL/QBY* BD13 ......44 A1
Kirby St *KGHY* BD21 ......7 G3
Kirkbourne Gv *BAIL* BD17 ......19 F4
Kirkburn Pl *GTHN* BD7 ......46 C1
Kirkby Leas *HFAX* HX1 ......5 G6
Kirk Dr *BAIL* BD17 ......19 E2
Kirkfields *BAIL* BD17 ......19 F2
Kirkgate *BFD* BD1 ......2 D5
  SHPY BD18 ......28 B2
Kirkham Rd *GTHN* * BD7 ......46 C1
Kirklands Av *BAIL* BD17 ......19 F4
  YEA LS19 ......11 F4
Kirklands Gdns *BAIL* BD17 ......19 F3
Kirklands La *BAIL* BD17 ......19 F4
Kirklands Rd *BAIL* BD17 ......19 E3
Kirklands Vls *BAIL* * BD17 ......19 F3
Kirk La *HIPP* HX3 ......61 F5
  YEA LS19 ......11 F4
Kirklees Rd *WIL/AL* BD15 ......37 G5
Kirklees Wy *BIRK/DRI* BD11 ......57 E5
  CLECK BD19 ......63 H2
  HUDN HD2 ......79 E5
Kirkley Av *LM/WK* BD12 ......62 D4
Kirkstall Gv *GIR* BD8 ......37 G5
Kirkstone Dr *CLECK* BD19 ......65 G5
  LUD/ILL HX2 ......58 A5
Kirkwall Dr *BOW* BD4 ......48 D4
Kismet Gdns *BFDE* BD3 ......40 B4
Kitchener St *LM/WK* BD12 ......55 H5
Kite Ms *GIR* BD8 ......37 F5
Kitson La *RPDN/SBR* HX6 ......74 C2
Kitson St *SHPY* BD18 ......28 D2
Kliffen Pl *HIPP* HX3 ......69 E4
Knightsbridge Wk *BOW* BD4 ......56 A2
Knight's Fold *GTHN* BD7 ......46 B3
Knight St *HFAX* HX1 ......4 B6
The Knoll *PDSY/CALV* LS28 ......41 F1
Knoll Park Dr *BAIL* BD17 ......18 C5

Knowle La *LM/WK* BD12 ......63 E3
Knowles Av *BOW* BD4 ......48 C5
Knowles La *BOW* BD4 ......48 C5
  CLECK BD19 ......65 G2
Knowles Rd *BRIG* HD6 ......78 B3
Knowles St *BOW* BD4 ......56 B1
  CUL/QBY BD13 ......34 C4
Knowles Vw *BOW* BD4 ......48 C5
Knowle Top Dr *HIPP* HX3 ......61 H5
Knowle Top Rd *HIPP* HX3 ......61 H5
Knowsley St *BFDE* BD3 ......3 H6
Knutsford Gv *BOW* BD4 ......48 D5
Knutsford Ms *BOW* * BD4 ......48 D5
Komla Cl *BFD* BD1 ......3 F4
Kyffin Pl *BOW* BD4 ......48 D2

L

Laburnum Dr *BAIL* BD17 ......19 E2
Laburnum Gv *BRIG* HD6 ......71 F2
  CLECK BD19 ......65 F4
  HWTH BD22 ......23 F1
Laburnum Pl *GIR* BD8 ......38 D3
  IDLE BD10 ......30 D1
Laburnum Rd *SHPY* BD18 ......29 E4
  PDSY/CALV LS28 ......41 H4
Laceby Cl *IDLE* BD10 ......30 B1
Lacy Wy *ELL* HX5 ......76 D3
Ladbroke Gv *BOW* * BD4 ......48 C5
Ladderbanks La *BAIL* BD17 ......19 E2
Lady La *BGLY* BD16 ......9 H5
Lady Park Av *BGLY* BD16 ......9 H5
Ladyroyd Dr *BIRK/DRI* BD11 ......56 D4
Ladysmith Rd *CUL/QBY* BD13 ......51 H2
Ladywell Cl *WBOW* BD5 ......47 F4
Ladywell La *LVSG* WF15 ......73 E5
Ladywood Ter *HFAX* HX1 ......4 C1
Laisterdyke *BFDE* BD3 ......48 C1
Laisteridge La *WBOW* BD5 ......46 D2
Laithe Gv *WBSY* BD6 ......46 B5
Laithe Rd *WBSY* BD6 ......54 C1
Lake Rw *BOW* BD4 ......48 A2
Lakeside *AIRE* BD20 ......9 F1
Lakeside Cha *YEA* LS19 ......21 H2
Lakeside Gdns *YEA* LS19 ......21 H2
Lakeside Ter *YEA* LS19 ......21 H2
Lakeside Vw *YEA* LS19 ......21 H2
Lake St *BOW* BD4 ......48 A2
  KGHY BD21 ......7 F2
Lake Vw *HFAX* HX1 ......5 F1
Lamb Cote Rd *HUDN* HD2 ......79 E5
Lambert Cl *GTL/HWG* HX4 ......76 A4
Lambert Pl *ECHL* BD2 ......40 A2
Lambert St *GTL/HWG* HX4 ......76 A4
Lambourne Av *IDLE* BD10 ......30 C4
Lampards Cl *WIL/AL* BD15 ......36 D2
Lancaster Ct *KGHY* BD21 ......14 A1
Landor St *KGHY* * BD21 ......7 G3
Landscove Av *BOW* BD4 ......48 D5
Lands Head La *HIPP* HX3 ......60 C1
Landsholme Ct *BOW* BD4 ......48 E5
Lands La *GSLY* LS20 ......10 D2
  IDLE BD10 ......30 B4
Landsmoor Gv *BGLY* BD16 ......16 C1
Lane End *CUL/QBY* BD13 ......44 A1
Lane Ends *LUD/ILL* HX2 ......58 D3
Lane Ends Cl *GIR* BD8 ......37 H4
Lane Ends Gn *HIPP* HX3 ......61 E5
Lane Head La *LUD/ILL* HX2 ......50 B2
Lane Side *CUL/QBY* BD13 ......44 A4
  WIL/AL BD15 ......25 G5
Lane Side Cl *LM/WK* BD12 ......62 D1
Lane Top *BRIG* * HD6 ......72 A1
Langbar Av *HTON* BD9 ......37 G1
Langdale Av *GIR* BD8 ......37 H4
  LM/WK BD12 ......63 F4
Langdale Cs *BGLY* BD16 ......16 D2
Langdale Crs *LUD/ILL* HX2 ......58 D4
Langdale Dr *CUL/QBY* BD13 ......52 A1
Langdale Rd *IDLE* BD10 ......30 D5
Langdale St *ELL* HX5 ......76 C5
Langlands Rd *BGLY* BD16 ......26 D2
Lang La *AIRE* * BD2 ......29 E5
Langley Av *BGLY* BD16 ......16 D2
  BOW BD4 ......56 A4
Langley Crs *BAIL* BD17 ......19 F3
Langley Gv *BGLY* BD16 ......16 D2
Langley La *BAIL* BD17 ......19 F2
Langley Pl *BGLY* BD16 ......16 D2
Langport Cl *CUL/QBY* BD13 ......52 D2
Langton Av *BOW* BD4 ......56 A4
Langton Cl *CLECK* BD19 ......65 F3
Langton St *RPDN/SBR* HX6 ......67 E3
Lansdale Ct *BOW* BD4 ......49 E5

Lansdowne Cl BAIL BD17 ....19 G3
Lansdowne Pl WBOW BD5 ....2 B7
Lapage St BFDE BD3 ....40 B5
Lapage Ter BFDE * BD3 ....40 B5
Lapwing Cl IGR BD8 ....37 E4
Larch Cl HWTH BD22 ....13 E3
Larch Dr WBSY BD6 ....54 D3
Larch Gv BGLY BD16 ....16 C1
Larch Hl WBSY BD6 ....55 E3
Larch Hill Crs WBSY BD6 ....55 E2
Larchmont CLAY BD14 ....45 F3
Larch St KGHY BD21 ....14 A2
Larkfield Av YEA LS19 ....21 H2
Larkfield Crs YEA LS19 ....21 H2
Larkfield Dr YEA LS19 ....21 H2
Larkfield Mt YEA LS19 ....21 H2
Larkfield Rd YEA LS19 ....21 H2
Larkfield Ter KGHY BD21 ....7 H5
Lark Hill Av CLECK BD19 ....73 G2
Lark Hill Dr CLECK BD19 ....73 E1
Lark St BGLY BD16 ....16 C3
  HWTH BD22 ....13 E4
  HWTH BD22 ....3 E4
  KGHY BD21 ....7 E4
Larwood Av IDLE BD10 ....30 D5
Lastingham Gn WBSY * BD6 ....53 H1
Latham St CLECK BD19 ....65 G3
Latham La CLECK BD19 ....65 F2
Latham Lea CLECK BD19 ....65 F4
Latimer St BFDE BD3 ....48 C1
Launceston Dr BOW BD4 ....48 D5
Launton Wy WBOW BD5 ....47 E3
Laura St BRIG HD6 ....78 B2
  HIPP HX3 ....59 H4
Laurel Bank BGLY * BD16 ....17 G2
Laurel Bank Cl LUD/ILL HX2 ....51 F4
Laurel Cl ELL HX5 ....76 B5
  HIPP HX3 ....53 F3
Laurel Crs KGHY BD21 ....7 E3
Laurel Gv BGLY BD16 ....16 B1
  KGHY BD21 ....7 E3
Laurel Mt HFAX * HX1 ....4 D7
Laurel Pk WIL/AL BD15 ....25 H5
The Laurels BGLY * BD16 ....17 E3
Laurel St BFDE BD3 ....48 B1
  HFAX HX1 ....4 D7
Lavender Hl IDLE BD10 ....30 D7
Laverhills LVSG WF15 ....73 G3
Laverock Crs BRIG HD6 ....71 E3
Laverock La BRIG HD6 ....71 E3
Laverton Rd BOW BD4 ....48 A3
Lavinia Ter CLAY BD14 ....45 G3
Lawcliffe Crs HWTH BD22 ....23 E1
Lawkholme Crs KGHY * BD21 ....7 F4
Lawkholme La KGHY BD21 ....7 F4
Law La HIPP HX3 ....69 H3
Lawnswood Rd KGHY BD21 ....13 H1
Lawrence Dr GTHN BD7 ....45 H5
Lawrence Rd HIPP HX3 ....68 C5
Lawrence St HIPP * HX3 ....59 F4
Lawson Rd BRIG HD6 ....78 C1
Lawson St BFDE BD3 ....2 E2
Law St BOW BD4 ....48 B5
  CLECK BD19 ....64 C4
Lea Av HIPP HX3 ....68 D5
Leach Crs AIRE BD20 ....7 H1
Leache's Br AIRE BD20 ....7 G1
Leach Ri AIRE BD20 ....7 H1
Leach Rd AIRE BD20 ....7 G1
Leach Wy AIRE BD20 ....7 H1
Lea Cl BRIG HD6 ....71 F4
Lea Ct HIPP HX3 ....45 H5
Leadenhall St HFAX HX1 ....4 B7
Leafield Av ECHL BD2 ....40 B1
Leafield Crs ECHL BD2 ....40 A1
Leafield Dr ECHL BD2 ....30 B5
Leafield Gv ECHL BD2 ....40 B1
Leafield Ter ECHL BD2 ....40 A1
Leafield Wy ECHL BD2 ....40 B1
Leafland St HFAX HX1 ....4 C4
Leaf St HWTH * BD22 ....23 F1
Leafsway WBSY * BD6 ....54 A4
Lea Mill Park Cl YEA LS19 ....11 F4
Lea Mill Park Dr YEA LS19 ....11 F4
Leamington Dr IDLE BD10 ....30 B1
Leamington St HTON BD9 ....38 C2
Leamside Wk BOW BD4 ....48 D5
Leaside Dr CUL/QBY BD13 ....36 A5
The Leavens IDLE BD10 ....30 C1
Leaventhorpe Av GIR BD8 ....37 F5
Leaventhorpe Cl GIR BD8 ....37 G5
Leaventhorpe Gv
  CUL/QBY BD13 ....45 F1
Leaventhorpe La
  CUL/QBY BD13 ....45 F1
Leaventhorpe Wy GIR BD8 ....37 G5
Leavington Cl LM/WK BD12 ....54 C1
Ledbury Pl BOW BD4 ....47 H3

Lee Bank HIPP HX3 ....59 G4
Lee Br HFAX HX1 ....5 F1
Leech La BGLY BD16 ....25 E1
Lee Cl WIL/AL BD15 ....25 H3
Lee Ct KGHY BD21 ....8 A5
Leeds Country Wy
  PDSY/CALV LS28 ....41 E1
Leeds Old Rd BFDE BD3 ....40 C4
Leeds Rd BFD BD1 ....3 F5
  ECHL BD2 ....40 A1
  GSLY LS20 ....10 D3
  HIPP HX3 ....60 D4
  HIPP HX3 ....61 G5
  SHPY BD18 ....29 E1
  YEA LS19 ....21 H3
Leeds St KGHY BD21 ....7 E4
Lee La HIPP HX3 ....60 A2
  HWTH BD22 ....32 A1
  WIL/AL BD15 ....25 G3
Leeming St BFD BD1 ....2 E3
Lee Mount Gdns HIPP HX3 ....59 F4
Lee Mount Rd HIPP HX3 ....59 F4
Lees Bank Av HWTH BD22 ....23 F1
Lees Bank Dr HWTH * BD22 ....23 F1
Lees Bank Hl HWTH BD22 ....23 F1
Lees Bank Rd HWTH BD22 ....23 F1
Lees Cl CUL/QBY BD13 ....24 B3
Lees La HWTH BD22 ....23 F1
Lees Moor Rd CUL/QBY BD13 ....24 B3
Lee St BFD BD1 ....2 C6
  BRIG HD6 ....71 F4
  CUL/QBY BD13 ....52 A2
Leesworth Ct HWTH * BD22 ....23 F1
Legrams Av GTHN BD7 ....46 A2
Legrams La GTHN BD7 ....46 B1
Legrams Mill La GTHN BD7 ....46 B1
Legrams St GTHN BD7 ....38 C5
Legrams Ter GTHN BD7 ....38 D5
Leicester St BOW BD4 ....47 H3
Leicester Ter HIPP BD7 ....68 C4
Leigh St RPDN/SBR HX6 ....67 F3
Leith St KGHY BD21 ....7 E3
Lemington Av HFAX HX1 ....4 D6
Lemon St HFAX HX1 ....4 D6
  WBOW BD5 ....46 D5
Lennie St KGHY BD21 ....7 E5
Lennon Dr GIR BD8 ....38 C5
Lens Dr BAIL BD17 ....18 D2
Lentilfield St HIPP HX3 ....59 F3
Lentilfield Ter HIPP HX3 ....59 F3
Lenton Vls IDLE BD10 ....20 A5
Leonard's Pl BGLY BD16 ....16 C4
Leonard St BGLY BD16 ....16 D4
  LM/WK BD12 ....63 E2
Leslie Av YEA LS19 ....11 G3
Lesmere Gv GTHN BD7 ....46 A5
Lessarna Ct BOW * BD4 ....48 B2
Lever St WBSY BD6 ....54 B1
Levita Gv BOW BD4 ....48 C3
Levita Pl BOW BD4 ....48 C3
Lewis Cl CUL/QBY BD13 ....52 A1
Lewis St HFAX HX1 ....5 F2
Lexington Cl BOW BD4 ....56 A2
Leyburn Av HIPP HX3 ....61 G5
Leyburne St GIR BD8 ....38 D3
Leyburn Gv BGLY BD16 ....16 D2
  SHPY BD18 ....28 B2
Leyden Ri WIL/AL BD15 ....37 E4
Leyfield BAIL BD17 ....18 B3
Ley Fleaks Rd IDLE BD10 ....30 A2
Leylands Av HTON BD9 ....38 A1
Leylands Gv HTON BD9 ....38 A1
Leylands La HTON BD9 ....38 A1
  KGHY BD21 ....7 G5
Leylands Ter HTON BD9 ....38 A1
Leys Cl IDLE BD10 ....19 H5
Leyside Dr WIL/AL BD15 ....37 E2
Leyton Crs IDLE * BD10 ....30 A2
Leyton Dr IDLE BD10 ....30 A2
Leyton Gv IDLE BD10 ....30 A2
Leyton Ter IDLE BD10 ....30 A2
Ley Top La WIL/AL BD15 ....37 F4
Libbey St GIR BD8 ....38 C3
Lichen Cl GTHN BD7 ....46 B4
Lichfield Mt ECHL BD2 ....29 F5
Lightcliffe Rd BRIG HD6 ....71 F4
Lightcliffe Royd La
  GTL/HWG HX4 ....74 B5
Lightowler Cl HFAX HX1 ....4 D3
Lightowler Rd HFAX HX1 ....4 D3
Lightowler St WBSY BD6 ....54 D1
Lilac Cl BRIG HD6 ....71 H5
Lilac Gv BOW BD4 ....48 C1
  CLECK BD19 ....65 F4

SHPY BD18 ....29 E4
The Lilacs GSLY LS20 ....10 D2
Lilac St HIPP HX3 ....59 F4
Lilian St BOW BD4 ....48 B4
Lillands Av BRIG HD6 ....78 A1
Lillands La BRIG HD6 ....78 A1
Lillands Ter BRIG HD6 ....78 A1
Lilly La HIPP HX3 ....5 J5
Lilly Cft GIR BD8 ....38 C2
Lilly St RPDN/SBR HX6 ....67 G5
Lilycroft Rd GIR BD8 ....38 B3
Lilycroft Wk HTON BD9 ....38 B2
Lily St GIR BD8 ....38 C2
Lilythorne Av IDLE BD10 ....30 B1
Lime Cl KGHY BD21 ....6 D2
Lime Gv YEA LS19 ....21 F2
Limes Av HIPP HX3 ....68 D4
Lime St BGLY BD16 ....16 C3
  GTHN BD7 ....46 B3
  HWTH BD22 ....22 D3
  KGHY BD21 ....7 G4
Lime Tree Gv BIRK/DRI * BD11 ....57 F3
Lime Tree Sq SHPY BD18 ....27 G1
Lincoln Rd GIR BD8 ....38 D3
Lincoln Wy HIPP HX3 ....59 G4
Lincs Wold LVSG WF15 ....73 E4
Linden Av BFDE BD3 ....40 D4
Linden Cl BRIG HD6 ....71 H5
Linden Ri KGHY BD21 ....14 D1
Linden Rd ELL HX5 ....76 B5
  HIPP HX3 ....68 D4
Lindisfarne Rd SHPY BD18 ....28 A2
Lindley Dr GTHN BD7 ....46 A5
Lindley Rd WBOW BD5 ....47 E4
Lindrick Gv LUD/ILL HX2 ....51 E3
Lindrick Wk LUD/ILL HX2 ....51 E3
Lindrick Wy LUD/ILL HX2 ....51 E3
Lindwell Av GTL/HWG HX4 ....75 H4
Lindwell Gv GTL/HWG HX4 ....75 H4
Lingard St BFD BD1 ....2 E3
Ling Bob LUD/ILL HX2 ....58 C5
Ling Bob Cft LUD/ILL HX2 ....58 C4
Lingdale Rd LM/WK BD12 ....54 B4
Lingfield Crs WBSY BD6 ....45 F5
Lingfield Dr HWTH BD22 ....13 H5
Lingfield Gv WIL/AL BD15 ....26 A4
Lingfield Rd WIL/AL BD15 ....25 H5
Lingfield Ter WBSY BD6 ....45 F5
Ling Park Ap WIL/AL BD15 ....25 H5
Ling Park Av WIL/AL BD15 ....25 H5
Ling Royd Av LUD/ILL HX2 ....58 C5
Lingwood Av GIR BD8 ....38 A3
Lingwood Rd GIR BD8 ....38 A4
Lingwood Ter GIR BD8 ....38 A4
Links Av CLECK BD19 ....64 C4
Linkway BGLY BD16 ....26 D2
Linnet Cl GIR * BD8 ....37 F4
Linnet St KGHY BD21 ....7 F3
Linnhe Av WBSY BD6 ....54 A4
Linton Gv BRIG HD6 ....77 H3
Linton St BOW BD4 ....47 G3
  HWTH BD22 ....13 G1
Lismore Rd KGHY BD21 ....7 E3
Lister Av BOW BD4 ....48 A4
Lister Ct HFAX HX1 ....5 G4
Lister Gdns GIR BD8 ....38 D2
Listerhills Rd BFD BD1 ....2 A5
  GTHN BD7 ....38 D5
Lister La ECHL BD2 ....39 G2
  HFAX HX1 ....4 D4
Lister's Rd HIPP HX3 ....60 B5
Lister St BOW BD4 ....48 B5
  BRIG HD6 ....71 F5
  HFAX HX1 ....5 H3
  KGHY BD21 ....7 E5
Lister Vw GIR BD8 ....38 D3
Little Baines St HFAX HX1 ....4 C3
Littlebeck Dr BGLY BD16 ....17 F3
Little Bradley GTL/HWG HX4 ....75 H5
Little Cote IDLE BD10 ....19 H5
Little Cross St WBSY BD6 ....47 F5
Littlefield Wk WBSY BD6 ....54 C2
Little Hew Royd IDLE BD10 ....29 G1
Little Horton Gn WBOW BD5 ....46 D2
Little Horton La WBOW BD5 ....2 C6
Littlelands BGLY BD16 ....26 D2
Littlelands Ct BGLY * BD16 ....26 D2
Little La AIRE BD20 ....9 F3
  HTON BD9 ....38 A2
Littlemoor CUL/QBY BD13 ....52 D1
Littlemoor Gdns LUD/ILL HX2 ....50 D4
Littlemoor Rd LUD/ILL HX2 ....50 D4
Little Pk IDLE BD10 ....20 D5
Littlewood Cl WBSY BD6 ....54 D3
Little Wood Dr CLECK BD19 ....64 C3
Little Woodhouse BRIG HD6 ....78 B1
Littondale Cl BAIL BD17 ....19 F2

Litton Rd HWTH BD22 ....6 D5
Livingstone Cl ECHL BD2 ....29 G3
Livingstone Rd SHPY BD18 ....29 E5
Livingstone St HIPP HX3 ....59 F4
Livingstone St North
  LUD/ILL HX2 ....51 F5
Lloyds Dr LM/WK BD12 ....55 F4
Locarno Av HTON BD9 ....37 H2
Locherbie Gn WIL/AL * BD15 ....36 D3
Lochy Rd WBSY BD6 ....54 A4
The Locks BGLY BD16 ....16 C2
Locksley Rd BRIG HD6 ....79 E2
Lock St HIPP * HX3 ....5 K6
Lock Vw ELL HX5 ....77 F4
Lockwood St LM/WK BD12 ....55 F5
  SHPY * BD18 ....28 A1
  WBSY BD6 ....54 D1
Lode Pit La BGLY BD16 ....17 G2
Lodge Av ELL HX5 ....77 F4
Lodge Dr ELL HX5 ....77 F4
Lodge Gate Cl CUL/QBY BD13 ....34 D3
Lodge Hl LUD/ILL HX2 ....18 A3
Lodge Pl ELL * HX5 ....77 F4
Lodge St CUL/QBY BD13 ....24 C3
Lodore Pl ECHL BD2 ....40 A1
Lodore Rd ECHL BD2 ....39 H1
Loft St GIR BD8 ....38 A4
Lombard St HFAX HX1 ....4 B7
  YEA LS19 ....21 F2
London La YEA LS19 ....21 F2
London Rd RPDN/SBR HX6 ....67 G5
London St YEA LS19 ....21 F2
Longacre La HWTH BD22 ....23 E1
Longacres HWTH BD22 ....23 F1
Longbottom Av RPDN/SBR HX6 ....66 B5
Longbottom Ter HIPP * HX3 ....69 E4
Long Cswy HWTH BD22 ....33 H3
Long Cl LM/WK BD12 ....62 C1
Longcroft KGHY BD21 ....7 F5
Longcroft Pl BFD BD1 ....2 B5
Long Fallas Crs BRIG HD6 ....78 C4
Longfield Av BOW BD4 ....48 A4
Longfield Dr BOW BD4 ....48 B4
Longford Ter BRIG HD6 ....46 A2
Long Heys GTL/HWG HX4 ....75 H2
Longhouse Dr CUL/QBY BD13 ....34 C4
Longhouse La CUL/QBY BD13 ....34 C4
Long House Rd LUD/ILL HX2 ....50 B4
Longlands Av CUL/QBY BD13 ....34 C3
Longlands Dr HWTH BD22 ....23 E1
Longlands St BFD BD1 ....2 B4
Long La BGLY BD16 ....15 F5
  CUL/QBY BD13 ....52 B3
  HIPP HX3 ....58 D3
  HIPP HX3 ....69 G2
  HTON BD9 ....27 G4
  WIL/AL BD15 ....36 C1
Long Lee La KGHY BD21 ....14 C1
Long Lee Ter KGHY BD21 ....14 D1
Long Mdw ECHL BD2 ....29 F5
Long Preston Cha IDLE * BD10 ....30 D2
Long Rdg BRIG HD6 ....78 B4
Long Rw LM/WK BD12 ....55 E5
Long Royd Dr BAIL BD17 ....19 F2
Longroyde Cl BRIG HD6 ....78 A3
Longroyde Gv BRIG HD6 ....78 A3
Longroyde Rd BRIG HD6 ....78 A2
Longside La GTHN BD7 ....46 D1
Long St BOW BD4 ....48 A2
Long Wall ELL HX5 ....76 B5
Longwood Av BGLY BD16 ....16 B1
Longwood Vw BGLY BD16 ....16 B1
Lonsdale St BFDE BD3 ....3 J3
Lord La HWTH BD22 ....22 C1
Lordsfield Pl BOW BD4 ....56 C1
Lord's La BRIG HD6 ....78 C2
Lord St HFAX HX1 ....5 F4
  KGHY BD21 ....7 F4
  RPDN/SBR HX6 ....67 F3
Loris St BOW BD4 ....56 C1
Lorne St BOW BD4 ....48 A4
  HWTH BD22 ....23 G1
  HIPP HX3 ....7 H3
Loughrigg St WBOW BD5 ....47 F4
Louisa St IDLE * BD10 ....30 A1
Louis Av WBOW BD5 ....46 D3
Love La HFAX HX1 ....5 F6
Low Ash Av SHPY BD18 ....29 E2
Low Ash Crs SHPY BD18 ....29 E2
Low Ash Dr SHPY BD18 ....29 E2
Low Ash Gv SHPY BD18 ....29 E2
Low Ash Rd SHPY BD18 ....29 F2
Low Bank Dr HWTH BD22 ....12 C3
Low Bank La HWTH BD22 ....12 C3
Low Banks AIRE * BD20 ....8 A1
Low Bank St PDSY/CALV LS28 ....41 H1
Low Cl BGLY BD16 ....17 E4

Lowell Av GTHN BD7 ....46 A2
Lower Ashgrove WBOW BD5 .....2 B7
Lower Clifton St
  RPDN/SBR * HX6 ....67 F4
Lower Clyde St RPDN/SBR HX6 ...67 E5
Lower Cow St LM/WK BD12 ....63 G3
Lower Cross St HFAX HX1 ....5 J2
Lower Crow Nest Dr BRIG HD6 ...71 G1
Lower Edge Rd ELL HX5 ....77 E4
Lower Ellistones
  GTL/HWG * HX4 ....75 H4
Lower Finkil St BRIG HD6 ....70 D3
Lower Fold BRIG HD6 ....78 A5
Lower George St WBSY * BD6 ......54 C1
Lower Globe St GIR BD8 ....38 D4
Lower Gra HUDN HD2 ....79 F5
Lower Grattan Rd BFD BD1 ....2 A5
Lower Green Av CLECK BD19 ......63 G5
Lower Heights Rd
  CUL/QBY BD13 ....35 H4
Lower Holme BAIL BD17 ....18 D5
Lower House Cl SHPY BD18 ....19 G5
Lower Kipping La
  CUL/QBY BD13 ....44 A1
Lower Kirkgate HFAX HX1 ....5 K4
Lower Lane BIRK/DRI BD11 ....56 C5
  BOW BD4 ....48 B3
Lower Lark HI CLECK BD19 ....73 E1
Lower Newlands BRIG HD6 ....78 C2
Lower Quarry Rd HUDN HD2 ....79 F5
Lower Range HIPP HX3 ....59 H4
Lower Rushton Rd BFDE BD3 ......40 D5
Lower School St LM/WK BD12 ......54 D4
  SHPY * BD18 ....28 A1
Lowertown HWTH BD22 ....32 D2
Lower Westfield Rd GIR * BD8 ......38 B3
Lower Wyke Gn LM/WK BD12 ....62 C5
Lower Wyke La LM/WK BD12 ....62 D5
Loweswater Av WBSY BD6 ....54 A4
Lowfield Cl LM/WK BD12 ....55 F5
Lowfields Cl ELL HX5 ....76 D3
Lowfields Wy ELL HX5 ....76 D3
Low Fold CLECK BD19 ....63 G5
  ECHL BD2 ....39 G2
  YEA LS19 ....21 H3
Low Gn GTHN BD7 ....46 B3
Low Green Ter GTHN BD7 ....46 B3
Low La BRIG HD6 ....71 H2
  CLAY BD14 ....44 D2
  CUL/QBY BD13 ....43 H4
Low Mill La KGHY BD21 ....7 G4
Low Mills GSLY * LS20 ....10 D3
Low Moor St LM/WK * BD12 ....55 E4
Low Moor Ter LUD/ILL HX2 ....67 G2
Lowry Vw KGHY BD21 ....7 F5
Low Spring Rd KGHY BD21 ....7 H5
Low St KGHY BD21 ....7 F4
Lowther St ECHL BD2 ....40 A3
Low Well Rd WBOW * BD5 ....47 E4
Low Wd WIL/AL BD15 ....26 A5
Lucy Hall Dr BAIL BD17 ....17 H4
Lucy St HIPP HX3 ....5 K1
Luddenden La LUD/ILL HX2 ....66 A1
Ludlam St WBOW BD5 ....47 F2
Luke Rd WBOW BD5 ....46 D3
Lulworth Gv BOW BD4 ....38 D3
Lumb La GIR BD8 ....38 D3
  HIPP HX3 ....59 G3
Lumbrook Cl HIPP HX3 ....61 F2
Lumby St IDLE * BD10 ....30 A1
Lund St BGLY BD16 ....16 D3
  GIR BD8 ....37 H5
  KGHY BD21 ....7 F3
Lupton St GIR BD8 ....2 B1
Lustre St KGHY BD21 ....6 D4
Luther Wy ECHL BD2 ....39 G1
Luton St HFAX HX1 ....4 B3
  KGHY BD21 ....7 E4
Lydbrook Pk HIPP HX3 ....75 F1
Lydgate Av BRIG HD6 ....78 B4
Lydgate Dr SHPY BD18 ....60 D2
Lydgate Pk HIPP HX3 ....70 D1
Lydgate Pl PDSY/CALV LS28 ....31 F2
Lydgate St PDSY/CALV LS28 ....31 F2
Lydget Ct AIRE BD20 ....6 D2
Lymington Dr BOW BD4 ....48 D3
Lynch Av GTHN BD7 ....46 A4
Lyncroft ECHL BD2 ....29 G5
Lyndale Dr SHPY BD18 ....29 G2
Lyndale Pk SHPY BD18 ....29 G2
Lynden Av SHPY BD18 ....29 F1
Lynden Ct WBSY BD6 ....54 B3
Lyndhurst Av BRIG HD6 ....78 B4
Lyndhurst Cl WBSY BD6 ....16 C2
Lyndhurst Gv WIL/AL BD15 ....37 F3
Lyndhurst Grove Rd BRIG HD6 ....78 B4
Lyndhurst Rd BRIG HD6 ....78 B4
Lyndon Ter BGLY BD16 ....16 D3

Lynfield Dr HTON BD9 ....37 G1
  LVSG WF15 ....73 E3
Lynfield Mt SHPY BD18 ....29 F1
Lynmoor Ct IDLE BD10 ....29 H2
Lynwood Gdns
  PDSY/CALV LS28 ....49 H1
Lynsey Gdns BOW BD4 ....56 A3
Lynthorne Rd HTON BD9 ....28 D5
Lynton Av HTON BD9 ....38 A1
Lynton Dr AIRE BD20 ....8 A2
  HTON BD9 ....37 H2
Lynton St BFD BD1 ....28 B2
Lynton Gv LUD/ILL HX2 ....51 E1
Lynton Ter CLECK * BD19 ....64 C5
Lynton Vls HTON BD9 ....38 A2
Lynwood Av SHPY BD18 ....25 H4
Lynwood Cl BIRK/DRI BD11 ....57 G5
Lynwood Ct HWTH BD22 ....13 F1
Lynwood Crs HFAX HX1 ....4 A7
Lynwood Ms BOW BD4 ....49 E5
Lyon St CUL/QBY BD13 ....36 A5
  CUL/QBY BD13 ....52 C1
Lytham Dr CUL/QBY BD13 ....45 E5
Lytton Rd GIR BD8 ....38 A4
Lytton St HIPP * HX3 ....59 H4

M

Mabel Royd GTHN BD7 ....46 A2
Mackingstone Dr HWTH BD22 ......12 C3
Mackingstone La HWTH BD22 ......12 C3
Mackintosh Gv GIR * BD8 ....38 B3
Mackintosh Homes LUD/ILL HX2 ..68 B4
Macturk Gv GIR * BD8 ....38 B3
Maddocks St SHPY BD18 ....28 B1
Madison Av BOW BD4 ....56 D1
Madni Cl HFAX HX1 ....4 E4
Magpie Cl WBSY BD6 ....53 F1
Maidstone St BFDE BD3 ....40 B5
Maidwell Wy WBSY BD6 ....54 B4
Main Rd AIRE BD20 ....8 C3
  CUL/QBY BD13 ....34 C4
Mainspring Rd WIL/AL BD15 ....25 H4
Main St BAIL BD17 ....20 B1
  BGLY BD16 ....16 C3
  BGLY BD16 ....27 E3
  HWTH BD22 ....22 D2
  LM/WK BD12 ....55 F4
  LM/WK BD12 ....62 D1
  WIL/AL BD15 ....25 H4
Maister Pl HWTH BD22 ....12 C3
Maitland Cl WIL/AL BD15 ....37 E5
Maize St HWTH * BD22 ....13 H2
Malham Av BRIG HD6 ....78 B4
  HTON BD9 ....37 F1
Malham Rd BRIG HD6 ....78 B4
Mallard Cl IDLE BD10 ....30 B4
Mallard St BFDE BD3 ....37 F5
Mallard Vw HWTH BD22 ....32 D2
Mallory Cl GTHN BD7 ....37 H5
Malmesbury Cl BOW BD4 ....48 D5
Malsis Crs KGHY * BD21 ....6 D5
Malsis Rd KGHY BD21 ....6 D5
Maltings Rd LUD/ILL HX2 ....58 C3
Malt Kiln La CUL/QBY BD13 ....43 G2
Malton St HIPP HX3 ....59 H5
  RPDN/SBR HX6 ....?
Malt St HWTH * BD22 ....13 H2
Malvern Brow HTON BD9 ....37 G2
Malvern Gv HTON BD9 ....37 G3
Malvern Rd HTON BD9 ....37 G3
Manchester Rd WBSY BD6 ....55 E4
Mandale Gv WBSY BD6 ....53 G2
Mandale Rd WBSY BD6 ....53 G2
Mandeville Crs WBSY BD6 ....54 A2
Manley St BRIG HD6 ....71 F5
Mannheim Rd HTON BD9 ....38 B2
Manningham La GIR BD8 ....38 D2
Mannville Gv HWTH BD22 ....6 D5
Mannville Pl HWTH BD22 ....6 D5
Mannville Rd KGHY BD21 ....13 H1
Mannville St HWTH BD22 ....6 D5
Mannville Ter GTHN BD7 ....2 B7
Mannville Wk HWTH * BD22 ....6 D5
Mannville Wy HWTH * BD22 ....6 D5
Manor Cl GIR BD8 ....37 G4
  HIPP HX3 ....68 C4
  YEA LS19 ....11 G4
Manor Ct BGLY * BD16 ....26 B2
Manor Dr BGLY BD16 ....26 B2
  HIPP HX3 ....68 C4
Manor Farm Cl BGLY BD16 ....27 E3
Manor Fold BGLY BD16 ....27 E3
Manor Gdns CUL/QBY BD13 ....24 C4
Manor Gv AIRE BD20 ....8 B3
Manor Heath Rd HIPP HX3 ....68 C4
Manor House Rd WIL/AL BD15 .....25 H3

Manor La SHPY BD18 ....28 C2
Manorley La HIPP HX3 ....53 H4
Manor Pk GIR BD8 ....37 G4
  HWTH BD22 ....12 D4
Manor Park Gdns CLECK BD19 .....65 F2
Manor Rd AIRE BD20 ....6 D1
  BGLY BD16 ....27 E2
Manor Rw BFD BD1 ....2 C3
  WBSY BD6 ....54 D3
Manor Sq YEA LS19 ....11 G4
Manor St CLECK BD19 ....72 C2
  ECHL BD2 ....40 A1
Manor Ter ECHL BD2 ....40 A1
Manscombe Rd WIL/AL BD15 ....37 F3
Mansel Ms BOW BD4 ....56 D1
Manse St BFDE BD3 ....40 B5
Mansfield Av BGLY BD16 ....17 F5
Mansfield Rd GIR BD8 ....38 D2
Mansion La HIPP HX3 ....68 D4
Manywells Brow CUL/QBY BD13 ...24 B4
Manywells Crs CUL/QBY BD13 .....24 C4
Manywells La CUL/QBY BD13 ....24 A4
Maple Av BFDE BD3 ....40 D4
  HWTH BD22 ....13 E4
Maple Gv CLECK BD19 ....65 F4
  KGHY BD21 ....6 D2
Maple St HFAX HX1 ....4 B7
Marbridge Ct WBSY BD6 ....46 C5
Marchbank Rd BFDE BD3 ....40 B4
March Cote La BGLY BD16 ....26 D3
Marchwood Gv CLAY BD14 ....45 G2
Margaret St HFAX HX1 ....4 A7
  KGHY BD21 ....7 F2
Margate Rd BOW BD4 ....47 H3
Margate St RPDN/SBR HX6 ....66 D5
Marion Dr SHPY BD18 ....28 D2
Marion St BGLY * BD16 ....16 D3
  BRIG HD6 ....71 H4
  GTHN BD7 ....38 D5
Mark Cl IDLE BD10 ....30 B1
Market Ar CLECK * BD19 ....73 H1
Market Balcony HFAX * HX1 ....5 H4
Market Ct CUL/QBY BD13 ....44 B1
Market Pl CLECK BD19 ....73 H1
  KGHY BD21 ....7 F4
Market Sq SHPY BD18 ....28 C1
Market Stall HFAX * HX1 ....5 H4
Market St BFD BD1 ....5 F4
  BGLY BD16 ....16 C3
  BRIG HD6 ....78 C1
  CLECK BD19 ....73 H1
  CUL/QBY BD13 ....44 B1
  HFAX HX1 ....5 H4
  KGHY BD21 ....7 F3
  SHPY BD18 ....28 C2
  WBSY * BD6 ....54 D1
Markfield Av LM/WK BD12 ....54 D5
Markfield Cl LM/WK BD12 ....54 D5
Markfield Crs LM/WK BD12 ....54 D5
Markfield Dr LM/WK BD12 ....54 D5
Markham Av YEA LS19 ....21 H1
Markham Crs YEA LS19 ....21 H1
Markham Cft YEA LS19 ....21 H1
Mark St WBOW BD5 ....47 F4
Marland Rd KGHY BD21 ....7 H3
Marlborough Av HIPP HX3 ....68 C4
Marlborough Rd GIR BD8 ....38 D3
  SHPY BD18 ....28 B2
Marlborough St KGHY BD21 ....7 F3
Maridon Rd HIPP HX3 ....60 D4
Marley Cl GIR BD8 ....37 H4
Marley Cottages KGHY * BD21 ....8 A4
Marley Ct AIRE BD20 ....9 E4
Marley La CUL/QBY BD13 ....44 B4
Marley Rd KGHY BD21 ....8 A3
Marley St BFDE BD3 ....3 E5
  KGHY BD21 ....7 E5
Marley Vw AIRE BD20 ....9 E4
Marlott Rd SHPY BD18 ....29 E1
Marlow St KGHY BD21 ....7 E4
Marmion Av GIR BD8 ....37 F5
Marne Av CLAY BD14 ....45 F4
Marne Crs IDLE BD10 ....30 A2
Marquis Av LM/WK BD12 ....56 A5
Marriner Rd KGHY BD21 ....7 F5
Marriner's Dr HTON BD9 ....28 C5
Marriner's Wk KGHY BD21 ....14 B1
Marriner Wk KGHY BD21 ....14 B1
Marsh PDSY/CALV LS28 ....41 H5
Marshall St KGHY BD21 ....7 E2
  YEA LS19 ....11 G4
Marsh Ct PDSY/CALV LS28 ....41 H5
Marsh Delves La HIPP HX3 ....69 G2
Marshfield Pl WBOW BD5 ....47 E4
Marshfield St WBOW BD5 ....47 E4
Marsh Gv WBOW BD5 ....46 D4
Marsh La BIRK/DRI BD11 ....65 F1
  HIPP HX3 ....69 G2

Marsh St CLECK BD19 ....73 H2
  WBOW BD5 ....46 D4
Marsh Ter PDSY/CALV LS28 ....41 H5
Marshway HFAX HX1 ....4 D2
Marsland Ct CLECK BD19 ....64 C3
Marsland Pl BFDE BD3 ....40 C5
Marston Cl CUL/QBY BD13 ....52 C3
Marten Rd WBOW BD5 ....46 D4
Martin Green La GTL/HWG HX4 ....75 H4
Martin St BRIG * HD6 ....71 G5
Martlett Dr WBOW BD5 ....47 G5
Marton Ct BFDE BD3 ....40 C5
Mary St BOW BD4 ....48 B2
  BRIG HD6 ....71 F4
  CUL/QBY BD13 ....34 D3
  CUL/QBY BD13 ....44 A1
  ECHL BD2 ....32 D2
  LM/WK BD12 ....62 D1
  SHPY BD18 ....28 A1
Maryville Av BRIG HD6 ....71 E3
Masefield Av HTON BD9 ....37 F1
Masefield St GSLY LS20 ....11 E3
Masham Pl HTON BD9 ....38 A2
Masonic St HFAX HX1 ....67 G2
Massey Flds HWTH BD22 ....23 E1
Master La LUD/ILL HX2 ....68 A4
Matlock St HIPP HX3 ....59 F4
Matthew Cl AIRE BD20 ....7 H2
Maude Av BAIL BD17 ....18 D4
Maude Crs RPDN/SBR HX6 ....66 B5
Maude St GTL/HWG HX4 ....76 A4
  HIPP HX3 ....59 F1
Maudsley St BFDE BD3 ....3 H5
Maud St BFDE BD3 ....3 J6
Maurice Av BRIG HD6 ....79 G1
Mavis St BFDE BD3 ....3 J4
Mawcroft Cl YEA LS19 ....21 F1
Mawcroft Grange Dr YEA LS19 .....21 F1
Mawson St SHPY BD18 ....28 A1
Maw St BOW BD4 ....47 G2
Maxwell Rd WBSY BD6 ....54 A2
May Av CUL/QBY BD13 ....44 B1
Mayfair WBOW BD5 ....47 E3
Mayfair Wy BOW BD4 ....48 C2
Mayfield Av BRIG HD6 ....62 C5
  HFAX HX1 ....4 C6
  LM/WK BD12 ....62 D2
Mayfield Dr AIRE BD20 ....8 D3
  HFAX HX1 ....4 C6
Mayfield Gdns HFAX HX1 ....4 C6
Mayfield Gv BAIL BD17 ....19 E3
  BRIG HD6 ....62 C5
  HFAX HX1 ....4 C6
  WIL/AL BD15 ....25 G3
Mayfield Mt HFAX * HX1 ....4 C6
Mayfield Pl LM/WK BD12 ....62 D2
Mayfield Ri LM/WK BD12 ....63 E2
Mayfield Rd KGHY BD21 ....7 E3
Mayfield St HFAX HX1 ....4 C6
Mayfield Ter CLAY BD14 ....45 F3
  HFAX HX1 ....4 C6
  LM/WK BD12 ....63 E2
Mayfield Ter South HFAX * HX1 ......4 D6
Mayfield Vw LM/WK BD12 ....63 E2
Mayo Av WBOW BD5 ....47 E5
Mayo Crs WBOW BD5 ....55 F1
Mayo Dr WBOW BD5 ....55 F1
Mayo Gv WBOW BD5 ....55 F1
Mayo Rd WBOW BD5 ....55 F1
Mayster Gv BRIG HD6 ....77 H4
Mayster Rd BRIG HD6 ....77 H4
May St CLECK BD19 ....64 C5
  HWTH BD22 ....23 E3
  KGHY BD21 ....7 F3
Maythorne Crs CLAY BD14 ....45 G3
Maythorne Dr CLAY BD14 ....45 H3
May Tree Cl CLAY BD14 ....45 G2
Mayville Av AIRE BD20 ....8 D3
Mazebrook Av CLECK BD19 ....64 D3
Mazebrook Crs CLECK BD19 ....64 C3
McMahon Dr CUL/QBY BD13 ....45 F5
McMillan Gdns WBSY BD6 ....55 G4
Meadowbank Av WIL/AL BD15 ......37 E3
Meadow Cl BGLY BD16 ....15 G5
  HIPP HX3 ....53 G4
Meadow Cft BRIG HD6 ....79 F1
  WIL/AL BD15 ....26 D5
Meadow Crs HIPP HX3 ....58 D3
Meadow Cft HWTH BD22 ....6 B5
Meadow Croft Cl IDLE BD10 ....29 G1
Meadowcroft Ri BOW BD4 ....56 B2
Meadow Dr HIPP HX3 ....58 D3
Meadowlands CLECK BD19 ....63 G4
Meadow La HIPP HX3 ....58 D3
Meadow Park Crs
  PDSY/CALV LS28 ....41 G2

Meadow Park Dr
  PDSY/CALV LS28 .....41 G2
Meadow Rd IDLE BD10 .....30 D1
The Meadows WBSY BD6 .....54 D1
Meadow Vw HWTH BD22 .....13 E4
  LM/WK BD12 .....62 D4
Meadow Wk HIPP HX3 .....58 D3
Mead Vw BOW * BD4 .....48 D4
Meadway WBSY BD6 .....53 H4
Mearclough Rd RPDN/SBR HX6...67 G4
Medley La HIPP HX3 .....60 C1
Medway PDSY/CALV LS28 .....41 H3
Medway CUL/QBY BD13 .....52 C2
Meggison Gv WBOW BD5 .....46 D3
Megnaway WBOW BD5. .....47 F3
Melba Rd GTHN BD7 .....46 C4
Melbourne Gv BFDE BD3 .....40 D4
Melbourne Pl WBOW BD5. .....47 E2
Melbourne St HIPP HX3 .....59 F4
  SHPY BD18 .....28 B1
Melbourne Ter WBOW BD5 .....47 E2
Melcombe Wk BOW BD4 .....48 D3
Melford St BOW BD4 .....48 B5
  HFAX HX1 .....68 B3
Mellor St BRIG * HD6 .....78 C1
  HFAX HX1 .....68 B3
Melrose St GTHN BD7 .....46 B3
  HIPP HX3 .....59 F4
Melrose Ter ELL * HX5 .....76 C5
Melton Ms HWTH BD22 .....23 E2
Melton Ter IDLE BD10 .....30 D4
Melville St GTHN BD7 .....38 D5
Mendip Wy LM/WK BD12 .....54 C4
Menin Dr BAIL BD17 .....18 C1
Menstone St GIR BD8 .....38 D4
Merchants Ct BOW BD4 .....47 H2
Merlin Ct KGHY BD21 .....14 A1
Merlin Gv GIR BD8 .....37 F5
Merlinwood Dr BAIL BD17 .....19 E2
Merrivale Rd WIL/AL BD15 .....36 C4
Merrydale Rd BOW BD4 .....55 H4
Merton Dr PDSY/CALV LS28 .....41 H2
Merton Fold WBOW BD5 .....47 E3
Merton Gdns PDSY/CALV LS28 .....41 H2
Merton Rd GTHN BD7 .....46 D2
Merville Av BAIL BD17 .....18 D1
Metcalfe St BOW BD4 .....48 A3
Methuen Ov LM/WK BD12 .....62 D4
Miall St HFAX HX1 .....4 C2
Mickledore Cl GTHN * BD7 .....45 H4
Mickledore Rdg GTHN BD7...45 H4
Micklefield Ct YEA LS19 .....21 G2
Micklefield La YEA LS19 .....21 F2
Micklefield Ms YEA * LS19 .....21 F2
Micklefield Rd YEA LS19 .....21 G2
Micklemoss Dr CUL/QBY BD13...43 H5
Micklethwaite Dr
  CUL/QBY BD13 .....52 B2
Micklethwaite La BGLY BD16...9 F5
Middlebrook Cl GIR BD8 .....37 H5
Middlebrook Crs GIR BD8 .....45 G1
Middlebrook Dr GIR BD8 .....37 G5
Middlebrook Hl GIR BD8 .....37 G5
Middlebrook Ri GIR BD8 .....37 G5
Middlebrook Vw GIR BD8 .....37 H5
Middlebrook Wk GIR BD8 .....37 H5
Middlebrook Wy GIR BD8 .....45 G1
Middle Dean St GTL/HWG HX4...75 H4
Middlegate Ct BOW * BD4 .....56 A2
Middleham Ct BOW * BD4 .....48 C4
Middle La CLAY BD14 .....45 F2
Middleton Ct LVSG WF15 .....73 H4
Middleton St GIR BD8 .....38 C3
Middle Wy KGHY BD21 .....7 H3
Midgeham Gv BGLY BD16 .....15 F5
Midgeley Rd BAIL BD17 .....18 B5
Midland Hl BGLY BD16 .....16 C3
Midland Rd BAIL BD17 .....19 E4
  GIR BD8 .....39 E2
  HTON BD9 .....28 D4
Midland Ter ECHL BD2 .....39 F2
  HTON BD9 .....28 D4
  KGHY BD21 .....7 F3
Mid Point BFDE BD3 .....41 E4
Midway Av BGLY BD16 .....26 D2
Mile Cross Gdns HFAX HX1...67 H2
Mile Cross Pl HFAX HX1 .....67 H2
Mile Cross Rd HFAX HX1 .....67 H2
Mile Cross Ter HFAX HX1 .....67 H2
Miles Hill Crs BOW BD4 .....56 B1
Mile Hill Dr BOW BD4 .....56 B1
Mile Thorn St HFAX HX1 .....4 B4
Milford Gv CLECK BD19 .....65 F2
Milford Pl HTON BD9 .....38 B1
Millbeck Cl GIR BD8 .....45 F1
Millbeck Dr BGLY BD16 .....15 F5
Mill Carr Hill Rd BOW BD4...56 A4
Mill Ct HWTH BD22 .....32 D2
Millgate BFD BD1 .....2 C5

Millersdale Cl BOW BD4 .....55 H3
Millgate ELL HX5 .....76 C4
Mill Gv BRIG HD6 .....71 E4
Millhaven Ms GIR BD8 .....38 D2
Mill Hey HWTH BD22 .....23 E2
Mill Hl HWTH BD22 .....22 D2
Mill Hill La BRIG HD6 .....71 E4
  BRIG HD6 .....79 C2
Mill Hill Top BGLY BD16 .....25 C1
Mill House Ri BOW * BD4 .....56 A1
Milligan Av ECHL * BD2 .....29 G4
Milligan Ct CLECK BD19 .....15 F5
Mill La BIRK/DRI BD11 .....57 F4
  BRIG HD6 .....78 C1
  CLECK BD19 .....64 C2
  CUL/QBY BD13 .....43 H5
  HIPP HX3 .....59 G3
  HIPP HX3 .....53 G3
  HWTH BD22 .....12 C4
  HWTH BD22 .....32 D1
  LUD/ILL HX2 .....50 B3
  WBOW BD5 .....47 F2
Millmoor Cl HTON BD9 .....37 G2
Mill Royd St BRIG HD6 .....78 C1
Mill St BFD BD1 .....2 E5
  CUL/QBY BD13 .....24 C3
  HIPP HX3 .....75 F2
  WBSY BD6 .....54 B1
Milner Cl GTL/HWG HX4 .....75 H4
Milner Ing LM/WK BD12 .....62 D1
Milner La GTL/HWG HX4 .....75 H4
Milner Rd BAIL BD17 .....18 C5
Milner's Rd YEA LS19 .....11 E4
Milne St GTHN * BD7 .....38 D5
Milton Av RPDN/SBR HX6 .....67 F3
Milton Pl HFAX HX1 .....4 A4
Milton St CUL/QBY BD13 .....34 D4
  GTHN BD7 .....38 D5
  RPDN/SBR HX6 .....67 E3
Milton Ter CLECK BD19 .....64 B5
  HFAX * HX1 .....4 E4
Minnie St HWTH BD22 .....22 D3
Minorca Mt CUL/QBY BD13 .....34 C3
Mint St ECHL BD2 .....40 A2
Mirfield Av ECHL BD2 .....29 H4
Miry La LUD/ILL WF15 .....73 F4
  YEA LS19. .....11 G4
Mission St BRIG HD6 .....78 D2
Mistral Cl LM/WK BD12 .....62 D3
Mistral Gv LVSG WF15 .....73 E3
Mitcham Dr HTON BD9 .....38 B2
Mitchell Cl IDLE BD10 .....20 B5
Mitchell La IDLE BD10 .....20 B5
Mitchell Sq WBOW BD5 .....47 F3
Mitchell St BRIG HD6 .....71 F5
  KGHY BD21 .....7 G3
  RPDN/SBR HX6 .....67 F4
Mitchell Ter BGLY BD16 .....16 C4
Mitre Ct BOW BD4 .....48 C4
Mitton St WBOW BD5 .....46 D4
Mixenden Cl LUD/ILL HX2 .....50 B5
Mixenden La LUD/ILL HX2 .....50 B5
Mixenden Rd LUD/ILL HX2 .....50 B5
Moffat Cl WBSY BD6 .....54 A3
Mond Av BFDE BD3 .....40 C3
Monk Barn Cl BAIL * BD16 .....16 D2
Monk Ings Av BTLY WF17 .....65 H4
Monk St GTHN BD7 .....38 D5
Monson Av PDSY/CALV LS28...31 G3
Montague St RPDN/SBR HX6...66 D5
  WBOW BD5 .....46 D4
Montreal Av BGLY BD16 .....29 E5
Montserrat Rd BOW BD4 .....57 E1
Moody St BOW BD4 .....47 G2
Moorbottom CLECK BD19 .....73 E2
Moor Bottom La BGLY BD16...16 D3
  GTL/HWG HX4 .....75 F5
  KGHY BD21 .....14 A4
Moor Bottom Rd LUD/ILL HX2...51 H4
Moor Close Av CUL/QBY BD13...51 H2
Moor Close Farm Ms
  CUL/QBY BD13 .....51 H2
Moor Close La CUL/QBY BD13...51 H2
Moor Close Pde CUL/QBY BD13...51 H1
Moor Close Rd CUL/QBY BD13...51 H2
Moor Cft BGLY BD16 .....17 E1
Moorcroft Av BFDE BD3 .....40 C3
  HWTH BD22 .....13 E3
Moorcroft Dr BOW BD4 .....57 E1
Moorcroft Rd BOW BD4 .....57 E1
Moorcroft Ter BOW BD4 .....57 E1
Moor Dr HWTH BD22 .....12 D3
Moore Av GTHN BD7 .....46 A5
Moor Edge High Side
  BGLY BD16 .....15 F4
Moor End Av LUD/ILL HX2 .....58 B4

Moor End Gdns LUD/ILL HX2...58 C4
Moor End La RPDN/SBR HX6...74 C1
Moor End Rd LUD/ILL HX2 .....58 A3
Moor End Vw LUD/ILL HX2 .....58 D4
Moore St KGHY BD21 .....7 F5
Moore Vw GTHN BD7 .....46 A5
Moorfield Av BFDE BD3 .....40 C3
  CLECK BD19 .....72 B1
Moorfield Crs YEA LS19 .....11 H5
Moorfield Dr BAIL BD17 .....18 D1
  HWTH BD22 .....13 E3
Moorfield Gdns PDSY/CALV LS28...49 H1
Moorfield Gv PDSY/CALV LS28...49 H1
Moorfield Pl IDLE BD10 .....30 A1
Moorfield Rd BGLY BD16 .....26 D2
Moorfield St HFAX HX1 .....4 D7
Moorfield Wy CLECK BD19 .....72 B1
Moorgarth Av BFDE BD3 .....40 C3
Moorgate BAIL BD17 .....18 D2
Moorgate Av BFDE BD3 .....40 B3
Moorgate St HFAX * HX1 .....4 B7
Moor Gv HIPP HX3 .....53 F3
Moorhead Crs SHPY BD18 .....27 H2
Moorhead La SHPY BD18 .....27 H2
Moorhead Ter SHPY BD18 .....27 H2
Moorhouse Av ECHL BD2 .....29 H4
Moorhouse Cl HWTH BD22 .....32 D1
Moorhouse Ct HWTH BD22 .....32 D1
Moorhouse La HWTH BD22 .....22 C5
The Moorings IDLE BD10 .....30 C1
Moorland Av BAIL BD17 .....19 E2
  GSLY LS20 .....10 D2
Moorland Cl LUD/ILL HX2 .....58 D2
Moorland Crs BAIL BD17 .....19 E2
  GSLY LS20 .....10 D1
  ILK LS29 .....10 A1
Moorland Dr BIRK/DRI BD11...57 G3
  GSLY LS20 .....10 D1
  PDSY/CALV LS28 .....41 F4
Moorland Gv GTL/HWG HX4...28 A1
Moorland Pl LM/WK BD12 .....55 F5
Moorland Rd PDSY/CALV LS28...41 F4
Moorlands Av BFDE BD3 .....40 C3
  BIRK/DRI BD11 .....57 F3
  HWTH BD22 .....13 G2
  LUD/ILL HX2 .....58 D2
Moorlands Ct GTL/HWG * HX4...75 G3
Moorlands Dr LUD/ILL HX2...58 D3
Moorlands Pl HFAX HX1 .....68 C3
Moorlands Rd BIRK/DRI BD11...57 F3
  GTL/HWG HX4 .....75 G3
Moorlands Vw HFAX HX1 .....68 C3
Moorland Ter KGHY BD22 .....8 A5
Moorland Vw LM/WK BD12 .....55 F5
  RPDN/SBR HX6 .....66 C5
Moor La CLECK BD19 .....65 G3
  GSLY LS20 .....10 D1
  LUD/ILL HX2 .....58 D1
Moorlea Dr BAIL BD17 .....19 E3
Moor Park Dr BFDE BD3 .....40 C4
Moor Park Rd BFDE * BD3 .....40 B4
Moor Royd HIPP HX3 .....68 B4
Moorside BAIL BD17 .....19 E1
  CLECK BD19 .....72 D2
  HTON BD9 .....37 H2
Moorside Av BIRK/DRI BD11...57 F3
  ECHL BD2 .....40 C2
Moorside Cl ECHL BD2 .....40 B1
Moorside Cft ECHL BD2 .....40 B1
Moorside Gdns ECHL BD2 .....40 B1
  LUD/ILL HX2 .....59 E1
Moorside Gv BFDE BD3 .....40 C5
Moorside Pl BFDE BD3 .....40 C5
Moorside Ri CLECK BD19 .....73 E1
Moorside Rd BFDE BD3 .....40 C5
  ECHL BD2 .....30 B5
  WIL/AL BD15 .....25 H5
Moorside St ECHL BD2 .....40 C2
Moorside Ter ECHL BD2 .....40 C2
Moor Stone Pl HIPP HX3 .....53 F5
Moor St CUL/QBY * BD13 .....52 B1
  HWTH BD22 .....13 E3
Moor Ter ECHL BD2 .....40 B3
Moorthorpe Av BFDE BD3 .....40 C3
Moor Top Gdns LUD/ILL HX2...50 D3
Moor Top Rd LM/WK BD12 .....54 C4
  LUD/ILL HX2 .....58 A5
Moor Vw BOW * BD4 .....57 F2
Moor View Av SHPY BD18 .....28 B1
Moor View Ct AIRE BD20 .....8 D4
  IDLE * BD10 .....19 H5
Moorview Dr BGLY BD16 .....26 B3
  SHPY BD18 .....29 G2
Moorview Gv KGHY BD21 .....14 C1
Moorville Av BFDE BD3 .....40 C3
Moorville Dr BIRK/DRI BD11...57 F3
Moorway GSLY LS20 .....10 A2

Moor Wy HWTH BD22 .....12 D5
Moorwell Pl ECHL BD2 .....30 A1
Moravian Pl WBOW * BD5 .....47 E3
Moresby Rd WBSY BD6 .....53 H4
Morley Av BFDE BD3 .....40 C3
Morley Carr Rd LM/WK BD12...55 E5
Morley St GTHN BD7 .....2 B7
Morningside GIR BD8 .....38 C3
Morning St KGHY BD21 .....14 A2
Mornington Rd BGLY BD16 .....16 D3
Mornington St KGHY BD21 .....7 E5
Mornington Vls GIR BD8. .....39 E2
Morpeth St CUL/QBY BD13 .....52 B1
  GTHN BD7 .....38 D5
Mortimer Av BFDE BD3 .....40 C2
Mortimer Rw BFDE BD3 .....48 C2
Mortimer St CLECK * BD19 .....73 C2
  GIR BD8 .....38 A2
Morton Gv AIRE BD20 .....9 E1
Morton La AIRE BD20 .....9 E1
Morton Rd BOW BD4 .....48 C2
Mortons Cl HIPP HX3 .....69 F1
Moser Av ECHL BD2 .....29 H4
Moser Crs ECHL BD2 .....29 H4
Moss Carr Av LM/WK BD12 .....15 E5
Moss Carr Gv KGHY * BD21 .....15 E5
Moss Carr Rd KGHY BD21 .....15 E5
Mossdale Av HTON BD9 .....37 F2
Moss Dr LUD/ILL HX2 .....50 D4
Moss La LUD/ILL HX2 .....50 D4
Moss Rw WIL/AL BD15 .....25 H3
Moss Side HTON BD9 .....37 H2
Moss St CUL/QBY BD13 .....35 G3
  HWTH BD22 .....23 F3
Mosstree Cl CUL/QBY BD13 .....43 H5
Mossy Bank Cl CUL/QBY BD13...44 B5
Mostyn Gv WBSY BD6 .....54 B2
Mostyn Mt HIPP HX3 .....59 F2
Motley La GSLY LS20 .....10 A2
Moulson Ct WBOW BD5 .....47 F4
Mountain Vw LUD/ILL HX2 .....51 H4
  SHPY BD18 .....29 E3
Mount Av ECHL BD2 .....30 A4
  LUD/ILL HX2 .....67 F2
Mount Crs CLECK BD19 .....64 C5
  LUD/ILL HX2 .....67 F2
Mountfields HIPP HX3 .....61 H1
Mount Gdns CLECK BD19 .....64 C5
Mount Gv ECHL BD2 .....30 A4
Mount La BRIG HD6 .....77 H5
Mountleigh Cl BOW BD4 .....55 H4
Mount Pellon LUD/ILL HX2 .....4 A2
Mount Pellon Rd LUD/ILL HX2...58 D1
Mount Pl SHPY BD18 .....28 C1
Mount Pleasant AIRE BD20 .....8 D4
  CUL/QBY BD13 .....34 C2
  GIR * BD8 .....38 D2
  GSLY LS20 .....10 D2
  WBSY BD6 .....53 H3
Mount Pleasant Av HFAX HX1...4 E7
Mount Pleasant Rd WBSY BD6...30 A4
  WBSY BD6 .....54 B2
Mount Royd GIR BD8 .....38 D2
Mount St BFDE BD3 .....3 H2
  CLECK BD19 .....64 C5
  ECHL BD2 .....30 A4
  HFAX HX1 .....5 F4
  HWTH BD22 .....6 D4
  RPDN/SBR HX6 .....67 E4
Mount St West LUD/ILL * HX2...58 D1
Mount Tabor St
  PDSY/CALV * LS28 .....41 H1
Mount Ter ECHL BD2 .....30 A4
  LUD/ILL HX2 .....58 D1
Mount Vernon Rd YEA LS19 .....21 H2
Mount Vw HWTH BD22 .....12 C2
Mount View Ct CLECK BD19 .....64 B5
Mowat Ct LVSG WF15 .....73 E3
Mowbray Cl CUL/QBY BD13 .....24 B3
Mozley Dr LUD/ILL HX2 .....51 E3
Muff St BOW BD4 .....48 A2
Muirhead Ct BOW BD4 .....48 D5
Muirhead Dr BOW BD4 .....48 D5
Muirhead Fold BOW BD4 .....48 D5
Mulberry St KGHY * BD21 .....7 G5
Mulcture Hall Rd HFAX HX1 .....5 J5
Mulgrave St BFDE BD5 .....3 J1
Mumford St WBOW BD5 .....47 F4
Munby St GIR BD8 .....37 H5
Munster St BOW BD4 .....48 A3
Munton Cl WBSY * BD6 .....53 H4
Murdoch St KGHY BD21 .....8 A3
Murgatroyd St SHPY BD18 .....28 C1
  WBOW BD5 .....47 F4
Murray St WBOW * BD5 .....46 D3
Museum Ct ECHL BD2 .....40 B2
Musgrave Dr ECHL BD2 .....40 B2
Musgrave Gv ECHL BD2 .....40 B2

Musgrave Mt ECHL BD2 40 B2
Musgrave Rd ECHL BD2 40 B2
Musselburgh St GTHN BD7 38 D5
Mutton La WIL/AL BD15 36 A2
Myers Av ECHL BD2 29 H5
Myers La ECHL BD2 29 H5
Myrtle Av BGLY * BD16 16 C4
LUD/ILL HX2 58 D1
Myrtle Ct BGLY BD16 16 C4
Myrtle Dr HWTH BD22 13 G5
LUD/ILL HX2 58 D1
Myrtle Gdns LUD/ILL HX2 58 D1
Myrtle Gv BGLY BD16 16 C4
LUD/ILL HX2 58 D1
Myrtle Pl BGLY BD16 16 C3
LUD/ILL HX2 58 D1
Myrtle St BFDE BD3 48 B1
BGLY BD16 16 D3
Mytholmes La HWTH BD22 22 D2

N

Nab End La GTL/HWG HX4 76 A4
Nab La SHPY BD18 27 G2
Nab Wood Bank SHPY BD18 27 G2
Nab Wood Cl SHPY * BD18 27 H2
Nab Wood Crs SHPY BD18 27 G2
Nab Wood Dr BGLY BD16 27 G3
Nab Wood Gdns SHPY BD18 27 H2
Nab Wood Gv SHPY BD18 27 G2
Nab Wood Mt SHPY BD18 27 G2
Nab Wood Pl SHPY BD18 27 G2
Nab Wood Ri SHPY BD18 27 G2
Nab Wood Rd SHPY BD18 27 G3
Nab Wood Ter SHPY BD18 27 G2
Napier Rd BFDE BD3 40 C5
ELL HX5 76 B5
Napier St BFDE BD3 40 C5
CUL/QBY BD13 52 C1
KGHY * BD21 7 G5
Napier Ter BFDE BD3 40 C5
Naples St GIR BD8 38 C3
Nares St HWTH BD22 23 F1
KGHY BD21 7 E4
Nares St Upper KGHY * BD21 7 E4
Narrow La BGLY BD16 15 G5
The Narrows BGLY BD16 15 G5
Naseby Ri CUL/QBY BD13 52 C1
Nashville Rd HWTH BD22 6 D5
Nashville St HWTH BD22 6 D5
Nashville Ter HWTH BD22 6 D5
Natty Fields Cl LUD/ILL HX2 50 D3
Natty La LUD/ILL HX2 50 D3
Nature Wy WBSY BD6 53 H3
Navigation Cl ELL HX5 76 D3
Navigation Rd HIPP HX3 5 K5
Naylor St HFAX HX1 4 A3
Neal St WBOW BD5 2 C7
Nearcliffe Rd HTON BD9 38 B2
Near Crook SHPY BD18 19 G5
Necropolis Rd GTHN BD7 46 A2
Ned Hill Rd LUD/ILL HX2 42 D5
Ned La BOW BD4 49 E3
Nelson Pl CUL/QBY BD13 52 B1
Nelson St BFD BD1 2 D6
CUL/QBY BD13 52 B1
HWTH BD22 23 F1
RPDN/SBR HX6 67 G4
WIL/AL BD15 37 F3
Nene St WBOW BD5 46 D3
Nesfield St BFD BD1 2 B2
Nessfield Dr HWTH BD22 13 G1
Nessfield Gv HWTH BD22 13 G1
Nessfield Rd HWTH BD22 13 G1
Netherby St BFDE BD3 3 K5
Nethercliffe Rd GSLY LS20 10 C1
Netherfield Cl YEA LS19 11 G4
Netherfield Dr GSLY LS20 10 C1
Netherfield Pl CLECK BD19 73 H1
Netherfield Rd GSLY LS20 10 C1
Netherhall Rd BAIL BD17 19 E3
Netherlands Av WBSY BD6 54 D3
Netherlands Sq WBSY BD6 55 E3
Nether Moor Vw BGLY BD16 16 D3
Nettle Gv HIPP HX3 60 C4
Neville Av BOW BD4 56 A1
Neville Rd BOW BD4 48 A3
Neville St CLECK BD19 73 H2
KGHY * BD21 7 G3
Nevill Gv HTON BD9 37 G1
Newall St WBOW BD5 47 E3
Newark Rd BGLY BD16 16 B1
Newark St BOW BD4 47 H2
New Augustus St BFD BD1 3 F6
New Bank HIPP HX3 5 J1
New Bank Ri BOW BD4 48 C4
New Brighton BGLY BD16 27 F3
New Bond St HFAX HX1 5 F4
New Brunswick St HFAX HX1 5 F3
Newburn Rd GTHN BD7 46 C2
Newbury Rd BRIG HD6 78 A4
New Cl SHPY BD18 27 G2
New Close Rd SHPY BD18 27 G2
New Clough Rd
RPDN/SBR HX6 74 C1
New Cross St LM/WK BD12 56 A5
WBOW BD5 47 F5
New Fold WBSY BD6 53 H3
Newforth Gv WBOW * BD5 46 D5
Newhall Dr WBSY BD6 55 G2
Newhall Mt WBSY BD6 55 G2
Newhall Rd BOW * BD4 56 A1
New Hey Rd BOW BD4 47 H3
New Holme Rd HWTH BD22 23 E3
New House La CUL/QBY BD13 53 E2
New Houses CUL/QBY * BD13 52 C1
Newill Cl WBOW BD5 47 G5
New John St BFD * BD1 2 C5
New Kirkgate SHPY * BD18 28 C1
New Laithe Rd WBSY * BD6 54 B1
Newlands YEA LS19 11 F3
Newlands Av BFDE BD3 40 C3
HIPP HX3 60 D1
RPDN/SBR HX6 66 B5
YEA LS19 11 F4
Newlands Cl BRIG HD6 78 C2
Newlands Dr BGLY BD16 16 B1
HIPP HX3 60 D2
Newlands Gv HIPP HX3 60 D2
Newlands Pl BFDE BD3 3 H2
Newlands Ri YEA LS19 11 F4
Newlands Rd LUD/ILL HX2 67 E1
New La BOW BD4 48 C1
BOW BD4 49 G5
CLECK BD19 72 D2
HIPP HX3 69 E4
HIPP HX3 75 G1
Newlay Cl IDLE BD10 30 D2
New Line IDLE BD10 30 D2
Newlyn Rd AIRE BD20 8 B2
Newman St BOW BD4 48 A5
New Occupation La
PDSY/CALV LS28 49 H1
New Otley Rd BFDE BD3 3 G3
New Park Rd CUL/QBY BD13 52 A1
New Popplewell La CLECK BD19 63 G5
Newport Pl GIR BD8 38 D4
Newport Rd GIR BD8 38 D3
New Pudsey Sq
PDSY/CALV LS28 41 H3
New Rd CUL/QBY BD13 34 C4
GTL/HWG HX4 75 F4
HFAX HX1 5 H5
YEA LS19 11 E4
New Rd East CLECK BD19 63 F5
New Road Side YEA LS19 21 G2
New Road Sq BRIG * HD6 77 H5
New Rw HTON BD9 37 H2
Newroyd Rd WBOW BD5 47 F5
Newsholme New Rd
HWTH BD22 12 B2
Newstead Av HFAX HX1 67 H1
Newstead Gdns HFAX HX1 67 H1
Newstead Gv HFAX HX1 67 H1
Newstead Heath HFAX HX1 67 H1
Newstead Pl HFAX HX1 67 H1
Newstead Ter HFAX HX1 67 H1
Newstead Wk WBOW * BD5 47 E3
New St BOW BD4 56 A2
BRIG HD6 71 G1
BRIG HD6 79 E1
CUL/QBY BD13 34 C4
HIPP HX3 69 H4
HWTH BD22 22 D3
IDLE BD10 30 A1
LM/WK BD12 56 A5
LUD/ILL * HX2 58 D5
Newton Pk BRIG HD6 71 E2
Newton Pl WBOW BD5 47 E3
Newton St RPDN/SBR * HX6 67 E4
WBOW BD5 47 F4
Newton Wy BAIL * BD17 18 D2
New Town Ct HWTH BD22 6 D4
New Wy GSLY LS20 10 B2
New Works Rd LM/WK BD12 54 D5
Nibshaw La CLECK BD19 65 F5
Nibshaw Rd CLECK BD19 65 F5
Nicholas Cl GTHN BD7 38 A5
Nidderdale Wk BAIL BD17 19 F2
Nidd St BFDE BD3 3 K6
Nighthorne Av BFDE BD3 40 B3
Nightingale St KGHY * BD21 7 F3
Nightingale Wk BGLY BD16 17 F2
Nile Crs HWTH BD22 6 C5
Nile St HWTH BD22 6 C5
HWTH BD22 23 F1
Nina Rd GTHN BD7 46 A4
Ninth Av LVSG WF15 73 E3
Noble St GTHN BD7 46 C2
Nog La HTON BD9 28 B5
The Nook CLECK BD19 64 D5
RPDN/SBR HX6 67 E5
Norbeck Dr HWTH BD22 23 F1
Norbury Rd IDLE BD10 30 D4
Norcliffe La HIPP HX3 69 H2
Norcroft Brow GTHN BD7 2 A6
Norcroft St BFD BD1 38 D5
Norfolk Gdns BFD BD1 2 D6
Norfolk Pl HFAX HX1 4 D6
Norfolk St BGLY BD16 16 D3
Norham Gv LM/WK BD12 63 E3
Norland Rd RPDN/SBR HX6 67 E5
RPDN/SBR HX6 74 C2
Norland St GTHN BD7 46 A4
Norland Town Rd
RPDN/SBR HX6 74 C1
Norland Vw RPDN/SBR HX6 67 G4
Norman Av ECHL BD2 30 A4
ELL HX5 76 D5
Norman Crs ECHL BD2 30 A4
Norman Gv ECHL BD2 30 A4
ELL * HX5 76 D5
Norman La ECHL BD2 30 A4
Norman Mt ECHL BD2 30 A4
Norman St BGLY * BD16 16 D3
ELL HX5 76 D5
HFAX HX1 4 A7
SHPY BD18 29 E2
Norman Ter ECHL BD2 30 A4
ELL HX5 76 D5
Northallerton Rd BFDE BD3 3 F1
North Av HTON BD9 39 E1
North Bank Rd BGLY BD16 26 D4
North Bolton LUD/ILL HX2 50 C3
North Br HFAX HX1 5 H2
North Bridge St HFAX HX1 5 H2
North Brook St BFD BD1 2 E3
North Byland LUD/ILL HX2 50 D3
North Cliffe Av CUL/QBY BD13 44 C1
North Cliffe Cl CUL/QBY * BD13 44 B1
North Cliffe Dr CUL/QBY BD13 44 B1
North Cliffe Gv CUL/QBY BD13 36 B5
North Cliffe La CUL/QBY BD13 36 C5
Northcliffe Rd SHPY BD18 28 B3
Northcote Rd ECHL BD2 40 A2
Northcroft Ri HTON BD9 37 H3
North Cut BRIG HD6 77 H1
Northdale Av WBOW BD5 46 D5
Northdale Crs WBOW BD5 46 D5
Northdale Mt WBOW BD5 46 D5
Northdale Rd HTON BD9 28 C4
North Dean Av HWTH BD22 6 B4
North Dean Rd GTL/HWG HX4 75 E2
HWTH BD22 6 C4
Northedge La HIPP HX3 61 G4
Northedge Meadow IDLE BD10 30 A3
Northedge Pk HIPP HX3 61 G5
Northern Cl GTHN BD7 46 A5
Northfield Cl ELL * HX5 76 C5
Northfield Crs BGLY BD16 26 D2
Northfield Gdns WBSY BD6 54 D1
Northfield Gv WBSY BD6 54 D1
Northfield Pl GIR BD8 38 D3
Northfield Rd WBSY BD6 54 C1
Northfield Ter CUL/QBY BD13 52 D1
North Fold IDLE BD10 30 A1
Northgate BAIL BD17 18 D2
BFD BD1 2 C4
CLECK BD19 73 H1
ELL HX5 76 C4
HFAX HX1 5 H3
North Hall Av IDLE BD10 19 H4
North Holme St BFD BD1 2 D3
Northlea Av IDLE BD10 19 H5
Northowram Gn HIPP HX3 60 D1
North Pde BFD BD1 2 C4
HFAX HX1 5 G3
WIL/AL BD15 36 D2
North Park Rd HTON BD9 38 C1
North Park Ter HTON BD9 38 D2
North Pollard St HFAX HX1 5 H2
North Queen St KGHY BD21 7 F4
North Rd WBSY BD6 54 C2
Northrop Cl GIR BD8 38 B3
Northside Av GTHN BD7 46 B1
Northside Rd GTHN BD7 46 B1
Northside Ter GTHN BD7 46 A1
North St BFD BD1 3 F4
GTL/HWG HX4 76 A4
HWTH BD22 22 C2
IDLE BD10 20 A4
KGHY BD21 7 F4
LM/WK BD12 63 H1
YEA LS19 21 G2
North Ter YEA LS19 11 G4
North Vw WIL/AL BD15 25 H4
WIL/AL BD15 36 D3
North View Rd BFDE BD3 39 G2
BOW BD4 57 F3
North View St KGHY BD21 7 F2
North View Ter HWTH BD22 22 D1
North Wk BGLY BD16 15 F5
North Wing BFDE BD3 3 F3
Northwood Crs IDLE BD10 30 B2
Norton Cl LUD/ILL HX2 67 E1
Norton Dr LUD/ILL HX2 67 E1
Norton Fold ECHL * BD2 30 A4
Norwood Av BIRK/DRI BD11 65 G1
SHPY BD18 28 C3
Norwood Crs CLECK BD19 65 G1
Norwood Dr BIRK/DRI BD11 65 G1
Norwood Green Hl HIPP HX3 62 A3
Norwood Gv BIRK/DRI BD11 65 G1
Norwood Pl SHPY BD18 28 C3
Norwood Rd SHPY BD18 28 C3
Norwood St SHPY BD18 28 C3
WBOW BD5 47 E5
Norwood Ter SHPY BD18 28 C3
Nostell Cl GIR BD8 2 A2
Nottingham St BFDE BD3 40 D5
Nunburnholme Wk IDLE BD10 30 B3
Nunlea Royd BRIG HD6 71 F2
Nunnery La BRIG HD6 77 G4
Nunroyd Av GSLY LS20 11 E3
Nurser La WBOW BD5 46 D3
Nurser Pl WBOW BD5 46 D3
Nursery Av LUD/ILL HX2 59 E2
Nursery Cl BAIL * BD17 17 H4
Nursery Gv LUD/ILL HX2 59 E2
Nursery La HIPP HX3 59 E2
Nursery Rd GTHN BD7 46 A5
Nuttall Rd BFDE BD3 3 G4
Nutter La CLECK BD19 65 H3
Nutter St CLECK BD19 73 F1
Nutwood Wk WBSY BD6 53 H4

O

Oak Av BGLY BD16 16 C5
GIR BD8 38 D2
RPDN/SBR HX6 67 E3
Oak Bank BGLY BD16 16 D4
SHPY BD18 29 E4
Oakbank Av HWTH BD22 13 G1
Oakbank Broadway
HWTH BD22 13 G2
Oakbank Ct HWTH BD22 13 G2
Oakbank Crs HWTH BD22 13 G2
Oakbank Dr HWTH BD22 13 G1
Oakbank Gv HWTH BD22 13 G1
Oakbank La HWTH BD22 13 G2
Oakbank Mt HWTH BD22 13 G2
Oakdale BGLY BD16 16 D1
Oakdale Av SHPY BD18 29 E3
WBSY BD6 54 C1
Oakdale Cl HIPP HX3 59 F3
IDLE BD10 40 D1
Oakdale Crs WBSY BD6 54 C1
Oakdale Dr IDLE BD10 40 D1
SHPY BD18 29 F3
Oakdale Gv SHPY BD18 29 F3
Oakdale Rd SHPY BD18 29 F3
Oakdale Ter WBSY BD6 54 C1
Oakenshaw Ct LM/WK BD12 62 D3
Oakenshaw La CLECK BD19 63 H2
Oakfield Av BGLY BD16 17 F4
Oakfield Cl ELL HX5 76 B5
Oakfield Dr BAIL BD17 19 E4
Oakfield Gv HTON BD9 38 D2
Oakfield Rd KGHY BD21 13 H2
Oakfield Ter SHPY BD18 29 E2
Oak Gv HWTH BD22 13 H2
Oakhall Pk CUL/QBY BD13 36 A5
Oakhall Park Av
CUL/QBY BD13 36 A5
Oakham Wk BOW * BD4 47 H3
Oak Hill Rd BRIG HD6 71 G5
Oaklands BRIG HD6 78 A2
IDLE BD10 29 H1
SHPY BD18 27 G2
Oaklands Av HIPP HX3 60 D2
Oak La GIR BD8 38 D2
HFAX HX1 4 C3
Oakleigh Av CLAY BD14 45 E4
HIPP HX3 68 D5
Oakleigh Cl CLAY BD14 45 E3
Oakleigh Gdns CLAY * BD14 45 E4
Oakleigh Gv CLAY BD14 45 E4

Oakleigh Rd *CLAY* BD14 ....45 E4
Oakleigh Ter *CLAY* BD14 ....45 E3
Oakleigh Vw *BAIL* BD17 ....18 C3
Oak Mt *GIR* BD8 ....39 E2
  HIPP * HX3 ....70 D1
Oak Pl *HFAX* HX1 ....4 C4
  RPDN/SBR HX6 ....67 E3
Oakridge Ct *BGLY* BD16 ....16 D2
Oak Ri *CLECK* BD19 ....64 C3
Oakroyd Av *WBSY* BD6 ....54 D2
Oakroyd Cl *BIRK/DRI* BD11 ....57 F5
  BRIG HD6 ....71 G3
Oakroyd Dr *BIRK/DRI* BD11 ....65 F1
  BRIG HD6 ....71 G3
Oakroyd Rd *WBSY* BD6 ....54 D2
Oakroyd Ter *BAIL* BD17 ....19 E4
  GIR BD8 ....39 E2
Oakroyd Vls *GIR* BD8 ....39 E2
Oaks Dr *GIR* BD8 ....37 F4
Oaks Fold *WBOW* BD5 ....47 F4
Oaks Green Mt *BRIG* HD6 ....78 A4
Oaks La *GIR* BD8 ....37 F4
Oak St *CLAY* BD14 ....45 E3
  ELL HX5 ....76 C5
  HWTH BD22 ....23 E2
  HWTH BD22 ....32 D1
  PDSY/CALV LS28 ....41 H4
  RPDN/SBR HX6 ....67 E3
Oak Ter *HFAX* * HX1 ....4 C3
Oak Vls *GIR* BD8 ....39 E2
Oakway *BIRK/DRI* BD11 ....65 G1
Oakwell Cl *GTHN* BD7 ....46 C4
Oakwood Av *BIRK/DRI* BD11 ....57 F5
  ECHL BD2 ....29 E5
Oakwood Cottages
  BGLY BD16 ....9 H5
Oakwood Ct *GIR* BD8 ....38 D4
Oakwood Dr *BGLY* BD16 ....16 C1
Oakwood Gv *GIR* BD8 ....38 B3
Oakworth Hall *HWTH* BD22 ....12 D4
Oakworth Rd *HWTH* BD22 ....13 G2
Oasby Cft *BOW* BD4 ....56 D1
Oastler Pl *LM/WK* BD12 ....55 E4
Oastler Rd *PDSY/CALV* LS28 ....31 G3
  SHPY BD18 ....28 A1
Oat St *HWTH* * BD22 ....13 H2
Occupation La *HWTH* BD22 ....13 E2
  LUD/ILL HX2 ....50 D4
  PDSY/CALV LS28 ....49 H1
Octagon Ter *LUD/ILL* HX2 ....67 H4
Oddfellows' Ct *BFD* BD1 ....2 C5
Oddfellows St *BRIG* HD6 ....71 G5
  CLECK BD19 ....63 G5
Oddy Pl *WBSY* BD6 ....54 C1
Oddy St *BOW* BD4 ....56 D1
Odsal Pl *WBSY* BD6 ....55 E2
Odsal Rd *WBSY* BD6 ....54 D1
Ogden St *RPDN/SBR* HX6 ....66 D5
Ogden La *BRIG* HD6 ....78 A3
  CUL/QBY BD13 ....34 C2
  LUD/ILL HX2 ....42 C5
Ogden View Cl *LUD/ILL* HX2 ....50 C3
Old Allen Rd *CUL/QBY* BD13 ....35 F1
Old Bank *HIPP* HX3 ....5 K3
Old Bell Ct *HFAX* * HX1 ....5 G6
Old Canal Rd *BFD* BD1 ....2 D1
Old Cawsey *RPDN/SBR* HX6 ....67 H4
Old Cock Yd *HFAX* * HX1 ....5 H4
Old Corn Mill La *GTHN* * BD7 ....46 D4
Old Dalton La *KGHY* BD21 ....7 G4
Old Earth *ELL* HX5 ....77 E4
Old Farm Crs *BOW* * BD4 ....48 A4
Oldfield La *HWTH* BD22 ....22 B2
Oldfield St *HIPP* HX3 ....59 F1
Old Godley La *HIPP* HX3 ....60 B5
Old Guy Rd *CUL/QBY* BD13 ....43 H5
Old Hall Cl *HWTH* * BD22 ....22 D3
Old Haworth La *YEA* LS19 ....11 G4
Old Hollings Hi *BAIL* BD17 ....10 B5
Old La *BIRK/DRI* BD11 ....57 F5
  BRIG HD6 ....71 G5
  HIPP HX3 ....59 F3
Old Langley La *BAIL* BD17 ....19 F2
Old Lee Bank *HIPP* HX3 ....59 F4
Old Main St *BGLY* BD16 ....16 C3
Old Manse Cft *HWTH* * BD22 ....32 D1
Old Market *HFAX* * HX1 ....5 H4
Old Marsh *PDSY/CALV* LS28 ....41 H4
Old Mill Rd *BAIL* * BD17 ....28 B1
Old Oxenhope La *HWTH* BD22 ....22 C4
Old Park Rd *IDLE* BD10 ....30 B2
Old Popplewell La *CLECK* BD19 ....63 F5
Old Power Wy *ELL* HX5 ....76 D3
Old Rd *CUL/QBY* BD13 ....34 C4
  CUL/QBY BD13 ....44 C1
  GTHN BD7 ....45 H5
Old Schools Gdns *HIPP* HX3 ....59 H4

Old Side Ct *AIRE* BD20 ....9 F2
Old Souls Wy *BGLY* BD16 ....9 F5
Old Station Rd *LUD/ILL* HX2 ....66 A1
Old Well Head *HFAX* HX1 ....5 G6
Old Whack House La *YEA* LS19 ....11 E5
Olive Gv *GIR* BD8 ....37 H4
Oliver Mdw *ELL* HX5 ....76 D3
Oliver St *BOW* BD4 ....47 H2
Ollerdale Av *WIL/AL* BD15 ....36 D1
Ollerdale Cl *WIL/AL* BD15 ....36 D2
Olympic Pk *LM/WK* BD12 ....55 F5
Onslow Cv *BOW* BD4 ....48 A5
Opal St *HWTH* BD22 ....13 H2
Orange St *BFDE* BD3 ....48 B1
  HFAX HX1 ....5 G3
Orchard Cl *LUD/ILL* HX2 ....67 G2
Orchard Gv *IDLE* BD10 ....30 C2
The Orchards *BGLY* BD16 ....16 D1
  CLECK BD19 ....65 H5
The Orchard *KGHY* BD21 ....8 A4
Orchard Wy *BRIG* HD6 ....71 F4
Orchid Cl *SHPY* BD18 ....29 E4
Orleans St *WBSY* BD6 ....54 A3
Ormonde Dr *WIL/AL* BD15 ....36 D4
Ormond Rd *WBSY* BD6 ....54 C1
Ormondroyd Av *WBSY* BD6 ....54 D2
Ormond St *GTHN* BD7 ....46 B3
Osborne St *HFAX* HX1 ....4 B2
  WBOW BD5 ....47 E2
Osbourne Dr *CUL/QBY* BD13 ....52 B1
Osprey Ct *GIR* * BD8 ....37 F5
Osterley Gv *IDLE* BD10 ....30 D2
Oswald St *SHPY* BD18 ....29 E2
Oswaldthorpe Av *BFDE* BD3 ....40 C3
Otley La *YEA* LS19 ....11 G4
Otley Mt *AIRE* BD20 ....9 E3
Otley Rd *BAIL* BD17 ....19 G3
  BFDE BD3 ....3 F4
  BGLY BD16 ....9 H2
  SHPY BD18 ....28 C3
Otley St *HFAX* HX1 ....4 A3
  KGHY BD21 ....7 E5
Otterburn Cl *WBOW* BD5 ....47 E2
Otterburn St *KGHY* * BD21 ....7 F2
Oulton Ter *GTHN* BD7 ....46 D2
Ounsworth St *BOW* BD4 ....48 A3
Outlands Ri *IDLE* BD10 ....30 C1
Outside La *HWTH* BD22 ....32 A2
The Oval *BGLY* BD16 ....17 E4
  GIR BD8 ....37 H4
  GSLY LS20 ....10 B3
  LVSG WF15 ....73 F3
Ovenden Av *HIPP* HX3 ....59 F4
Ovenden Cl *HIPP* * HX3 ....59 F3
Ovenden Crs *HIPP* HX3 ....59 F3
Ovenden Gn *HIPP* HX3 ....59 F3
Ovenden Pk *LUD/ILL* * HX2 ....59 E1
Ovenden Rd *HIPP* HX3 ....59 F3
Ovenden Road Ter *HIPP* HX3 ....59 F3
Ovenden Ter *HIPP* HX3 ....59 F3
Ovenden Wy *HIPP* HX3 ....59 E3
Ovenden Wood Rd *LUD/ILL* HX2 ......58 B3
Overdale Dr *SHPY* BD18 ....19 G5
Overdale Mt *LUD/ILL* HX2 ....67 G3
Overdale Ter *HWTH* * BD22 ....22 D2
Overland Crs *IDLE* BD10 ....30 C1
Over La *YEA* LS19 ....21 H3
Overton Dr *WBSY* BD6 ....45 G5
Ovington Dr *BOW* BD4 ....48 D5
Owen Ct *BGLY* BD16 ....9 H5
Owlcotes Ct *PDSY/CALV* LS28 ....41 H4
Owlcotes Gdns *PDSY/CALV* LS28 ....41 H4
Owlcotes Garth
  PDSY/CALV LS28 ....41 G4
Owlcotes La *PDSY/CALV* LS28 ....41 G3
Owlcotes Rd *PDSY/CALV* LS28 ....41 G4
Owler Ings Rd *BRIG* HD6 ....78 B1
Owlet Rd *SHPY* BD18 ....28 D2
Owl St *KGHY* * BD21 ....7 G3
Oxford Av *GSLY* LS20 ....10 C2
Oxford Cl *CLECK* BD19 ....65 G5
  CUL/QBY BD13 ....51 H3
Oxford Crs *CLAY* BD14 ....45 E3
  HIPP HX3 ....69 E4
Oxford Dr *CLECK* BD19 ....65 G5
Oxford La *HIPP* HX3 ....69 E4
Oxford Pl *BAIL* BD17 ....19 E4
  BFDE BD3 ....3 F2
Oxford Rd *CLECK* BD19 ....65 H2
  CUL/QBY BD13 ....51 H2
  ECHL BD2 ....98 B2
  GSLY LS20 ....10 C2
  HFAX HX1 ....5 G6
Oxford St *CLAY* BD14 ....45 E3
  GSLY LS20 ....10 C2
  KGHY BD21 ....6 D5
  RPDN/SBR HX6 ....67 G3

Oxford Wk *CLECK* BD19 ....65 G5
Ox Heys Mdw *CUL/QBY* BD13 ....44 D1
Oxley Gdns *WBSY* BD6 ....54 D3
Oxley St *GIR* BD8 ....38 D4

P

Padan St *HIPP* HX3 ....69 E4
The Paddock *BAIL* BD17 ....19 G2
  CLECK * BD19 ....63 G5
  CUL/QBY BD13 ....24 C3
Paddock Cl *LM/WK* BD12 ....62 D4
Paddock La *LUD/ILL* HX2 ....58 B5
Paddock Rd *HIPP* HX3 ....52 B5
Paddocks Church *BRIG* HD6 ....79 F1
Padgum *BAIL* BD17 ....18 D2
Padma Cl *IDLE* BD7 ....38 C5
Page Hl *LUD/ILL* HX2 ....58 D3
Paget St *HIPP* * HX3 ....6 D4
Pagewood Ct *IDLE* BD10 ....19 H5
Pakington St *WBOW* BD5 ....47 E3
Paley Rd *BOW* BD4 ....47 H3
Paley Ter *BOW* BD4 ....47 H3
Palin Av *BFDE* BD3 ....40 C3
Palm Cl *WBSY* BD6 ....54 C2
Palmer Rd *BFDE* BD3 ....3 K3
Palmerston Dr *ECHL* * BD2 ....40 A2
Palm St *HIPP* HX3 ....59 G3
Panelagh Av *IDLE* BD10 ....30 D4
Pannal St *GTHN* BD7 ....46 B4
The Parade *BGLY* BD16 ....26 D2
  YEA * LS19 ....11 E5
Paradise La *LUD/ILL* HX2 ....67 E2
Paradise Rd *HIPP* BD9 ....28 A5
Paradise St *BFD* BD1 ....2 A4
  HFAX HX1 ....5 F5
Park Av *BGLY* BD16 ....16 C4
  ELL HX5 ....76 B5
  HWTH BD22 ....13 E4
  IDLE BD10 ....20 A4
  KGHY BD21 ....7 E5
  SHPY BD18 ....28 B1
  YEA LS19 ....11 F4
Park Crs *BFDE* BD3 ....39 H2
  GSLY LS20 ....10 B3
  HIPP HX3 ....59 F4
Park Dene *HFAX* * HX1 ....4 C5
Park Dr *BGLY* BD16 ....17 E1
  HTON BD9 ....28 C5
Park Drive Rd *KGHY* BD21 ....14 B1
Parkfield Av *ELL* HX5 ....76 C5
Parkfield Dr *CUL/QBY* BD13 ....52 A1
Parkfield La *RPDN/SBR* HX6 ....67 G5
Parkfield Rd *GIR* BD8 ....39 E2
  SHPY BD18 ....27 H1
Park Flds *LUD/ILL* HX2 ....58 A3
Park Gdns *LUD/ILL* HX2 ....67 G3
Park Ga *BFDE* BD3 ....3 F4
Park Ga West *HIPP* * HX3 ....76 B1
Park Gv *CUL/QBY* BD13 ....52 A1
  HIPP HX3 ....60 C4
  HTON BD9 ....28 D5
  SHPY BD18 ....28 A1
  YEA LS19 ....11 F4
Park Hl *HUDN* HD2 ....79 G5
Park Hill Cl *GIR* BD8 ....37 G3
Park Hill Dr *GIR* BD8 ....37 G3
Park House Cl *LM/WK* BD12 ....55 F3
Park House Crs *LM/WK* BD12 ....55 F3
Park House Gv *LM/WK* * BD12 ....55 F3
Park House Rd *LM/WK* BD12 ....55 F3
Park House Wk *LM/WK* BD12 ....55 F3
Parkin La *IDLE* BD10 ....31 E1
Parkinson Rd *CUL/QBY* BD13 ....34 D4
Parkinson St *WBOW* BD5 ....47 E3
Parkin St *LVSG* WF15 ....73 F3
Parkland Dr *IDLE* BD10 ....30 A4
Parkland Vw *YEA* LS19 ....11 G5
Park La *BAIL* BD17 ....19 G2
  CLAY BD14 ....45 E3
  CUL/QBY BD13 ....52 C1
  GSLY LS20 ....10 B4
  HIPP HX3 ....76 B1
  KGHY BD21 ....7 F5
  WBOW BD5 ....47 E3
Park Lea *HUDN* HD2 ....79 H5
Park Md *IDLE* BD10 ....20 A4
Parkmere Cl *BOW* BD4 ....56 A3

Park Mount Av *BAIL* BD17 ....19 F3
Park Pl *HFAX* * HX1 ....4 C6
  IDLE BD10 ....20 A4
Park Pl East *HIPP* HX3 ....70 D1
Park Pl West *HIPP* HX3 ....70 D1
Park Rd *BGLY* BD16 ....16 C3
  ELL HX5 ....76 C5
  GSLY LS20 ....10 C4
  HFAX HX1 ....4 E5
  IDLE BD10 ....20 A4
  IDLE BD10 ....30 C4
  RPDN/SBR HX6 ....67 F4
  SHPY BD18 ....28 D2
  WBOW BD5 ....47 F2
  WBSY BD6 ....54 D3
  YEA LS19 ....11 F4
  YEA LS19 ....21 G2
Park Rw *BRIG* * HD6 ....78 C1
Parkside *BGLY* BD16 ....16 D2
  CLECK BD19 ....73 E2
Parkside Av *CUL/QBY* BD13 ....52 A1
Parkside Ct *SHPY* BD20 ....23 F1
Parkside Gv *HTON* BD9 ....38 B1
Parkside Rd *WBOW* BD5 ....47 F2
Parkside Ter *CUL/QBY* BD13 ....24 C3
Park Sq *WBSY* BD6 ....54 A2
Parkstone *HUDN* HD2 ....79 C5
Parkstone Dr *IDLE* BD10 ....30 B4
Park Stone Ri *HIPP* HX3 ....53 E4
Park St *BRIG* HD6 ....79 F1
  CLECK BD19 ....65 H5
  CLECK BD19 ....73 E2
  HWTH BD22 ....23 E2
  RPDN/SBR HX6 ....67 F4
  SHPY BD18 ....28 B1
  YEA LS19 ....11 F4
Park Ter *HFAX* * HX1 ....4 C4
  HIPP HX3 ....60 C4
  KGHY BD21 ....7 G4
  SHPY BD18 ....28 B1
The Park Towngate *HIPP* HX3 ....69 H5
Park Vw *CLECK* BD19 ....64 B5
  HFAX HX1 ....4 C5
  HIPP HX3 ....70 D1
Park View Av *HIPP* HX3 ....60 D4
  HWTH BD22 ....23 F1
Parkview Ct *SHPY* * BD18 ....28 B2
Park View Rd *HTON* BD9 ....38 C2
Park View Ter *HTON* BD9 ....38 C1
  YEA LS19 ....21 G2
Park Wy *BAIL* BD17 ....18 A5
Parkway *CUL/QBY* BD13 ....52 A1
  KGHY BD21 ....14 B1
  WBOW BD5 ....55 G4
Park Willow *HIPP* HX3 ....55 G4
Parkwood Gdns
  PDSY/CALV LS28 ....31 G3
Parkwood Ri *KGHY* BD21 ....14 B1
Parkwood Rd *PDSY/CALV* LS28 ....31 G3
  SHPY BD18 ....28 A2
Parkwood St *KGHY* BD21 ....7 G5
Parma St *WBOW* BD5 ....47 F2
Parratt Rw *BFDE* BD3 ....40 C5
Parrott St *BOW* BD4 ....56 C1
Parry Cl *BGLY* * BD16 ....11 F5
Parry La *BOW* BD4 ....48 B2
Parsonage La *BRIG* HD6 ....71 F5
Parsonage Rd *BOW* BD4 ....48 C2
  WBOW BD5 ....47 F4
Parsonage St *HIPP* HX3 ....60 D4
Parsons Rd *HTON* BD9 ....28 B5
Parson St *KGHY* BD21 ....7 F5
Pasture Av *HWTH* BD22 ....12 D5
Pasture Cl *CLAY* BD14 ....45 G3
Pasture La *CLAY* BD14 ....45 G3
Pasture Ri *CLAY* BD14 ....45 G3
Pasture Rd *BAIL* BD17 ....19 E4
Pasture Side Ter East
  CLAY BD14 ....45 G3
Pasture Side Ter West
  CLAY BD14 ....45 F3
Pasture Wk *CLAY* BD14 ....45 F3
Patent St *HTON* BD9 ....38 C5
Paternoster La *GTHN* BD7 ....46 B3
Patricia Gdns *RPDN/SBR* * HX6 ....68 A4
Pattie St *KGHY* BD21 ....7 E2
Pavement La *LUD/ILL* HX2 ....50 D3
Paw La *CUL/QBY* BD13 ....52 C3
Pawson St *BOW* BD4 ....48 C1
Peabody St *HIPP* HX3 ....59 F4
Peace St *BOW* BD4 ....48 B2
Peacock Ct *YEA* LS19 ....11 H5
Pearl St *HWTH* BD22 ....13 H2
Pearson La *HTON* BD9 ....37 G3
Pearson Rd *WBSY* BD6 ....55 E2
Pearson Rw *LM/WK* BD12 ....63 E2
Pearson St *BFDE* BD3 ....48 B1
  CLECK BD19 ....73 E2

PDSY/CALV LS28 ......31 G2
Pear St HFAX HX1 ......4 A5
  HWTH BD22 ......13 H3
  HWTH * BD22 ......32 D2
Peasehill Cl YEA LS19 ......21 H2
Peasehill Pk YEA LS19 ......21 H2
Peaseland Av CLECK BD19 ......73 F1
Peaseland Cl CLECK BD19 ......73 G1
Peaseland Rd CLECK BD19 ......73 G1
Peckover Dr PDSY/CALV LS28 ......41 E3
Peckover St BFD BD1 ......3 F5
Peel Cl BOW BD4 ......48 D2
Peel Park Dr ECHL BD2 ......40 A2
Peel Park Ter ECHL BD2 ......39 H2
Peel Park Vw BFDE BD3 ......39 H3
Peel Rw GTHN BD7 ......46 B4
Peel Sq BFD BD1 ......2 B1
Peel St BGLY BD16 ......17 E3
  CUL/QBY BD13 ......44 A1
  CUL/QBY BD13 ......52 C1
  RPDN/SBR * HX6 ......67 E4
  WIL/AL BD15 ......25 H5
Peep Green Rd LVSG WF15 ......73 F5
Pelham Ct ECHL BD2 ......40 A1
Pelham Rd ECHL BD2 ......40 A1
Pellon La HFAX HX1 ......4 A1
Pellon New Rd LUD/ILL HX2 ......58 D1
Pellon Ter IDLE BD10 ......20 A5
Pellon Wk IDLE BD10 ......20 A5
Pemberton Dr GTHN BD7 ......2 A7
Pembroke St WBOW BD5 ......47 F3
Pendle Ct CUL/QBY BD13 ......52 B3
Pendle Rd BGLY BD16 ......17 E3
Pendragon ECHL * BD2 ......39 H1
Pendragon La ECHL BD2 ......40 A1
Penfield Gv CLAY BD14 ......45 F3
Pengarth BGLY BD16 ......17 E1
Penistone Ms HWTH * BD22 ......22 D2
Penn Cl ECHL BD2 ......40 A1
Penn Dr CLECK BD19 ......73 G2
Penn Gv CLECK BD19 ......73 G2
Pennine Cl CUL/QBY BD13 ......52 A3
Pennington Ter WBOW * BD5 ......46 D3
Pennithorne Av BAIL BD17 ......18 D2
Penn St HFAX HX1 ......4 C2
Penny Hill Dr CLAY BD14 ......45 G3
Penrose Dr GTHN BD7 ......46 A4
Pentland Av CLAY BD14 ......45 G3
Pentland Cl HWTH BD22 ......6 D1
Penzance Ct GIR BD8 ......38 C4
Percival St BFDE BD3 ......3 H1
Percy St BGLY BD16 ......16 D3
  KGHY BD21 ......14 A2
Peregrine Wy WBSY BD6 ......53 F1
Per La LUD/ILL HX2 ......50 C3
Perry Cl HWTH BD22 ......13 H1
Perseverance La GTHN BD7 ......46 B4
Perseverance Rd
  CUL/QBY BD13 ......43 F4
Perseverance St BAIL * BD17 ......19 E2
  LM/WK BD12 ......62 D1
  PDSY/CALV LS28 ......41 E3
  RPDN/SBR * HX6 ......67 E4
Perseverance Ter HFAX HX1 ......68 B3
Perth Av ECHL BD2 ......39 F1
Peterborough Pl ECHL BD2 ......40 A1
Peterborough Rd ECHL BD2 ......40 A2
Peterborough Ter ECHL BD2 ......40 A1
Petergate BFD BD1 ......2 D5
Peter La LUD/ILL HX2 ......67 C1
Petrel Cl WBSY BD6 ......53 F1
Petrie Gv BFDE BD3 ......40 D5
Petrie Rd BFDE BD3 ......40 D5
Peverell Cl BOW BD4 ......48 D4
Peveril Mt ECHL BD2 ......40 B2
Pheasant St KGHY BD21 ......7 G3
Phoebe La HIPP HX3 ......69 G4
Phoenix St BRIG HD6 ......78 C1
Phoenix Wy BOW BD4 ......48 D1
Piccadilly BFD BD1 ......2 D4
The Pickerings CUL/QBY BD13 ......52 B2
Pickles La GTHN BD7 ......46 A4
Pickles St KGHY BD21 ......14 A1
Pickwood La RPDN/SBR HX6 ......74 D1
Picton St GIR BD8 ......2 A1
Pictureville BFD BD1 ......2 D5
Piggott St BRIG HD6 ......71 F5
Pinebury Dr CUL/QBY BD13 ......51 H3
Pine Cft KGHY BD21 ......6 D2
Pinedale BGLY BD16 ......16 C1
Pine St BFD BD1 ......3 F4
  HFAX HX1 ......5 H1
  HWTH BD22 ......22 D3
Pinfold Cft CLAY BD14 ......45 F3
Pinfold La ELL HX5 ......77 G5
  RPDN/SBR HX6 ......66 A4
Pink St HWTH BD22 ......22 D3
Pinnar La HIPP HX3 ......69 G3

Pipercroft WBSY BD6 ......53 H4
Pirie Cl ECHL BD2 ......39 G1
Pitcliffe Wy WBOW BD5 ......47 F3
Pit Hl HIPP HX3 ......5 K6
Pit La CLECK BD19 ......65 G3
  CUL/QBY BD13 ......34 B3
  CUL/QBY BD13 ......43 H3
Pits La CLECK BD19 ......72 B2
Pitts St BOW BD4 ......48 C3
Pitt St KGHY BD21 ......7 G4
Plains La ELL HX5 ......76 C2
Plane Tree Nest La LUD/ILL HX2 ......67 H2
Plane Tree Rd RPDN/SBR HX6 ......67 E3
Plane Trees CLECK BD19 ......58 C5
Plane Trees Cl CLECK BD19 ......64 C2
Planetrees St WIL/AL BD15 ......36 D3
Plantation Pl BOW BD4 ......48 B3
Plantation Wy BAIL BD17 ......19 E3
Pleasant St GTHN BD7 ......46 B3
Plevna Ter BGLY BD16 ......16 C2
Plimsoll St BOW BD4 ......47 H3
Ploughcroft La HIPP HX3 ......59 G3
Ploughmans Cft ECHL BD2 ......29 F5
Plover St KGHY BD21 ......7 F3
  WBOW BD5 ......46 D4
Plumpton Av ECHL BD2 ......29 G3
Plumpton Cl ECHL BD2 ......29 H4
Plumpton Dr ECHL BD2 ......29 H3
Plumpton End ECHL BD2 ......29 H3
Plumpton Gdns ECHL BD2 ......29 G3
Plumpton Lea ECHL BD2 ......29 G3
Plumpton Md ECHL BD2 ......29 G3
Plumpton St GIR BD8 ......38 B4
Plumpton Wk ECHL BD2 ......29 G3
Plum St HFAX HX1 ......4 B6
  HWTH BD22 ......13 H3
Plymouth Gv HFAX * HX1 ......4 C1
Pohlman St HFAX * HX1 ......4 B7
Pollard Av BGLY BD16 ......17 E1
  CLECK BD19 ......65 G4
Pollard Cl CLECK BD19 ......65 G4
Pollard La BFDE BD3 ......40 A3
Pollard St BOW BD4 ......47 G2
Pollard Wy CLECK BD19 ......65 G4
Pollit Av RPDN/SBR HX6 ......66 C5
Pond St KGHY BD21 ......7 F3
Pool Ct BFDE BD3 ......3 H3
Pool St KGHY * BD21 ......7 H2
Pope St KGHY BD21 ......7 H2
Poplar Av GTHN BD7 ......46 A5
  RPDN/SBR HX6 ......67 E3
  SHPY BD18 ......28 D4
Poplar Ct ELL * HX5 ......76 C5
Poplar Crs LUD/ILL HX2 ......51 E3
  SHPY BD18 ......28 D4
Poplar Dr AIRE BD20 ......8 D4
  SHPY BD18 ......28 D4
Poplar Gv BGLY BD16 ......15 F5
  CLECK BD19 ......73 F2
  GTHN BD7 ......46 A5
  SHPY BD18 ......28 D4
Poplar Rd GTHN BD7 ......46 B5
  SHPY BD18 ......28 D4
The Poplars GSLY LS20 ......10 D1
Poplars Park Rd ECHL BD2 ......29 E5
Poplar St HIPP HX3 ......5 G1
Poplar Ter AIRE BD20 ......9 E4
Poplar Vw BRIG HD6 ......71 F2
  GTHN BD7 ......45 H5
Poplarwood Gdns IDLE BD10 ......30 D4
Popples Dr LUD/ILL HX2 ......51 E3
Popple Wells La LUD/ILL HX2 ......66 C1
Poppy Ct WBSY * BD6 ......54 A4
Porritt St CLECK BD19 ......64 C4
Portland Pl BGLY BD16 ......16 D4
  HFAX HX1 ......5 H6
Portland Rd HIPP HX3 ......5 H1
Portland St HFAX HX1 ......4 D4
  HWTH BD22 ......23 E2
  WBOW BD5 ......5 E2
Portman St PDSY/CALV LS28 ......31 G3
Portsmouth Av BFDE BD3 ......3 F1
Portwood St HTON BD9 ......37 G2
Post Office Rd IDLE BD10 ......30 B4
Pothouse Rd WBSY BD6 ......54 C2
Powell Av WBOW BD5 ......46 D3
Powell Rd BGLY BD16 ......16 D3
  SHPY BD18 ......29 E4
Powell St HFAX HX1 ......5 G4
Pratt La SHPY BD18 ......28 D3
Prescott St HFAX HX1 ......5 H6
Prescott Ter WIL/AL BD15 ......37 E3
Preston La LUD/ILL HX2 ......58 B3
Preston Pl HFAX HX1 ......4 D4
Preston St GIR BD8 ......38 D5
Priestthorpe Av PDSY/CALV LS28 ......41 G2

Priesthorpe La PDSY/CALV LS28 ......41 G1
Priesthorpe Rd PDSY/CALV LS28 ......31 H5
Priestley Av WBSY BD6 ......54 C2
Priestley Pl RPDN/SBR HX6 ......66 D5
Priestley St CUL/QBY BD13 ......44 A1
Priestley Ter WBSY BD6 ......54 C1
Priestman Cl GIR BD8 ......38 D3
Priestman St GIR BD8 ......38 D3
Priestthorpe Cl BGLY BD16 ......16 D2
Priestthorpe La BGLY BD16 ......16 D2
Priestthorpe Rd BGLY BD16 ......16 D3
Primrose Bank BGLY BD16 ......17 E4
Primrose Dr BGLY BD16 ......17 E5
Primrose Gv KGHY BD21 ......7 H4
Primrose La BGLY BD16 ......17 E5
  ECHL BD2 ......29 E5
Primrose St GIR BD8 ......38 D4
  KGHY BD21 ......7 H4
Primrose Wy HIPP HX3 ......53 G3
Princeroyd Wy GTHN BD7 ......38 B5
Prince's Crs ECHL BD2 ......39 F1
Prince's Ga HIPP HX3 ......68 C4
Princess St BRIG HD6 ......78 C1
  GTL/HWG HX4 ......76 A4
  HFAX HX1 ......5 H3
  RPDN/SBR HX6 ......67 F4
  YEA LS19 ......21 F2
Prince's La CUL/QBY BD13 ......44 A1
Prince's St WBSY BD6 ......53 H3
  WBSY BD6 ......54 C2
Prince St BOW BD4 ......56 B1
  HWTH BD22 ......23 E2
Prince's Wy WBOW BD5 ......2 C6
Princeville Rd GTHN BD7 ......38 B5
Princeville St GTHN BD7 ......38 C5
Prior St KGHY BD21 ......7 H3
Priory Cl BGLY BD16 ......16 D2
Priory Ct GIR * BD8 ......2 A2
Priory Gv BGLY BD16 ......16 D2
Priory Rd BRIG HD6 ......78 D2
Proctor St BOW BD4 ......56 C1
Prod Ga BAIL * BD17 ......18 A4
Prod La BAIL BD17 ......17 H4
Progress Av BGLY BD16 ......15 F5
Prospect Av LUD/ILL HX2 ......67 H4
  SHPY BD18 ......28 D2
Prospect Cl LUD/ILL HX2 ......67 H4
  SHPY BD18 ......28 D2
Prospect Ct LUD/ILL HX2 ......58 A5
Prospect Crs HWTH BD22 ......13 F1
Prospect Dr HWTH BD22 ......13 F1
Prospect Gv SHPY BD18 ......28 D2
Prospect La BIRK/DRI BD11 ......57 G5
Prospect Mt HWTH BD22 ......13 F1
  SHPY BD18 ......28 D2
Prospect Pl BRIG HD6 ......78 B1
  ECHL BD2 ......40 B2
  HTON BD9 ......38 A3
  LUD/ILL HX2 ......59 E2
  RPDN/SBR * HX6 ......66 A5
Prospect Rd BFDE BD3 ......2 E1
  BGLY BD16 ......17 F1
  CLECK BD19 ......64 C5
Prospect St BOW BD4 ......47 G2
  CLECK BD19 ......73 G1
  CUL/QBY * BD13 ......44 B1
  HIPP HX3 ......5 J1
  HWTH BD22 ......6 C5
  HWTH BD22 ......22 D3
  IDLE BD10 ......30 B4
  PDSY/CALV * LS28 ......41 H4
  SHPY BD18 ......28 D2
  WBSY BD6 ......54 A3
  YEA LS19 ......21 H3
Prospect Ter CLECK BD19 ......64 C5
  WIL/AL BD15 ......37 F3
Prospect Wk SHPY BD18 ......28 D2
Providence Av BAIL BD17 ......18 D2
Providence Crs HWTH BD22 ......12 D4
Providence La HWTH BD22 ......12 D4
Providence Pl * HD6 ......78 D2
Providence Rw BAIL BD17 ......18 D2
  LUD/ILL HX2 ......59 E2
Providence St BFD BD1 ......2 B5
  CLECK * BD19 ......63 F5
  CLECK * BD19 ......64 D5
  ELL HX5 ......76 C4
Providence Ter CUL/QBY BD13 ......44 A1
Prune Park La WIL/AL BD15 ......36 A5
Pule Green La HIPP HX3 ......59 G2
Pullan Av ECHL BD2 ......30 B5
Pullan Dr ECHL BD2 ......30 B5
Pullan Gv ECHL BD2 ......30 B5
Pullan La BAIL BD17 ......20 B1
Pullan St WBOW BD5 ......47 E2
Purbeck Ct BOW * BD4 ......48 D5
Purley Wk WBSY BD6 ......54 C2
Pye Nest Av LUD/ILL HX2 ......67 G4
Pye Nest Ct LVSG WF15 ......73 G4

Pye Nest Dr LUD/ILL HX2 ......67 H4
Pye Nest Gdns LUD/ILL HX2 ......67 H3
Pye Nest Gv LUD/ILL HX2 ......67 H4
Pye Nest Ri LUD/ILL HX2 ......67 H4
Pye Nest Rd RPDN/SBR HX6 ......67 G4
Pyenot Av CLECK BD19 ......73 H2
Pyenot Dr CLECK BD19 ......73 H2
Pyenot Gdns CLECK BD19 ......73 H2
Pyenot Hall La CLECK BD19 ......73 H1
Pyrah Rd LM/WK BD12 ......55 E3
Pyrah St LM/WK BD12 ......63 E1

Q

Quail St KGHY BD21 ......7 G3
Quaker La CLECK BD19 ......73 G2
  WBOW BD5 ......46 C4
Quakers La YEA LS19 ......21 G1
Quarry Hl RPDN/SBR HX6 ......67 E5
Quarry Pl ECHL BD2 ......40 A2
Quarry Rd CLECK BD19 ......73 F1
  HIPP HX3 ......58 D3
Quarry St HTON BD9 ......38 B5
  KGHY BD21 ......7 G4
Quayside BAIL BD17 ......28 C1
Quebec St ELL HX5 ......76 D5
Queen's Av ECHL BD2 ......39 G1
Queensbury Rd HIPP HX3 ......51 G5
Queensbury Sq CUL/QBY * BD13 ......52 B1
Queens Cl BGLY BD16 ......17 E4
Queens Dr HIPP HX3 ......69 H4
Queensgate BFD BD1 ......2 D5
Queen's Ga HIPP HX3 ......68 C4
Queens Gv KGHY BD21 ......14 A1
Queens Md HIPP * HX3 ......60 D2
Queens Pl SHPY BD18 ......28 A1
Queen's Ri ECHL BD2 ......39 G1
Queen's Rd BGLY BD16 ......9 F5
  ECHL BD2 ......39 F2
  HFAX HX1 ......4 B2
  HIPP HX3 ......62 A3
  KGHY BD21 ......13 H2
  SHPY BD18 ......28 A1
Queen St BAIL BD17 ......18 D5
  BGLY BD16 ......16 D2
  CLECK BD19 ......65 G3
  CLECK BD19 ......65 G3
  GTL/HWG HX4 ......75 H5
  IDLE BD10 ......30 C2
  RPDN/SBR HX6 ......66 B5
  WBSY BD6 ......53 H3
  WIL/AL BD15 ......25 H5
  YEA LS19 ......21 G2
Queensway BGLY BD16 ......17 E4
  GSLY LS20 ......11 E2
  HFAX HX1 ......4 A2
Queen Victoria Crs HIPP HX3 ......61 E3
Quincy Cl ECHL BD2 ......30 B5

R

Race Moor La HWTH BD22 ......12 C3
Radcliffe Av ECHL BD2 ......29 H4
Radfield Dr WBSY BD6 ......55 F2
Radnor St BFDE BD3 ......40 B5
Radwell Dr WBOW BD5 ......47 F2
Raeburn Dr WBSY BD6 ......54 B3
Rae Rd SHPY BD18 ......28 B3
Raglan Av HWTH BD22 ......4 C5
Raglan Ct HFAX HX1 ......4 D3
Raglan St BFDE BD3 ......3 H3
  CUL/QBY BD13 ......52 B1
  HFAX HX1 ......4 D3
  HWTH BD22 ......6 C5
Raglan Ter BFDE BD3 ......40 D5
Raikes La BOW BD4 ......49 F5
  BOW BD4 ......56 D3
Raikes Wood Dr BOW BD4 ......56 D3
Railway Rd IDLE BD10 ......30 A1
Railway St BOW BD4 ......56 B1
  BRIG HD6 ......78 C2
  CLECK BD19 ......73 G1
  KGHY * BD21 ......7 F2
Railway Ter HIPP HX3 ......75 F1
Rainbow Ms WBSY * BD6 ......54 A4
Raistrick Wy SHPY BD18 ......29 E1
Raleigh St HFAX * HX1 ......4 B7
Ramsden Av GTHN BD7 ......45 H2
Ramsden Ct GTHN BD7 ......46 B3
Ramsden Pl CLAY BD14 ......45 H2
Ramsden St HIPP HX3 ......58 D3
Ramsey St WBOW BD5 ......47 E4
Ramsgate St HFAX HX1 ......4 A3

Randall Pl *HTON* BD9......................38 B1
Randall Well St *BFD* BD1.................2 B6
Randolph St *BFDE* BD3..................40 D4
　HIPP HX3...5 G1
Random Cl *HWTH* BD22................13 C1
Rand Pl *GTHN* BD7.......................46 D2
Rand St *GTHN* BD7.......................46 D2
Ranelagh Av *IDLE* BD10................30 D4
Range Bank *HIPP* HX3..................59 H4
Range Bank Top *HIPP* HX3............59 H4
Range Gdns *HIPP* HX3...................59 H4
Range La *HIPP* HX3.......................5 H1
Range St *HIPP* HX3.......................59 H4
Ransdale Dr *WBOW* BD5................47 E4
Ransdale Gv *WBOW* BD5................47 E4
Ransdale Rd *WBOW* BD5................47 E4
Rastrick Common *BRIG* HD6........78 B3
Rathmell St *WBOW* BD5.................55 E1
Ravenscliffe Av *IDLE* BD10...........30 D4
Ravenscliffe Rd
　PDSY/CALV LS28.......................30 D3
Ravenstone Dr *GTL/HWG* HX4.....75 H3
Raven St *BGLY* BD16....................16 C3
　HFAX HX1..4 B3
　KGHY BD21.......................................7 E4
Ravensworth Av *IDLE* BD10..........30 D4
Raven Ter *GIR* BD8.......................37 F5
Rawdon Dr *YEA* LS19....................21 G3
Rawdon Hall Dr *YEA* LS19............21 G3
Rawdon Rd *HWTH* BD22...............22 D2
Rawdon St *HWTH* BD22..................6 D5
Rawfolds Wy *CLECK* BD19.............73 H2
Raw Hl *BRIG* * HD6.......................78 A3
Raw La *LUD/ILL* HX2....................50 C5
Rawling St *KGHY* BD21.................14 A1
Raw Nook *LM/WK* BD12................55 C5
Rawson Av *BFDE* BD3...................40 C4
　HIPP HX3.......................................68 C5
Rawson Pl *BFD* BD1........................2 C4
　RPDN/SBR HX6.............................66 D5
Rawson Rd *BFD* BD1........................2 B4
Rawson Sq *BFD* BD1........................2 C4
　IDLE BD10.....................................20 A5
Rawson St *HFAX* HX1......................5 G4
　LM/WK BD12..................................63 E1
Rawson St North *HIPP* HX3..........59 G4
Rayleigh St *BOW* BD4...................47 H3
Raymond Dr *WBOW* BD5...............47 F5
Raymond St *WBOW* BD5................47 F5
Raynbron Crs *WBOW* BD5.............47 G5
Rayner Av *GIR* BD8......................38 A3
Rayner Dr *BRIG* HD6....................71 F4
Rayner Mt *WIL/AL* BD15..............37 E4
Rayner Rd *BRIG* HD6....................71 F4
Rayners Av *LVSG* WF15.................73 F4
Raynham Crs *HWTH* BD22..............6 B3
Raywood Cl *YEA* LS19...................11 F3
Rebecca St *BFD* BD1.......................2 A3
Recreation La *ELL* HX5.................76 B5
Recreation Rd *RPDN/SBR* HX6.....67 E4
Rectory Rw *KGHY* BD21..................7 E4
Red Beck Rd *HIPP* HX3.................60 C4
Red Beck V *SHPY* BD18.................28 B4
Redburn Av *SHPY* BD18................28 B4
Redburn Dr *SHPY* BD18................28 B4
Redburn Rd *SHPY* BD18................28 B4
Redcar Rd *IDLE* BD10...................30 D3
Redcar St *HFAX* HX1......................4 A3
Redcliffe Av *KGHY* BD21...............6 D4
Redcliffe Gv *KGHY* BD21...............6 D4
Redcliffe St *KGHY* BD21................6 D4
Red La *PDSY/CALV* LS28...............41 H4
Redman Garth *HWTH* BD22..........22 C2
Redmire St *BFDE* BD3..................40 D5
Red V *CLECK* BD19.......................65 G3
Redwood Cl *KGHY* BD21................14 D1
Redwood Wy *YEA* LS19.................11 E4
Rees Wy *BFDE* BD3........................3 F2
Reeth Rd *BRIG* HD6......................77 H3
Reevy Av *WBSY* BD6.....................54 A2
Reevy Crs *WBSY* BD6...................53 H3
Reevy Dr *WBSY* BD6....................54 A2
Reevylands Dr *WBSY* BD6............54 B2
Reevy Rd *WBSY* BD6....................54 A2
Reevy Rd West *WBSY* BD6............53 H2
Reevy St *WBSY* BD6.....................54 B1
Reform St *CLECK* BD19.................65 G4
Regency Ct *GIR* BD8.....................38 B4
Regency Vw *BFDE* BD3.................39 H2
Regent Cl *BRIG* HD6.....................77 H5
Regent Pde *RPDN/SBR* * HX6.......67 F4
Regent Pl *IDLE* BD10....................19 H5
　RPDN/SBR HX6.............................67 E3
Regent St *CUL/QBY* BD13.............52 C1
　HFAX HX1..5 F5
　IDLE BD10.....................................19 H5
　IDLE * BD10...................................30 C2
Reginald St *WBOW* BD5................47 E4

Reighton Cft *IDLE* BD10...............30 D3
Reins Av *BAIL* BD17......................18 C5
Reins Rd *BRIG* HD6......................77 H3
Renee Cl *BOW* BD4.......................56 B2
Renshaw St *IDLE* BD10................20 A5
Renton Av *GSLY* LS20...................10 C2
Renton Dr *GSLY* LS20...................10 C3
Reservoir Pl *CUL/QBY* BD13........43 H5
Reservoir Rd *LUD/ILL* HX2..........58 D5
Reservoir Vw *CUL/QBY* BD13......36 A5
Retford Pl *GTHN* BD7...................46 D2
Reva Cl *BGLY* BD16......................17 E2
Reva Syke Rd *BGLY* BD14............45 E4
Reydon Wk *WBSY* BD6.................54 A1
Reyhill Gv *WBOW* BD5.................47 F2
Reyner House Ms *WBOW* BD5.......47 F2
Reynolds Av *GTHN* BD7...............45 H2
Rhine St *BOW* BD4.......................47 H2
Rhodesia Av *HIPP* HX3.................68 D5
　WIL/AL BD15................................37 F4
Rhodes Pl *SHPY* BD18.................28 C1
Rhodes St *HFAX* HX1.....................4 B1
　SHPY BD18....................................28 B1
Rhodes Wy *GIR* BD8....................37 G5
Rhodesway *GIR* BD8....................37 G5
Rhondda Pl *HFAX* HX1...................5 H1
Rhum Cl *WBSY* BD6.....................54 A4
Rhylstone Mt *GTHN* BD7.............38 A5
Ribble St *KGHY* BD21....................7 H3
Ribbleton Gv *BFDE* BD3.................3 G3
Riccall Nook *IDLE* BD10..............30 C3
Richardson Av *WBSY* BD6............54 D2
Richardson St *LM/WK* BD12........63 H1
Richard St *BFDE* BD3.....................3 G5
　BRIG HD6......................................79 F1
Richmond Av *RPDN/SBR* HX6......66 C5
Richmond Cl *HFAX* HX1..................5 F2
Richmond Gdns *RPDN/SBR* HX6..66 C5
Richmond Gv *CLECK* BD19...........65 G3
Richmond Ms *SHPY* BD18............28 A1
Richmond Pl *SHPY* BD18.............28 A1
Richmond Rd *GTHN* BD7..............46 D1
　HFAX HX1..5 F2
　PDSY/CALV LS28...........................41 H2
　SHPY * BD18..................................28 A1
Richmond St *CLECK* BD19...........73 C1
　HFAX HX1..5 F2
　KGHY BD21.....................................7 E3
Riddlesden St *AIRE* * BD20...........8 A2
Ridge Cl *GSLY* LS20......................10 B3
Ridge Hl *BRIG* HD6......................77 H2
Ridge Lea *BRIG* HD6....................78 A2
Ridgemount Rd *AIRE* BD20............7 H1
Ridge View Bank *IDLE* BD10.......30 B2
Ridge View Gdns *IDLE* BD10.......30 B2
Ridgeway *CUL/QBY* BD13............52 C2
　GSLY LS20.....................................10 A3
　SHPY BD18....................................29 F3
Ridgeway Gdns *BRIG* HD6...........70 D3
Ridgway Mt *HWTH* BD22.............23 F3
Ridgewood Cl *BAIL* BD17.............19 F5
Riding Hl *HIPP* HX3.....................53 H4
Riding La *LUD/ILL* HX2................58 B2
Ridings Wy *WBSY* BD6.................53 H2
Rievaulx Av *GIR* BD8...................38 D4
Rigton St *WBOW* BD5...................47 E4
Riley La *LUD/ILL* HX2..................51 E2
Rillington Md *IDLE* BD10.............30 C3
Rilston St *GTHN* BD7...................46 C1
Rimswell Holt *IDLE* BD10............30 D3
Ringby La *HIPP* HX3.....................59 G3
Ringby Ter *HIPP* * HX3................59 G3
Ring Rd Farsley
　PDSY/CALV LS28.......................41 H1
Ringwood Edge *GTL/HWG* HX4...75 H5
Ringwood Rd *WBOW* BD5.............46 C4
Ripley La *GSLY* LS20....................10 D1
Ripley Rd *BOW* BD4.....................47 G3
Ripley St *AIRE* BD20......................8 A2
　HIPP HX3.......................................71 F1
　WBOW BD5....................................47 F3
　WIL/AL BD15.................................36 D2
Ripon St *HFAX* HX1......................67 H2
Ripon Ter *HIPP* HX3.....................59 G3
The Rise *HIPP* HX3.......................60 D3
Rishworthian Ct *HIPP* * HX3.......75 F2
Rishworth St *HWTH* BD22..............6 C5
River Mt *AIRE* BD20.......................8 A2
Riverside *KGHY* BD21.....................7 H4
Riverside Dr *CLECK* BD19............64 C4
Riverside Est *BAIL* BD17..............28 B1
River St *BRIG* HD6.......................78 D2
　HWTH * BD22................................23 E2
　KGHY BD21.....................................7 H2
River Wk *BGLY* BD16....................16 C3
Riverwood Dr *HIPP* HX3...............75 G1
Rivock Gv *AIRE* BD20.....................6 C1
Roans Brae *IDLE* BD10.................30 D3

Roberson Ter *CLECK* BD19...........65 F5
Robertson Av *BRIG* HD6...............78 B3
Roberts Pl *BFD* BD1.......................2 B4
Robert's Ct *CLECK* BD19..............73 F1
Robert St *BFDE* BD3......................3 G1
　HIPP HX3.......................................59 F3
　HWTH BD22...................................23 C1
Robert St North *HIPP* HX3...........59 H3
Robin Cl *ECHL* BD2......................30 B5
Robin Dr *ECHL* BD2.....................30 B5
Robin Hood Wy *BRIG* HD6...........79 F1
Robinson Ct *GTHN* BD7...............46 A1
Robin St *WBOW* * BD5.................46 D3
Robin Wk *SHPY* BD18..................29 E3
Rochdale Rd *GTL/HWG* HX4........74 D4
　LUD/ILL HX2.................................67 G3
Rochester Pl *ELL* * HX5...............76 C5
Rochester St *BFDE* BD3...............40 B5
　SHPY BD18....................................28 D3
Rockcliffe Av *BAIL* BD17..............18 D5
Rockfield Ter *YEA* LS19................11 H4
Rockhill La *BOW* BD4..................55 H3
Rockland Crs *GTHN* BD7..............45 H2
Rocklands Av *BAIL* BD17..............18 D2
Rocklands Pl *BAIL* BD17..............18 D2
Rock La *CUL/QBY* BD13...............35 H4
Rocks Rd *HIPP* HX3......................68 B5
Rock St *BRIG* HD6........................71 F5
Rocks Vw *LUD/ILL* HX2...............68 B4
Rock Ter *CUL/QBY* BD13.............44 A1
　GIR BD8..39 E3
Rockville Ter *HFAX* HX1...............68 B3
Rockwell La *IDLE* BD10...............30 B3
Rockwood Cl *HUDN* HD2.............79 F5
Rockwood Crs *PDSY/CALV* LS28...41 F1
Rockwood Gv *PDSY/CALV* LS28...41 G1
Rockwood Hill Ct
　PDSY/CALV LS28.......................41 F2
Rockwood Rd *PDSY/CALV* LS28...41 F2
Rodin Av *GIR* BD8........................37 G5
Rodley La *PDSY/CALV* LS28.........31 H3
Roger Ct *ECHL* BD2......................40 A3
Rogerson Sq *BRIG* HD6...............71 F5
Roils Head Rd *LUD/ILL* HX2........67 E1
Rokeby Gdns *IDLE* BD10.............30 D3
Romanby Shaw *IDLE* BD10..........30 C3
Rombalds Dr *BGLY* BD16.............17 E3
Romsey Gdns *BOW* BD4...............48 C4
Romsey Ms *BOW* BD4..................48 C4
Ronald Dr *GTHN* BD7...................38 B5
Rookery La *HIPP* HX3...................69 E5
Rookes Av *WBSY* BD6..................54 D2
Rookes La *HIPP* HX3....................62 B4
Rook La *BOW* BD4........................48 A5
Rooks Av *CLECK* BD19.................64 B5
Rooks Cl *LM/WK* BD12.................63 E4
Rook St *BGLY* BD16......................16 C3
Rookwith Pde *IDLE* BD10............30 C3
Rooley Av *WBSY* BD6...................55 E2
Rooley Banks *RPDN/SBR* HX6......66 B5
Rooley Cl *WBOW* BD5...................55 F1
Rooley Crs *WBSY* BD6..................55 F2
Rooley Hts *RPDN/SBR* HX6..........66 A5
Rooley La *BOW* BD4.....................48 A5
　WBOW BD5....................................55 E1
Roper Gn *LUD/ILL* HX2................58 C1
Roper La *CUL/QBY* BD13.............43 G5
　LUD/ILL HX2.................................51 E2
Roper St *KGHY* BD21.....................7 E4
Rose Bank *GIR* BD8......................38 D2
Rose Bank Pl *GIR* BD8.................37 H5
Roseberry St *HWTH* BD22............13 E4
Rosebery Av *HIPP* HX3.................69 E4
　SHPY BD18....................................28 D2
Rosebery Mt *SHPY* BD18..............28 D2
Rosebery Rd *GIR* BD8..................38 D2
Rosebery St *ELL* HX5...................76 C5
　PDSY/CALV LS28...........................41 H4
Rosebery Ter *HFAX* HX1................4 C1
Rosechapel Cl *WBSY* * BD6.........54 A4
Rosedale Av *WIL/AL* BD15...........36 C2
Rosedale Cl *BAIL* BD17................18 B4
Rose Gv *RPDN/SBR* HX6..............66 C3
Rose Heath *LUD/ILL* HX2............50 C3
Rosehill Crs *LM/WK* BD12............62 D1
Roselee Cl *HIPP* HX3...................69 F5
Rosemary La *BRIG* HD6...............78 B3
　HIPP HX3.......................................69 F5
Rose Mdw *HWTH* BD22................13 F1
Rosemont La *BAIL* BD17..............19 E4
Rose Mt *BOW* * BD4....................57 F2
　ECHL BD2......................................39 H1
　LUD/ILL * HX2..............................68 B4
Rosemount Av *ELL* HX5...............76 D5
Rosemount Cl *KGHY* * BD21..........7 E4
Rosemount Wk *KGHY* * BD21........7 E4
Rose Pl *LUD/ILL* HX2...................66 B3

Rose St *GIR* BD8..........................38 C3
　HFAX HX1..4 B4
　KGHY BD21.....................................4 A4
Rose Ter *HFAX* HX1........................4 C3
　LUD/ILL * HX2...............................68 B4
Rosewood Av *KGHY* BD21..............8 A2
Rosewood Gv *BOW* BD4...............48 C2
Rosley Mt *WBSY* BD6...................54 A4
Roslyn Pl *GTHN* BD7...................46 C1
Rossefield Pk *HTON* BD9.............28 C5
Rossefield Rd *HTON* BD9.............28 B5
Rossendale Pl *SHPY* BD18...........28 B4
Rosse St *GIR* BD8.........................38 B5
　SHPY BD18....................................28 C1
Rosslyn Gv *HWTH* BD22..............22 D3
Rossmore Dr *WIL/AL* BD15.........37 F3
Rosy St *HWTH* BD22....................23 C1
Rothery Ct *HFAX* * HX1.................4 D2
Rothesay Ter *GTHN* BD7.............46 D2
Roth St *HWTH* BD22....................23 F1
Rothwell Mt *HFAX* HX1..................4 C1
Rothwell Rd *HFAX* HX1..................4 C1
Roundell Av *BOW* BD4.................56 A2
Roundhead Fold *IDLE* BD10.........30 D1
Round Hl *LUD/ILL* HX2................51 E4
Roundhill Av *BGLY* BD16.............27 E2
Round Hill Cl *CUL/QBY* BD13......45 E5
Roundhill Mt *BGLY* BD16.............27 E2
Roundhill Pl *BFD* BD1....................2 B4
Roundhill St *WBOW* BD5.............47 E3
Round St *WBOW* BD5...................47 F4
Round Thorn Pl *GIR* * BD8...........38 B4
Roundwell Rd *LVSG* WF15...........73 F3
Roundwood *SHPY* BD18...............27 H2
Roundwood Av *BAIL* BD17...........19 G3
　IDLE BD10.....................................30 D4
Roundwood Gln *BAIL* BD17..........30 D3
Roundwood Rd *BAIL* BD17...........19 F3
Roundwood Vw *IDLE* BD10..........30 D3
Rouse Fold *BOW* BD4...................47 G2
Rowan Av *BFDE* BD3....................40 D5
Rowanberry Cl *ECHL* BD2............30 A4
Rowan Ct *ECHL* * BD2.................40 B3
　YEA LS19.......................................21 G1
Rowan Dr *BRIG* HD6....................71 H5
The Rowans *BAIL* BD17...............18 A3
Rowan St *AIRE* BD20.....................6 D1
Rowantree Av *BAIL* BD17.............18 C2
Rowantree Dr *IDLE* BD10............30 B3
Rowanwood Gdns *IDLE* * BD10....30 D4
Row La *RPDN/SBR* HX6................66 A5
Rowlestone Ri *IDLE* BD10............30 D3
Rowsley St *KGHY* BD21..................7 H4
Rowton Thorpe *IDLE* BD10..........30 D3
Roxburgh Gv *WIL/AL* BD15.........37 E4
Roxby St *WBOW* BD5...................47 E4
Royal Cl *GTHN* BD7.....................46 A4
Royd Av *BGLY* BD16.....................17 E3
Royd Crs *HFAX* * HX1....................4 A2
Royden Gv *HTON* BD9..................38 B2
Royd House Gv *KGHY* BD21.........14 D1
Royd House Rd *KGHY* BD21.........14 D1
Royd House Wk *KGHY* BD21........14 D1
Royd Ings Av *KGHY* BD21............17 G2
Roydlands St *HIPP* HX3................61 G5
Royd La *HIPP* HX3........................59 F2
　KGHY BD21.....................................7 E2
　LUD/ILL HX2.................................50 D3
Royd Moor Rd *BOW* BD4.............57 H2
Royd Mt *HIPP* HX3.......................59 H3
Roydon Gv *HTON* BD9.................38 B2
Royd Pl *HIPP* HX3........................59 H3
Royds Av *BIRK/DRI* BD11............57 G5
　BRIG HD6......................................62 C5
Roydscliffe Dr *HTON* BD9............28 A5
Roydscliffe Rd *HTON* BD9...........37 H1
Royds Crs *BRIG* HD6....................71 G1
Roydsdale Wy *BOW* BD4.............55 H4
Royds Hall Av *WBSY* BD6............54 B5
Royds Hall La *LM/WK* BD12........54 B5
Royds Park Crs *LM/WK* BD12......63 E1
Roydstone Rd *BFDE* BD3.............40 C4
Roydstone Ter *BFDE* BD3............40 C4
Royd St *CUL/QBY* BD13...............43 H1
　KGHY BD21.....................................7 E1
　WIL/AL BD15.................................25 H4
Royd Wy *KGHY* BD21.....................7 F2
Royd Wd *CLECK* BD19.................73 G2
Roydwood Ter *CUL/QBY* BD13....24 C3
Roydwood Ter Back
　CUL/QBY BD13..........................24 C3
Roy Rd *WBSY* BD6.......................53 G1
Ruby St *HWTH* BD22....................13 H2
Rudding Av *WIL/AL* BD15............36 D3
Rudding Crs *WIL/AL* BD15...........36 D3
Rudd St *GTHN* BD7......................46 B4
Ruffield Side *LM/WK* BD12..........54 D5

Rufford Av YEA LS19 ...11 G5
Rufford Bank YEA LS19 ...11 H5
Rufford Cl YEA LS19 ...11 H5
Rufford Crs YEA LS19 ...11 H5
Rufford Dr YEA LS19 ...11 H5
Rufford Pl HFAX * HX1 ...68 C4
Rufford Rdg YEA LS19 ...11 H5
Rufford Ri YEA LS19 ...11 G5
Rufford Rd ELL HX5 ...76 B5
  HIPP HX3 ...68 C4
Rufford St BFDE BD3 ...40 B5
Rufford Vis HIPP HX3 ...68 C4
Rufus St KGHY BD21 ...7 F3
  WBOW BD5 ...46 C4
Rugby Av HIPP HX3 ...59 E2
Rugby Dr HIPP HX3 ...59 E2
Rugby Gdns HIPP HX3 ...59 E2
Rugby Mt HIPP HX3 ...59 E2
Rugby Pl GTHN BD7 ...46 C1
Rugby Ter HIPP HX3 ...59 E2
Runswick Gv WBOW BD5 ...55 E1
Runswick St WBOW BD5 ...55 E1
Runswick Ter WBOW BD5 ...55 E1
Rupert St HWTH BD22 ...23 G1
  KGHY * BD21 ...7 F3
Rush Cft IDLE BD10 ...19 G5
Rushdene Ct LM/WK BD12 ...62 D4
Rushmoor Rd BOW BD4 ...48 C5
Rusholme Dr PDSY/CALV LS28 ...41 H1
Rushton Av BFDE BD3 ...40 D4
Rushton Hill Cl LUD/ILL HX2 ...58 B4
Rushton Rd BFDE BD3 ...40 C4
Rushton St HFAX HX1 ...4 B7
  PDSY/CALV LS28 ...31 C3
Rushton Ter BFDE BD3 ...40 D5
Rushworth St HIPP * HX3 ...59 F4
Ruskin Av HTON BD9 ...37 G1
Ruskin Crs GSLY LS20 ...11 E3
Ruskin Rd PDSY/CALV LS28 ...41 H3
Ruskin Ter HIPP HX3 ...59 F4
Russell Av CUL/QBY BD13 ...52 B2
Russell Hall La CUL/QBY BD13 ...52 B1
Russell Rd CUL/QBY BD13 ...52 A2
Russell St CUL/QBY BD13 ...52 B1
  HFAX HX1 ...5 H4
  KGHY BD21 ...7 F4
  SHPY BD18 ...28 D4
  WBOW BD5 ...47 E2
Russell Wy BRIG HD6 ...71 F4
Rustic Av HIPP HX3 ...69 H4
Ruswarp Crs IDLE BD10 ...30 C3
Rutland St BOW BD4 ...47 F3
  KGHY BD21 ...14 A1
Ryan Gv HWTH BD22 ...6 A3
Ryan St WBOW BD5 ...47 E4
Ryburn Ct HFAX HX1 ...4 B5
Ryburn St RPDN/SBR HX6 ...67 E5
Ryburn Ter HFAX HX1 ...4 B5
Ryburn Vw LUD/ILL HX2 ...67 H3
Rycroft Av BGLY BD16 ...26 D3
Rycroft St SHPY BD18 ...28 D5
Rydal Av HTON BD9 ...28 D5
Rydal St KGHY BD21 ...6 D5
Rydings Av BRIG HD6 ...71 F5
Rydings Cl BRIG HD6 ...71 F5
Rydings Dr BRIG HD6 ...71 G5
Ryecroft BGLY BD16 ...15 E5
Rye Cft LUD/ILL HX2 ...51 E4
Ryecroft Crs LUD/ILL HX2 ...58 C4
Ryecroft La LUD/ILL HX2 ...58 C5
Ryecroft Rd BGLY BD16 ...14 C4
Ryecroft Ter LUD/ILL HX2 ...58 C5
Ryedale Wy WIL/AL BD15 ...36 D2
Ryefield Av CLAY BD14 ...45 E2
Ryelands Gv HTON BD9 ...27 G5
Rye La LUD/ILL HX2 ...67 H2
Rye St HWTH BD22 ...14 A2
Rylands Av BGLY BD16 ...17 E3
Rylands Meadow HWTH BD22 ...23 F1
Rylstone Gdns BFDE BD3 ...39 H3
Rylstone Rd BAIL BD17 ...18 A4
Rylstone St KGHY BD21 ...7 G3
Ryshworth Av AIRE BD20 ...9 E4
Ryton Dl IDLE BD10 ...30 D3

S

Sable Crest ECHL BD2 ...29 G5
Sackville St BFD BD1 ...5 F3
Saddler La LM/WK BD12 ...62 D1
Saddleworth Rd GTL/HWG HX4 ...76 B4
Saffron Dr WIL/AL BD15 ...36 D3
Sage St WBOW BD5 ...46 D3
Sahara Ct GIR BD8 ...39 E2
St Abbs Cl WBSY BD6 ...54 D3
St Abbs Dr WBSY BD6 ...54 D3

St Abbs Fold WBSY BD6 ...54 D3
St Abbs Ga WBSY BD6 ...54 D3
St Abbs Wk WBSY BD6 ...54 D3
St Abbs Wy WBSY BD6 ...54 D3
St Aidan's Rd BAIL BD17 ...19 E4
St Alban's Av HIPP HX3 ...68 D5
St Albans Cft HIPP HX3 ...69 E4
St Albans Pl HIPP HX3 ...68 D5
St Andrews Cl YEA LS19 ...11 H4
St Andrew's Crs LM/WK BD12 ...63 H1
St Andrew's Dr BRIG HD6 ...71 F4
St Andrew's Pl GTHN * BD7 ...46 D1
St Andrews Rd YEA LS19 ...11 H4
St Andrew's Vls GTHN BD7 ...38 D5
St Anne's Av HIPP HX3 ...75 H1
St Anns Sq RPDN/SBR HX6 ...67 F4
St Anuil GIR * BD8 ...38 C3
St Augustine's Ter BFDE BD3 ...3 C1
  HFAX * HX1 ...4 C3
St Barnabas Rd LVSG WF15 ...73 F3
St Bevan's Rd HIPP HX3 ...68 D5
St Blaise Ct WBOW BD5 ...2 D7
St Blaise Wy BFD BD1 ...2 D4
St Chad's Av BRIG * HD6 ...70 D3
St Chad's Rd GIR BD8 ...38 C3
St Clare's Av ECHL BD2 ...40 C2
St Eloi Av BAIL BD17 ...18 D2
St Enoch's Rd WBSY BD6 ...54 C1
St George's Crs HFAX HX1 ...4 D7
St George's Pl WBOW * BD5 ...47 F2
St George's Rd HIPP HX3 ...59 F4
St Giles Cl BRIG HD6 ...70 D2
St Giles Rd HIPP HX3 ...70 D2
St Helena Rd WBSY BD6 ...54 C1
St Helier Gv BAIL BD17 ...19 E2
St Hilda's Ter BFDE BD3 ...40 D4
St Ive's Gdns HIPP * HX3 ...68 D5
St Ives Gv BGLY BD16 ...15 H4
St Ives Pl BGLY BD16 ...15 H4
St Ives Rd BGLY BD16 ...15 H4
  HIPP HX3 ...68 C5
St James Ct HFAX HX1 ...5 G3
St James Crs PDSY/CALV LS28 ...41 G5
St James Rd HFAX HX1 ...5 G3
St James's Market BFDE * BD3 ...3 G7
St James's Sq WBOW * BD5 ...47 F2
St James St HFAX HX1 ...5 G3
St Johns Cl CLECK * BD19 ...73 H1
St John's Ct BAIL BD17 ...19 F4
  YEA LS19 ...11 F5
St John's Crs GIR BD8 ...37 H4
St John's Dr YEA LS19 ...11 F5
St John's La HFAX HX1 ...5 G6
St John's Pl BIRK/DRI * BD11 ...57 F4
  HFAX * HX1 ...5 G6
St John's Rd AIRE BD20 ...6 D1
  YEA LS19 ...11 F5
St John St BRIG HD6 ...78 B2
St Johns Wy HWTH BD22 ...6 C5
  YEA LS19 ...11 F5
St Jude's Pl GIR BD8 ...2 B2
St Jude's St BFD BD1 ...2 A2
  HFAX HX1 ...68 C3
St Laurence's Cl SHPY BD18 ...29 E4
St Leonards Ct HTON BD9 ...38 A3
St Leonard's Gv GIR BD8 ...38 A3
St Leonard's Rd GIR BD8 ...38 A3
St Luke's Cl CLECK BD19 ...73 E1
  WBOW BD5 ...47 E2
St Margaret's Av BOW BD4 ...48 C5
St Margaret's Pl GTHN BD7 ...46 C2
St Margaret's Ter GTHN BD7 ...46 C1
St Mark's Av LM/WK BD12 ...54 D5
St Mark's Ter LM/WK BD12 ...54 D5
St Martins Av GTHN BD7 ...38 D5
St Martin's Vw BRIG HD6 ...71 F5
St Mary Magdalenes Cl
  GIR * BD8 ...38 D4
St Mary's Av LM/WK BD12 ...62 D3
St Mary's Cl LM/WK BD12 ...62 C3
St Mary's Crs LM/WK BD12 ...62 C4
St Mary's Dr LM/WK BD12 ...62 D3
St Mary's Gdns LM/WK BD12 ...62 D3
St Marys Ga ELL HX5 ...76 C4
St Mary's Mt LM/WK BD12 ...62 C4
St Mary's Rd AIRE BD20 ...8 A1
  BOW BD4 ...48 C3
  HTON BD9 ...38 D2
St Mary's Sq LM/WK BD12 ...62 C3
St Mary St HFAX HX1 ...4 E5
St Matthews Cl WIL/AL BD15 ...25 G5
St Matthew's Dr HIPP HX3 ...70 D3
St Matthews Gv WIL/AL BD15 ...25 G5
St Matthew's Rd WBSY BD6 ...55 E1
St Merrion Crs HIPP HX3 ...69 F3
St Michael's Rd GIR BD8 ...38 C4
St Oswalds Garth GSLY LS20 ...10 D2

St Paul's Av BIRK/DRI BD11 ...57 G5
  WBSY BD6 ...54 C2
St Pauls Cl GIR BD8 ...38 D3
St Pauls Gv WBSY BD6 ...54 C2
St Paul's Rd BIRK/DRI BD11 ...57 F5
  GIR BD8 ...38 D2
  HFAX HX1 ...4 A7
  KGHY BD21 ...7 G5
  SHPY BD18 ...28 B2
  WBSY BD6 ...54 C2
St Peg Cl CLECK BD19 ...73 H1
St Peg La CLECK BD19 ...73 H1
St Peter's Av RPDN/SBR HX6 ...66 C5
St Phillips Ct GIR BD8 ...38 A3
St Stephens Ct HIPP * HX3 ...75 F1
St Stephen's Rd
  PDSY/CALV LS28 ...31 F2
  WBOW BD5 ...47 F4
St Stephen's St HIPP HX3 ...75 F1
St Stephen's Ter WBOW * BD5 ...47 F4
Saint St GTHN BD7 ...46 B3
St Thomas Gdns HUDN HD2 ...79 G5
St Wilfred's St PDSY/CALV LS28 ...31 G2
St Wilfrid's Cl GTHN BD7 ...46 A2
St Wilfrid's Crs GTHN BD7 ...46 A2
St Wilfrid's Rd GTHN BD7 ...46 A2
St Winifred's Cl LUD/ILL * HX2 ...50 C5
Salcombe Pl BOW BD4 ...48 D5
Salem St BFD BD1 ...2 C4
  CUL/QBY BD13 ...52 A1
Salisbury Av BAIL BD17 ...18 D3
Salisbury Pl HIPP HX3 ...59 G4
  PDSY/CALV LS28 ...31 F3
Salisbury Rd CLECK BD19 ...63 G5
  HTON BD9 ...28 D4
  HWTH BD22 ...6 D5
  LM/WK BD12 ...54 D4
Salisbury St PDSY/CALV LS28 ...31 F3
  RPDN/SBR HX6 ...66 C5
  YEA LS19 ...21 G2
Salisbury Ter HIPP HX3 ...59 G4
Sal Nook Cl LM/WK BD12 ...55 E3
Sal Royd Rd LM/WK BD12 ...55 F5
Saltaire Rd BGLY BD16 ...17 G1
  SHPY BD18 ...28 B1
Saltburn Pl HTON BD9 ...38 A2
Saltburn St HFAX HX1 ...4 A3
Salterhebble Hl HIPP HX3 ...76 A1
Salterlee HIPP HX3 ...60 B3
Salt Horn Cl LM/WK BD12 ...55 G5
Salts Mill Rd BAIL BD17 ...28 C1
Salt St GIR BD8 ...38 D3
  HFAX HX1 ...4 C2
Samuel St KGHY BD21 ...7 F3
Sandale Wk WBSY BD6 ...54 A3
Sandall Magna WBSY BD6 ...53 H3
Sandals Rd BAIL BD17 ...18 D4
Sand Beds CUL/QBY BD13 ...52 B3
Sandbeds Crs LUD/ILL HX2 ...58 D4
Sandbeds Rd LUD/ILL HX2 ...58 D4
Sandbeds Ter LUD/ILL HX2 ...58 D4
Sanderling Ct GIR * BD8 ...37 F5
Sanderson Av WBSY BD6 ...54 D1
Sandfield Rd IDLE BD10 ...30 A3
Sandford Rd BFDE BD3 ...40 B5
Sandforth Av HIPP HX3 ...59 F5
Sandhall Av LUD/ILL HX2 ...67 G1
Sandhall Dr LUD/ILL HX2 ...67 G1
Sandhall Gn LUD/ILL HX2 ...58 C5
Sandhall La LUD/ILL HX2 ...67 G1
Sandhill Fold IDLE BD10 ...29 H2
Sandhill Mt IDLE BD10 ...30 A3
Sandholme Crs HIPP HX3 ...70 C1
Sandholme Dr IDLE BD10 ...30 B3
Sandmead Cl BOW BD4 ...48 C5
Sandmoor Cl CUL/QBY BD13 ...44 B1
Sandmoor Gdns HIPP HX3 ...61 E1
Sandmoor Garth IDLE BD10 ...20 A5
Sandown Av LUD/ILL HX2 ...58 C1
Sandown Rd LUD/ILL HX2 ...58 D1
Sandpiper Ms GIR BD8 ...37 F5
Sandringham Cl CLAY BD14 ...45 G2
Sandringham Ct CLAY BD14 ...45 G2
Sandringham Rd CLAY BD14 ...45 G2
Sandsend Cl HTON BD9 ...37 G1
Sandside Cl WBOW BD5 ...47 G5
Sand St HWTH BD22 ...22 D3
  KGHY BD21 ...7 F5
Sandy Banks BGLY BD16 ...25 G1
Sandy Beck WIL/AL BD15 ...36 D1
Sandy Ga KGHY BD21 ...7 H3
Sandygate Ter BOW BD4 ...48 C2
Sandymoor WIL/AL BD15 ...26 D5
Sandy Wy YEA LS19 ...11 G4
Sandywood St KGHY BD21 ...7 F5
Sangster Wy WBOW BD5 ...55 H1
Santa Monica Crs IDLE BD10 ...29 H2
Santa Monica Gv IDLE BD10 ...29 H2

Santa Monica Rd IDLE BD10 ...29 H2
Sapgate La CUL/QBY BD13 ...44 B1
Saplin St GIR BD8 ...38 C3
Savile Av IDLE BD10 ...30 B3
Savile Cl BRIG HD6 ...72 A5
Savile Crs HFAX HX1 ...5 F6
Savile Dr HFAX HX1 ...4 E6
Savile Gln HFAX HX1 ...5 F6
Savile Gn HFAX HX1 ...5 G6
Savile Lea HFAX HX1 ...5 F6
Savile Pde HFAX HX1 ...68 C3
Savile Pk HFAX HX1 ...68 B3
Savile Park Gdns HFAX HX1 ...4 C7
Savile Park Rd CLECK BD19 ...64 C2
  HFAX HX1 ...5 F6
Savile Park St HFAX HX1 ...68 B3
Savile Park Ter HFAX * HX1 ...68 B3
Savile Rd ELL HX5 ...76 C5
Savile Royd HFAX HX1 ...4 E7
Savile St CLECK BD19 ...64 C4
Savile Ter HFAX HX1 ...5 F6
Savile Wy ELL HX5 ...76 D3
Saville Park Rd HFAX HX1 ...4 E7
Sawley St KGHY BD21 ...7 E5
Sawood La HWTH BD22 ...33 G4
Sawrey Pl WBOW BD5 ...2 B7
Saxon St GIR BD8 ...38 D4
  HFAX HX1 ...4 A3
Saxton Av WBSY BD6 ...54 A1
Sayle Av BOW BD4 ...56 A2
Scaley St BFDE BD3 ...40 C5
Scarborough Gv SHPY BD18 ...28 B2
Scarborough Rd SHPY BD18 ...28 B2
Scar Bottom La GTL/HWG HX4 ...75 E4
Scar Head Rd RPDN/SBR HX6 ...74 A1
Scarlet Hts CUL/QBY BD13 ...52 C1
Scarr Bottom Rd LUD/ILL HX2 ...68 A4
Scar Top GTL/HWG * HX4 ...75 E4
Scarwood Cl BGLY BD16 ...16 D2
Scholars Wk ECHL BD2 ...40 A1
Scholebrook La BOW BD4 ...49 H4
Scholemoor Av GTHN BD7 ...45 H2
Scholemoor La GTHN BD7 ...45 H2
Scholemoor Rd GTHN BD7 ...46 A2
Scholes La CLECK BD19 ...63 G5
  GTL/HWG HX4 ...75 E4
Scholes St WBOW BD5 ...47 E5
Scholey Av BRIG HD6 ...78 B3
Scholey Rd BRIG HD6 ...78 B3
School Cl LUD/ILL HX2 ...51 E3
School Cote Brow LUD/ILL HX2 ...51 G4
School Crs LUD/ILL HX2 ...51 E3
School Gn BRIG HD6 ...78 B3
  CUL/QBY BD13 ...44 C1
School Green Av CUL/QBY BD13 ...44 C1
School La HIPP HX3 ...59 H5
  LUD/ILL HX2 ...51 E2
  LUD/ILL HX2 ...51 E4
School Pl LM/WK * BD12 ...62 D1
School Rd HWTH BD22 ...6 C4
School Sq BFDE BD3 ...40 C5
School St AIRE BD20 ...6 D1
  BGLY BD16 ...27 E2
  BOW BD4 ...48 B4
  BOW BD4 ...56 A2
  CLAY BD14 ...45 E3
  CLECK BD19 ...73 F2
  CUL/QBY BD13 ...24 C3
  CUL/QBY BD13 ...34 D4
  CUL/QBY * BD13 ...34 D4
  GTL/HWG HX4 ...75 G3
  HFAX HX1 ...5 J5
  LM/WK BD12 ...54 D4
  LM/WK BD12 ...63 H1
  WIL/AL BD15 ...25 H4
School Wk HWTH BD22 ...6 C4
School Yard Vw HIPP HX3 ...59 H4
Score Hl HIPP HX3 ...60 D1
Scoresby St BFD BD1 ...3 F5
Scotchman Rd HTON BD9 ...38 A2
Scotland St CLECK BD19 ...65 H4
Scott La AIRE BD20 ...7 H1
  CLECK BD19 ...64 C5
  CLECK BD19 ...65 G4
Scott La West AIRE BD20 ...7 G1
Scott St KGHY BD21 ...7 E4
Scotty Bank BRIG * HD6 ...78 B1
Scotty Croft La BRIG HD6 ...78 B1
Seaton St BFDE BD3 ...3 J4
Second Av BFDE BD3 ...40 B3
  HIPP HX3 ...68 C4
  KGHY BD21 ...7 E4
  LVSG WF15 ...73 E4
  YEA LS19 ...21 H1
Second St LM/WK BD12 ...55 F4

Sedan St HFAX * HX1 ....5 G5
Sedburgh Rd HIPP HX3 ....5 J7
Sedge Gv HWTH BD22 ....22 D1
Sedgwick Cl GIR BD8 ....2 A3
Seed Hill Ter LUD/ILL HX2 ....50 B4
Seed St LM/WK BD5 ....55 E4
Sefton Av BRIG HD6 ....71 E3
Sefton Cres BRIG HD6 ....71 E3
Sefton Dr BRIG HD6 ....71 E3
Sefton Gv ECHL BD2 ....40 A1
Sefton Pl KGHY * BD21 ....7 F3
Sefton St HFAX HX1 ....4 D2
  KGHY BD21 ....7 F3
Sefton Ter HFAX HX1 ....4 D2
  KGHY BD21 ....13 H1
Selborne Gv HTON BD9 ....38 C1
Selborne Mt HTON BD9 ....38 D2
Selborne Ter HTON BD9 ....38 C2
  SHPY BD18 ....28 C3
Selborne Vls CLAY BD14 ....45 F4
  HTON BD9 ....38 C2
Selby LUD/ILL HX2 ....50 C3
Seldon St WBOW BD5 ....46 C4
Selene Cl CLECK BD19 ....65 H3
Sellars Fold GTHN * BD7 ....46 B3
Sellerdale Av LM/WK BD12 ....63 E4
Sellerdale Dr LM/WK BD12 ....63 E3
Sellerdale Ri LM/WK BD12 ....63 E3
Sellerdale Wy LM/WK BD12 ....63 E4
Semon Av ECHL BD2 ....29 G4
Senior Wy WBOW BD5 ....2 C7
Serpentine Rd CLECK BD19 ....64 D3
Sevenoaks Md WIL/AL BD15 ....37 E3
Seventh Av LVSG WF15 ....73 E3
Severn Rd ECHL BD2 ....39 H2
Sewell Rd BFDE BD3 ....3 K6
Seymour St BRIG HD6 ....3 H5
Shaftesbury Av BRIG HD6 ....78 D4
  HTON BD9 ....37 G2
  SHPY BD18 ....28 D2
Shakespeare Rd GSLY LS20 ....10 D3
Shakespeare St HFAX HX1 ....5 H5
Shalimar St HFAX HX1 ....4 A3
Shann Av KGHY BD21 ....6 C3
Shann Crs KGHY BD21 ....6 C3
Shann La KGHY BD21 ....6 C3
Shannon Cl BRIG HD6 ....77 H4
Shannon Rd BRIG HD6 ....77 H4
Shann St SHPY BD18 ....29 E3
Shapla Cl HWTH BD22 ....6 D5
Sharp Av WBSY BD6 ....54 D2
Sharpe St BFD BD1 ....2 C7
Sharp St WBSY BD6 ....54 D1
Shaw Hl HFAX HX1 ....5 J7
Shaw Hill La HIPP HX3 ....5 J7
Shaw La ELL HX5 ....77 F4
  GSLY LS20 ....11 E2
  HIPP HX3 ....52 C4
  HIPP HX3 ....69 E4
  KGHY BD21 ....14 C3
  RPDN/SBR HX6 ....74 B2
Shaw Lane Gdns GSLY LS20 ....11 E2
Shaw Leys LS19 ....11 F3
Shaw Royd YEA LS19 ....11 F3
Shaw St CLECK * BD19 ....73 E1
  LM/WK BD12 ....54 C4
Shay Cl HTON BD9 ....28 A5
Shay Crs HTON BD9 ....27 H5
Shay Dr HTON BD9 ....27 H5
Shay Fold HTON BD9 ....27 H5
Shay Ga WIL/AL * BD15 ....26 B5
Shay Gra HTON BD9 ....27 H4
Shay Gv HTON BD9 ....28 A5
Shay La HTON BD9 ....27 H4
  LUD/ILL HX2 ....59 F1
  WIL/AL BD15 ....26 B5
Shay Syke HFAX HX1 ....5 J6
Shearbridge Gn GTHN BD7 ....46 D1
Shearbridge Rd GTHN BD7 ....46 D1
Shearbridge Ter GTHN BD7 ....46 D1
Shed St KGHY * BD21 ....7 F4
Sheep Hill La CUL/QBY BD13 ....45 E5
Sheldon Rdg BOW BD4 ....56 A3
Sheldrake Av GIR BD8 ....37 F5
Shelf Hall La HIPP HX3 ....53 E5
Shelf Moor HIPP HX3 ....53 F3
Shelf Moor Rd HIPP HX3 ....53 F3
Shelley Ct BGLY BD16 ....16 D3
Shelley Gv GIR BD8 ....37 H4
Shell La PDSY/CALV LS28 ....31 C3
Shepherds Thorn La HUDN HD2 ....78 D5
Sherborne Rd HWTH BD22 ....13 F1
Sherborne St GTHN * BD7 ....46 D1
  IDLE BD10 ....20 A5
Sherburn Cl BIRK/DRI BD11 ....57 G4
Sherburn Gv BIRK/DRI BD11 ....57 G4
Sherburn Rd BRIG HD6 ....77 G3
Sheridan St BOW BD4 ....47 H3

Sheriff La BGLY BD16 ....17 F2
Sherwell Gv WIL/AL BD15 ....37 F3
Sherwell La WIL/AL BD15 ....37 F3
Sherwood Av CLECK BD19 ....65 G5
Sherwood Cl BGLY BD16 ....17 F1
  CLECK BD19 ....65 G5
Sherwood Gv SHPY BD18 ....27 H1
Sherwood Pl ECHL BD2 ....40 A2
Sherwood Rd BRIG HD6 ....78 D1
Shetcliffe La BOW BD4 ....56 B2
Shetcliffe Rd BOW BD4 ....56 A2
Shetland Cl ECHL BD2 ....29 G5
Shibden Garth HIPP HX3 ....60 D5
Shibden Grange Dr HIPP HX3 ....60 C4
Shibden Hall Cft HIPP HX3 ....60 C4
Shibden Hall Rd HIPP HX3 ....60 C5
Shibden Head La
  CUL/QBY BD13 ....51 H3
Shibden Vw CUL/QBY BD13 ....52 A3
Shipley Airedale Rd BFDE BD3 ....2 E2
Shipley Fields Rd SHPY BD18 ....28 C4
Ship St BRIG HD6 ....78 B1
Shire Cl WBSY BD6 ....54 A3
Shirley Av CLECK BD19 ....65 G5
  LM/WK BD12 ....62 C4
Shirley Crs LM/WK BD12 ....62 C4
Shirley Gv CLECK BD19 ....65 G5
  HIPP HX3 ....71 F1
Shirley Mt CLECK BD19 ....65 G5
Shirley Pde CLECK BD19 ....65 F5
Shirley Pl CLECK BD19 ....65 F5
  LM/WK BD12 ....62 D4
Shirley Rd BOW BD4 ....56 C1
  CLECK BD19 ....65 G5
  GTHN BD7 ....46 C1
Shirley St HWTH BD22 ....22 C2
  SHPY BD18 ....28 A1
Shirley Ter CLECK BD19 ....65 G5
Shirley Wk CLECK BD19 ....65 G5
Short Cl LM/WK BD12 ....54 C5
Shortway CUL/QBY BD13 ....44 D1
  PDSY/CALV LS28 ....41 F3
Shroggs Rd HFAX HX1 ....4 D1
Shroggs St HFAX HX1 ....4 D2
Shroggs Vue Ter HFAX HX1 ....4 D2
Shuttleworth La GIR BD8 ....37 H4
Shutts La HIPP HX3 ....61 H3
Sickle St CLECK BD19 ....64 D5
Siddal Gv HIPP HX3 ....69 F4
Siddal La HIPP HX3 ....69 F4
Siddal New Rd HIPP HX3 ....69 E3
Siddal St HIPP HX3 ....69 F5
Siddal Top La HIPP HX3 ....69 F4
The Sidings LS20 ....10 C2
  SHPY * BD18 ....28 D1
Silk St HTON BD9 ....38 B2
Silson La BAIL BD17 ....19 F2
Silver Birch Av LM/WK BD12 ....63 E3
Silver Birch Cl LM/WK BD12 ....63 E3
Silver Birch Dr LM/WK BD12 ....63 E3
Silver Birch Gv LM/WK BD12 ....63 E3
Silverdale Av AIRE BD20 ....7 G2
  GSLY LS20 ....10 D3
Silverdale Cl GSLY LS20 ....10 D4
Silverdale Dr GSLY LS20 ....10 D4
Silverdale Gra GSLY LS20 ....10 D4
Silverdale Gv GSLY LS20 ....10 C4
Silverdale Mt GSLY LS20 ....10 D4
Silverdale Rd GSLY LS20 ....10 C4
  WBOW BD5 ....47 G5
Silverhill Dr BFDE BD3 ....40 C4
Silverhill Rd BFDE BD3 ....40 B3
Silver La YEA LS19 ....11 G4
Silver St GIR BD8 ....38 C3
  HFAX HX1 ....5 G4
Silverwood Av LUD/ILL HX2 ....58 B4
Silwood Dr ECHL BD2 ....40 B1
Simes St BFD BD1 ....2 B4
Simm Carr La HIPP HX3 ....60 A1
Simmonds La HFAX HX1 ....5 J7
Simms Dene WIL/AL BD15 ....26 D5
Simon Cl BOW BD4 ....49 E5
Simpson Gv IDLE BD10 ....20 B5
Simpson St HIPP HX3 ....59 G3
  KGHY BD21 ....6 D3
Sinclair Rd ECHL BD2 ....29 G4
Sinden Ms IDLE BD10 ....20 A4
Singleton St BFD BD1 ....2 D5
Sion Hl HIPP HX3 ....69 H5
Sir Isaac Holden Pl GTHN BD7 ....38 C5
Sir Wilfred Pl IDLE * BD10 ....30 A1
Sixth Av BFDE BD3 ....40 B3
  LVSG WF15 ....73 E3
Sizers Ct YEA LS19 ....21 F1
Skelton Wk IDLE BD10 ....30 C2
Skinner La GIR BD8 ....38 C4
Skipton Rd KGHY BD21 ....7 F3
Skircoat Gn HIPP HX3 ....75 H1

Skircoat Green Rd HIPP HX3 ....75 H1
Skircoat Moor Cl LUD/ILL * HX2 ....68 B4
Skircoat Moor Rd LUD/ILL HX2 ....68 B4
Skircoat Rd HFAX HX1 ....5 H7
Skirrow St BGLY BD16 ....27 E3
Skye Rd HTON BD9 ....38 B1
Slack Bottom Rd WBSY BD6 ....54 B2
Slack La HWTH BD22 ....12 C3
Sladdin Rw CUL/QBY BD13 ....51 H2
Slade La AIRE BD20 ....7 H1
  BRIG HD6 ....78 A5
Sladen St KGHY BD21 ....6 D4
Slaymaker La HWTH BD22 ....12 D3
Slead Av BRIG HD6 ....71 E4
Slead Ct BRIG HD6 ....71 E4
Slead Crs BRIG HD6 ....71 E4
Slead Gv BRIG HD6 ....71 E4
Slead Royd BRIG HD6 ....71 E4
Sleningford Gv SHPY BD18 ....27 H1
Sleningford Ri BGLY BD16 ....16 C1
Sleningford Rd BGLY BD16 ....16 C1
  SHPY BD18 ....27 H1
Slingsby Cl IDLE BD10 ....30 C1
Slippy La LUD/ILL HX2 ....50 B5
Sloan Sq GIR BD8 ....38 C4
Smalewell Dr PDSY/CALV LS28 ....49 H1
Smalewell Gdns
  PDSY/CALV LS28 ....49 H1
Smalewell Rd PDSY/CALV LS28 ....49 G1
Small Page Fold
  CUL/QBY * BD13 ....52 B1
Smiddles La WBOW BD5 ....46 D5
Smith Av WBSY BD6 ....54 D2
Smith Crs BRIG HD6 ....77 H3
Smitherds St KGHY BD21 ....7 E5
Smithfield Av HIPP HX3 ....61 F5
Smith House Crs BRIG HD6 ....71 E3
Smith House Gv BRIG HD6 ....71 F3
Smith House La BRIG HD6 ....71 F3
Smith La HTON BD9 ....37 H2
Smith Rd GTHN BD7 ....46 C4
Smith's Ter HIPP HX3 ....59 F2
Smith St BGLY BD16 ....27 E3
  BOW BD4 ....56 A2
  GTHN BD7 ....2 A5
  KGHY BD21 ....6 D3
Smithville AIRE BD20 ....8 A2
Smithy Carr La BRIG HD6 ....71 F4
Smithy Hl CUL/QBY BD13 ....42 D1
  WBSY BD6 ....54 D1
Smithy La WIL/AL BD15 ....25 H3
Smithy St HFAX HX1 ....5 J3
Snaith Wood Dr YEA LS19 ....21 H5
Snaith Wood Ms YEA LS19 ....21 H5
Snape Dr GTHN BD7 ....45 G5
Snape St KGHY BD21 ....14 B3
Snelsins La CLECK BD19 ....64 B4
Snelsins Rd CLECK BD19 ....64 B4
Snowden Rd SHPY BD18 ....29 E3
Snowden St BFD BD1 ....2 C3
Snowdens Wk CLAY BD14 ....45 G3
Snowdrop Ms WIL/AL BD15 ....37 E4
Soaper House La HIPP HX3 ....61 F3
Soaper La HIPP HX3 ....53 C3
Sod House Gn HIPP HX3 ....59 F2
Soho St BFD BD1 ....2 B5
  HFAX HX1 ....4 B4
Somerset Av BAIL BD17 ....18 C2
  BRIG HD6 ....78 C4
Somerton Dr BOW BD4 ....48 C5
Somerville Av WBSY BD6 ....54 C3
Somerville Pk WBSY BD6 ....54 C3
Sonning Rd WIL/AL BD15 ....37 E4
Sorrin Cl IDLE BD10 ....29 H2
Soureby Cross Wy BOW BD4 ....57 E3
Southampton St BFDE BD3 ....3 F1
South Bank CUL/QBY BD13 ....52 C1
South Bolton LUD/ILL HX2 ....50 C3
South Brook Ter GTHN * BD7 ....2 B6
South Cliffe CUL/QBY BD13 ....44 A1
Southcliffe Dr BAIL BD17 ....18 C5
Southcliffe Wy BAIL BD17 ....18 D5
South Cl GSLY LS20 ....10 A3
South Clough Head
  LUD/ILL HX2 ....66 D1
Southcote Pl IDLE BD10 ....30 A1
South Croft Av BIRK/DRI BD11 ....57 F4
South Croft Dr BIRK/DRI BD11 ....57 F3
South Croft Ga BIRK/DRI BD11 ....57 F4
Southdown Cl HTON BD9 ....37 H2
Southdown Rd BAIL BD17 ....18 C5
South Dr GSLY LS20 ....10 A3
South Edge KGHY BD21 ....6 D3
  SHPY BD18 ....27 H2
Southedge Cl HIPP HX3 ....70 B1
Southfield Av AIRE BD20 ....8 A1
  WBSY BD6 ....54 D2

Southfield Dr AIRE BD20 ....8 B1
Southfield La GTHN BD7 ....46 B4
Southfield Mt AIRE BD20 ....8 B1
Southfield Rd BGLY BD16 ....16 D5
  WBOW BD5 ....46 D4
Southfield Sq GIR BD8 ....38 D3
Southfield Ter BIRK/DRI BD11 ....57 F4
  HIPP HX3 ....61 F4
Southfield Vw AIRE BD20 ....8 B1
Southgate BFD BD1 ....2 C6
  ELL HX5 ....76 C4
  GSLY LS20 ....10 A4
  HFAX HX1 ....5 H4
South Gv BRIG HD6 ....70 C3
  SHPY BD18 ....27 G2
South Hill Dr BGLY BD16 ....17 E3
Southlands BAIL BD17 ....18 C5
  LUD/ILL HX2 ....51 E1
Southlands Av AIRE * BD20 ....8 B2
  BGLY BD16 ....16 D5
  CUL/QBY BD13 ....45 F1
Southlands Dr AIRE * BD20 ....8 B2
Southlands Gv AIRE BD20 ....8 B2
  BGLY BD16 ....16 C5
  CUL/QBY BD13 ....45 F1
Southlands Gv West AIRE BD20 ....8 B1
Southlands Mt AIRE * BD20 ....8 B2
Southlands Rd AIRE BD20 ....8 B1
South La HIPP HX3 ....53 E3
Southlea Av HWTH BD22 ....13 F4
Southlea Cl LM/WK BD12 ....55 H5
Southmere Av GTHN BD7 ....46 B4
Southmere Crs GTHN BD7 ....46 B4
Southmere Dr GTHN BD7 ....46 B4
Southmere Gv GTHN BD7 ....46 B4
Southmere Ov GTHN BD7 ....46 A5
Southmere Rd GTHN BD7 ....46 B4
Southmere Ter GTHN BD7 ....46 B4
Southowram Bank HIPP HX3 ....69 F2
South Pde CLECK BD19 ....64 B5
  GIR BD8 ....2 B1
  HFAX HX1 ....5 J6
South Rd CUL/QBY BD13 ....24 C4
  HTON BD9 ....28 D5
South Royde Av HIPP HX3 ....68 D3
South Sq CUL/QBY BD13 ....44 A1
South St BRIG HD6 ....71 F5
  CUL/QBY BD13 ....34 C4
  CUL/QBY BD13 ....36 A5
  HFAX HX1 ....5 F5
  KGHY BD21 ....7 E5
  LM/WK BD12 ....63 H1
  WBOW BD5 ....46 D4
South Vw AIRE BD20 ....8 C2
  BAIL BD17 ....18 D3
  HIPP HX3 ....69 H4
  HWTH BD22 ....22 D2
  IDLE BD10 ....30 C2
  PDSY/CALV LS28 ....41 H3
  YEA LS19 ....11 H4
South View Cl BOW BD4 ....56 D3
  YEA LS19 ....10 D4
South View Ct HIPP HX3 ....70 C2
South View Dr BOW BD4 ....57 E3
South View Rd BOW BD4 ....57 E3
  YEA LS19 ....11 G4
South View Ter BAIL * BD17 ....18 D3
  HFAX HX1 ....4 B2
  YEA LS19 ....11 H5
South Wk BGLY BD16 ....15 F5
South Wy BOW BD4 ....56 D3
  SHPY BD18 ....27 G2
Southway BGLY BD16 ....17 E3
  GSLY LS20 ....10 A3
Sovereign St HFAX * HX1 ....5 F4
Sowden Buildings ECHL BD2 ....40 A2
Sowden Gra CUL/QBY BD13 ....44 A3
Sowden Rd HTON BD9 ....37 G1
Sowden St GTHN * BD7 ....46 C4
Sowerby Croft La
  RPDN/SBR HX6 ....67 G5
Sowerby New Rd
  RPDN/SBR HX6 ....66 B5
Sowerby St RPDN/SBR HX6 ....67 G5
Spa La BGLY BD16 ....16 D1
Spark House La RPDN/SBR HX6 ....67 F5
Spartan Rd LM/WK BD12 ....55 H5
Spearhead Wy KGHY BD21 ....7 F3
Speeton Av WBSY BD6 ....45 H5
Speeton Gv GTHN BD7 ....45 G5
Spencer Av GTHN BD7 ....46 B2
Spencer Rd GSLY LS20 ....11 E3
  GTHN BD7 ....46 C2
Spencer St KGHY BD21 ....6 D4
Spen Cl BOW BD4 ....56 A3
Spen La CLECK BD19 ....65 G5
Spenser Ri GSLY LS20 ....11 E3
Spenser Rd GSLY LS20 ....11 E3

Spen Valley Heritage Trail
BIRK/DRI BD11 ....56 D4
CLECK BD19 ....64 D3
Spen View La *BOW* BD4 ....56 A3
Spicer St *WBOW* * BD5 ....46 D4
Spiers Garth *WBSY* BD6 ....55 E1
Spindle St *LUD/ILL* HX2 ....51 F5
The Spinners *HWTH* BD22 ....22 D3
Spinners Wy *CLECK* BD19 ....63 G5
The Spinney *AIRE* BD20......9 E3
BRIG HD6 ....71 F3
IDLE BD10 ....21 F4
Spinning Mill Ct *SHPY* BD18 ....27 H1
Spout HI *BRIG* HD6............77 H5
Spout House La *BRIG* HD6 ....70 D2
Spring Av *KGHY* BD21 ....7 H5
Spring Bank PI *GIR* BD8 ....39 E3
Spring Bank Ri *KGHY* BD21 ....14 B2
Springcliffe *GIR* BD8 ....38 C3
Springcliffe St *GIR* BD8 ....38 C3
Spring CI *BGLY* BD16 ....17 E4
KGHY BD21..................7 H5
Spring Ct *WIL/AL* * BD15 ....36 D1
Springdale Crs *IDLE* BD10 ....30 B1
Spring Dr *KGHY* BD21 ....7 H5
Spring Edge North *HFAX* HX1 ....4 C7
Spring Edge South *HFAX* HX1 ....68 B3
Spring Edge West *HFAX* HX1 ....68 A3
Spring Farm La *BGLY* BD16 ....15 F5
Spring Farm Ms *WIL/AL* BD15 ....25 H4
Springfield *KGHY* BD21 ......66 D5
Springfield Av *GTHN* BD7 ....46 A2
Springfield Bungalows
CLECK * BD19................73 H1
Springfield Ct *KGHY* BD21 ......6 D3
Springfield Dr *LVSG* WF15......3 F2
Springfield Gdns *KGHY* BD21 ....6 D3
Springfield Gv *BGLY* BD16 ....16 C2
BRIG HD6 ....71 F4
Springfield La *LVSG* WF15 ....73 H3
Springfield PI *GIR* BD8 ....2 B2
Springfield Rd *BAIL* BD17 ....18 C2
ELL HX5 ....77 E4
GSLY LS20 ....10 D3
KGHY LS20 ....6 D3
Springfield St *CUL/QBY* BD13 ....44 D1
GIR BD8 ....38 D4
Springfield Ter *CLECK* BD19 ....63 G4
GSLY LS20 ....10 C2
Spring Garden St
CUL/QBY BD13 ....52 B1
Spring Gv *HFAX* HX1 ....67 H1
Spring Hall CI *HIPP* HX3 ....53 E5
Spring Hall Ct *HFAX* HX1 ....58 D5
Spring Hall Dr *HFAX* HX1 ....67 H1
Spring Hall Gdns *HFAX* HX1 ....67 H1
Spring Hall Gv *LUD/ILL* HX2 ....67 H1
Spring Hall La *HFAX* HX1 ....67 H1
Spring Hall PI *HFAX* HX1 ....67 H1
Spring Head Rd *CUL/QBY* BD13 ....44 B1
HWTH BD22 ....22 D1
Spring HI *BAIL* BD17 ....18 A3
SHPY BD18 ....28 D2
Spring Holes La *CUL/QBY* BD13 ....35 H5
Springhurst Rd *SHPY* BD18 ....28 B2
Spring La *GTL/HWG* HX4 ....75 F4
Springlodge PI *GIR* BD8 ......2 B3
Spring Mill St *WBOW* BD5 ....47 F2
Spring Mt *KGHY* BD21 ....14 D1
Spring Park Rd *WIL/AL* BD15 ....25 H4
Spring PI *GTHN* BD7..........46 D2
KGHY BD21 ....14 D1
Spring Ri *KGHY* BD21 ....7 H5
Spring Rw *BGLY* BD16 ....15 G5
KGHY * BD21 ....7 H5
Springroyd Ter *GIR* BD8 ....38 A4
Springs Rd *BAIL* BD17 ......20 D1
Spring St *BRIG* HD6 ......78 B1
IDLE BD10 ....30 A3
KGHY BD21..................7 H5
Springswood Av *SHPY* BD18 ....28 B2
Springswood PI *SHPY* BD18 ....28 B2
Springswood Rd *SHPY* BD18 ....28 B2
Spring Ter *HIPP* HX3 ....5 J3
KGHY BD21..................7 H5
RPDN/SBR HX6 ....74 B1
Spring Wy *KGHY* BD21 ....7 H5
Springwell CI *YEA* LS19 ....11 H5
Springwell Dr *WBOW* BD5 ....47 F3
Spring Wood Av *HIPP* HX3 ....75 G1
Springwood Av *WBOW* BD5 ....47 G4
Spring Wood Dr *HIPP* HX3 ....75 G1
Spring Wood Gdns *HIPP* * HX3 ....75 G2

WBOW BD5 ....47 G5
Springwood Rd *YEA* LS19 ....21 F3
Springwood Ter *ECHL* BD2 ....39 F2
Sprinkwell CI *BFDE* BD3......2 E1
Spruce Hts *BRIG* HD6 ....71 F2
Spruce St *KGHY* BD21..........7 G3
The Square *GIR* BD8 ....37 F5
Square Rd *HFAX* HX1 ....5 J4
Square St *BOW* BD4 ....47 H2
Squire Gn *GIR* BD8 ....38 A3
Squire La *HTON* BD9 ....38 A3
Squirrel La *CUL/QBY* BD13 ....43 G2
Stable Fold *LM/WK* BD12 ....63 E3
Stable La *HIPP* HX3 ....59 G4
Stackgarth *BRIG* HD6 ....78 B3
Stadium Rd *WBSY* BD6 ......55 E2
Stafford Av *HIPP* HX3 ....68 C4
Stafford Pde *HIPP* HX3 ......68 D5
Stafford Rd *HIPP* HX3 ....68 C5
Stafford Sq *HIPP* HX3 ....69 E5
Stafford St *BOW* BD4 ....48 A3
Stainbeck Gdns *WBSY* BD6 ....53 G2
Stainland Rd *GTL/HWG* HX4 ....75 H5
Stainton La *WBSY* BD6 ......53 H2
Staithgate La *WBSY* BD6 ....55 G2
Stallabrass St *GIR* BD8 ....38 D4
Stamford St *BOW* BD4 ....48 A2
Stanacre PI *BFDE* BD3........3 F1
Stanage La *HIPP* HX3 ....53 F3
Stanley Rd *ECHL* BD2 ....29 E5
HFAX HX1 ....4 A6
HWTH BD22 ....13 H2
Stanley St *BGLY* BD16 ......16 D3
BRIG HD6 ....71 G5
CLECK BD19 ....64 C5
HWTH BD22 ....23 F1
IDLE BD10 ....30 A1
KGHY * BD21 ....7 E3
RPDN/SBR HX6 ....67 H4
SHPY BD18 ....28 D4
Stanmore PI *GTHN* BD7 ....46 B2
Stannary PI *HFAX* HX1 ....5 F2
Stanningley Av *LUD/ILL* HX2 ....50 A5
Stanningley By-Pass
PDSY/CALV LS28 ....41 H3
Stanningley Rd *LUD/ILL* HX2 ....50 A5
Stansfield CI *HFAX* HX1 ......4 D3
Stansfield Ct *RPDN/SBR* HX6 ....67 E5
Stapper Gn *WIL/AL* BD15 ....25 G3
Starkie St *KGHY* BD21 ....7 E5
Station Ct *GSLY* * LS20 ....10 C2
Station Forecourt *BFD* * BD1 ....2 D5
Station La *BIRK/DRI* BD11 ....57 G4
Station Rd *BAIL* BD17 ....10 A5
BAIL BD17 ....19 E3
BRIG HD6 ....78 D1
CLAY BD14 ....45 F3
CUL/QBY BD13 ....24 B3
CUL/QBY BD13 ....34 D4
CUL/QBY BD13 ....52 B1
GSLY LS20 ....10 C2
HIPP HX3 ....62 B3
HIPP HX3 ....70 B1
HWTH BD22 ....13 E4
HWTH BD22 ....22 D1
HWTH BD22 ....32 D2
LM/WK BD12 ....55 F5
LUD/ILL HX2 ....66 A1
RPDN/SBR HX6 ....67 F1
SHPY BD18 ....28 C1
WIL/AL BD15 ....35 E1
Station Vw *HWTH* BD22 ....32 D1
Station Works *KGHY* * BD21 ....7 H4
Staups La *HIPP* HX3 ....60 C4
Staveley Dr *SHPY* BD18 ....27 G2
Staveley Gv *HWTH* BD22 ....13 H3
Staveley Ms *BGLY* * BD16 ....16 D2
Staveley Rd *BGLY* BD16 ....16 C2
GTHN BD7 ....46 C1
HWTH BD22 ....13 H3
SHPY BD18 ....27 G1
Staveley Wy *HWTH* BD22 ....13 H3
Stavely Ms *BGLY* * BD16 ....16 D2
Staverton Gv *CUL/QBY* BD13 ....36 B5
Staverton St *LUD/ILL* HX2 ....67 H1
Staybrite Av *BGLY* BD16 ....26 D2
Staygate Gn *WBSY* BD6 ....55 F1
Stead Hill Wy *IDLE* BD10 ....19 G5
Steadman St *BFDE* BD3 ......3 K6
Steadman Ter *BFDE* BD3 ......3 K6
Stead Rd *BOW* BD4 ....56 D2
Stead St *BAIL* BD17 ....28 C1
HFAX * HX1 ....5 F4
Steeplands *HUDN* HD2 ......79 D4
Stell HI *HWTH* BD22 ....13 E1
Stephen CI *HIPP* HX3 ....60 D4

Stephen Crs *ECHL* BD2 ......39 F1
Stephen Rd *WBSY* BD6 ......46 A5
Stephenson Rd *WIL/AL* BD15 ....36 A2
Stephenson St *GTHN* BD7......46 C4
Stepping Stones *AIRE* BD20......9 F3
Sterne HI *LUD/ILL* HX2 ......68 A4
Stewart CI *ECHL* BD2 ....30 B4
Stewart St *HWTH* BD22 ....23 F1
Sticker La *BOW* BD4 ....48 A1
Stirling Crs *BOW* BD4 ....48 D4
Stirling St *HFAX* HX1 ....4 E5
Stirrup Gv *ECHL* BD2 ....29 G5
Stirton St *WBOW* BD5 ....47 E4
Stockhill Fold *IDLE* BD10 ....30 C1
Stockhill Rd *IDLE* BD10 ....30 C1
Stock La *LUD/ILL* HX2 ......67 G2
Stocks Hill CI *AIRE* * BD20......9 E2
Stocks La *CUL/QBY* BD13 ....53 E1
RPDN/SBR HX6 ....66 B5
Stod Fold *LUD/ILL* HX2 ......50 B2
Stone Arches *WBOW* BD5 ....47 F3
Stonecliffe *LUD/ILL* HX2 ....68 A4
Stone Ct *AIRE* BD20..........9 E3
Stonecroft *ECHL* BD2 ....30 B5
Stonecroft Mt *LUD/ILL* HX2 ....67 F3
Stonefield CI *IDLE* BD10 ....30 A4
Stonefield St *CLECK* BD19 ....72 D2
Stonegate *BGLY* BD16 ....16 D1
Stonegate Rd *IDLE* BD10 ....30 A5
Stone Hall Rd *ECHL* BD2 ....30 A5
Stone HI *BGLY* BD16 ....17 E2
Stonehouse Dr *CUL/QBY* BD13 ....51 H2
Stone La *HWTH* BD22 ....32 C2
Stoneleigh *CUL/QBY* BD13 ....52 C1
Stone St *BAIL* BD17 ....19 F4
BFD BD1 ....2 D4
WIL/AL BD15 ....36 D1
Stoney Battery *HFAX* HX1 ....5 H1
Stoneycroft La *AIRE* BD20......7 E1
Stoney HI *BRIG* HD6 ....78 B1
Stoneyhurst Sq *BOW* BD4 ....48 D4
Stoney La *HIPP* HX3 ....59 F2
HIPP HX3 ....71 F1
Stoney Ridge Av *WIL/AL* BD15 ....27 E5
Stoney Ridge Rd *BGLY* BD16 ....27 F4
Stoney Royd Ter *HIPP* HX3 ....69 E4
Stoneys Fold *WIL/AL* BD15 ....25 G3
Stoneys St *AIRE* BD20........7 E1
Stony La *ECHL* BD2 ....30 B4
GTL/HWG HX4 ....75 F1
HIPP HX3 ....70 B4
WIL/AL BD15 ....36 C2
Stony Royd *PDSY/CALV* LS28 ....41 H1
Stoodley Ter *LUD/ILL* HX2 ....67 H2
Stormer Hill La *RPDN/SBR* HX6 ....74 C1
Storr HI *LM/WK* BD12 ......62 D1
Stott HI *BFD* BD1 ....2 E4
Stott Ter *ECHL* BD2 ....30 C5
Stowell Mill St *WBOW* BD5 ....47 E3
Stradmore Rd *CUL/QBY* BD13 ....34 C4
Strafford Wy *IDLE* BD10 ....30 D1
Straightacres La *IDLE* BD10 ....30 C4
Straight La *LUD/ILL* HX2 ....50 C5
Straits *BAIL* BD17 ....18 D2
Strangford Ct *IDLE* BD10 ....30 C1
Stratford Rd *GTHN* BD7 ....46 C2
Strathallan Dr *BAIL* BD17 ....19 E3
Strathmore Dr *BAIL* BD17 ....18 C2
Stratton CI *BRIG* HD6..........78 C2
Stratton Pk *BRIG* HD6 ....78 C2
Stratton Rd *BRIG* HD6 ....78 C2
Stratton Vw *BOW* * BD4 ....48 D3
Strawberry Flds *KGHY* BD21 ....7 F3
Strawberry St *KGHY* BD21 ....7 F3
Stream Head Rd *CUL/QBY* BD13 ....35 G2
Street La *AIRE* BD20..........9 E2
Strensall Gn *WBSY* BD6 ......53 H2
Stretchgate La *LUD/ILL* HX2 ....58 D5
Strong Close Gv *KGHY* BD21 ....7 H4
Strong Close Rd *KGHY* BD21 ....7 H4
Strong Close Wy *KGHY* BD21 ....7 H4
Stubbings Rd *BAIL* BD17 ....18 A4
Stubbing Wy *SHPY* BD18 ....28 D3
Stubs Beck La *CLECK* BD19 ....64 B3
Studley Av *WBSY* BD6 ......54 C3
Studley CI *AIRE* BD20..........9 E2
Studley Crs *BGLY* BD16 ....17 E3
Studley Rd *ECHL* BD2 ....39 G2
Stump Cross *HIPP* HX3 ......60 C4
Stunsteds Rd *CLECK* BD19 ....64 C5
Sturges Gv *ECHL* BD2 ....40 A2
Sturton Gv *LUD/ILL* HX2 ....50 D3
Sturton La *LUD/ILL* HX2 ....50 D4
Styes La *LUD/ILL* HX2 ......66 A4
Sty La *BGLY* BD16 ....9 G5

Sugden CI *BRIG* HD6 ....78 B3
Sugden St *BFD* BD1 ....38 D5
LM/WK BD12 ....63 G1
Sulby Gv *IDLE* BD10 ....30 C5
Summerbridge Crs *CLECK* BD19 ....65 E3
IDLE BD10 ....30 C4
Summerbridge Dr *IDLE* BD10 ....30 C4
Summerdale *CLECK* BD19 ....65 C3
Summerfield Av *BRIG* HD6 ....71 G2
Summerfield CI *BAIL* BD17 ....18 B3
Summerfield Dr *BAIL* BD17 ....18 B3
Summerfield Gn *BAIL* BD17 ....18 C3
Summerfield Gv *BAIL* BD17 ....18 C3
Summerfield Pk *BAIL* BD17 ....18 B3
Summerfield Rd *IDLE* BD10 ....30 B3
Summergate PI *HFAX* HX1 ....4 A6
Summergate St *HFAX* HX1 ....4 B6
Summer Hall Ing *LM/WK* BD12 ....62 C1
Summerlands Gv *WBOW* BD5 ....47 H5
Summer Lea *IDLE* BD10 ......29 H1
Summerscale St *HFAX* * HX1 ....4 C2
Summerseat PI *GTHN* BD7 ....46 C2
Summer St *HFAX* HX1 ....4 B7
Summerville Rd *GTHN* BD7 ....46 D1
PDSY/CALV LS28 ....41 H2
Summit St *KGHY* BD21........7 E3
Sunbridge Rd *BFD* BD1 ......2 C5
GIR BD8 ....38 D4
Sunderland Ct *BRIG* HD6 ....71 F3
Sunderland Rd *HTON* BD9 ....38 C2
Sunderland St *HFAX* HX1 ....5 F4
HWTH BD22 ....23 G1
KGHY BD21 ....7 E5
Sundown Av *GTHN* BD7 ....45 H3
Sun Fold *HFAX* HX1 ....5 J6
Sun Hill Dr *BAIL* BD17 ......17 H3
Sunhurst CI *HWTH* BD22 ....12 D4
Sunhurst Dr *HWTH* BD22 ....12 D4
Sunningdale *IDLE* BD10 ....37 G4
Sunningdale Crs *CUL/QBY* BD13 ....24 D4
Sunny Bank *SHPY* BD18 ....28 C2
Sunnybank Av *BFDE* BD3 ....41 E3
Sunny Bank Av *WBOW* * BD5 ....55 E1
Sunnybank CI *CLECK* BD19 ....72 E4
Sunnybank Crs *GTL/HWG* HX4 ....75 G4
Sunny Bank Dr *RPDN/SBR* HX6 ....67 F1
Sunnybank Gv *BFDE* BD3 ....41 E3
Sunnybank La *BFDE* BD3 ....41 E3
GTL/HWG HX4 ....75 G4
Sunny Bank La *HIPP* HX3 ....70 A3
Sunny Bank Rd *BRIG* HD6 ....71 E5
LUD/ILL HX2 ....50 A5
SHPY BD18 ....55 E1
Sunnybank Rd *GTL/HWG* HX4 ....75 H4
Sunny Bank St *RPDN/SBR* HX6 ....67 F4
Sunny Bank Ter *HIPP* * HX3 ....59 H4
Sunnybrae Crs *BGLY* BD16 ....17 E4
Sunny Brow La *HTON* BD9 ....37 G2
Sunnycliffe *AIRE* BD20..........9 E3
Sunnydale Av *BRIG* HD6 ....78 B3
Sunnydale Gv *KGHY* BD21 ....8 A5
Sunnydale Pk *AIRE* BD20......9 F2
Sunny Hill Av *HWTH* BD22 ....13 G1
Sunny Hill Gv *HWTH* BD22 ....13 G1
Sunny Lea Ter *WBSY* * BD6 ....55 E2
Sunny Mt *AIRE* BD20..........8 D4
BGLY BD16 ....15 G5
KGHY BD21 ....7 E5
Sunnymount *HWTH* BD22 ......6 A3
Sunnyridge Av *PDSY/CALV* LS28 ....41 G5
Sunnyside *BRIG* HD6 ....79 E5
Sunnyside La *BFDE* BD3 ....39 G3
Sunny Side St *HIPP* * HX3 ....59 H4
Sunny View Ter *CUL/QBY* BD13 ....51 H2
Sunshine Ct *WBSY* BD6 ....54 A3
Sun St *BFDE* BD3 ....7 F5
KGHY BD21..................7 F5
YEA LS19 ....11 H4
Sun Wy *HIPP* HX3 ....69 G3
Sun Wood Av *HIPP* HX3 ......61 E1
Suresnes Rd *KGHY* BD21 ....7 E4
Surgery St *HWTH* BD22 ......23 E3
Surrey Gv *WBOW* BD5 ....67 F4
Surrey St *HFAX* HX1 ....67 H2
KGHY BD21 ....7 H3
Sussex St *KGHY* BD21........7 H3
Sutcliffe St *LUD/ILL* HX2 ....58 D5
Sutcliffe Wood La *HIPP* HX3 ....70 D4
Sutherland Rd *HIPP* HX3 ....61 H5
Sutton Av *ECHL* BD2 ....29 G4
Sutton Crs *BOW* BD4 ....48 D3
Sutton Dr *CUL/QBY* BD13 ....24 C4
Sutton Gv *BOW* BD4 ....48 D2
Sutton Rd *BOW* BD4 ....48 D2
Swaine Hill Crs *YEA* LS19 ....11 F4
Swaine Hill St *YEA* LS19 ....11 F4

Swaine Hill Ter *YEA* LS19 .... 11 F4
Swain House Crs *ECHL* BD2 .... 29 H4
Swain House Rd *ECHL* BD2 .... 29 H4
Swain Mt *ECHL* BD2 .... 29 H4
Swales Moor Rd *HIPP* HX3 .... 51 H5
Swallow Fold *GIR* BD8 .... 37 F5
Swallow St *KGHY* BD21 .... 7 G3
Swan Av *BGLY* BD16 .... 17 F3
Swan Bank La *HIPP* HX3 .... 5 K7
Swarland Gv *WBOW* BD5 .... 47 F2
Swincar Av *YEA* LS19 .... 11 G4
Swincliffe Cl *CLECK* BD19 .... 65 F1
Swincliffe Crs *CLECK* BD19 .... 65 F2
Swine La *AIRE* BD20 .... 8 C3
Swine Lane Br *AIRE* BD20 .... 8 D3
Swinton Gl *GTHN* BD7 .... 46 C2
Swinton Ter *HFAX* HX1 .... 4 A6
Swires Rd *ECHL* BD2 .... 40 A3
  HFAX HX1 .... 4 E6
Swires Ter *HFAX* HX1 .... 5 F6
Sycamore Av *BGLY* BD16 .... 16 C4
  GTHN BD7 .... 38 A5
Sycamore Cl *BFDE* BD3 .... 3 C2
Sycamore Dr *BRIG* HD6 .... 71 F2
  CLECK BD19 .... 73 E1
  ELL HX5 .... 76 A3
The Sycamores *GSLY* LS20 .... 10 D1
  WIL/AL * BD15 .... 25 H5
Sycamore Vw *HWTH* BD22 .... 4 B7
Sydenham Pl *BFDE* BD3 .... 39 H2
Sydney St *BGLY* BD16 .... 16 D3
Syke House La *GTL/HWG* HX4 .... 75 E5
Syke La *CUL/QBY* BD13 .... 52 B3
  HIPP HX3 .... 61 H4
  LUD/ILL HX2 .... 42 C5
  RPDN/SBR HX6 .... 66 D5
Syke Side *AIRE* BD20 .... 7 E1
Sykes La *HWTH* BD22 .... 13 E3
  LM/WK BD12 .... 63 H1
Sykes St *CLECK* BD19 .... 73 G1
Sylhet Cl *BFD* D1 .... 2 B3
Sylvan Av *CUL/QBY* BD13 .... 52 A2
Syringa Av *WIL/AL* BD15 .... 26 D1

T

Tabbs Ct *CLECK* BD19 .... 63 G4
Tabbs La *CLECK* BD19 .... 63 H4
Tagore Ct *BOW* BD4 .... 48 C1
Talbot St *GTHN* BD7 .... 38 C5
  KGHY 6 D4
Tamar St *WBOW* BD5 .... 46 D3
Tamworth St *BOW* BD4 .... 48 D1
Tanglewood Ct *WBSY* BD6 .... 54 B1
Tanhouse Hl *HIPP* HX3 .... 70 D1
Tan House La *HIPP* HX3 .... 60 D1
  WIL/AL BD15 .... 25 F4
Tanhouse Pk *HIPP* HX3 .... 70 B1
Tanhouse Vw *HIPP* * HX3 .... 70 B1
Tan La *BOW* BD4 .... 56 A4
Tannerbrook Cl *CLAY* BD14 .... 45 G3
Tanner Hill Rd *GTHN* BD7 .... 45 H4
Tanner St *LVSG* WF15 .... 73 E3
Tannery Ct *IDLE* BD10 .... 30 C1
Tanton Crs *CLAY* BD14 .... 45 G3
Tanton Wk *CLAY* BD14 .... 45 G3
Tarn *BAIL* * BD17 .... 19 H2
Tarn Ct *HWTH* BD22 .... 2 C5
Tarnhill Ms *WBOW* BD5 .... 47 F3
Tarn View Rd *YEA* LS19 .... 11 H4
Taunton St *SHPY* BD18 .... 28 B1
Tawny Cl *BOW* BD4 .... 56 D1
Taylor La *LUD/ILL* HX2 .... 43 F1
Taylor Rd *WBSY* BD6 .... 55 E2
Taylor St *CLECK* BD19 .... 73 F1
Teasdale St *BOW* BD4 .... 48 A4
Teasel Cl *LM/WK* BD12 .... 63 H1
Tees St *WBOW* BD5 .... 46 D4
Telscombe Dr *BOW* BD4 .... 48 C5
Temperance Flds *CLECK* BD19 .... 63 G5
Templars Cl *GTL/HWG* HX4 .... 75 F4
Templar's Wy *GIR* BD8 .... 37 H4
Temple Rhydding Dr *BAIL* BD17 .... 18 D4
Temple St *HTON* BD9 .... 38 C2
  KGHY BD21 .... 7 E4
Tenbury Fold *BOW* BD4 .... 48 D1
Tenby Ter *HFAX* * HX1 .... 5 F5
Tennis Av *BOW* BD4 .... 56 D1
Tennis Wy *BAIL* BD17 .... 18 B5
Tennyson Av *RPDN/SBR* HX6 .... 66 C5
Tennyson Pl *BFDE* BD3 .... 3 J2
  CLECK BD19 .... 64 C5
Tennyson Rd *WBSY* BD6 .... 54 C2
Tennyson St *GSLY* LS20 .... 11 E3
  HIPP HX3 .... 59 F4
  KGHY BD21 .... 14 A1

Tenterfield Ri *HIPP* HX3 .... 60 D4
Tenterfields *IDLE* BD10 .... 30 D1
  LUD/ILL HX2 .... 66 B3
Tenter Hl *CLAY* BD14 .... 45 E3
Tenter Av *LVSG* WF15 .... 73 E3
Ten Yards La *CUL/QBY* BD13 .... 35 E3
Ternhill Gv *WBOW* BD5 .... 47 F2
Tern St *WBOW* BD5 .... 46 D4
Terrace Gdns *HIPP* HX3 .... 59 G4
Terrington Crest *CLAY* BD14 .... 45 G3
Terry Rd *LM/WK* BD12 .... 55 F5
Tetley Dr *BIRK/DRI* BD11 .... 65 G1
Tetley La *HIPP* HX3 .... 60 D3
Tetley Pl *ECHL* BD2 .... 39 G1
Tetley St *BFD* D1 .... 2 B5
Teville Ct *BOW* BD4 .... 47 H3
Tewit Cl *LUD/ILL* HX2 .... 51 E3
Tewit Gn *LUD/ILL* HX2 .... 51 E3
Tewit Hall Gdns *LUD/ILL* HX2 .... 51 E4
Tewit Hall Rd *BFD* BD3 .... 40 B4
Tewit La *LUD/ILL* HX2 .... 51 E3
Tewitt La *CUL/QBY* BD13 .... 35 F2
Thackeray Rd *IDLE* BD10 .... 30 C5
Thackley Av *IDLE* BD10 .... 19 H4
Thackley Ct *BAIL* BD17 .... 28 D1
Thackley Old Rd *SHPY* BD18 .... 29 E1
Thackley Rd *IDLE* BD10 .... 19 H4
Thackley Vw *IDLE* BD10 .... 19 H4
Thackray St *LUD/ILL* HX2 .... 67 G1
Thatchers Wy *CLECK* BD19 .... 65 F4
Theakston Rd *CLAY* BD14 .... 45 F2
Thearne Gn *CLAY* BD14 .... 45 G3
Third Av *BFDE* BD3 .... 40 B3
  HIPP HX3 .... 68 C4
  KGHY BD21 .... 7 E5
  LVSG WF15 .... 73 E3
Third St *LM/WK* BD12 .... 55 F4
Thirkleby Royd *CLAY* BD14 .... 45 F3
Thirlmere Av *ELL* HX5 .... 77 E4
  LM/WK BD12 .... 63 F4
Thirlmere Gdns *ECHL* BD2 .... 40 A2
Thirsk Gra *CLAY* BD14 .... 45 F3
Thirteenth Av *LVSG* WF15 .... 73 E3
Thomas Ct *WBSY* BD6 .... 54 D1
Thomas St *BRIG* HD6 .... 78 B2
  ELL HX5 .... 76 D5
  HFAX HX1 .... 5 H4
  HWTH BD22 .... 23 E3
Thomas St South *HFAX* HX1 .... 4 B5
Thomas St West *HFAX* HX1 .... 68 B3
Thompson Av *ECHL* BD2 .... 29 G4
Thompson Gn *BAIL* BD17 .... 18 B4
Thompson La *BAIL* BD17 .... 18 B5
Thompson St *HFAX* HX1 .... 5 F3
  SHPY BD18 .... 28 B1
Thoresby Dr *CLECK* BD19 .... 65 G5
Thoresby Gv *GTHN* BD7 .... 45 H4
Thornaby Dr *CLAY* BD14 .... 45 F3
Thornacre Crs *SHPY* BD18 .... 29 F3
Thornacre Rd *SHPY* BD18 .... 29 F2
Thorn Av *HTON* BD9 .... 27 F5
Thorn Bank Av *HWTH* BD22 .... 13 F2
Thornberry Dr *LVSG* WF15 .... 73 E3
Thornbridge Ms *ECHL* BD2 .... 30 A5
Thornbury Av *BFDE* BD3 .... 40 C4
Thornbury Crs *BFDE* BD3 .... 40 C4
Thornbury Dr *BFDE* BD3 .... 40 C4
Thornbury Gv *BFDE* BD3 .... 40 C4
Thornbury Rd *BFDE* BD3 .... 40 C5
Thornbury St *BFDE* BD3 .... 40 C5
Thorncliffe Rd *GIR* BD8 .... 39 E3
  HWTH BD22 .... 6 C5
Thorn Cl *SHPY* BD18 .... 29 F3
Thorncroft Rd *WBSY* BD6 .... 54 B1
Thorndale Ri *ECHL* BD2 .... 29 F5
Thorndene Wy *BOW* BD4 .... 57 F3
Thorn Dr *CUL/QBY* BD13 .... 51 H3
  HTON BD9 .... 27 G5
Thorne Cl *PDSY/CALV* LS28 .... 41 C4
Thornes Pk *BRIG* HD6 .... 78 B2
  SHPY BD18 .... 29 E4
Thornfield *BGLY* BD16 .... 16 B2
Thornfield Av *PDSY/CALV* LS28 .... 41 H1
  WBSY BD6 .... 54 D2
Thornfield Ms *BGLY* BD16 .... 9 F4
Thornfield Pl *ECHL* BD2 .... 40 B1
Thornfield Ri *GTL/HWG* HX4 .... 75 G4
Thornfield Sq *GTL/HWG* HX4 .... 75 G4
Thorn Garth *CLECK* BD19 .... 73 F2
  KGHY BD21 .... 6 D2
Thorn Gv *HTON* BD9 .... 27 G5
Thornhill Av *HWTH* BD22 .... 13 F5
  SHPY BD18 .... 29 E4
Thornhill Bridge La *BRIG* HD6 .... 71 F5
Thornhill Cl *PDSY/CALV* LS28 .... 31 G2
Thornhill Dr *PDSY/CALV* LS28 .... 31 F1
  SHPY BD18 .... 29 E4
Thornhill Gv *PDSY/CALV* LS28 .... 31 G2

  SHPY BD18 .... 29 E4
Thornhill Pl *BFDE* BD3 .... 40 D4
Thornhill Rd *BRIG* HD6 .... 78 A3
Thornhills Beck La *BRIG* HD6 .... 71 G4
Thornhills La *BRIG* HD6 .... 71 G4
Thornhill St *PDSY/CALV* LS28 .... 31 G3
Thornhill Ter *BFDE* BD3 .... 40 C4
Thorn La *HTON* BD9 .... 27 G5
Thornlea Cl *YEA* LS19 .... 21 E1
Thornmead Rd *BAIL* BD17 .... 19 E4
Thorn Royd Dr *BOW* BD4 .... 49 E5
Thornsgill Av *BOW* BD4 .... 48 B4
Thorn St *GIR* BD8 .... 38 A3
  HWTH BD22 .... 23 F1
Thornton Ct *GIR* BD8 .... 38 A4
Thornton La *WBOW* BD5 .... 46 D4
Thornton Moor Rd *HWTH* BD22 .... 33 H5
Thornton Old Rd *GIR* BD8 .... 37 G5
Thornton Rd *BRIG* HD6 .... 77 H3
  CUL/QBY BD13 .... 44 C1
  GIR BD8 .... 38 C4
Thornton St *BFD* D1 .... 38 D5
  CLECK BD19 .... 72 D2
  HFAX HX1 .... 4 B7
Thornton Ter *HFAX* HX1 .... 4 B7
Thornton View Rd *CLAY* BD14 .... 45 F3
Thorn Tree St *HFAX* HX1 .... 5 H4
Thorn Vw *HIPP* HX3 .... 59 H3
Thorpe Av *CUL/QBY* BD13 .... 44 D1
Thorpe Cl *GSLY* LS20 .... 10 A3
Thorpe Dr *GSLY* LS20 .... 10 A2
Thorpe Gv *CUL/QBY* BD13 .... 45 E1
Thorpe Rd *CUL/QBY* BD13 .... 44 D1
Thorpe St *HIPP* HX3 .... 59 G3
  KGHY * BD21 .... 7 F3
Thorp Garth *IDLE* BD10 .... 30 A2
Thorverton Dr *BOW* BD4 .... 56 D2
Thorverton Gv *BOW* BD4 .... 56 D2
Threshfield Crs *BIRK/DRI* BD11 .... 57 F4
Thrice Fold *IDLE* BD10 .... 19 G5
Thrift Wy *BGLY* BD16 .... 16 C4
Throstle Bank *LUD/ILL* HX2 .... 68 A3
Throstle Mt *LUD/ILL* HX2 .... 66 C3
Throxenby Wy *CLAY* BD14 .... 45 F3
Thrum Hall Cl *HFAX* HX1 .... 67 H1
Thrum Hall Dr *HFAX* HX1 .... 4 A3
Thrum Hall La *HFAX* HX1 .... 4 A3
Thrush St *KGHY* BD21 .... 7 G3
Thryberg St *BFDE* BD3 .... 3 H6
Thurley Dr *BOW* BD4 .... 48 A5
Thurley Rd *BOW* BD4 .... 48 A5
Thurnscoe Rd *BFD* D1 .... 2 B2
Thursby St *BFDE* BD3 .... 3 J5
Thurston Gdns *WIL/AL* BD15 .... 37 E4
Thwaites Br *KGHY* BD21 .... 7 H4
Thwaites Brow Rd *KGHY* BD21 .... 8 A4
Thwaites La *KGHY* BD21 .... 7 H4
Tichborne Rd *WBOW* * BD5 .... 47 F4
Tichborne Rd West *WBOW* BD5 .... 47 F4
Tichborne St *LVSG* WF15 .... 73 H4
Tickhill St *BFDE* BD3 .... 3 J6
Tile St *GIR* BD8 .... 38 C3
Tiley Sq *WBOW* BD5 .... 46 D4
Till Carr La *HIPP* HX3 .... 71 F1
Tillotson Av *RPDN/SBR* HX6 .... 66 D5
Timber St *ELL* HX5 .... 76 C5
  KGHY BD21 .... 7 H3
Timble Dr *BGLY* BD16 .... 17 E2
Tim La *HWTH* BD22 .... 12 C5
Timmey La *RPDN/SBR* HX6 .... 66 D3
Tinkler Stile *SHPY* BD18 .... 29 G1
Tintern Av *GIR* BD8 .... 37 G5
Tisma Dr *BOW* BD4 .... 56 B2
Tithe Barn Vw *BRIG* HD6 .... 78 D3
Tithe House Wy *HUDN* HD2 .... 79 F5
Titus St *SHPY* BD18 .... 28 A1
Tivoli Pl *WBOW* BD5 .... 46 D4
Toby La *GTHN* BD7 .... 46 B2
Todd Ter *GTHN* * BD7 .... 46 C3
Todwell La *WBOW* BD5 .... 46 B4
Tofts Av *LM/WK* BD12 .... 62 D3
Tofts Gv *BGLY* BD16 .... 5 G6
Tofts Grove Gdns *BRIG* HD6 .... 78 A4
Toftshaw Fold *BOW* BD4 .... 56 C2
Toftshaw La *BOW* BD4 .... 56 C2
Toftshaw New Rd *BOW* BD4 .... 56 C2
Tofts Rd *CLECK* BD19 .... 73 G1
Toller Dr *HTON* BD9 .... 37 H1
Toller Gv *HTON* BD9 .... 38 A1
Toller La *HTON* BD9 .... 38 A1
Toller Pk *HTON* BD9 .... 38 A1
Tolworth Fold *WIL/AL* BD15 .... 36 D4
Tonbridge Cl *WBSY* BD6 .... 54 A2
Tong La *BOW* BD4 .... 57 H2
Tong St *BOW* BD4 .... 56 C1
Toothill Av *BRIG* HD6 .... 78 B4
Toothill Bank *BRIG* HD6 .... 78 B4
Toothill La *BRIG* HD6 .... 78 B5

Tor Av *LM/WK* BD12 .... 62 D4
Tordoff Av *GTHN* BD7 .... 45 H2
Tordoff Gn *WBSY* BD6 .... 54 C2
Tordoff Rd *LM/WK* BD12 .... 55 F5
Torre Crs *WBSY* BD6 .... 53 G1
Torre Gv *WBSY* BD6 .... 53 G1
Torre Rd *WBSY* BD6 .... 53 G1
Torridon Crs *WBSY* BD6 .... 53 H4
Tower Gdns *LUD/ILL* HX2 .... 68 A4
Tower Hl *RPDN/SBR* HX6 .... 67 E4
Tower Rd *SHPY* BD18 .... 27 H1
Tower St *ECHL* BD2 .... 40 A2
Tower Vw *HFAX* HX1 .... 67 H3
Town End *GTHN* BD7 .... 46 B3
Town End Rd *CLAY* BD14 .... 45 E2
Townfield *WIL/AL* BD15 .... 25 H4
Town Fields Rd *ELL* HX5 .... 76 B5
Town Ga *CLECK* BD19 .... 63 G5
  GSLY LS20 .... 10 D2
  HIPP HX3 .... 60 D2
  PDSY/CALV LS28 .... 31 G2
  RPDN/SBR HX6 .... 66 A5
Towngate *BRIG* HD6 .... 72 A3
  HIPP HX3 .... 61 F5
  HX3 .... 69 H4
  LM/WK BD12 .... 62 D3
  SHPY BD18 .... 29 E2
Towngate Av *BRIG* HD6 .... 72 A3
Town Gate Cl *GSLY* LS20 .... 10 D2
Town Hall Sq *YEA* LS19 .... 11 G4
Town Hall St *ELL* HX5 .... 76 C5
  KGHY BD21 .... 7 F4
  RPDN/SBR HX6 .... 67 E5
Town Hall St East *HFAX* * HX1 .... 5 H3
Town Hill St *BGLY* * BD16 .... 27 E3
Town La *IDLE* BD10 .... 20 A5
Townley Av *HIPP* HX3 .... 69 H4
Town St *BIRK/DRI* BD11 .... 57 F4
  GSLY LS20 .... 10 D2
  YEA LS19 .... 11 G4
Town Wells Dr *PDSY/CALV* LS28 .... 31 G3
Trafalgar Sq *HFAX* HX1 .... 4 C7
Trafalgar St *BFD* D1 .... 2 C5
  HFAX HX1 .... 4 C7
Tramways *LM/WK* BD12 .... 55 G5
Tranbeck Rd *GSLY* LS20 .... 10 A2
Tranfield Av *GSLY* LS20 .... 10 B2
Tranfield Cl *GSLY* LS20 .... 10 B2
Tranfield Gdns *GSLY* LS20 .... 10 B2
Tranmere Ct *GSLY* LS20 .... 10 B2
Tranmere Dr *GSLY* LS20 .... 10 A2
Transperience Wy *LM/WK* BD12 .... 55 G4
Tranter Gv *BOW* BD4 .... 48 D2
Trees St *GIR* BD8 .... 38 D3
Tree Top Vw *CUL/QBY* BD13 .... 43 H5
Trenam Park Dr *IDLE* BD10 .... 19 H4
Trenance Dr *SHPY* BD18 .... 28 A2
Trenance Gdns *GTL/HWG* HX4 .... 75 E4
Trenholme Av *LM/WK* BD12 .... 54 C4
Trenton Dr *GIR* BD8 .... 38 D3
Trevelyan St *BRIG* HD6 .... 71 F3
Trimmingham La *LUD/ILL* HX2 .... 67 G2
Trimmingham Rd *LUD/ILL* HX2 .... 67 G2
Trimmingham Vls *LUD/ILL* * HX2 .... 67 H2
Trinity Cl *LUD/ILL* HX2 .... 51 F4
Trinity Fold *HFAX* * HX1 .... 5 G5
Trinity Gv *BRIG* * HD6 .... 71 F4
Trinity Pl *BGLY* BD16 .... 16 D4
  HFAX HX1 .... 5 G5
Trinity Rd *HFAX* HX1 .... 5 G5
  WBOW BD5 .... 47 E2
Trinity St *HFAX* HX1 .... 5 G5
  KGHY BD21 .... 7 F3
Trinity Vw *HIPP* HX3 .... 5 K6
  LM/WK BD12 .... 55 F3
Trinity Wk *LM/WK* BD12 .... 55 F3
Tristram Av *WBOW* BD5 .... 47 H5
Trooper La *HIPP* HX3 .... 5 K6
Trooper Ter *HIPP* HX3 .... 5 K6
Trough La *HWTH* BD22 .... 33 H3
Trueman Ct *LM/WK* BD12 .... 55 F4
Truncliffe *WBSY* BD6 .... 55 E1
Tudor Barn Ct *SHPY* BD18 .... 29 E4
Tudor Cl *PDSY/CALV* LS28 .... 41 H2
Tudor St *WBOW* BD5 .... 47 E3
Tuel La *RPDN/SBR* HX6 .... 67 E4
Tulip St *HWTH* BD22 .... 22 D3
Tumbling Hill St *GTHN* BD7 .... 2 A6
Tunnel St *CUL/QBY* BD13 .... 34 C4
Tunstall Gn *BOW* BD4 .... 48 D4
Tunwell La *ECHL* BD2 .... 30 B5
Tunwell St *ECHL* BD2 .... 30 B5
Turbury La *GTL/HWG* HX4 .... 74 D3
Turf Ct *CUL/QBY* BD13 .... 24 B4
Turf La *CUL/QBY* BD13 .... 24 B4
Turner Av *GTHN* BD7 .... 46 A2
Turner Av North *LUD/ILL* HX2 .... 50 C5
Turner Av South *LUD/ILL* HX2 .... 58 D1

Turner La HIPP HX3 .....60 A4
Turner Pl GTHN BD7 .....46 C2
LUD/ILL HX2 .....58 D1
Turner's Ct HIPP HX3 .....59 G3
Turner Vw LUD/ILL * HX2 .....58 D1
Turney St HIPP HX3 .....59 F3
Turnpike St ELL HX5 .....76 D4
Turnshaw Rd HWTH BD22 .....12 A4
Turnsteads Av CLECK BD19 .....64 A5
Turnsteads Cl CLECK BD19 .....64 B5
Turnsteads Crs CLECK BD19 .....64 B5
Turnsteads Dr CLECK BD19 .....64 B5
Turnsteads Mt CLECK BD19 .....64 B5
Tweedy St WIL/AL BD15 .....25 H4
Twelfth Av LVSG WF15 .....73 E3
Twickenham Ct GIR BD8 .....39 E2
Tyersal Av BOW BD4 .....41 E5
Tyersal Cl BOW BD4 .....41 E5
Tyersal Ct BOW BD4 .....49 E1
Tyersal Crs BOW BD4 .....49 E1
Tyersal Dr BOW BD4 .....49 E1
Tyersal Garth BOW BD4 .....49 E1
Tyersal Gn BOW BD4 .....49 E1
Tyersal Gv BOW BD4 .....41 E5
Tyersal La BOW BD4 .....49 E1
Tyersal Pk BOW BD4 .....49 E1
Tyersal Rd BOW BD4 .....49 E1
Tyersal Ter BOW BD4 .....48 D1
Tyersal Vw BOW BD4 .....48 D1
Tyersal Wk BOW BD4 .....49 E1
Tyne St BFDE BD3 .....3 F3
KGHY BD21 .....7 G4
Tyrrel St BFD BD1 .....2 D5
Tyson St HX1 .....67 H2

U

Ullswater Dr WBSY BD6 .....54 A4
Undercliffe La BAIL BD17 .....3 G1
Undercliffe Rd ECHL BD2 .....40 A1
Undercliffe St BFDE BD3 .....3 J1
Underwood Dr YEA LS19 .....21 G5
Union House La CLAY BD14 .....45 F5
Union La LUD/ILL HX2 .....50 C1
Union St BAIL BD17 .....19 E4
BGLY BD16 .....9 F4
CUL/QBY BD13 .....52 B1
GTL/HWG HX4 .....76 A4
HFAX HX1 .....5 H5
RPDN/SBR HX6 .....67 F3
Union St South HFAX * HX1 .....5 H6
Union Yd IDLE BD10 .....30 A1
Unity St AIRE BD20 .....8 A1
Unity St North BGLY BD16 .....16 C4
Unity St South BGLY BD16 .....16 C4
Unity Ter HFAX HX1 .....67 H2
Unwin Pl HTON BD9 .....37 H2
Uplands CUL/QBY BD13 .....6 D2
Uplands Av CUL/QBY BD13 .....45 E5
Uplands Cl CUL/QBY BD13 .....45 E5
Uplands Crs CUL/QBY BD13 .....45 E5
Uplands Gv CUL/QBY BD13 .....45 E5
Upper Ada St SHPY BD18 .....28 A1
Upper Addison St BOW BD4 .....47 G2
Upper Allerton La WIL/AL BD15 .....36 B4
Upper Ashley La SHPY * BD18 .....28 C1
Upper Bell Hall HFAX HX1 .....68 B3
Upper Bolton Brow
RPDN/SBR HX6 .....67 G3
Upper Butts CLECK BD19 .....73 G1
Upper Calton St KGHY BD21 .....14 A1
Upper Carr La PDSY/CALV LS28 .....31 F3
Upper Castle St WBOW BD5 .....47 F2
Upper Chelsea St KGHY BD21 .....14 A1
Upper Ellistones Ct
GTL/HWG HX4 .....75 F5
Upper Ferndown Gn
WIL/AL * BD15 .....36 D3
Upper Forge HFAX HX1 .....5 G4
Upper Fountain St
RPDN/SBR HX6 .....67 G3
Upper Fyfe La BAIL BD17 .....19 F3
Upper George St SHPY * BD6 .....54 C1
Upper Grange Av WIL/AL BD15 .....37 E4
Upper Green Av CLECK BD19 .....63 G5
Upper Green La BRIG HD6 .....70 D3
Upper Hall Vw HIPP HX3 .....60 D2
Upper Haugh Shaw HFAX HX1 .....4 D7
Upper Headley CUL/QBY * BD13 .....44 A2
Upper Heights Rd
CUL/QBY BD13 .....35 H4
Upper Hird St KGHY BD21 .....13 H1
Upper House La LVSG WF15 .....73 F4

Upper House St BOW BD4 .....48 A2
Upper Kirkgate HFAX HX1 .....5 J4
Upper La HIPP HX3 .....60 C1
Upper Lombard St YEA LS19 .....21 F2
Upper Marsh HFAX 69 G3
Upper Marsh La HWTH BD22 .....22 A4
Upper Martin Gn GTL/HWG HX4 .....75 F4
Upper Mary St SHPY BD18 .....28 A1
Upper Mdw CUL/QBY BD13 .....52 B2
Upper Mosscar St BFDE BD3 .....3 H5
Upper Nidd St BFDE BD3 .....3 K6
Upper Park Ga BFDE BD3 .....3 F4
Upper Piccadilly BFD * BD1 .....2 C4
Upper Quarry Rd HUDN HD2 .....79 H5
Upper Range HIPP HX3 .....59 H4
Upper Royd HIPP * HX3 .....61 F5
Upper Rushton Rd BFDE BD3 .....40 C3
Upper Seymour St BFDE BD3 .....3 J6
Upper Sutherland Rd HIPP HX3 .....61 H5
Upper Washer La LUD/ILL HX2 .....68 A3
Upper Willow Hall LUD/ILL HX2 .....67 G2
Upper Woodlands Rd GIR BD8 .....38 B3
Upwood La AIRE BD20 .....9 E1
Usher St BOW BD4 .....47 H2
Uttley St HIPP * HX3 .....59 G3

V

Vale Gv CUL/QBY BD13 .....52 C2
Vale Mill La HWTH BD22 .....13 E5
Valentine Ct CUL/QBY BD13 .....36 B5
Vale St BRIG HD6 .....71 F5
KGHY BD21 .....7 H2
Valley HIPP HX3 .....62 A5
Valley Ct BFDE BD3 .....39 F5
Valley Fold CUL/QBY BD13 .....52 B2
Valley Gv LUD/ILL HX2 .....51 E3
Valley Pde GIR BD8 .....2 B1
Valley Pl BFD BD1 .....39 F3
Valley Rd BFD BD1 .....2 D1
CLECK BD19 .....64 D5
KGHY BD21 .....7 H4
SHPY BD18 .....28 C3
Valley Vw BAIL BD17 .....18 C5
BGLY BD16 .....15 F5
LUD/ILL HX2 .....51 E3
Valley View Cl HWTH BD22 .....13 E5
Valley View Gdns HWTH * BD22 .....23 F1
Valley View Gv ECHL BD2 .....39 H2
Valley Wy LUD/ILL HX2 .....51 E3
Vaughan St BFD BD1 .....2 A4
HFAX HX1 .....4 A7
Ventnor Cl CLECK BD19 .....65 C3
Ventnor St BFDE BD3 .....3 H5
Ventnor Ter HIPP BD3 .....68 C4
Vento Cl WBSY BD6 .....54 C2
Verdun Rd WBSY BD6 .....54 B2
Vere Sq WBOW BD5 .....47 F3
Verity St BOW BD4 .....57 E3
Vernon Ct KGHY BD21 .....7 E4
Vernon Pl ECHL BD2 .....40 A2
Vernon St HWTH BD22 .....23 G1
Vestry St BOW BD4 .....48 A4
Vicarage Cl LM/WK BD12 .....62 D3
Vicarage Ct CLECK BD19 .....64 C5
Vicarage Gdns BIRK/DRI BD11 .....57 F5
BRIG HD6 .....78 A3
Vicarage Rd SHPY BD18 .....29 F1
Vicar La BFD BD1 .....2 E6
Vicar Park Dr LUD/ILL HX2 .....58 A5
Vickerman St HFAX HX1 .....4 B6
Victor Dr GSLY LS20 .....10 D3
Victoria Av BRIG HD6 .....71 H5
CLECK * BD19 .....73 G1
ECHL BD2 .....30 C5
ELL HX5 .....76 B5
HFAX HX1 .....4 A6
HWTH BD22 .....22 D1
KGHY BD21 .....7 F3
RPDN/SBR HX6 .....67 G3
SHPY BD18 .....28 A1
Victoria Ct KGHY BD21 .....7 E4
Victoria Crs ELL HX5 .....76 C5
PDSY/CALV LS28 .....41 H5
Victoria Dr ECHL BD2 .....30 C5
HIPP HX3 .....61 E2
Victoria Gdns PDSY/CALV LS28 .....41 H5
Victoria Ms ELL * HX5 .....76 C5
KGHY BD21 .....7 G3
Victoria Pk HFAX * HX1 .....4 C3
SHPY BD18 .....28 A2
Victoria Park St KGHY BD21 .....7 G3
Victoria Park Vw KGHY BD21 .....7 G3
Victoria Pl BRIG HD6 .....78 C2
YEA LS19 .....11 F4

Victoria Ri PDSY/CALV LS28 .....41 H5
Victoria Rd BRIG HD6 .....71 G1
CLECK BD19 .....65 H5
ECHL BD2 .....30 B5
ELL HX5 .....76 B5
GSLY LS20 .....10 C3
HFAX HX1 .....4 C3
HIPP HX3 .....70 C1
HWTH BD22 .....13 E4
HWTH BD22 .....23 E2
KGHY BD21 .....7 E5
PDSY/CALV LS28 .....41 H5
RPDN/SBR HX6 .....67 G5
SHPY BD18 .....28 A1
WBSY BD6 .....54 B2
Victoria St BAIL BD17 .....28 C1
BFD BD1 .....2 B5
BRIG HD6 .....78 C2
CLAY BD14 .....45 E3
CLECK BD19 .....64 C5
CUL/QBY BD13 .....24 D3
CUL/QBY BD13 .....52 C1
ECHL BD2 .....40 B2
GTL/HWG HX4 .....76 A4
HFAX HX1 .....5 G3
IDLE BD10 .....20 A4
PDSY/CALV LS28 .....31 F3
RPDN/SBR HX6 .....67 G5
WIL/AL BD15 .....25 H5
WIL/AL BD15 .....36 D1
Victoria Ter HFAX * HX1 .....4 C5
KGHY BD21 .....7 F3
LUD/ILL HX2 .....66 B3
Victor Rd HTON BD9 .....38 C2
Victor St BFDE BD3 .....40 D5
HTON BD9 .....38 C2
Victor Ter HFAX HX1 .....4 C1
HTON BD9 .....38 C2
View Croft Rd BAIL BD17 .....28 C1
View Rd KGHY BD21 .....6 D3
Vignola Ter CLAY BD14 .....45 F2
Village Ms WIL/AL * BD15 .....25 H4
Village St HIPP HX3 .....62 A3
Villa Gv BGLY BD16 .....16 C3
Villa Mt LM/WK BD12 .....62 D4
Villa Rd BGLY BD16 .....16 C3
Villa St RPDN/SBR HX6 .....67 F4
Villier Ct WIL/AL BD15 .....37 E3
Vincent St BFD * BD1 .....2 B5
HFAX HX1 .....4 B5
Vine Av CLECK BD19 .....64 B5
Vine Cl BRIG HD6 .....79 E1
Vine Ct BRIG HD6 .....79 E1
Vine Crs CLECK BD19 .....64 B5
Vine Garth BRIG HD6 .....79 E1
Vine Gv BRIG HD6 .....79 E1
Vine St CLECK BD19 .....64 C5
GTHN BD7 .....46 C2
Vine Ter CUL/QBY BD13 .....44 A1
HFAX HX1 .....5 F6
Vine Ter East GIR BD8 .....37 H4
Vine Ter West GIR BD8 .....37 H4
Violet St HFAX HX1 .....4 C3
HWTH BD22 .....22 D3
Violet St North HFAX HX1 .....4 C2
Virginia St CLAY BD14 .....45 F4
Vivian Pl GTHN BD7 .....46 B4
Vivien Rd GIR BD8 .....37 F4
Vulcan St BOW BD4 .....56 C1
BRIG HD6 .....78 D2

W

Waddington St KGHY BD21 .....7 F5
Wade House Av HIPP HX3 .....53 F4
Wade House Rd HIPP HX3 .....53 F5
Wade St BFD BD1 .....2 C6
HFAX HX1 .....5 H3
Wadlands Cl PDSY/CALV LS28 .....31 H1
Wadlands Dr PDSY/CALV LS28 .....41 H1
Wadlands Gv PDSY/CALV LS28 .....31 H1
Wadlands Ri PDSY/CALV LS28 .....41 H1
Wadsworth St HFAX HX1 .....4 B2
Wagon La BGLY BD16 .....16 D5
Wainhouse Rd HFAX HX1 .....4 A7
Wainman St BAIL BD17 .....19 E2
BAIL BD17 .....28 C1
HFAX HX1 .....4 B3
Wakefield Ga LUD/ILL HX2 .....68 A4
Wakefield Rd BFD BD1 .....2 E7
BOW BD4 .....48 A3
BRIG HD6 .....79 E4
HIPP HX3 .....71 E1
HIPP HX3 .....75 F1
RPDN/SBR HX6 .....67 H4
Walden Dr HTON BD9 .....37 F1

The Walk KGHY BD21 .....7 F5
PDSY/CALV LS28 .....41 H2
Walker Av GTHN BD7 .....45 H2
Walker Dr GIR BD8 .....38 B4
Walker La RPDN/SBR HX6 .....67 G4
Walker Pl SHPY BD18 .....29 E1
Walker Rd LM/WK BD12 .....63 G1
Walkers Rw YEA LS19 .....11 F5
Walker St BOW BD4 .....56 A2
CLECK BD19 .....63 G4
CLECK BD19 .....64 C5
Walker Ter BOW BD4 .....47 H3
CUL/QBY BD13 .....24 C4
Walker Wd BAIL BD17 .....18 A4
Wallace St HFAX HX1 .....4 A5
Wallbank Dr SHPY BD18 .....28 D3
Wallingford Mt WIL/AL BD15 .....37 E5
Wallis St GIR BD8 .....38 B5
RPDN/SBR HX6 .....67 E4
Wall St HWTH BD22 .....6 C5
Walmer Vls GIR BD8 .....39 E3
Walnut St BFDE BD3 .....48 B1
HFAX HX1 .....4 C4
KGHY BD21 .....14 A2
Walshaw St GTHN BD7 .....46 B3
Walsh La BGLY BD16 .....9 G5
HIPP HX3 .....59 G4
Walsh Sq HFAX * HX1 .....68 B3
Walsh St HFAX HX1 .....4 B3
Walter Clough La HIPP HX3 .....70 A3
Walter St ECHL BD2 .....29 E5
IDLE BD10 .....30 A1
Walton La BRIG HD6 .....72 B3
Walton St BOW BD4 .....47 G2
RPDN/SBR HX6 .....67 E4
Waltroyd Rd CLECK BD19 .....73 F1
Wansford Cl BOW BD4 .....48 D5
Wanstead Crs WIL/AL BD15 .....37 E4
Wapping Rd BFDE BD3 .....2 E2
Wardle Crs KGHY BD21 .....6 C3
Wardman St KGHY BD21 .....7 H2
Ward's End HFAX HX1 .....5 H5
Ward St GTHN BD7 .....46 B4
KGHY BD21 .....7 E5
Wareham Cnr BOW BD4 .....48 D5
Warhurst Rd ELL HX5 .....76 D3
Warley Av BFDE BD3 .....40 C4
Warley Dene LUD/ILL HX2 .....67 G2
Warley Dr BFDE BD3 .....40 C5
Warley Edge La LUD/ILL HX2 .....67 E1
Warley Gv BFDE BD3 .....40 C4
LUD/ILL HX2 .....67 G2
Warley Rd LUD/ILL HX2 .....67 G2
Warley St HFAX * HX1 .....4 C5
Warley Town La LUD/ILL HX2 .....66 D1
Warley Vw LUD/ILL HX2 .....67 G1
Warley Wood Av LUD/ILL HX2 .....66 C3
Warley Wood La LUD/ILL HX2 .....66 C3
Warm La YEA LS19 .....21 F1
Warmliegh Pk CUL/QBY BD13 .....51 G1
Warren Av BGLY BD16 .....17 E1
Warren Dr BGLY BD16 .....17 E2
Warren La BGLY BD16 .....17 E2
Warren Pk BRIG HD6 .....70 D2
Warren Park Cl BRIG HD6 .....70 D3
Warrenton Pl GTHN * BD7 .....46 B2
Warton Av BOW BD4 .....56 A1
Warwick Cl BOW BD4 .....48 A3
HFAX * HX1 .....4 A3
Warwick Dr BOW BD4 .....48 A3
Warwick Rd BOW BD4 .....48 A3
Washer La LUD/ILL HX2 .....68 A4
Washington St GIR BD8 .....38 A3
HIPP * HX3 .....59 F4
Waterslack Dr WBSY BD6 .....54 A4
Watercock St BOW BD4 .....47 H2
Waterfront Ms IDLE BD10 .....30 D1
Watergate HIPP HX3 .....70 B1
Water Hill La RPDN/SBR HX6 .....66 D3
Waterhouse St HFAX HX1 .....5 G4
KGHY BD21 .....6 D4
Water La BFD BD1 .....2 A4
HFAX HX1 .....5 J6
KGHY BD21 .....7 E5
Waterloo Crs IDLE BD10 .....31 E1
Waterloo Fold LM/WK BD12 .....63 E3
Waterloo Gv PDSY/CALV LS28 .....41 G5
Waterloo Mt PDSY/CALV LS28 .....41 G5
Waterloo Rd BGLY BD16 .....16 C3
BRIG HD6 .....71 G1
PDSY/CALV LS28 .....41 G4
Waterloo Ter LUD/ILL HX2 .....67 F2
Waterside BGLY BD16 .....16 A1
HIPP HX3 .....5 J6
HWTH BD22 .....32 D2
Water St BRIG HD6 .....71 G5
RPDN/SBR HX6 .....67 E5
Watford Av HIPP HX3 .....62 A5

Watkin Av *CUL/QBY* BD13 ....44 C1
Watkinson Av *LUD/ILL* HX2 ......59 E1
Watkinson Dr *LUD/ILL* HX2 ......59 E1
Watkinson Rd *LUD/ILL* HX2 ......59 E1
Watmough St *GTHN* BD7 ......46 B4
Watson Mill La *RPDN/SBR* HX6 ...67 E5
Watts St *CLAY* BD14 ......45 E3
Watt St *BOW* BD4 ......48 C2
Watty Hall Av *WBSY* BD6 ......46 B5
Watty Hall La *WBSY* BD6 ......46 B5
Watty Hall Rd *WBSY* BD6 ......46 B5
Wauds Gates *BAIL* BD17 ......18 D5
Waverley Av *AIRE* BD20 ......8 C3
  GTHN BD7 ......46 C2
Waverley Crs *HIPP* HX3 ......70 B1
Waverley Pl *GTHN* BD7 ......46 C2
Waverley Rd *GTHN* BD7 ......46 C2
Waverley Ter *GTHN* BD7 ......46 C2
Waverton Gn *WBSY* BD6 ......53 H3
Wavertree Park Gdns
  LM/WK BD12 ......62 D1
Wayside Crs *IDLE* * BD10 ......30 A4
Weardale Cl *BOW* BD4 ......56 B1
Weatherhouse Ter *LUD/ILL* HX2 ...58 C4
Weavers Cft *IDLE* BD10 ......19 H4
Weavers Gra *GSLY* LS20 ......10 C2
Weavers Hl *HWTH* BD22 ......22 D3
Weaverthorpe Rd *BOW* BD4 ......56 D2
Webb Dr *ECHL* BD2 ......39 H2
Webb's Ter *HIPP* HX3 ......5 K1
Weber Ct *BFDE* * BD3 ......40 B5
Webster St *BFDE* BD3 ......3 J3
Wedgemoor Cl *LM/WK* BD12 ......62 D1
Weetwood Rd *GIR* BD8 ......38 B4
Welbeck Dr *GTHN* BD7 ......45 H3
Welbeck Ri *GTHN* BD7 ......45 G3
Welburn Av *HIPP* HX3 ......70 C1
Welburn Mt *WBSY* BD6 ......53 H2
Welbury Dr *GIR* BD8 ......38 D2
Weldon Ct *BOW* BD4 ......48 D3
Welham Wk *BFDE* BD3 ......3 G2
Wellands Gn *CLECK* BD19 ......73 E1
Wellands La *CLECK* BD19 ......63 G5
Wellands Ter *BFDE* BD3 ......40 B5
Well Cl *YEA* LS19 ......21 H3
Well Close St *BRIG* HD6 ......71 F5
Well Cft *SHPY* BD18 ......28 C2
Wellesley Pk *LUD/ILL* * HX2 ......67 H1
Wellgarth *HFAX* HX1 ......5 F7
Wellgate *GTL/HWG* HX4 ......75 H3
Well Green La *BRIG* HD6 ......71 E3
Well Gv *BRIG* HD6 ......71 E3
Well Head Rd *HFAX* HX1 ......5 G6
Well Head La *HFAX* HX1 ......5 G6
Well Heads *CUL/QBY* BD13 ......43 F1
Well Hl *YEA* LS19 ......11 G4
Wellholme *BRIG* HD6 ......71 G5
Wellington Ar *BRIG* * HD6 ......78 B1
  LUD/ILL HX2 ......58 D4
Wellington Crs *SHPY* BD18 ......28 B2
Wellington Gv *ECHL* BD2 ......40 A2
  PDSY/CALV LS28 ......41 H5
  KGHY BD21 ......7 E5
  WIL/AL BD15 ......25 H5
Wellington St *BFD* BD1 ......2 E4
  BGLY BD16 ......16 C3
  BOW BD4 ......48 C1
  CUL/QBY BD13 ......52 C1
  ECHL BD2 ......40 A1
  IDLE BD10 ......30 A2
  WIL/AL BD15 ......37 F3
Wellington St South *HFAX* HX1 ...5 J5
Wellington St West *HFAX* HX1 ......4 E6
Well La *BRIG* HD6 ......79 F1
  GSLY LS20 ......10 D2
  HFAX HX1 ......5 J3
  YEA LS19 ......11 G5
  YEA LS19 ......21 H3
Well Road *LUD/ILL* HX2 ......67 G1
Well Royd Av *LUD/ILL* HX2 ......67 F1
Wells Rd *GSLY* LS20 ......10 D2
The Wells *LUD/ILL* HX2 ......67 F1
  LUD/ILL * HX2 ......67 H3
Well St *BFD* BD1 ......2 E5
  CUL/QBY BD13 ......34 C4
  KGHY BD21 ......7 E4
  WIL/AL BD15 ......25 H4
Well Vw *GSLY* LS20 ......10 D2
Welwyn Av *SHPY* BD18 ......29 G2
Welwyn Dr *BAIL* BD17 ......18 D4
  SHPY BD18 ......29 G2
Wembly Av *CUL/QBY* BD13 ......44 C1
Wenborough La *BOW* BD4 ......49 E3
Wendron Wy *IDLE* BD10 ......30 A2
Wenlock St *BFDE* BD3 ......3 G6

Wenning St *KGHY* BD21 ......7 H3
Wensley Av *SHPY* BD18 ......28 B2
Wensley Bank *CUL/QBY* BD13 ......43 H1
Wensley Bank Ter
  CUL/QBY BD13 ......43 H1
Wensley Bank West
  CUL/QBY BD13 ......43 H1
Wensleydale Ri *BAIL* BD17 ......19 F2
Wensleydale Rd *BFDE* BD3 ......40 D5
Wensley Gv *BRIG* HD6 ......77 H3
Wentworth Ct *BRIG* HD6 ......78 A4
Wentworth Dr *LUD/ILL* HX2 ......51 E3
Wentworth Gv *LUD/ILL* HX2 ......51 E3
Wesley Av *LM/WK* BD12 ......55 E3
Wesley Av South *LM/WK* BD12 ...55 F4
Wesley Ct *HFAX* * HX1 ......5 H3
Wesley Dr *LM/WK* BD12 ......55 F3
Wesley Gv *IDLE* BD10 ......20 B5
Wesley Pl *KGHY* BD21 ......14 A3
Wesley Rd *PDSY/CALV* LS28 ......41 H3
Wesley St *CLECK* BD19 ......64 C5
West Av *BAIL* BD17 ......18 D2
  HIPP HX3 ......68 C4
  HIPP HX3 ......71 F1
West Bank *HWTH* BD22 ......6 C3
  LUD/ILL HX2 ......58 C1
West Bank Cl *HWTH* BD22 ......6 C3
West Bank Gv *AIRE* BD20 ......7 H1
West Bank Ri *HWTH* BD22 ......6 C3
West Bank Rd *AIRE* BD20 ......7 G1
West Bolton *LUD/ILL* HX2 ......50 C5
Westborough Dr *LUD/ILL* HX2 ...67 G1
Westbourne Dr *GSLY* LS20 ......10 B2
Westbourne Gv *HIPP* HX3 ......69 E5
Westbourne Rd *GIR* * BD8 ......38 C2
Westbourne Ter *HIPP* HX3 ......69 E5
West Brook Ct *HFAX* HX1 ......5 F2
Westburn Av *HWTH* BD22 ......13 G1
Westburn Crs *HWTH* BD22 ......13 G1
Westburn Gv *HWTH* BD22 ......13 G1
Westburn Wy *HWTH* BD22 ......13 G1
Westbury Cl *BOW* BD4 ......48 C2
Westbury Pl *HFAX* HX1 ......67 H2
Westbury Rd *WBSY* BD6 ......53 C1
Westbury St *BOW* BD4 ......48 C2
  ELL HX5 ......76 D4
Westbury Ter *HFAX* HX1 ......67 H2
West Byland *LUD/ILL* HX2 ......50 C3
Westcliffe Av *BAIL* BD17 ......18 C2
Westcliffe Dr *LUD/ILL* HX2 ......67 G1
Westcliffe Ri *CLECK* BD19 ......67 G1
Westcliffe Rd *CLECK* BD19 ......64 B5
  SHPY BD18 ......28 C3
Westcombe Ct *LM/WK* BD12 ......62 D1
West Cote Dr *IDLE* BD10 ......19 G5
West Cft *LM/WK* BD12 ......62 D2
Westcroft Av *HIPP* HX3 ......61 G1
Westcroft Rd *GTHN* BD7 ......46 B3
West Dr *HWTH* BD22 ......32 D1
West End *CUL/QBY* BD13 ......52 D1
  HFAX * HX1 ......67 H2
West End Dr *CLECK* BD19 ......73 E2
West End Rd *HFAX* HX1 ......67 H2
  PDSY/CALV LS28 ......31 G3
Westend St *BFD* BD1 ......2 B4
West End Ter *ECHL* BD2 ......30 A4
  GSLY LS20 ......10 B2
  SHPY BD18 ......28 B1
Westercroft La *HIPP* HX3 ......61 G2
Westercroft Vw *HIPP* HX3 ......61 G2
Western Pl *CUL/QBY* BD13 ......53 E1
Western Wy *WBSY* BD6 ......54 B3
Westerton Ct *LM/WK* BD12 ......56 A5
Westfell Cl *HWTH* BD22 ......6 C5
Westfell Rd *HWTH* BD22 ......6 C5
Westfell Wy *HWTH* BD22 ......6 C5
Westfield *CUL/QBY* BD13 ......44 D1
Westfield Av *HIPP* HX3 ......70 C1
  YEA LS19 ......11 E5
Westfield Cl *YEA* LS19 ......11 E5
Westfield Crs *AIRE* BD20 ......8 A1
  SHPY BD18 ......29 F3
Westfield Dr *AIRE* BD20 ......8 A2
  HIPP HX3 ......70 C1
  YEA LS19 ......10 D5
Westfield Gdns *HIPP* HX3 ......70 C1
Westfield Gv *IDLE* BD10 ......29 H1
  SHPY BD18 ......29 F1
Westfield La *ECHL* BD2 ......29 G2
  LM/WK BD12 ......63 E4
Westfield Mt *YEA* LS19 ......10 D5
Westfield Ov *YEA* LS19 ......10 D5
Westfield Pl *CLECK* BD19 ......63 F4
  HFAX HX1 ......4 C5
Westfield Rd *AIRE* BD20 ......8 A2
  CLAY BD14 ......45 E3
  HTON BD9 ......38 B2

Westfield St *HFAX* HX1 ......4 E5
Westfield Ter *BAIL* BD17 ......18 D2
  CLAY BD14 ......45 E3
  ECHL BD2 ......40 A3
  HFAX HX1 ......4 C1
Westgate *BAIL* BD17 ......18 D2
  BRIG HD6 ......79 F1
  CLECK BD19 ......73 F1
  ECHL BD2 ......30 B5
  ELL HX5 ......76 C4
  GIR BD8 ......2 A3
  GSLY LS20 ......10 A3
  HFAX HX1 ......5 H4
  SHPY BD18 ......28 C1
Westgate Gdns *KGHY* BD21 ......7 E5
Westgate Hill St *BOW* BD4 ......57 F2
Westgate Market *HFAX* HX1 ......5 H4
Westgate Ter *BOW* BD4 ......57 F2
West Gv *BAIL* BD17 ......18 D2
Westgrove Ct *CLECK* BD19 ......64 B5
West Grove Ter *HFAX* HX1 ......4 E4
Westhill Av *CUL/QBY* BD13 ......24 D4
West Hill St *HFAX* HX1 ......4 D4
Westholme Rd *HTON* BD9 ......2 A1
Westholme St *BFD* BD1 ......2 B6
Westlands Dr *WIL/AL* BD15 ......37 E3
Westlands Gv *WIL/AL* BD15 ......37 F3
West La *BAIL* BD17 ......18 B4
  CLECK BD19 ......65 G4
  CUL/QBY BD13 ......36 A5
  HIPP HX3 ......69 G5
  HWTH BD22 ......6 C5
  HWTH BD22 ......22 C2
Westlea Av *KGHY* BD21 ......8 A2
West Lea Crs *YEA* LS19 ......11 E5
West Lea Gv *YEA* LS19 ......11 E5
West Leeds St *HWTH* BD22 ......6 D4
Westleigh *BGLY* BD16 ......16 D3
Westleigh Cl *BAIL* * BD17 ......18 B4
Westleigh Dr *BAIL* BD17 ......18 B4
Westleigh Rd *BAIL* BD17 ......18 B3
Westleigh Wy *BAIL* BD17 ......18 A4
Westminster Av *CLAY* BD14 ......44 D3
Westminster Crs *CLAY* BD14 ......44 D3
Westminster Dr *CLAY* BD14 ......44 D3
Westminster Gdns *CLAY* BD14 ...44 D3
Westminster Pl *BFDE* BD3 ......3 F1
Westminster Rd *BFDE* BD3 ......3 F1
Westminster Ter *BFDE* BD3 ......3 F2
Westmoor Av *BAIL* BD17 ......18 C2
Westmoor Cl *BAIL* * BD17 ......18 C2
West Mount Pl *HFAX* HX1 ......4 C3
Weston Av *CUL/QBY* BD13 ......52 A2
Weston St *HWTH* BD22 ......13 G1
Weston Vale Rd *CUL/QBY* BD13 ...51 D2
Westover Gdns *PDSY/CALV* LS28 ...41 H5
West Pde *HFAX* HX1 ......4 E5
  RPDN/SBR HX6 ......67 G4
West Pk *GSLY* LS20 ......10 B1
West Park Rd *GIR* BD8 ......38 A4
West Park St *BRIG* HD6 ......78 C1
West Park Ter *GIR* * BD8 ......38 A4
Westroyd *PDSY/CALV* LS28 ......49 H1
West Royd *WIL/AL* BD15 ......25 H4
West Royd Av *ECHL* * BD2 ......30 A5
  HFAX HX1 ......4 B7
  SHPY BD18 ......29 E1
Westroyd Av *CLECK* BD19 ......64 C2
  PDSY/CALV LS28 ......49 H1
West Royd Cl *HFAX* HX1 ......4 C7
  SHPY BD18 ......29 F1
Westroyd Crs *SHPY* BD18 ......29 F1
West Royd Crs *SHPY* BD18 ......29 F1
West Royd Dr *SHPY* BD18 ......29 F1
Westroyd Gdns *PDSY/CALV* LS28 ...49 H1
West Royd Gv *SHPY* BD18 ......29 F1
West Royd Mt *SHPY* BD18 ......29 F1
West Royd Rd *SHPY* BD18 ......29 F1
West Royd Ter *SHPY* BD18 ......29 F1
West Royd Vis *HFAX* HX1 ......4 C7
West Royd Wk *SHPY* BD18 ......29 F1
West Scausby Pk *LUD/ILL* HX2 ...50 D3
West Shaw La *HWTH* BD22 ......32 B1
West Side Ct *GIR* BD8 ......38 A3
West St *BAIL* BD17 ......18 D2
  BFD BD1 ......2 E6
  BRIG HD6 ......71 F5
  BRIG HD6 ......71 G1
  CLECK BD19 ......65 F4
  CLECK BD19 ......73 G1
  ECHL BD2 ......40 A1
  HFAX HX1 ......4 C3
  HIPP HX3 ......61 G1
  RPDN/SBR HX6 ......67 E5
West Vw *BOW* BD4 ......47 H3
  HIPP HX3 ......59 G3
  YEA LS19 ......11 E4
West View Av *HFAX* HX1 ......67 H1

  SHPY BD18 ......29 F2
West View Cl *SHPY* BD18 ......29 F2
West View Ct *KGHY* BD21 ......6 D3
West View Ct *YEA* * LS19 ......11 E4
West View Crs *HFAX* HX1 ......67 G1
West View Dr *LUD/ILL* HX2 ......67 G1
West View Gv *KGHY* BD21 ......6 D3
West View Rd *HIPP* * HX3 ......59 G3
West View Ter *GIR* * BD8 ......37 H5
  LUD/ILL * HX2 ......58 D5
Westview Wy *KGHY* BD21 ......7 E2
West Villa Rd *GSLY* LS20 ......10 D2
Westville Wy *CUL/QBY* BD13 ......44 A1
Westward Ho *HIPP* HX3 ......59 F1
Westway *GSLY* LS20 ......10 A3
  HTON BD9 ......37 F2
  KGHY BD21 ......6 C2
  PDSY/CALV LS28 ......41 H1
West Wy *SHPY* BD18 ......27 G2
Westwood Av *ECHL* BD2 ......30 A4
Westwood Crs *BGLY* BD16 ......26 D1
Westwood Gv *ECHL* BD2 ......30 A4
Westwood St *HUDN* * HD2 ......79 H5
Wetton Ct *BFDE* BD3 ......40 C5
Weyhill Dr *WIL/AL* BD15 ......37 E4
Weymouth Av *WIL/AL* BD15 ......36 D4
Whack House Cl *YEA* LS19 ......11 F5
Whalley La *CUL/QBY* BD13 ......34 C2
Wharfedale Gdns *BAIL* BD17 ......19 F2
Wharfedale Mt *HIPP* HX3 ......53 E4
Wharfedale Ri *HTON* BD9 ......37 F2
Wharfedale Rd *BOW* BD4 ......55 H3
Wharf St *BAIL* BD17 ......28 C1
  BFDE BD3 ......2 E3
  BRIG HD6 ......78 C1
  RPDN/SBR HX6 ......67 F4
Wharncliffe Crs *ECHL* BD2 ......30 C5
Wharncliffe Dr *ECHL* BD2 ......30 C5
Wharncliffe Gv *ECHL* BD2 ......30 C5
  SHPY BD18 ......28 C3
Wharncliffe Rd *SHPY* BD18 ......28 C3
Wheater Rd *GTHN* * BD7 ......46 B2
Wheathead Crs *HWTH* BD22 ......13 F1
Wheathead Dr *HWTH* BD22 ......13 G1
Wheathead La *HWTH* BD22 ......13 F1
Wheatlands *PDSY/CALV* LS28 ......41 H1
Wheatlands Av *HTON* BD9 ......37 H2
Wheatlands Crs *HTON* BD9 ......37 H2
Wheatlands Dr *HTON* BD9 ......37 H2
Wheatlands Gv *HTON* BD9 ......37 H2
Wheatlands Sq *HTON* BD9 ......37 H2
Wheatley Cl *HIPP* * HX3 ......59 E4
Wheatley La *HIPP* HX3 ......59 F4
Wheatley Rd *HIPP* HX3 ......59 E3
Wheat St *HWTH* BD22 ......13 H2
Wherneside Mt *GTHN* BD7 ......45 H5
Wherwell Rd *BRIG* HD6 ......78 C2
Whetley Cl *GIR* BD8 ......38 D4
Whetley Gv *GIR* BD8 ......38 B3
Whetley Hl *GIR* BD8 ......38 C3
Whetley La *GIR* BD8 ......38 B4
Whetley Ter *GIR* BD8 ......38 B3
Whimbrel Cl *GIR* BD8 ......37 F5
Whinfield Av *HWTH* BD22 ......6 B3
Whinfield Cl *HWTH* BD22 ......6 C3
Whinfield Dr *HWTH* BD22 ......6 B3
Whin Knoll Av *KGHY* BD21 ......6 C5
Whinney Brow *IDLE* BD10 ......29 G1
Whinney Hill Pk *BRIG* HD6 ......71 G5
Whinney Royd La *HIPP* HX3 ......52 D5
Whin St *HWTH* BD22 ......6 D5
Whiskers La *HIPP* HX3 ......60 B2
Whitaker Av *ECHL* BD2 ......40 B1
Whitaker Cl *ECHL* BD2 ......40 B1
Whitaker Wk *HWTH* * BD22 ......32 D1
Whitby Rd *GIR* BD8 ......38 B3
Whitby Ter *GIR* BD8 ......38 B3
Whitcliffe Rd *CLECK* BD19 ......64 B5
Whitcliffe Sq *CLECK* BD19 ......64 C5
White Abbey Rd *GIR* BD8 ......38 C4
White Birch Ter *HIPP* HX3 ......59 E3
White Castle Ct *CUL/QBY* BD13 ...43 C5
Whitechapel Gv *CLECK* BD19 ......63 H4
Whitechapel Rd *CLECK* BD19 ......63 H5
Whitefield Pl *GIR* BD8 ......38 B4
Whitegate *HIPP* HX3 ......69 G5
White Ga *LUD/ILL* HX2 ......50 C3
Whitegate Dr *HIPP* HX3 ......69 E4
Whitegate Rd *HIPP* HX3 ......69 E3
Whitegate Ter *HIPP* HX3 ......69 E3
Whitegate Top *HIPP* HX3 ......69 E4
Whitehall Av *LM/WK* BD12 ......62 D4
Whitehall Gv *BIRK/DRI* BD11 ......57 G5
Whitehall Rd *CLECK* BD19 ......63 G4
Whitehall Rd East
  BIRK/DRI BD11 ......57 G5
Whitehall Rd West *CLECK* BD19 ...64 D3

Whitehall St HIPP HX3 ....61 C5
Whitehaven Cl WBSY BD6 ....54 A3
Whitehead Gv ECHL BD2 ....40 B3
Whitehead Pl ECHL BD2 ....40 B2
Whitehead's Ter HFAX * HX1 ....4 B3
Whitehead St BFDE BD3 ....3 K6
Whitehill Cottages
LUD/ILL * HX2 ....50 D5
Whitehill Crs LUD/ILL HX2 ....50 D5
Whitehill Dr LUD/ILL HX2 ....50 D4
Whitehill Gn LUD/ILL HX2 ....51 E4
Whitehill Rd LUD/ILL HX2 ....50 D5
White Lands YEA LS19 ....21 F2
Whitelands Crs BAIL BD17 ....19 E3
Whitelands Rd BAIL BD17 ....19 E3
White La HWTH BD22 ....12 A4
WBSY BD6 ....55 E2
Whiteley Av RPDN/SBR HX6 ....66 C5
Whiteley St HFAX HX1 ....5 F5
White's Ter GIR BD8 ....38 C5
Whitestone Crs YEA LS19 ....11 G4
Whitestone Dr AIRE BD20 ....9 E3
White's Vw GIR BD8 ....38 C4
Whiteways ECHL BD2 ....39 F1
Whitewell Green La ELL HX5 ....77 E4
Whitfield St CLECK BD19 ....64 C5
Whitlam St SHPY BD18 ....28 A1
Whitley Dr LUD/ILL HX2 ....51 E4
Whitley La HIPP HX3 ....19 H3
Whitley Rd KGHY BD21 ....13 H1
Whitley St BFDE BD3 ....3 C5
BGLY BD16 ....16 C3
Whittle Crs CLAY BD14 ....45 E2
Whitty La LUD/ILL HX2 ....67 E2
Whitwell Av ELL HX5 ....77 E4
Whitwell Ct ELL HX5 ....77 E4
Whitwell Gv ELL HX5 ....77 E4
Whitwell St BOW BD4 ....47 H2
Whitwood La CLECK BD19 ....71 H1
Whytecote End LM/WK BD12 ....62 D1
Wibsey Bank WBSY BD6 ....55 E1
Wibsey Park Av WBSY BD6 ....54 A2
Wicken Cl IDLE BD10 ....30 B3
Wicken La CUL/QBY BD13 ....35 H5
Wickets Cl WBSY BD6 ....55 E2
Wickham Av WBSY * BD6 ....54 D2
Wickham St CLECK BD19 ....64 C4
Wide La HWTH BD22 ....12 B3
Wigan St BFD BD1 ....2 C4
Wightman St BFDE BD3 ....39 H2
Wignall St KGHY BD21 ....7 E2
Wild Gv PDSY/CALV LS28 ....41 F5
Wilfred St CLAY BD14 ....45 G3
Wilkinson Fold LM/WK * BD12 ....62 D3
Wilkinson Ter GTHN BD7 ....46 A1
Wilkin St KGHY BD21 ....7 E4
Willgutter La HWTH BD22 ....12 A5
William Henry St BRIC * HD6 ....71 F5
SHPY BD18 ....28 A1
Williamson St HFAX HX1 ....4 C2
William St BOW BD4 ....48 C2
BOW BD4 ....56 C1
BRIC HD6 ....78 B2
CUL/QBY BD13 ....34 C3
CUL/QBY * BD13 ....34 C3
WBOW * BD5 ....2 C7
WBSY BD6 ....54 A3
Willow Av ECHL BD2 ....29 H3
Willow Bank HFAX HX1 ....4 C7
Willow Cl LUD/ILL HX2 ....67 G2
WBSY BD6 ....54 D1
Willow Crs ECHL BD2 ....29 H3
RPDN/SBR HX6 ....66 C5
Willow Cft CLECK BD19 ....73 F1
Willow Dene Av LUD/ILL HX2 ....67 G2
Willow Dr LUD/ILL HX2 ....67 G2
WBSY BD6 ....54 D1
Willow Gdns ECHL BD2 ....29 H3
GSLY LS20 ....10 D2
Willow Gv ECHL BD2 ....29 H3
Willow Hall La RPDN/SBR HX6 ....67 F3
Willow Hall La RPDN/SBR HX6 ....67 F3
Willow Ri LUD/ILL HX2 ....67 G2
Willow Rd PDSY/CALV LS28 ....41 H2
The Willows BGLY BD16 ....16 C4
LUD/ILL HX2 ....50 D3
Willow St CLECK BD19 ....64 C4
GIR BD8 ....38 B4
HFAX HX1 ....4 C4

RPDN/SBR HX6 ....67 F4
Willow Tree Cl KGHY BD21 ....14 C1
Willow Tree Gdns BGLY BD16 ....17 F1
Willow Vls IDLE BD10 ....29 H3
Wills Gill GSLY LS20 ....11 E2
Wilmer Dr HTON BD9 ....28 B5
Wilmer Rd HTON BD9 ....38 B1
Wilsden Hill Rd WIL/AL BD15 ....25 G4
Wilsden Old Rd BGLY BD16 ....15 G5
Wilsden St BGLY BD16 ....15 G5
WIL/AL BD15 ....36 B1
Wilson Rd BGLY BD16 ....16 C2
HFAX * HX1 ....4 A7
LM/WK BD12 ....63 E1
Wilton St GIR BD8 ....38 D3
Wilton Av HUDN HD2 ....79 F5
Wilton St BRIC HD6 ....71 E5
GTHN BD7 ....2 B7
Wilton Ter CLECK BD19 ....73 G1
Wimborne Dr HWTH BD22 ....6 B3
WIL/AL BD15 ....37 F3
Winbrooke Ter WBSY BD6 ....54 B1
Winburg Rd GTHN BD7 ....46 B2
Windermere Rd GTHN BD7 ....45 H4
Windermere Ter GTHN BD7 ....45 H4
Windhill Old Rd IDLE BD10 ....19 G4
Winding Rd HFAX HX1 ....5 H3
Windle Royd La LUD/ILL HX2 ....67 F1
Windmill Crs HIPP HX3 ....60 D3
Windmill Dr HIPP HX3 ....60 D3
Windmill Hl PDSY/CALV LS28 ....49 H1
WBSY BD6 ....54 B1
Windmill La WBSY BD6 ....54 D1
YEA LS19 ....11 H5
Windsor Crs HWTH BD22 ....12 C4
LUD/ILL HX2 ....58 D4
Windsor Gv CUL/QBY BD13 ....44 A1
HWTH BD22 ....12 C4
Windsor Rd HWTH BD22 ....12 C4
SHPY * BD18 ....28 C1
Windsor St BOW * BD4 ....47 H2
HFAX HX1 ....5 G6
Windsor Wk BRIC HD6 ....71 F2
Windy Bank La HIPP HX3 ....51 G4
LVSG WF15 ....73 E4
Windy Gv WIL/AL BD15 ....36 A1
Windy Rdg CUL/QBY BD13 ....35 H5
Winfield Gv BIRK/DRI BD11 ....56 D4
Wingate Av HWTH BD22 ....6 C5
Wingate Wy HWTH BD22 ....6 C5
Wingfield Ct BGLY BD16 ....16 D2
Wingfield Mt BFDE BD3 ....3 J2
Wingfield St BFDE BD3 ....3 J3
Winnard Rw WBOW * BD5 ....47 G4
Winrose Cl LM/WK BD12 ....62 D1
Winslow Rd IDLE BD10 ....30 D5
Winston Ter GTHN BD7 ....46 B2
Winterburn La LUD/ILL HX2 ....66 D2
Winterburn St KGHY BD21 ....7 F3
Winter Ct WIL/AL BD15 ....36 D1
Winter St HFAX HX1 ....4 B7
Winterton Dr LM/WK BD12 ....54 D5
Wistons La ELL HX5 ....76 D4
Witchfield Hl HIPP HX3 ....53 G4
Witham Rd SHPY BD18 ....27 H1
Withens Hill Cft LUD/ILL HX2 ....50 C3
Within Flds HIPP HX3 ....69 H4
Withins Cl GTHN BD7 ....46 C5
Woburn Ter CLAY BD14 ....45 E3
Wold Cl CUL/QBY BD13 ....44 A1
Wolseley St CLAY BD14 ....45 F2
Wolseley Ter HFAX * HX1 ....4 B3
Wolston Cl BOW BD4 ....48 D5
Womersley St HFAX HX1 ....4 B3
Woodale Av HTON BD9 ....37 G1
Woodbine Gv IDLE BD10 ....30 A2
Woodbine St BFDE BD3 ....5 H4
HFAX * HX1 ....4 C7
Woodbine Ter HFAX * HX1 ....4 C7
IDLE BD10 ....30 A2
Wood Bottom La BRIC HD6 ....70 D3
Woodbrook Av LUD/ILL HX2 ....50 B5
Woodbrook Cl LUD/ILL HX2 ....50 B5
Woodbrook Pl LUD/ILL HX2 ....50 B5
Woodbrook Rd LUD/ILL HX2 ....50 B5
Woodbury Rd GIR BD8 ....38 C2
Wood Cft BAIL BD17 ....18 C4
Woodcot Av BAIL BD17 ....19 E4
Wood Cft BRIC HD6 ....78 A4
RPDN/SBR HX6 ....66 B5
Wood End Cl HIPP HX3 ....68 C5
Woodend Ct WBOW BD5 ....47 G5
Wood End Crs SHPY BD18 ....29 E1
Woodfield Av GTL/HWG HX4 ....75 G4
Woodfield Cl IDLE BD10 ....30 A1
Woodfield Cottages
HIPP * HX3 ....59 G4
Woodfield Dr GTL/HWG HX4 ....75 G5

Woodfield Rd CUL/QBY BD13 ....24 D2
Woodford Av WBOW HIPP HX3 ....69 E4
Woodford Cl WIL/AL BD15 ....36 D4
Woodgarth Gdns BOW BD4 ....49 E4
Woodhall Av BFDE BD3 ....40 D4
Woodhall Cl PDSY/CALV LS28 ....41 F2
Woodhall Ct PDSY/CALV LS28 ....31 F4
Woodhall Cft PDSY/CALV LS28 ....41 F2
Woodhall La PDSY/CALV LS28 ....41 F1
Woodhall Park Av
PDSY/CALV LS28 ....41 F2
Woodhall Park Crs West
PDSY/CALV * LS28 ....41 F3
Woodhall Park Cft
PDSY/CALV * LS28 ....41 G3
Woodhall Park Dr
PDSY/CALV LS28 ....41 F3
Woodhall Park Gv
PDSY/CALV LS28 ....41 F3
Woodhall Park Mt
PDSY/CALV LS28 ....41 F2
Woodhall Pl BFDE BD3 ....40 D3
Woodhall Rd PDSY/CALV LS28 ....31 F5
Woodhall Ter BFDE BD3 ....40 D4
Woodhall Vw BFDE BD3 ....41 E3
Woodhead La BRIC HD6 ....79 F2
Woodhead Rd GTHN BD7 ....46 C1
Woodhead St CLECK BD19 ....73 H2
LUD/ILL HX2 ....58 D5
Woodhill Ri IDLE BD10 ....30 D1
Woodhouse Av KGHY BD21 ....14 B1
Woodhouse Cl KGHY BD21 ....14 B1
Woodhouse Dr KGHY BD21 ....14 B2
Woodhouse Gdns BRIG HD6 ....78 D3
Woodhouse Gv KGHY BD21 ....14 B1
Woodhouse La BRIG HD6 ....78 D3
HIPP HX3 ....68 B5
Woodhouse Rd KGHY BD21 ....14 A1
Woodhouse Ter WBSY BD6 ....55 E2
Woodhouse Wk KGHY BD21 ....14 B1
Woodhouse Wy KGHY BD21 ....14 B1
Woodkirk Gv LM/WK BD12 ....62 D4
Woodland Cl HTON BD9 ....27 F5
Woodland La BGLY BD16 ....16 A1
Woodland Crs BGLY BD16 ....27 E5
Woodland Dr BRIG HD6 ....71 E5
LUD/ILL HX2 ....67 G3
Woodland Gv HTON BD9 ....27 F4
Woodlands BAIL * BD17 ....19 F2
HWTH * BD22 ....12 D4
Woodlands Av CLECK BD19 ....65 F4
HIPP HX3 ....59 H4
PDSY/CALV LS28 ....41 H3
Woodlands Cl HUDN HD2 ....79 H5
IDLE BD10 ....21 E5
Woodlands Crs CLECK BD19 ....65 F5
Woodlands Dr CLECK BD19 ....65 F4
IDLE BD10 ....21 E5
Woodlands Fold BIRK/DRI BD11 .....57 G5
Woodlands Gv BAIL BD17 ....18 A4
BGLY BD16 ....27 E2
CUL/QBY BD13 ....52 D1
HIPP HX3 ....59 H4
PDSY/CALV LS28 ....41 H3
Woodlands Mt HIPP HX3 ....59 H3
Woodlands Pk CLECK BD19 ....64 A2
Woodland Sq BRIG * HD6 ....78 D2
Woodlands Ri HWTH BD22 ....22 D3
Woodlands Rd BGLY BD16 ....17 F2
CLECK BD19 ....65 F4
CUL/QBY BD13 ....52 D1
ELL HX5 ....76 D3
GIR * BD8 ....38 B3
HIPP HX3 ....59 H4
Woodlands St GIR BD8 ....38 D4
Woodlands Ter PDSY/CALV LS28 ....41 H3
Woodlands Vw HIPP HX3 ....59 H4
Woodland Vw PDSY/CALV LS28 ......31 F3
Wood La ECHL BD2 ....29 G4
HIPP HX3 ....61 E4
HIPP * HX3 ....77 G1
LUD/ILL HX2 ....54 C4
PDSY/CALV LS28 ....31 G2
RPDN/SBR HX6 ....66 B4
Woodlea Ap YEA LS19 ....11 G5
Woodlea Cl YEA LS19 ....21 E1
Woodlea Dr YEA LS19 ....21 E1
Woodlea Gv YEA LS19 ....11 G5
Woodlea Mt YEA LS19 ....11 G5
Woodlea Rd YEA LS19 ....11 G5
Woodleigh Av WBOW BD5 ....55 F1
Woodlesford Crs LUD/ILL HX2 ....58 A3
Woodman St WBSY BD6 ....53 H4
Wood Nook La RPDN/SBR HX6 ....67 F3
Wood Nook Ter PDSY/CALV LS28 ...41 H3
Wood Pl GIR BD8 ....38 D4
Wood Rd HTON BD9 ....28 D5
WBOW BD5 ....47 F3

Woodrow Dr LM/WK BD12 ....55 F5
Woodroyd Av WBOW * BD5 ....47 G5
Woodroyd Dr HIPP HX3 ....58 D3
Woodroyd Gdns RPDN/SBR HX6 ....66 C3
Woodroyd Rd WBOW BD5 ....47 F5
Woodroyd Ter WBOW BD5 ....47 G4
Woodside KGHY BD21 ....6 D2
SHPY BD18 ....29 E1
Woodside Av BGLY BD16 ....26 C2
SHPY BD18 ....27 H1
Woodside Ct CUL/QBY BD13 ....24 C3
Woodside Crs BGLY BD16 ....26 C3
HIPP HX3 ....59 G4
Woodside Dr BGLY BD16 ....26 C2
Woodside Gv GTL/HWG HX4 ....75 H5
HIPP HX3 ....59 H4
Woodside Mt HIPP * HX3 ....59 F1
Woodside Pl HIPP HX3 ....59 G4
Woodside Rd LM/WK BD12 ....62 D1
Woodside Ter HIPP HX3 ....59 H4
Woodside Vw BGLY BD16 ....26 C2
HIPP HX3 ....59 G4
Wood St North HIPP * HX3 ....59 G3
Wood Top BRIG HD6 ....70 D3
Woodvale Cl BOW BD4 ....48 D2
Woodvale Crs BGLY BD16 ....16 D1
Woodvale Gv GTHN BD7 ....45 H2
Woodvale Rd BRIG HD6 ....71 G5
Woodvale Wy CLAY BD14 ....45 H2
Wood Vw HWTH * BD22 ....13 G2
Woodview Av BAIL BD17 ....19 G2
Wood View Dr ECHL BD2 ....40 B2
Wood View Gv BRIG HD6 ....71 E4
Woodview Rd HWTH BD22 ....13 G2
Wood View Ter KGHY BD21 ....14 A2
Woodville Gv HWTH BD22 ....23 G1
Woodville Pl HTON BD9 ....28 A5
HUDN HD2 ....79 F5
Woodville Rd KGHY BD21 ....7 E3
Woodville St HIPP HX3 ....59 F4
SHPY BD18 ....29 E1
Woodville Ter WBOW BD5 ....47 E2
Wood Vine Rd PDSY/CALV LS28 .....41 H3
Woodway BGLY BD16 ....26 C2
Woodworth Gv KGHY BD21 ....14 B1
Woolcomb Ct HTON BD9 ....38 B2
The Wool Ex BFD BD1 ....5 E5
Wooller Rd LM/WK BD12 ....55 E5
Woolrow La BRIG HD6 ....71 H2
Woolshops Sq HFAX HX1 ....5 H4
Wootton St WBOW BD5 ....47 E3
Worcester Pl BOW BD4 ....47 H3
Worden Gv CLAY BD14 ....45 H3
Workhouse La GTL/HWG HX4 ....76 A5
LUD/ILL HX2 ....66 D1
Worsnop Buildings
LM/WK BD12 ....62 D1
Worsnop St LM/WK BD12 ....55 E4
Worstead Rd HWTH BD22 ....23 G1
Worth Av KGHY BD21 ....7 H1
Worth Bridge Rd KGHY BD21 ....7 H3
Worthing Head Cl LM/WK BD12 ......63 E2
Worthing Head Rd
LM/WK BD12 ....62 D2
Worthing St LM/WK BD12 ....63 E2
Worthington St GIR BD8 ....38 D4
Worthville Cl KGHY BD21 ....14 B1
Worth Wy HWTH BD22 ....23 E5
HWTH BD22 ....23 H1
KGHY BD21 ....7 F5
Wortley St BGLY BD16 ....17 E3
Wren Av GTHN BD7 ....45 H2
Wren St KGHY BD21 ....7 F3
Wright Av HWTH BD22 ....13 E3
Wright St HWTH BD22 ....13 E4
Wrigley Av BOW BD4 ....56 A1
Wrigley Hl LUD/ILL HX2 ....50 D4
Wroe Crs LM/WK BD12 ....62 D2
Wroe Pl LM/WK BD12 ....62 D2
Wroe Ter LM/WK BD12 ....62 D2
Wrose Av SHPY BD18 ....29 E3
Wrose Brow Rd SHPY BD18 ....29 E1
Wrosecliffe Gv SHPY BD18 ....29 G1
Wrose Dr SHPY BD18 ....29 E3
Wrose Gv SHPY BD18 ....29 E3
Wrose Hill Pl SHPY BD18 ....29 E4
Wrose Mt SHPY BD18 ....29 F3

Wrose Rd *SHPY* BD18 ....29 E3
Wrose Vw *SHPY* BD18 ....29 E3
Wycliffe Gdns *SHPY* BD18 ....28 B1
Wycliffe Rd *SHPY* BD18 ....28 B1
Wycoller Rd *LM/WK* BD12 ....62 D1
Wycombe Gn *BOW* BD4 ....48 D4
Wyke Crs *LM/WK* BD12 ....63 E3
Wyke La *LM/WK* BD12 ....63 E3
Wykelea Cl *LM/WK* BD12 ....63 E3
Wyke Old La *BRIG* HD6 ....71 G1
Wyncroft Ri *SHPY* BD18 ....29 E4
Wyndham Av *ECHL* BD2 ....39 G1
Wynford Wy *WBSY* BD6 ....55 F2
Wyvern Cl *GTHN* BD7 ....46 A1

Wyvern Pl *LUD/ILL* HX2 ....58 D5
Wyvern Ter *LUD/ILL* HX2 ....58 D5

Y

Yarborough Cft *HIPP* HX3 ....60 D1
Yardley Wy *LM/WK* BD12 ....55 F4
Yarwood Gv *GTHN* BD7 ....45 H4
Yate La *HWTH* BD22 ....32 D1
Yates Flat *SHPY* BD18 ....29 E3
Yeadon Dr *HIPP* HX3 ....69 H4
Ye Farre Cl *BRIG* HD6 ....71 E4

Yewdall Wy *IDLE* BD10 ....30 B3
Yew Tree Av *GIR* BD8 ....37 G3
Yew Tree Cl *SHPY* BD18 ....28 D3
Yew Tree Crs *GIR* BD8 ....37 H3
Yew Tree La *WIL/AL* BD15 ....36 B4
Yew Trees Av *HIPP* HX3 ....60 D2
York Crs *BGLY* * BD16 ....16 D4
York Pl *CLECK* BD19 ....64 C5
Yorkshire Wy *GTHN* BD7 ....46 C4

York St *BGLY* BD16 ....16 D4
    BRIG HD6 ....78 B2
    CUL/QBY BD13 ....52 B1
    GIR BD8 ....37 H5

HFAX HX1 ....5 F5
York Ter *HIPP* HX3 ....59 G4
Young St *GIR* BD8 ....38 A5

Z

Zealand St *BOW* BD4 ....48 C3

Index - featured places

Abbey Park School
    LUD/ILL HX2 ....50 C4
ABC Cinema
    HFAX HX1 ....5 H5
Acorn Park Industrial Estate
    BAIL BD17 ....19 F4
Adult Education Centre
    BRIG HD6 ....71 F5
Adwalton Moor Business Park
    BOW BD4 ....57 G3
Aireborough Leisure Centre
    GSLY LS20 ....10 D2
Airedale Centre
    KGHY BD21 ....7 F4
Aire Valley Business Centre
    KGHY BD21 ....7 F3
Aireview Business Centre
    BAIL BD17 ....28 B1
Alhambra Theatre
    BFD BD1 ....2 C6
Allerton Clinic
    WIL/AL BD15 ....37 E4
Allerton First & Middle School
    WIL/AL BD15 ....37 E3
All Saints CE First School
    WBOW BD5 ....47 E3
All Saints CE J & I School
    HIPP HX3 ....75 H1
Alston Retail Park
    KGHY BD21 ....7 G2
Amateurs FC
    ELL HX5 ....77 E3
Armytage Road
    Industrial Estate
    BRIG HD6 ....78 D1
Arndale Shopping Centre
    SHPY BD18 ....28 C2
Ashfield School
    IDLE BD10 ....20 B5
Ash Tree County Infant School
    LUD/ILL HX2 ....50 B5
Atlas First School
    GIR BD8 ....38 D3
Aylesham Industrial Estate
    LM/WK BD12 ....55 E4
Baildon CE First School
    BAIL BD17 ....19 E2
Baildon Golf Club
    BAIL BD17 ....18 D1
Baildon Recreation Centre
    BAIL BD17 ....18 C5
Bailiff Bridge Primary School
    BRIG HD6 ....71 G1
Bankfield Museum
    HIPP HX3 ....59 H4
Bankfoot First School
    WBOW BD5 ....47 E5
Barkerend First School
    BFDE BD3 ....3 H3
Barplas Industrial Park
    WBOW BD5 ....47 F4
BBC North Studio
    BFD BD1 ....2 D6
Beacon Business Centre
    HIPP HX3 ....69 F2
The Beaconsfield Centre
    HIPP HX3 ....69 F3
Beckfoot Upper School
    BGLY BD16 ....16 D5
Beech Hill County
    Primary School
    HFAX HX1 ....4 E2
Belle Vue Boys School
    HTON BD9 ....27 G5
Belle Vue Girls Upper School
    BGLY BD16 ....27 F4
Belmont Business Centre
    BFD BD1 ....2 E5

Belmont Middle School
    BAIL BD17 ....18 C3
Benton Park School
    YEA LS19 ....21 G1
Bierley CE First School
    BOW BD4 ....56 A1
Bilton Medical Centre
    GIR BD8 ....38 D4
Bingley Grammar School
    BGLY BD16 ....16 B2
Bingley Health Centre
    BGLY BD16 ....16 B3
Bingley Hospital
    BGLY BD16 ....16 D3
Bingley Little Theatre
    BGLY BD16 ....16 C3
Bingley St Ives Golf Club
    BGLY BD16 ....15 H3
Birch Lane Medical Centre
    WBOW BD5 ....47 F4
Birkenshaw CE F & N School
    BIRK/DRI BD11 ....57 F4
Birkenshaw Health Centre
    BIRK/DRI BD11 ....57 F4
Birkenshaw Middle School
    BIRK/DRI BD11 ....65 G1
Birksland Industrial Estate
    BOW BD4 ....48 A2
Blakehill First School
    IDLE BD10 ....29 H3
Bolling Hall
    BOW BD4 ....47 H4
Bolton Brow Primary School
    RPDN/SBR HX6 ....67 G4
Bolton Lane First School
    ECHL BD2 ....39 H1
Bolton Royd College of
    Further Education
    GIR BD8 ....39 E2
Bolton Royd Primary School
    PDSY/CALV LS28 ....41 F4
Bolton Villas Cricket Club
    IDLE BD10 ....29 H3
Bolton Woods First School
    SHPY BD18 ....29 E4
Borough Market
    HFAX HX1 ....5 H4
Bowling Community College &
    Swimming Pool
    BOW BD4 ....47 H4
Bowling Court Industrial Estate
    BOW BD4 ....48 B2
Bowling Park First School
    WBOW BD5 ....47 G4
Bowling Special School
    BOW BD4 ....48 A4
Brackenhill First School
    GTHN BD7 ....46 A3
Bradford & Bingley RFC
    BGLY BD16 ....17 E5
Bradford Bulls RLFC
    (Odsal Stadium)
    WBSY BD6 ....55 F2
Bradford Business Park
    BFDE BD3 ....2 D1
Bradford Cathedral Community
    College
    BOW BD4 ....48 A4
Bradford City FC
    (Bradford & Bingley Stadium)
    GIR BD8 ....39 E3
Bradford Girls Grammar School
    GIR BD8 ....37 H3
Bradford Grammar School
    HTON BD9 ....38 D1
Bradford & Ilkley College
    BFD BD1 ....2 B6

Bradford & Ilkley
    Community College
    GTHN BD7 ....46 D1
    GTHN BD7 ....46 C3
Bradford Industrial &
    Horses at Work Museum
    ECHL BD2 ....40 B1
Bradford Moor First School
    BFDE BD3 ....40 B4
Bradford Moor Golf Club
    BFDE BD3 ....40 A3
Bradford Royal Infirmary
    HTON BD9 ....38 A2
Bradford Royal Infirmary
    Remedial Unit
    HTON BD9 ....37 H2
Bradford Salem RFC
    HTON BD9 ....27 H5
Bradford University
    GTHN BD7 ....46 D1
    PDSY/CALV LS28 ....41 F3
Bradley Park Golf Club
    HUDN HD2 ....79 E5
Bradshaw School
    LUD/ILL HX2 ....50 D2
Braithwaite Special School
    HWTH BD22 ....6 B3
Bramall Business Park
    WBOW BD5 ....47 F3
Branshaw Golf Club
    HWTH BD22 ....13 E3
Branshaw School
    HWTH BD22 ....6 D5
Branxholme Industrial Estate
    BRIG HD6 ....71 H1
Brighouse High School
    BRIG HD6 ....71 F5
Brighouse Sports Centre
    BRIG HD6 ....71 E3
Brighouse Sports Club
    BRIG HD6 ....71 G5
Bronte House School
    IDLE BD10 ....21 E4
Bronte Parsonage Museum
    HWTH BD22 ....22 C2
Bronte School
    HWTH BD22 ....13 F3
Brookfield Infant School
    IDLE BD10 ....30 D3
Brookfoot Industrial Estate
    BRIG HD6 ....78 A1
Broomwood Middle School
    BOW BD4 ....56 B1
Brow Quarry Industrial Estate
    HIPP HX3 ....70 C2
Brunswick Industrial Estate
    HFAX HX1 ....4 E6
Bull Royd Industrial Estate
    GIR BD8 ....37 H4
Business Enterprise Centre
    BFDE BD3 ....2 E4
Bus Station (Interchange)
    BFD BD1 ....2 D6
Butterfield Industrial Estate
    BAIL BD17 ....19 E5
Buttershaw Middle School
    WBSY BD6 ....54 A3
Buttershaw Upper School
    WBSY BD6 ....54 A2
Byron Primary School
    BFDE BD3 ....3 K3
Calderdale Business Centre
    HFAX HX1 ....4 B4
Calderdale Business Park
    LUD/ILL HX2 ....59 E2
Calderdale Industrial Museum
    HFAX HX1 ....5 J4

The Calderdale Royal Hospital
    HIPP HX3 ....68 D5
Calder Industrial Estate
    BRIG HD6 ....71 G2
Calder Trading Estate
    HUDN HD2 ....79 H5
    RPDN/SBR HX6 ....67 F5
Calverley CE Primary School
    PDSY/CALV LS28 ....31 G2
Calverley Golf Club
    PDSY/CALV LS28 ....41 F1
Calverley Medical Centre
    PDSY/CALV LS28 ....31 F3
Calverley Parkside
    Primary School
    PDSY/CALV LS28 ....31 F3
Calversyke Middle School
    HWTH BD22 ....6 B4
Carlisle Mills Business Centre
    GIR BD8 ....38 D3
Carlton Bolling College &
    Sports Centre
    BFDE BD3 ....3 H2
Carr Green County
    Primary School
    BRIG HD6 ....78 A4
Cartwright Hall Art Gallery
    HTON BD9 ....38 D1
Castlefields Industrial Estate
    BGLY BD16 ....16 A1
Chapel Grange Special School
    GIR BD8 ....37 F4
Chellow Dene Middle School
    GIR BD8 ....37 G4
Chesham Building
    GTHN BD7 ....46 D1
Chohan Medical Centre
    WBOW BD5 ....47 E3
Christ Church J & I School
    LUD/ILL HX2 ....58 C5
Christ Church Junior School
    RPDN/SBR HX6 ....67 F3
Church School
    CUL/QBY BD13 ....44 B1
Cineworld
    BFD BD1 ....2 E5
City Link Industrial Park
    BOW BD4 ....40 D5
Clayton CE First School
    CLAY BD14 ....45 E3
Clayton Cemetery
    CLAY BD14 ....45 G2
Clayton CE First School
    CLAY BD14 ....45 E3
Clayton Golf Club
    CLAY BD14 ....45 F4
Clayton Middle School
    CLAY BD14 ....45 F3
Cleckheaton & District Golf Club
    CLECK BD19 ....64 A3
Cleckheaton Sports Club
    CLECK BD19 ....64 B3
Cliffe Castle Museum & Gallery
    KGHY BD21 ....7 E2
Cliffe Hill School
    HIPP HX3 ....71 F2
Cliffe Middle School
    BFDE BD3 ....39 G3
Clifton Cemetery
    BRIG HD6 ....79 F1
Colour Museum
    BFD BD1 ....2 B5
Common Road Industrial Estate
    LM/WK BD12 ....55 E4
Co-operative Shopping Parade
    HIPP HX3 ....61 G5
Cooper Lane First School
    WBSY BD6 ....53 F1

Copley Primary School
HIPP HX3 .... 75 G2
Copthorne First School
GTHN BD7 .... 46 D2
Copwood Mental Health Clinic
BOW BD4 .... 48 D3
The Coronation Business Centre
KGHY BD21 .... 7 G2
Cottingley Clinic
BGLY BD16 .... 26 D2
Cottingley First School
BGLY BD16 .... 27 E2
Crossflatts Cricket Club
BGLY BD16 .... 9 E5
Crossflatts First School
BGLY BD16 .... 9 F5
Crossley Hall First &
Middle School
GIR BD8 .... 37 H5
Crossley Heath School
HFAX HX1 .... 68 B4
Crossley Retail Park
HFAX HX1 .... 4 E2
Cuckoo Nest Industrial Estate
GTHN BD7 .... 38 D5
Cullingworth First School
CUL/QBY BD13 .... 24 C3
Cullingworth Medical Centre
CUL/QBY BD13 .... 24 C3
Deanfield County
Primary School
LUD/ILL HX2 .... 58 D2
Delf Hill Middle School
LM/WK BD12 .... 54 D4
Denholme Clinic
CUL/QBY BD13 .... 34 C3
Denholme First School
CUL/QBY BD13 .... 34 C3
Dixons City Technology College
WBOW BD5 .... 47 F3
Dockfield Industrial Estate
BAIL BD17 .... 28 D1
Dominion Industrial Park
HIPP HX3 .... 61 F5
Drakes Industrial Estate
LUD/ILL HX2 .... 59 F1
Drummond Middle School
GIR BD8 .... 38 D3
Drummond Trading Estate
GIR BD8 .... 2 A2
Dudley Hill First School
BOW BD4 .... 48 B4
East Bierley CE First School
BOW BD4 .... 57 E3
East Bierley Cricket Club
BIRK/DRI BD11 .... 56 D4
East Bierley Golf Club
BOW BD4 .... 56 D3
East Morton First School
AIRE BD20 .... 8 D2
Eastwood First School
KGHY BD21 .... 7 G3
Eccleshill Clinic &
Health Centre
IDLE BD10 .... 30 C3
Eccleshill Cricket Club
IDLE BD10 .... 30 C4
Eccleshill North Middle School
IDLE BD10 .... 30 D3
Eccleshill School
IDLE BD10 .... 30 D4
Eccleshill United Sports Club
ECHL BD2 .... 29 G3
Eldwick First School
BGLY BD16 .... 17 F1
Elizabeth Industrial Estate
HFAX HX1 .... 4 D1
Elland CE School
ELL HX5 .... 76 C4
Elland Old Earth School
ELL HX5 .... 77 F4
Ellen Royde Health Centre
ELL HX5 .... 76 B4
Empire Business Centre
LUD/ILL HX2 .... 51 F5
Esholt & Aire Bronians
Sports Club
BAIL BD17 .... 20 A1
Essex Park Industrial Estate
BFDE BD3 .... 3 G7
Eureka the Museum for Children
HIPP HX3 .... 5 J5
Euroway Trading Estate
BOW BD4 .... 55 H4
The Eye Clinic
GTHN BD7 .... 46 D1
Fagley First School
ECHL BD2 .... 40 C2

Farfield Primary School
PDSY/CALV LS28 .... 41 G2
Farnham First School
GTHN BD7 .... 46 C2
Farrow Medical Centre
BFDE BD3 .... 3 F2
Farsley Community Clinic
PDSY/CALV LS28 .... 41 H1
Fentham Industrial Estate
BRIG HD6 .... 78 B2
Ferniehurst First School
BAIL BD17 .... 18 D4
Feversham College
BFDE BD3 .... 3 G6
Feversham Street First School
BFDE BD3 .... 3 K5
Fieldhead Business Centre
GTHN BD7 .... 46 D1
Forster Square Retail Park
BFD BD1 .... 2 C2
Four Lanes Business Park
GIR BD8 .... 38 A5
Fowler Street Industrial Estate
BOW BD4 .... 48 A2
Foxhill First School
CUL/QBY BD13 .... 44 A1
Friars Industrial Estate
IDLE BD10 .... 30 A2
Frizinghall First &
Middle School
HTON BD9 .... 28 D4
Frizinghall Medical Centre
HTON BD9 .... 28 C5
Fulford Grange Hospital
YEA LS19 .... 21 F3
Gilstead Middle School
BGLY BD16 .... 17 F2
Girlington First School
GIR BD8 .... 38 B4
Girlington Industrial Centre
GIR BD8 .... 38 A4
The Gleddings School
HIPP HX3 .... 68 B5
Glenaire First School
BAIL BD17 .... 18 B4
Glen Cable Tramway
BAIL BD17 .... 18 A4
Gomersal CE Middle School
CLECK BD19 .... 65 H4
Gomersal First School
CLECK BD19 .... 65 G4
Grange Middle School
AIRE BD20 .... 7 H2
Grange Upper School
WBOW BD5 .... 46 C5
Great Horton Cricket Club
GTHN BD7 .... 46 B4
Great Horton Industrial Estate
WBSY BD6 .... 45 G5
Great Horton Middle School
GTHN BD7 .... 46 B3
Greenfield School
IDLE BD10 .... 20 A5
Greengates First School
IDLE BD10 .... 30 D2
Greenhead Athletics Track
KGHY BD21 .... 7 E2
Greenhead Grammar School
AIRE BD20 .... 6 D1
Green Meadows School
GSLY LS20 .... 10 B2
Green Mount Retail Park
HFAX HX1 .... 4 E3
Greetland Cricket &
Bowling Club
GTL/HWG HX4 .... 75 H4
Greetland J & I School
GTL/HWG HX4 .... 75 F4
Greetland Mixed School
GTL/HWG HX4 .... 75 G4
Gregory Middle School
WBOW BD5 .... 55 H1
Gresley Road Industrial Estate
KGHY BD21 .... 7 F4
Grove House First School
ECHL BD2 .... 29 H5
Grove Mills Industrial Estate
ELL HX5 .... 76 C4
Guiseley AFC
GSLY LS20 .... 10 B2
Guiseley County Infant School
GSLY LS20 .... 10 D2
Guiseley School
GSLY LS20 .... 10 C3
Haigh Hall Medical Centre
IDLE BD10 .... 30 C2
Hainsworth Moor J & I School
CUL/QBY BD13 .... 52 A2

Halifax Building Society
HFAX HX1 .... 5 G5
Halifax Catholic High School
LUD/ILL HX2 .... 51 F4
Halifax Cricket Ground
HFAX HX1 .... 67 H1
Halifax Golf Club
LUD/ILL HX2 .... 50 B1
Halifax High School
HFAX HX1 .... 5 G6
Halifax Industrial Centre
HFAX HX1 .... 4 D2
Halifax Leisure Centre
HFAX HX1 .... 5 H5
Halifax RUFC
LUD/ILL HX2 .... 59 E1
Halifax Swimming Pool
HFAX HX1 .... 5 H6
Halifax Town FC Blue Sox RLFC
(The Shay Stadium)
HFAX HX1 .... 5 H7
Halton Building
GTHN BD7 .... 2 A6
Hambledon First School
BOW BD4 .... 56 A2
Hanson Upper School
ECHL BD2 .... 29 G5
Harden First School
BGLY BD16 .... 15 F5
Hartington Middle School
HWTH BD22 .... 22 D2
Haworth School
HWTH BD22 .... 22 D2
Haycliffe Special School
WBSY BD6 .... 46 C5
Headley Golf Club
CUL/QBY BD13 .... 44 A2
Health Studies School
WBOW BD5 .... 47 E2
Heather Grove First School
HTON BD9 .... 37 G1
Heathfield Industrial Estate
ELL HX5 .... 76 D5
Heaton Middle School
HTON BD9 .... 27 G5
Heaton Royds Hospital
HTON BD9 .... 27 G4
Heaton Royds Special School
SHPY BD18 .... 28 B4
Hebble Brook Business Park
LUD/ILL HX2 .... 50 B3
Highbank First School
LVSG WF15 .... 73 E3
High Crags First School
SHPY BD18 .... 28 D3
High Fernley First School
LM/WK BD12 .... 62 D2
Highfield Middle School
KGHY BD21 .... 6 D4
High Royds Hospital
ILK LS29 .... 10 A1
Hightown School
LVSG WF15 .... 73 F3
Hillside Works Industrial Estate
CLECK BD19 .... 64 C3
Hill Top CE First School
LM/WK BD12 .... 54 D4
Hipperholme Clinic
HIPP HX3 .... 61 G5
Hipperholme Grammar School
HIPP HX3 .... 61 F5
Hipperholme & Lightcliffe
High School
HIPP HX3 .... 71 E1
Hockney Road
Industrial Estate
GIR BD8 .... 38 C4
IDLE BD10 .... 30 A4
Hollingwood First School
GTHN BD7 .... 45 H4
Holmefield First School
BOW BD4 .... 49 E3
Holme Middle School
BOW BD4 .... 48 C4
Holme Wood Health Centre
BOW BD4 .... 48 D4
Holmfield Industrial Estate
LUD/ILL HX2 .... 51 F3
Holycroft First School
KGHY BD21 .... 7 E5
Holy Family School
KGHY BD21 .... 6 D2
Holy Trinity CE First School
BGLY BD16 .... 16 D4
Holy Trinity CE Senior School
LUD/ILL HX2 .... 51 E4
Holy Trinity Infant School
HFAX HX1 .... 4 E6

Holy Trinity Junior School
HFAX HX1 .... 4 E6
Horsfall Stadium
WBSY BD6 .... 54 C3
Horton Bank Top First School
GTHN BD7 .... 45 H5
Horton Park First School
WBOW BD5 .... 46 C3
Hoyle Court First School
BAIL BD17 .... 19 F3
Huddersfield Crematorium
HUDN HD2 .... 78 B5
Hutton J & I School
IDLE BD10 .... 30 B4
Hutton Middle School
ECHL BD2 .... 30 B4
Idle CE School
IDLE BD10 .... 20 A5
Idle Cricket Club
IDLE BD10 .... 30 A2
Idle Medical Centre
IDLE BD10 .... 30 A1
Ingrow First & Infant School
HWTH BD22 .... 13 H2
Inland Revenue Office
BFD BD1 .... 2 D4
John Street Market
BFD BD1 .... 2 C4
Keelham First School
CUL/QBY BD13 .... 43 E2
Keighley & Worth Valley Railway
HWTH BD22 .... 13 C4
HWTH BD22 .... 22 D2
KGHY BD21 .... 14 A2
Keighley Business Centre
KGHY BD21 .... 14 A1
Keighley College
KGHY BD21 .... 7 F4
Keighley Crematorium
HWTH BD22 .... 12 B3
Keighley Cricket Club
KGHY BD21 .... 7 F2
Keighley Industrial Park
KGHY BD21 .... 7 F2
Keighley Leisure Centre
KGHY BD21 .... 7 G3
Keighley Retail Park
KGHY BD21 .... 7 F2
Keighley St Andrew's
Primary School
HWTH BD22 .... 6 D5
Keighley & Worth
Valley Railway
KGHY BD21 .... 14 B1
Kensington Street
Health Centre
GIR BD8 .... 38 B4
Kents Sports Club
ECHL BD2 .... 30 A5
Killinghall First School
BFDE BD3 .... 40 B3
Kirkfields Business Centre
YEA LS19 .... 11 F4
Kirkgate Shopping
Centre & Market
BFD BD1 .... 2 C5
Knowle Spring
Industrial Estate
KGHY BD21 .... 14 A1
Ladderbank Middle School
BAIL BD17 .... 19 F2
Lady Lane Park School
BGLY BD16 .... 16 D1
Laisterdyke Clinic
BFDE BD3 .... 40 C5
Laisterdyke Middle School
BFDE BD3 .... 40 C5
Lapage Middle School
BFDE BD3 .... 40 C5
Laura Mitchell Health Centre
HFAX HX1 .... 5 G3
Leaventhorpe Middle School
WIL/AL BD15 .... 37 E5
Lee Bridge Industrial Estate
HFAX HX1 .... 4 D1
Leeds Road Hospital
BFDE BD3 .... 3 J5
Lee Mills Industrial Estate
HFAX HX1 .... 4 E1
Lee Mount County
Primary School
HIPP HX3 .... 59 G2
Lees First School
HWTH BD22 .... 23 F1
Lidget Green First School
GTHN BD7 .... 46 A1
Lidget Green Middle School
GTHN BD7 .... 46 A1

Lightcliffe CE Primary School
HIPP HX3 .... **70** D1

Lightcliffe Golf Club
HIPP HX3 .... **61** H5

Lightcliffe Preparatory School
HIPP HX3 .... **61** G5

Lilycroft First School
HTON BD9 .... **38** C2

Littlemoor Primary School
YEA LS19 .... **21** H4

Long Lee J & I School
KGHY BD21 .... **14** C1

Longroyde Junior School
BRIG HD6 .... **78** A2

Lorne First School
BOW BD4 .... **48** A3

Low Ash First School
SHPY BD18 .... **29** E3

Lowerfields Middle School
BOW BD4 .... **48** B3

Lower Grange Medical Centre
GIR BD8 .... **37** F5

Lowfields Business Park
ELL HX5 .... **77** E3

Low Moor Business Park
LM/WK BD12 .... **55** F4

Low Moor CE First School
LM/WK BD12 .... **55** E4

Luddendenfoot J & I School
LUD/ILL HX2 .... **66** B3

Lynfield Mount Hospital
HTON BD9 .... **37** G2

Mandale Middle School
WBSY BD6 .... **53** G2

Manningham Baths &
Sports Centre
GIR BD8 .... **38** C3

Manningham Clinic
GIR BD8 .... **38** D3

Manningham Middle School
GIR BD8 .... **2** A1

Manor Leisure Centre
YEA LS19 .... **11** F4

Mantra House Business Centre
KGHY BD21 .... **7** F5

Manywells Brow
Industrial Estate
CUL/QBY BD13 .... **24** C4

Margaret McMillan First School
HTON BD9 .... **38** B2

Margram Business Centre
HFAX HX1 .... **4** E3

Marshfield First School
WBOW BD5 .... **46** D4

Mid Point Business Park
PDSY/CALV LS28 .... **41** E4

Miriam Lord First School
GIR BD8 .... **38** C3

Mixenden Clinic
LUD/ILL HX2 .... **58** C1

Mixenden County
Primary School
LUD/ILL HX2 .... **50** A4

Moorfield First School
BFDE BD3 .... **40** B5

Moorlands Small
Business Centre
CLECK BD19 .... **64** C4

Moorside School
LUD/ILL HX2 .... **59** E1

Moorview Business Park
IDLE BD10 .... **19** H5

Mount Pellon J & I School
HFAX HX1 .... **4** A2

Municipal Baths
BRIG HD6 .... **78** C1

Myrtle Park Primary School
BGLY BD16 .... **16** C4

Nab Wood Cemetery
SHPY BD18 .... **27** G1

Nab Wood Grammar School
BGLY BD16 .... **27** F2

Nab Wood Middle School
BGLY BD16 .... **27** F2

Napoleon Business Park
BOW BD4 .... **48** A2

National Museum of
Photography, Film & Television
WBOW BD5 .... **2** C7

Neil Hunt
Memorial Ground & RFC
BOW BD4 .... **48** B2

Nessfield First School
HWTH BD22 .... **13** G1

Netherleigh School
HTON BD9 .... **38** A2

Newbridge Industrial Estate
KGHY BD21 .... **7** G4

Newby First School
WBOW BD5 .... **47** E4

New Cross Street Health Centre
WBOW BD5 .... **47** E4

Newlands County Junior School
RPDN/SBR HX6 .... **66** B5

Newlands Industrial Estate
BAIL BD17 .... **28** D1

New Line Clinic
IDLE BD10 .... **30** D2

Newspaper Office
BFD BD1 .... **2** E5

Norcroft Industrial Estate
BFD BD1 .... **38** D5

Norland CE J & I School
RPDN/SBR HX6 .... **74** C1

North Bridge Leisure Centre
HFAX HX1 .... **5** H2

Northcliffe Golf Club
SHPY BD18 .... **27** H3

North Dean Business Park
GTL/HWG HX4 .... **76** A3

North Dean RFC
GTL/HWG HX4 .... **76** A4

The North Halifax
Grammar School
LUD/ILL HX2 .... **51** E4

Northowram Hall Hospital
HIPP HX3 .... **60** D1

Northowram School
HIPP HX3 .... **60** D2

Norwood Business Park
LM/WK BD12 .... **62** C3

Oakbank School
HWTH BD22 .... **13** G2

Oakdale First School
SHPY BD18 .... **29** E3

Oakwell Hall
BTLY WF17 .... **65** H2

Oakworth Health Centre
HWTH BD22 .... **13** E4

Oakworth J & I School
HWTH BD22 .... **12** D4

Odeon Cinema
BFD BD1 .... **2** C6
BFDE BD3 .... **41** E4

Old Rishworthians RUFC
HIPP HX3 .... **75** F1

Our Lady of Victories
RC J & I School
HWTH BD22 .... **6** C4

Oxenhope CE First School
HWTH BD22 .... **32** C1

Parkhouse Industrial Estate
LM/WK BD12 .... **55** F4

Parkinson Lane School
HFAX HX1 .... **4** C6

Parkland First & Middle School
IDLE BD10 .... **30** B2

Park Road Medical Centre
WBOW BD5 .... **47** F2

Parkside Middle School
CUL/QBY BD13 .... **24** D3

Park Wood Crematorium
ELL HX5 .... **76** C2

Parkwood First School
KGHY BD21 .... **7** G5

Parkwood Primary School
KGHY BD21 .... **7** G5

Parkwood Street
Industrial Estate
KGHY BD21 .... **7** H4

Pecketwell College
HFAX HX1 .... **5** F3

Pellon Industrial Estate
HFAX HX1 .... **4** B2

Penistone Hill
HWTH BD22 .... **22** B3

Percival Whitley
College of Education
(Halifax New College)
HFAX HX1 .... **4** D5

Phoebe Lane Industrial Estate
HIPP HX3 .... **69** E4

Pictureville Cinema
BFD BD1 .... **2** C7

Piece Hall Art Gallery
HFAX HX1 .... **5** J4

Pitt Street Business Centre
KGHY BD21 .... **7** G4

Playhouse & Film Theatre
BFD BD1 .... **3** F6

Playhouse Theatre
HFAX HX1 .... **5** F4

Pollard Park Health Centre
BFDE BD3 .... **3** G2

Pollard Park Middle School
BFDE BD3 .... **3** K3

Poplars Farm First School
ECHL BD2 .... **29** F5

Priesthorpe School
PDSY/CALV LS28 .... **41** G2

Priestley Centre
BFD BD1 .... **3** F5

Priestman Middle School
WBOW BD5 .... **46** D5

Priesthorpe First School
BGLY BD16 .... **16** D3

Priesthorpe Medical Centre
BGLY BD16 .... **16** C2

Prince of Wales Business Park
BRIG HD6 .... **78** C1

Princes Mary Campus
(Halifax New College)
HFAX HX1 .... **4** C5

Princeville First School
GTHN BD7 .... **38** C5

Princeville Road
Industrial Estate
GIR BD8 .... **38** B5

Pudsey Tyersal
Primary School
BOW BD4 .... **49** E2

Q F Industrial Estate
BOW BD4 .... **48** A3

Quality Foods Industrial Park
BOW BD4 .... **48** C2

Queensbury Golf Club
CUL/QBY BD13 .... **52** C2

Queensbury Health Centre
CUL/QBY BD13 .... **52** A1

Queensbury School
CUL/QBY BD13 .... **52** B2

Queens Road School
HFAX HX1 .... **4** A3

Queens Sports Club
HFAX HX1 .... **4** E7

Queensway Primary School
GSLY LS20 .... **11** F3

Rastrick High School
BRIG HD6 .... **78** A2

Rastrick Squash Centre
BRIG HD6 .... **78** B2

Ravenscliffe First School
IDLE BD10 .... **30** D5

Ravenscliffe High School
HIPP HX3 .... **75** G1

Rawdon Cricket Club
YEA LS19 .... **21** H2

Rawdon Golf &
Lawn Tennis Club
YEA LS19 .... **21** F3

Rawson J & I School
HIPP HX3 .... **59** G3

Rawson Market
BFD BD1 .... **2** B4

Red House
CLECK BD19 .... **65** G4

Reevy Hill Primary School
WBSY BD6 .... **54** A1

Revival Industrial Estate
BOW BD4 .... **47** H2

Rex Cinema
ELL HX5 .... **76** C5

Rhodesway School
GIR BD8 .... **37** F4

Richard Dunn Sports Centre
WBOW BD5 .... **55** E1

Richmond Building
GTHN BD7 .... **2** A6

Riddlesden CE School
AIRE BD20 .... **8** A1

Riddlesden Infants School
AIRE BD20 .... **8** A1

Ridings Business Park
HFAX HX1 .... **4** A5

The Ridings School
LUD/ILL HX2 .... **58** D2

Riverside Business Park
BAIL BD17 .... **28** D1

Rossefield School
HTON BD9 .... **28** B5

Royal Halifax Infirmary
HFAX HX1 .... **68** D3

Royal Industrial Park
HFAX HX1 .... **4** E4

Royd Mill Business Park
BRIG HD6 .... **78** C1

Royd Mount Middle School
CUL/QBY BD13 .... **43** H1

Russell Hall First School
CUL/QBY BD13 .... **52** B1

Ryan Middle School
BOW BD4 .... **47** G4

Ryburn Golf Club
RPDN/SBR HX6 .... **74** B2

Ryecroft First School
BOW BD4 .... **49** E5

Ryshworth Middle School
BGLY BD16 .... **9** F4

Sai Medical Centre
GIR BD8 .... **38** D2

St Andrew CE Infant School
BRIG HD6 .... **71** F4

St Andrews CE Junior School
BRIG HD6 .... **71** F5

St Annes RC School
KGHY BD21 .... **7** E3

St Anthonys RC First School
CLAY BD14 .... **45** G2

St Anthonys RC J & I School
SHPY BD18 .... **29** G1

St Augustines CE First School
BFDE BD3 .... **3** G1

St Augustines CE Primary School
HFAX HX1 .... **4** C2

St Barnabas CE School
HTON BD9 .... **28** B5

St Bedes Grammar School
HTON BD9 .... **38** B1

St Chads CE Primary School
BRIG HD6 .... **70** D3

St Clares Roman Catholic School
ECHL BD2 .... **40** C2

St Columbas RC Primary School
BOW BD4 .... **48** C5

St Cuthberts & First Martyrs
First School
HTON BD9 .... **38** B2

St Francis RC First School
ECHL BD2 .... **29** H5

St George's Hall
BFD BD1 .... **2** E6

St James Business Park
BFD BD1 .... **3** F6

St James Market
BFDE BD3 .... **3** G7

St Johns CE Primary School
BRIG HD6 .... **79** F1

St Johns CE First School
BOW BD4 .... **56** C1

St Johns Health Centre
HFAX HX1 .... **4** C3

St John the Evangelist
RC School
WBSY BD6 .... **53** H1

St Josephs College
HTON BD9 .... **38** D1

St Josephs RC First School
WBOW BD5 .... **47** E3

St Josephs RC Primary School
BRIG HD6 .... **71** E3

St Josephs RC School
BGLY BD16 .... **16** D3
HIPP HX3 .... **5** J1
KGHY BD21 .... **14** A1

St Lukes CE First School
CLECK BD19 .... **73** E1

St Lukes Eccleshill
CE First School
ECHL BD2 .... **30** C5

St Lukes Hospital
WBOW BD5 .... **47** E3

St Malachys RC School
LUD/ILL HX2 .... **58** D2

St Marys RC Infant School
HFAX HX1 .... **4** D5

St Marys RC Primary School
BFD BD1 .... **2** E4

St Matthews CE First School
WBOW BD5 .... **55** F1

St Matthews RC Primary School
WIL/AL BD15 .... **37** E4

St Michael & All Angels
CE Primary School
HIPP HX3 .... **53** G4

St Oswald's CE Primary School
WBOW BD5 .... **46** D4

St Oswalds CE Junior School
GSLY LS20 .... **10** D3

St Patricks RC Primary School
ELL HX5 .... **76** A5

St Peters Cathedral
BFD BD1 .... **2** E4

St Peters CE Infant School
RPDN/SBR HX6 .... **66** B5

St Peters RC First School
BFDE BD3 .... **3** K5

St Philips CE First School
WIL/AL BD15 .... **36** D2

St Stephens Special School
WBOW BD5 .... **47** F4

St Walburgas RC First School
SHPY BD18 .... **28** A2

St Williams RC Primary School
GIR BD8 .... 38 B5
Saltaire First School
SHPY BD18 .... 28 A1
Saltaire Medical Centre
SHPY BD18 .... 28 A1
Salterhebble School
HIPP HX3 .... 69 E5
Salter Lee School
HIPP HX3 .... 60 C3
Salt Grammar School
BAIL BD17 .... 18 A4
Sandal First School
BAIL BD17 .... 18 D3
Sandy Lane First School
WIL/AL BD15 .... 26 D5
Savile Park J & I School
HFAX HX1 .... 68 B3
Scholemoor Cemetery
GTHN BD7 .... 45 H1
Scholemoor Crematorium
GTHN BD7 .... 45 H1
Scotchman Middle School
HTON BD9 .... 38 B2
Shaw House School
HTON BD9 .... 38 B1
Sheibarg Industrial Estate
BOW BD4 .... 48 C3
Shelf Health Centre
HIPP HX3 .... 53 F4
Shibden Hall & Folk Museum
HIPP HX3 .... 60 C5
Shibden Head First School
CUL/QBY BD13 .... 51 H3
Shipley Baths
SHPY BD18 .... 28 C2
Shipley CE First School
SHPY BD18 .... 28 C3
Shipley College
SHPY BD18 .... 28 B1
Shipley College of Education
SHPY BD18 .... 18 A5
Shipley Golf Club
BGLY BD16 .... 16 C5
Shipley Health Centre
SHPY BD18 .... 28 B2
Shipley Hospital
SHPY BD18 .... 28 B2
Shires Business Park
GTHN BD7 .... 46 B3
Siddal Infant School
HIPP HX3 .... 69 F5
Siddal Junior School
HIPP HX3 .... 69 F5
Silver Blades Ice Rink
WBOW BD5 .... 2 C7
Smith Art Gallery
BRIG HD6 .... 71 F5
South Bradford Golf Club
WBSY BD6 .... 55 F2
South Halifax High School
HIPP HX3 .... 76 B1
Southmere First School
GTHN BD7 .... 46 B4
South View Business Centre
GSLY LS20 .... 10 D1
Southview Business Park
GSLY LS20 .... 10 D1
South View Infant School
YEA LS19 .... 11 G5
South View Junior School
YEA LS19 .... 11 G5
Sowerby Bridge Clinic
RPDN/SBR HX6 .... 67 F5
Sowerby Bridge CE
Junior School
RPDN/SBR HX6 .... 67 E4
Sowerby Bridge Cricket Club
RPDN/SBR HX6 .... 66 D4
Sowerby Bridge High School
RPDN/SBR HX6 .... 67 F3

Spenborough Moorend
CE School
CLECK BD19 .... 64 B4
Spenborough Whitcliffe
Mount School
CLECK BD19 .... 64 A5
Spen Valley Industrial Park
CLECK BD19 .... 73 H2
Spen Victoria Cricket
Bowling & Athletic Club
CLECK BD19 .... 65 E5
Springwood First School
GIR BD8 .... 38 D4
Standard Industrial Estate
ECHL BD2 .... 40 B1
Station Industrial Park
LUD/ILL HX2 .... 66 A1
Station Works Industrial Park
KGHY BD21 .... 7 H4
Stocks Lane First School
CUL/QBY BD13 .... 45 E5
Stoney Lee Middle School
BGLY BD16 .... 27 E3
Stoney Ridge Hospital
BGLY BD16 .... 27 F4
Stoney Royd Cemetery
HIPP HX3 .... 69 E3
Swain House Middle School
ECHL BD2 .... 29 H5
Swire Smith Middle School
KGHY BD21 .... 7 H5
Taison Industrial Park
GTHN BD7 .... 46 A4
Tannery Business Park
HIPP HX3 .... 60 D2
Temple Bank Special School
HTON BD9 .... 37 H2
Tenterfields Business Park
LUD/ILL HX2 .... 66 B3
Thackley AFC
IDLE BD10 .... 19 H4
Thackley Cricket Club
IDLE BD10 .... 20 A4
Thackley First School
IDLE BD10 .... 20 A4
Thornbury First School
BFDE BD3 .... 40 C4
Thornbury Middle School
BFDE BD3 .... 40 D4
Thorncliffe Square
Industrial Estate
GIR BD8 .... 39 E3
Thorn Park School
HTON BD9 .... 27 G5
Thornton Baths
CUL/QBY BD13 .... 44 B1
Thornton First School
CUL/QBY BD13 .... 44 A1
Thornton Medical Centre
CUL/QBY BD13 .... 44 B1
Thornton Upper School
CUL/QBY BD13 .... 45 E1
Thorpe First & Middle School
IDLE BD10 .... 30 A1
Thrum Hall Industrial Park
LUD/ILL HX2 .... 67 H1
Tong Park First School
BAIL BD17 .... 19 G2
Tong Sports Centre
BOW BD4 .... 57 F2
Top Rank Theatre
HFAX HX1 .... 5 G3
Tranmere Park Primary School
GSLY LS20 .... 10 A3
Tuel Lane County
Primary School
RPDN/SBR HX6 .... 67 E4
Tyersal Family Clinic
BOW BD4 .... 49 E1
Tyersal First School
BOW BD4 .... 48 C2
Undercliffe Cemetery
BFDE BD3 .... 39 H3

Undercliffe Cricket Club
ECHL BD2 .... 40 B2
Undercliffe First School
ECHL BD2 .... 40 A2
Union Business Centre
ECHL BD2 .... 30 C5
University of Bradford
GTHN BD7 .... 2 A6
Usher Street First School
BOW BD4 .... 47 H2
Utley J & I School
AIRE BD20 .... 7 E1
Valley Mills Industrial Estate
IDLE BD10 .... 30 D1
Venlo Industrial Estate
BOW BD4 .... 48 B5
Victoria Baths
ELL HX5 .... 76 D5
Victoria Industrial Estate
ECHL BD2 .... 30 B5
The Victoria Theatre
HFAX HX1 .... 5 G4
Vine Industrial Estate
BRIG HD6 .... 71 E5
Vintage Railway Carriage Museum
HWTH BD22 .... 22 D2
Walnut Business Park
HFAX HX1 .... 4 C4
Wapping First School
BFDE BD3 .... 3 F2
Warley Road J & I School
LUD/ILL HX2 .... 67 H2
Warley Town School
LUD/ILL HX2 .... 67 E2
Waterloo Infant School
PDSY/CALV LS28 .... 41 H5
Waterloo Junior School
PDSY/CALV LS28 .... 41 H5
Waverley First School
GTHN BD7 .... 46 B2
Waverley Middle School
GTHN BD7 .... 46 C2
Wax Museum
BFD BD1 .... 2 B4
Wellington Business Centre
ELL HX5 .... 76 D4
Wellington First School
ECHL BD2 .... 40 A1
Wellington Middle School
ECHL BD2 .... 40 A1
Wellington Shopping Arcade
BRIG HD6 .... 78 B1
Wellwoman Clinic
HFAX HX1 .... 5 G5
West Bowling Golf Club
WBOW BD5 .... 55 H1
West Bradford Golf Club
HTON BD9 .... 37 E1
Westcliffe Medical Centre
SHPY BD18 .... 28 B2
West End Golf Club
LUD/ILL HX2 .... 58 B5
West End Middle School
CLECK BD19 .... 73 E1
Westfield Industrial Estate
YEA LS19 .... 11 F5
Westgate Hill First School
BOW BD4 .... 57 F3
West Side Retail Park
GSLY LS20 .... 11 E4
West Vale J & I School
GTL/HWG HX4 .... 76 A4
West Yorkshire Industrial Estate
BOW BD4 .... 56 C1
Wharfedale Business Park
BOW BD4 .... 56 C1
Whetley Middle School
GIR BD8 .... 38 B4
Whinburn Residential School
AIRE BD20 .... 6 C1
Whitechapel Middle School
CLECK BD19 .... 64 B4

Whitehill County Infant School
LUD/ILL HX2 .... 50 D4
Wibsey First School
WBSY BD6 .... 54 C1
Wibsey Middle School
WBSY BD6 .... 54 C1
William Henry Smith School
BRIG HD6 .... 77 H3
Willow Industrial Complex
RPDN/SBR HX6 .... 67 E5
The Willows Medical Centre
CUL/QBY BD13 .... 52 B1
Willow Valley Golf &
Country Club
BRIG HD6 .... 72 B3
Wilsden Primary School
WIL/AL BD15 .... 25 H4
Windhill CE First School
SHPY BD18 .... 29 E1
Windhill Cricket Club
SHPY BD18 .... 19 E5
Windhill Green Medical Centre
SHPY BD18 .... 28 D1
Withinfields J & I School
HIPP HX3 .... 69 G3
Woodhall Hills Golf Club
PDSY/CALV LS28 .... 31 E5
Woodhill Middle School
SHPY BD18 .... 29 E1
Woodhouse Grove School
IDLE BD10 .... 21 E5
Woodhouse Primary School
BRIG HD6 .... 78 C3
Woodlands CE First School
LM/WK BD12 .... 55 H5
Woodlands Cricket Club
LM/WK BD12 .... 55 G5
Woodroyd Industrial Estate
LM/WK BD12 .... 55 F5
Woodroyd Middle School
WBOW BD5 .... 47 F4
Woodside Clinic
WBSY BD6 .... 54 B4
Woodside First School
WBSY BD6 .... 54 B4
Woodside Middle School
WBSY BD6 .... 54 B4
Woolshops Shopping Centre
HFAX HX1 .... 5 H4
Worthinghead First School
LM/WK BD12 .... 63 E2
Worth Valley Middle School
HWTH BD22 .... 13 H3
Wrose Health Centre
ECHL BD2 .... 29 G4
Wyclciffe Middle School
SHPY BD18 .... 28 B1
Wyke Manor Upper School
LM/WK BD12 .... 63 E2
Wyke Middle School
LM/WK BD12 .... 62 D2
Yeadon Cemetery
YEA LS19 .... 11 H3
Yeadon Cricket Club
YEA LS19 .... 11 H4
Yeadon Health Centre
YEA LS19 .... 11 G4
Yeadon Westfield
Junior School
YEA LS19 .... 11 E5
Yorkshire Clinic
BGLY BD16 .... 27 F2
Yorkshire Martyrs
Collegiate School
BOW BD4 .... 57 F2
Young Street Industrial Estate
GIR BD8 .... 38 A4

 **AA** **Street by Street**   QUESTIONNAIRE

Dear Atlas User
Your comments, opinions and recommendations are very important to us.
So please help us to improve our street atlases by taking a few minutes
to complete this simple questionnaire.

You do NOT need a stamp (unless posted outside the UK). If you do not want to remove this page from your street atlas, then photocopy it or write your answers on a plain sheet of paper.

Send to: The Editor, AA Street by Street, FREEPOST SCE 4598,
Basingstoke RG21 4GY

ABOUT THE ATLAS...

Which city/town/county did you buy?

_____

Are there any features of the atlas or mapping that you find particularly useful?

_____
_____
_____

Is there anything we could have done better?

_____
_____
_____

Why did you choose an AA Street by Street atlas?

_____
_____
_____

Did it meet your expectations?

Exceeded ☐   **Met all** ☐   **Met most** ☐   **Fell below** ☐

Please give your reasons

_____
_____
_____
_____
_____

ML013   _continued overleaf_

Where did you buy it?

For what purpose? (please tick all applicable)

To use in your own local area ☐   To use on business or at work ☐

Visiting a strange place ☐   In the car ☐   On foot ☐

Other (please state)

LOCAL KNOWLEDGE...

Local knowledge is invaluable. Whilst every attempt has been made to make the information contained in this atlas as accurate as possible, should you notice any inaccuracies, please detail them below (if necessary, use a blank piece of paper) or e-mail us at *streetbystreet@theAA.com*

ABOUT YOU...

Name (Mr/Mrs/Ms)

Address
                                                                    Postcode

Daytime tel no

E-mail address

Which age group are you in?

Under 25 ☐   25-34 ☐   35-44 ☐   45-54 ☐   55-64 ☐   65+ ☐

Are you an AA member?   YES ☐   NO ☐

Do you have Internet access?   YES ☐   NO ☐

Thank you for taking the time to complete this questionnaire. Please send it to us as soon as possible, and remember, you do not need a stamp (unless posted outside the UK).

ML